Words and Buildings

Words and Buildings

A Vocabulary of Modern Architecture

Adrian Forty

With 216 illustrations

Thames & Hudson

To my parents, Ray and Gerald Forty, with whom I first discovered the pleasures of language

© 2000 Adrian Forty

First published in hardcover in the United States of America in 2000 by
Thames & Hudson Inc., 500 Fifth Avenue, New York, New York 10110

Library of Congress Catalog Card Number 99-70945
ISBN 0-500-34172-9

Printed and bound in Singapore

Design by Keith Lovegrove

Contents

Acknowledgments

Many people have helped in the writing of this book, not all of them knowingly. In particular, though, I would like to thank the following for their various contributions, advice and encouragement. For conversations in the initial stages of formulating the project, David Dunster, Andrew Saint and Mark Swenarton. For their generosity in reading and making suggestions on early drafts of individual chapters and parts, Robert Gutman, Richard Hill, Peter Kohane, Katerina Rüedi, Andrew Saint, Mark Swenarton, Alex Potts, Jeremy Till, and my colleagues at the Bartlett, Iain Borden and Bill Hillier. Robin Middleton read an early version of the whole book, and made invaluable suggestions on the shape and orientation of the whole. Neil Levine read the final manuscript and gave helpful advice and criticism. For conversations and assistance on a variety of questions, I thank Davide Deriu, Robert Elwall, Susannah Hagan, Jonathan Hill, Tanis Hinchcliffe, Robert Maxwell, Jeremy Melvin, Alessandra Ponte, Jane Rendell, David Solkin, Philip Steadman and Tom Weaver. For advice on translations, I would like to thank my mother, Ray Forty. It would be impossible to mention by name all the students at the Bartlett who have over the years provided me with material or suggested ideas, but among them in particular I would like to thank Halldora Arna, Alex Buchanan, Romaine Govett, Javier Sanchez-Merina, and Ellie de Gory (who provided the idea, and some of the material for the entry on 'Flexibility'). For his encouragement throughout the duration of the project, and his optimism that I would finish it, Nikos Stangos at Thames and Hudson; and for making sure I had time to finish it, the then Head of the Bartlett, Patrick O'Sullivan. For their tolerance towards me while writing the book, I cannot thank my children, Francesca and Olivia, too much; nor my wife, Briony, both for her patience, her advice, and for her support throughout.

An earlier version of chapter 4 appeared in *Desiring Practices*, edited by Katerina Rüedi, Sarah Wigglesworth and Duncan McCorquodale, and published by Black Dog Publishing in 1996; and chapter 6 appeared previously in *The Architecture of Science*, edited by Peter Galison and Emily Thompson, published by MIT Press in 1999.

The initial stages of the research were made possible by a Fellowship awarded by the Leverhulme Trust, which also contributed towards the cost of illustrations.

This book has two parts. Part I is an enquiry into the spoken and written language of modern architecture. It is about some of the general tasks that verbal language performs in architecture; about language's own processes relative to those of architecture; and about the formation of metaphors. It asks what language gives to architecture – and where language lets architecture down.

Part II is a historical and critical dictionary of the words that formed the core vocabulary of modernist architectural criticism. The story it tells is one of words always being inadequate to meanings, of meanings escaping words to find new metaphors. One of the models for Part II was Raymond Williams's *Keywords*. If the result bears little resemblance to Williams's admirably concise book, it is in part because Williams was concerned with language in general, whereas this is an enquiry into the language system of one particular practice – modern architecture – and to ask the task of words within that practice becomes necessarily a discourse about the practice itself.

Few things being definite in the world of language, there is nothing final about the book's contents; I am confident that every reader will be able to find something with which to disagree.

Part One

'When *I* use a word,' Humpty Dumpty said in rather a scornful tone, 'it means just what I choose it to mean – neither more nor less.'

'The question is,' said Alice, 'whether you *can* make words mean so many different things.'

Lewis Carroll, *Through the Looking Glass*, Chapter VI

G. B. Lenardi, Allegory of the arts of
architectural representation (detail).
From G. G. Ciampini, *Vetera Monimenta*,
Rome, 1690

Introduction

What happens when people talk about architecture? Are sullen lumps of concrete, steel and glass animated by the words that we shower upon them? Or does every word spoken or written about it diminish a work of architecture, and deprive it of a part of its being? These are not new questions. The seventeenth century French author Fréart de Chambray in his *Parallel of the Antient Architecture with the Modern*, the first comparative study of the orders, took a strong view of the matter, writing that 'the *Art* of *Architecture* does not consist in *words*; the demonstration ought to be sensible and ocular' (11). But Fréart's English translator, John Evelyn, in the *Account of Architects and Architecture* which he appended to his edition of Fréart's *Parallel*, approached the matter differently. Evelyn asserted that the art of architecture was embodied in four kinds of person. First was *architectus ingenio*, the superintending architect, a man of ideas, familiar with the history of architecture, skilled in geometry and drawing techniques, and with a sufficient knowledge of astronomy, law, medicine, optics and so on. Secondly, the *architectus sumptuarius*, 'with a full and overflowing purse' – the patron. Thirdly, *architectus manuarius*, 'in him I comprehend the several artizans and workmen'. And fourthly, *architectus verborum* – in whom he classed himself – the architect of words, skilled in the craft of language, and whose task was to talk about the work and interpret it to others. Evelyn's personification of the parts of architecture expressed an important idea: that architecture consisted not just of one or two of these activities, but of all four of them in concert. The critical language through which a work of architecture's qualities were explored was no less a part of architecture than the idea conceived by the *architectus ingenio* or the craftsmanship of the artisan. In this divergence, between seeing language as lying within architecture, or as foreign to it, we have a problem that underlies what this book is about. In terms of Evelyn's personification, can *architectus verborum* be admitted to the company of architects, or must he for ever remain outside? How are we to think about these questions? And indeed, do they matter?

The relationship between architecture and verbal language has not been much talked about, even though, as one architectural theorist, Tom Markus, recently

'Build, don't talk'. Suspicion of language, coupled with a compulsion to talk about architecture, has been a common trait amongst modern architects. Mies van der Rohe in conversation with Stephan Waetzoldt, with Dirk Lohan in the background, Berlin, 1967.

pointed out, 'Language is at the core of making, using and understanding buildings' (4). That the relationship has had so little attention is partly due to the modern tendency to identify architecture primarily with the mental work of creative invention – with Evelyn's *architectus ingenio* – at the expense of its other constituents. More particularly, architecture has, like all other art practices, been affected by the longstanding assumption in Western thought that experiences mediated through the senses are fundamentally incompatible with those mediated through language: that seeing something bears no relation to being told about it. Nowhere was this assumption more evident than in early twentieth-century modernist art, where it was held that the particular property of every art was to offer an experience unique to its own particular medium, uncommunicable through any other medium. For the visual arts, this led to the view, as the Bauhaus artist and pedagogue László Moholy-Nagy wrote in his book *The New Vision* (1928), that 'Language is inadequate to formulate the exact meaning and the rich variations of the realm of sensory experiences' (63). In every visual art, language fell under suspicion – and architecture was no exception: one might recall Mies van der Rohe's terse remark 'Build – don't talk' (Bonta, 1990, 13), a sentiment whose echo was to be heard throughout modernist architectural circles. Under these circumstances, there was something of an interdict upon serious investigation into the architecture–language relationship.

Although recently the part played by language in the pictorial arts has been questioned, and doubt cast upon the modernist belief that an art could be purely visual, nothing comparable has happened within architecture.[1] In so far as the issue is thought about at all, it is generally supposed that what is spoken or written about works of architecture is merely a tracing of them, an always less than adequate reflection of their 'reality': yet language itself constitutes a 'reality', which, while not the same as that formed through the other senses, is nonetheless equivalent.

If language is a necessary part of architecture, the difficulty is to describe the relationship in such a way as not to make language simply an accessory – for as well as being a part of architecture, language is unquestionably also a system in its own right. As an example of how to think about the place of language within a complex social practice, Roland Barthes's *The Fashion System* (1967) provides a model that has not been equalled. And Barthes's opening questions – 'Why does Fashion utter clothing so abundantly? Why does it interpose, between the object and its user, such a luxury of words (not to mention images), such a network of meaning?' (xi) – may just as well be asked of architecture. Though the differences between architecture and fashion are great, the similarities are sufficient to make Barthes's analysis of fashion an inspiration in investigating such questions in relation to architecture. For in particular, just as fashion is a system with three parts – a material product (the garment), images (the fashion photograph) and words (the fashion commentary) – so architecture is a three-part system constituted out of the building, its image (photograph or drawing), and its accompanying critical discourse (whether presented by the architect, client or critic). What the analogy of architecture with *The Fashion System* makes clear is that language is not something that simply gets in the way of architecture, but is a system of its own on a par with that of buildings.

In two important respects, though, architecture is more complex than Barthes's model of the fashion system. Firstly, its images are of two kinds, one of which – photography – is a universal code, but the other of which – drawing – is a code restricted to those within the system. The differences between these two types of image are sufficiently great for it to be more accurate to describe architecture as a four-part system, within which one of the main tensions, as we shall see in chapter 2, is that between language and drawing. The second way in which the architecture system differs from the fashion system is that whereas in fashion, the verbal component is produced almost entirely by fashion commentators and journalists, in architecture, architects themselves do much of the talking and writing – which indeed constitutes a significant and sometimes major component of their 'production'; one of the features of the architecture system – apparently absent from fashion – is the contest between architects and the press for control over the verbal element. Although language is vital to architects – their success in gaining commissions, and achieving the realization of projects frequently depends upon verbal presentation and persuasiveness – it is striking how little discussed language has been compared to architecture's other principal medium, drawing. Part of the reason for this disparity must surely be that whereas drawing is a code over which architects hold a large measure of control, their command of language will always be disputed by every other language user.

Language and History

Considered as a system, the phenomenon within language with which this book is mainly concerned is the constant flux between words and meanings, of meanings' pursuit of words, and words' escape from meanings. We can see this both in historical terms occurring over time, but also as occurring between one language and another. The history of architecture, as distinct from its present-day practice and criticism, is faced with the unique and special problem of seeing the work as it was seen by people in the past, and of attempting to recover their experience of it. This task is full of difficulties – so many as to make it seem close to impossible.[2] Whose experience do we succeed in recovering? For who else did those persons speak? How are we to grasp the distinctiveness of their mode of vision, which being not a timeless, universal faculty of the mind, but a historically determined property, must certainly be different from our own? By what means can we gain access to the lived experience of someone dead long ago? To consider this last question alone, the most reasonable, and most regularly followed solution is by appeal to drawn or photographic images, and above all to what people at the time, or others for them, wrote down. But even this evidence is not straightforward: for just as architecture is a historical phenomenon, so are drawings and photographs, whose meaning can only be interpreted through the conventions of representation available at the time – and so too is language. The very medium through which we stand in greatest hope of reliving the experiences

Suit by Valentino Garavani, 1964. 'Why does Fashion utter clothing so abundantly? Why does it interpose, between the object and its user, such a luxury of words?' Barthes's questions apply no less to architecture.

of the past itself escapes us, for nothing is more fugitive, more subject to the processes of historical change than language itself. In terms of language, the past is no less foreign than is abroad. We cannot expect that to a nineteenth-century person the words 'design', or 'form', meant the same as they would to us. It is almost certain that they did not.

Our problem, then, is to recover the past meanings of words so that we can interpret what those who uttered them intended to say. But this is no simple matter, for the history of language is not one of the straightforward replacement of one meaning by another, like a car manufacturer's model changes, but rather a process of accumulation as new meanings and inflections are added to existing words without necessarily displacing the old ones. To find the meaning of a word at any one time is to know the available possibilities: meanings cannot be identified the way one looks up a word up in a dictionary. Critical vocabulary is not about things, it is about encounters with things, and it is above all as a means of structuring those experiences that language is of value. The particular resource of language, itself a system of differences, is its capacity to make distinctions, between one thing and another thing, between one kind of experience and another. The significance of much critical vocabulary lies not so much in any specific meaning a term might have, but rather in all the things that it does *not* mean, that it excludes. Architects and critics do not always choose words for the sake of their positive denotations, but for their force of resistance to other ideas or terms – such, for example, has been the case with the architectural usage of 'history', and of 'type'. The historical enquiry into critical terms in Part II, becomes therefore not simply a record of meanings, but also of changing oppositions and shifting 'not-meanings'.

Language and Languages

Between European languages, there has always been a brisk trade in critical vocabulary. Few of the words discussed in Part II first took on life as architectural terms in English, and none have remained impervious to meanings and inflections developed elsewhere. Any account of 'space' in architecture that did not take into account its origins in German, or of 'structure' that overlooked its development in French would be manifestly incomplete and inadequate. It has been necessary therefore to give a good deal of attention to terms as they developed in languages other than English, and this would be so whatever art one was discussing – critical vocabulary travels fast and easily, often more rapidly than knowledge of the works about which it was spoken. In some respects, this is a problem, for one might well ask, what language is this book primarily about? I am not keen to encourage the impression that the language of architecture is 'international', that it is some kind of Esperanto understood identically wherever it is spoken: the fact is we can only speak in one language at a time, and the words necessarily take their meaning from the particular language in which they are uttered. It would be unwise to assume that the word *Form* in German will mean quite the same thing as 'form' in English – yet as the English use of the word in relation to architecture owes a great deal to its translation from German, it would at the same time be a mistake to overlook its German sense. Although the trade between languages is in some respects a difficulty in a book like this, in another sense the problem of translation is simply another manifestation of the transitoriness of meaning that is central to the whole enquiry: the migration of ideas and words from one language to another is another aspect of what goes on within a single language as one metaphor is displaced by another. Because this book is written in English, the terms with which it deals are terms as they exist in the English language. Quotations from other languages have been translated into English, which, although this contradicts the very point that words mean particular things within the language they are spoken, and tends towards the impression of a universal language of architecture, seemed necessary to make the book at all readable. But we should not regard the act of translation, as it often is regarded, as 'a problem', for through translation words gain as well as lose.

1 See Baxendall, *Patterns of Intention*, 1985; W. J. T. Mitchell, *Iconology: Image, Text, Ideology*, 1986; and W. J. T. Mitchell, *Picture Theory*, 1994.
2 See Podro, *The Critical Historians of Art*, 1982, especially chapter 1, on this question.

Just as photographs – images made
according to their own conventions –
are not 'tracings of reality', neither is
language. Le Corbusier, Pavilion Suisse,
Paris, 1930 © FLC L3(10)3-21

*" Did I really understand you, Miss Wilson, to use the expression,
' A cosy nook ' in connection with the house you wish me to
design for you?"*

Modern architecture, as well as being a
new style of building, also created a new
and distinctive way of talking about
architecture. (From Pont, *The British at
Home*, 1939)

1

Modernist architecture, as well as being a new style of building, was also a new way of talking about architecture, instantly recognizable by a distinctive vocabulary. Wherever two or more of the words 'form', 'space', 'design', 'order' or 'structure' are found in company, one can be sure that one is in the world of modernist discourse. When Kevin Lynch announced at the beginning of *The Image of the City* (1960) that 'giving visual form to the city is a special kind of design problem' (v), we know that we are in for a demonstration of modernist thinking – fully confirmed when he later announces that 'the objective here is to uncover the role of form itself' (46). These five words, the constellation of modernist architectural discourse, are discussed individually in Part II, but they do not give up their meanings easily: frequently defined through each other – 'The ultimate object of design is form' (Alexander, 1964, 15), or 'Design is form-making in order' (Kahn, 1961) and the like – they exist in a delicate, precariously balanced relationship to one another. Disturb one and you disturb the lot. It is this feature in particular of the vocabulary that suggests that modernist discourse was indeed a *system*.

For a style of architecture to be accompanied by its own distinctive critical vocabulary is not itself remarkable. The classical tradition that dominated European architecture between the sixteenth and nineteenth centuries had its own terminology, which by the late eighteenth century was highly evolved and even codified. We have good analytical studies of the classical vocabulary in three recent books, Werner Szambien's *Symétrie, Goût, Caractère* (1986), Anthony Vidler's *Claude-Nicolas Ledoux* (1990) and David Watkin's *Sir John Soane* (1996), but no equivalent for modernism. Although some modern critics (Alan Colquhoun in particular) have made interesting and observant remarks about particular terms, one of the aims of this book is not only to examine the meaning of individual words, but to also to look at the whole phenomenon of modernist language, considered more generally as a system. But the critical language of modernism presents a problem that does not arise within the classical system, for one of the most distinctive features of modernism has been its suspicion of language; however we approach the critical vocabulary of modernism, we have to take into account this tension that denies language any place in the practice that it purports to discuss. What, in that case, is the role allotted to language within modernism?

Although the new way of building developed by modernism might appear, because of the physical presence of the works, to have been the more durable, the most 'real' aspect of modernism, ironically it may be its language – seemingly more ephemeral, more fugitive – that turns out to be the more permanent feature. Even now, those who claim their liberation from modernism nonetheless persist in talking about architecture with a vocabulary which is wholly modernist – and indeed they have no choice, for modernism drove out all previous vocabularies, and there is none to take its place. While we might be free to choose between this way of building and that, words and concepts once absorbed seem to make an unconditional conquest of our mental apparatus, and to deny any right of coexistence to those belonging to previous schemes of thought. This state of affairs will continue until the modernist way of thinking and talking architecture is, in its turn, overpowered and subjugated by some new discourse. Despite the efforts of some individuals to bring this about, it has not yet happened.

The Horror of Language

Suspicion of language was a feature of modernism in all the visual arts. When Picasso said, 'A painting, for me, speaks by itself; what good does it do, after all, to impart explanations? A painter has only one language…' (Ashton, 97), he could equally well have been speaking about any other form of art. The general expectation of modernism that each art demonstrate its uniqueness through its own medium, and its own medium alone, ruled out resort to language. If, as Moholy-Nagy wrote, 'Any artistic creation must involve a consideration of the specific potentialities of its medium if it is to achieve an intrinsic, "organic" quality' (1947, 271), what place could there be for language anywhere but in literature?

Nor was suspicion of language within architecture restricted only to the modernist era. Certain earlier architects and critics resisted language's intrusion into architecture, as demonstrated by the eighteenth-century French architect E.-L. Boullée in his 'Architecture, Essay on Art':

> The only way that artists should communicate among themselves is by recalling forcefully and vividly what has aroused their sensibility; it is this attraction, which belongs to them alone, that will permit them to stimulate the fire of their genius. They should beware of entering into explanations which belong to the realm of reason, for the impression an image makes on our senses is subdued when we dwell on the cause that has produced the effect. To describe one's pleasures is to cease living under their influence, to cease to enjoy them, to cease to exist. (114)

But Boullée's reservations about language are not total: he was simply concerned to distinguish those aspects of architecture which could be described in language from those which could or should not. We shall find nothing from the eighteenth or nineteenth century that prepares us for the level of paranoia about language demonstrated by architectural modernists. It is worth reflecting a little further on the stages that led to this, and its possible causes.

Between the late eighteenth century and the early twentieth, criticism itself changed. In the eighteenth century, criticism concerned itself with objects; it was entirely proper, as Boullée said, for artists to discuss the objects which 'aroused their sensibility', but entirely wrong for them to attempt to describe the pleasures of those sensations – for to do so 'was to cease to exist'. By the twentieth century, the convention of which Boullée spoke had been almost completely inverted: the description of objects was regarded as an improper role for criticism, while 'the description of pleasures' was to be its principal domain. Language's colonization of a territory from which it had hitherto been excluded may be part of the reason for the hostility shown to language; but at the same time, ironically, it was in the colonization of this particular area that language found its legitimation within the modernist scheme.

The transformation of criticism was in part a result of the revolution in aesthetics brought about by Kant in his *Critique of Judgment*. Kant's definition of the aesthetic – as what constitutes reference to the subject, not the object – directed attention towards the particular form of experience induced by works of art. The particularity of this experience was that it excluded all cognition, all the facts one might know about an object: so, for example, 'as to the prospect of the ocean, we are not to regard it as we, with our minds stored with knowledge on a variety of matters (which, however, is not contained in the immediate intuition), are wont to represent it in *thought*, as, let us say, a spacious realm of aquatic creatures… Instead of this we must be able to see sublimity in the ocean, regarding it, as the poets do, according to what the impression upon the eye reveals…' (122). But, as Kant saw, the 'impression upon the eye' also invokes certain attributes, 'a multiplicity of partial representations', which 'allows a concept to be supplemented in thought by much that is indefinable in words' (179). The substance of Kant's aesthetics lay in the space between 'the impression upon the eye' and the indefinable multiplicity of partial representations it induced.

As the area of philosophical interest, this also was to become the area of critical interest in art – yet as Kant had warned, 'language, as a mere thing of the spirit, binds up the spirit also' (179): the ultimate experience of art lay beyond language. This difficulty, that the most interesting thing about art was also beyond language, created a problem of which at least some of the critics and historians within the German tradition of Kantian aesthetics were well aware: for example, the historian Heinrich Wölfflin writing in 1921 observed that 'If it were possible to express in words the deepest content or idea of a work of art, art itself would be superfluous, and all buildings, statues and paintings could have remained unbuilt, unfashioned and unpainted' (quoted in Antoni, 244). Yet this recognition of the ultimate inaccessibility of art to language, reminiscent of Picasso's own remarks, comes after criticism had established itself in the realm of experience. Like the feeling of emptiness experienced by the anthropologist who travels to a primitive people in a remote region only to discover that the strangeness he hopes to study is lost as soon as he learns what it consists of, Wölfflin's remark was a warning against trying to explain the very thing criticism aims to expose. The extraordinary degree of hostility shown by artists and architects towards language can perhaps be understood as one response to this conundrum.

Between Seeing and Understanding

What are the features of modernist critical writing? In the vocabulary itself there is, as we have said, the privilege accorded to the five key words 'space', 'form', 'design', 'structure' and 'order'. Corresponding to the adoption of these terms, there was a general purge of metaphors, particularly those derived from literary and art criticism that had played a large part in the classical critical vocabulary. Evicted were terms descriptive of character attributes, such as 'bold', 'noble', 'masculine', and 'affected'; and compositional terms like 'repose', 'strength' and 'massiveness'. In the pursuit of a language free from metaphor, modernism tolerated only two particular classes of metaphor, those drawn from language, and those drawn from science. These are discussed in more detail in chapters 4 and 5. Otherwise, criticism proceeded through a series of abstractions – not only those of the five key terms, but also a marked tendency to turn particulars into abstract generalities; so, for example, walls become 'the wall', streets 'the street', a path becomes 'the route', a house 'the dwelling', and so on.

In so far as we can discern a method in modernist critical writing, it has the same general tendency to render what is concrete abstract. If we take, for example, a passage from a classic modernist text, Edmund Bacon's *Design of Cities* (1967), we can observe this process at work. Modernist criticism is by no means restricted to modern architecture, and many of its finest examples relate to historical architecture. This passage refers to the centre of the Italian medieval town of Todi:

> Spectacular among the architectural works of medieval cities is the design of the two interlocking squares in Todi. The smaller of the squares, with a statue of Garibaldi at its center, overlooks the rolling Umbrian plains and draws the spirit of the countryside into the town. It was conceived as a space, with one corner overlapping the area of the principal center square, the Piazza del Popolo, thus establishing a small volume of space common to the two squares, of special intensity and impact. The towers of the Palazzo del Popolo and the Palazzo dei Priori flank this abstractly defined space and provide vertical forces that hold down the two corner points at the position of greatest intensity of design.

The positions of the buildings representing the two principal functions of communal life are precisely determined in the design both in plan and in a vertical relationship. The entrances to both the Palazzo del Popolo and to the cathedral are raised above the plane of the public square onto a level of their own, accessible by a large flight of steps. The simplicity of this over-all design is such that the citizen never loses his feeling of relationship with the city as a design entity while he is participating in his function as a member of the church or as a member of the political community. (1978, 95)

Leaving aside for the moment any doubts we might have about the 'design' intentions Bacon attributes to the builders of the squares, what is particularly striking about this passage is the way that each thing he describes is given a corresponding abstraction. The area common to the two *piazze* becomes 'a volume of space'; the towers of the Palazzi are 'vertical forces'; the pavement of the square is a 'plane'; the city is a 'design entity'. Why this compulsion to render everything of substance as an empty abstraction? Throughout, Bacon refuses to be satisfied with what can simply be seen by the eye, and to describe just that. His purpose is to reveal an invisible order which is concealed beneath the surface flux of objects; Bacon's use of the word 'design' – that most idealist of terms – no less than five times in the passage quoted, betrays only too well his obsession with what cannot be perceived directly.

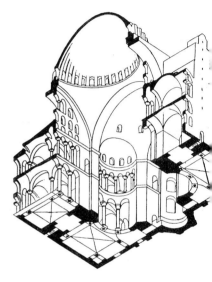

A. Choisy, Hagia Sophia, from *Histoire d'Architecture* (1899). Choisy's drawings showed buildings as the eye could never see them – sliced open and from below.

Just as the remarkable diagrams (see ill. p. 24) in Bacon's book drain all life out of heavily inhabited parts of cities, turning dense masses of building into blank white paper, so his text rejects the actuality of experience. In this he repeats, as Robert Maxwell has put it, 'the time-honoured formula of the modern architect, who always aspired to see through the trees to the wood, to uncover the soul of the project' (1993, 107). Much as Auguste Choisy's analytical drawings in his *Histoire de l'Architecture* (1899) showed buildings as the eye could never see them – sliced open and from below – modernist writing fastens itself on an abstract world, invisible except as 'idea'. But if Bacon, for the moment our 'typical' modernist writer, declined the visible town of Todi in favour of a 'design structure', neither did he try to interpret its 'meaning'. Just as to describe the physical properties of architecture only demonstrated the redundancy of language – because it simply became a substitute medium for architecture's own – so too would any attempt to render the 'meaning' of the work into words signal the utter superfluousness of language: for, as Roland Barthes wrote (in relation to literature), 'The critic cannot claim to "translate" the work, and particularly not to make it clearer, for nothing is clearer than the work' (1987, 80).

No writer has understood better the limitations placed upon language by modernism, nor exploited those restrictions to more effect, than the English critic Colin Rowe. Rowe's highly influential *oeuvre*, a series of critical essays and articles written since the late 1940s upon a very limited range of topics –

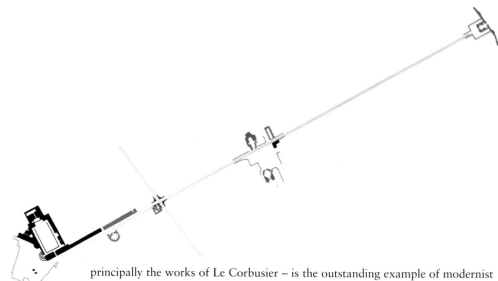

Rome, Acqua Felice and Via Quirinale,
from Edmund Bacon, *Design of Cities*
(1967). Modernist analysis
characteristically reduced complex
phenomena to a few general abstractions.

principally the works of Le Corbusier – is the outstanding example of modernist
critical writing on architecture, an equivalent to Clement Greenberg's on painting.

In Rowe's essays the recurrent theme is the tension a work of architecture
creates between what the senses experience, and what the intellect knows; between
what 'a man of moderate sophistication' (1982, 175) sees with his eyes, and the
mind's knowledge gained from the scrutiny of plans and sections. As Rowe
explains the distinction between the two components of architectural 'seeing':

> For while the plan, as a document addressed to the mind, will always be the
> primary concept, the vertical surface, as a presentation addressed to the eye,
> will always be the primary percept, will never be other than the beginning of
> comprehension. (1984, 22)

Writing about architecture, Rowe habitually describes the optical experience, but
aware that this alone is not enough, is an insufficient role for language to play in
relation to architecture, he will turn abruptly to the mental concept, and out of the
differences between these two ways of seeing will develop his argument. Nowhere
is this switch from visual to mental perception more abrupt than in his essay on
Le Corbusier's 'La Tourette' (1961). Only by transferring attention to the mental
conception of the building does the optical experience, recounted verbally, take
on any significance at all, as the optical testimony starts to weaken and be called
into question under cross examination from the mental concept. Only 'when the
senses are confounded by what is apparently arbitrary and the intellect is more
than convinced by the intuitive knowledge that, despite all to the contrary, here
problems have been both recognized and answered and that here there is a
reasonable order' (1982, 15) does the work start to hold critical interest.
The telling of this dialectical relationship is a privilege of language alone,

and it is in this special role that language's value within the modernist system of the arts is assured.

In 'The Mathematics of the Ideal Villa' (1947), we can see how Rowe plays off the tensions between the visual and the mental. The theme of the essay is the comparison of two pairs of villas – Palladio's Villa Rotonda and Le Corbusier's Villa Savoie, and Palladio's Villa Malcontenta and Le Corbusier's Villa Stein at Garches. The central theme of the essay emerges from the contrast of the latter pair. Having compared the different rhythms of the façades, Rowe turns to the internal differences which result from the differing structural systems of load-bearing wall in the Villa Malcontenta and reinforced concrete slab in the Villa Stein. The effect of the reinforced concrete slab construction of Le Corbusier's villa is that all the architectural freedoms occur on the horizontal plane of the plan, whereas in Palladio's villa they occurred vertically, in the elevations and section. Rowe develops this as follows:

> The spatial audacities of the Garches plan continue to thrill; but it may sometimes seem to be an interior which is acceptable to the intellect alone – to the intellect operating from within a stage vacuum. Thus there is at Garches a permanent tension between the organized and the apparently fortuitous. Conceptually, all is clear; but, sensuously, all is deeply perplexing. There are statements of a hierarchical ideal; there are counter statements of an egalitarian one. Both houses may seem to be apprehensible from without; but, from within, in the cruciform hall of the Malcontenta, there is a clue to the whole building; while, at Garches, it is never possible to stand at any point and receive a total impression. For at Garches the necessary equidistance between floor and ceiling conveys an equal importance to all parts of the volume in between; and thus the development of absolute focus becomes an arbitrary, if not an impossible proceeding. This is the dilemma propounded by the system; and Le Corbusier responds to it. He accepts the principal of horizontal extension; thus, at Garches central focus is consistently broken up, concentration at any one point is disintegrated, and the dismembered fragments of the center become a peripheral dispersion of incident, a serial installation of interest around the extremities of the plan.

> But it is now that this system of horizontal extension which is *conceptually* logical comes up against the rigid boundary of the block which, almost certainly, is felt to be *perceptually* requisite; and, consequently, with horizontal extension checked, Le Corbusier is obliged to employ an opposite resource. That is, by gouging out large volumes of the block as terrace and roof garden, he introduces a contrary impulse of energy; and by opposing an explosive moment with an implosive one, by introducing inversive gestures alongside expansive ones, he again makes simultaneous use of conflicting strategies.

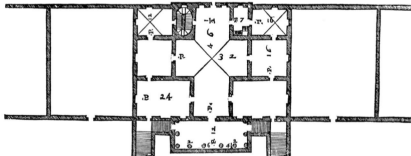

By its complexities, the resultant system (or symbiosis of systems) throws into intense relief the elementary, geometrical substructure of the building; and, as a sequel, the peripheral incident which substitutes for the Palladian focus can also become compounded with the inversions (of terrace and roof garden) which represent an essentially analogous development to Palladio's strategy of vertical extension. (1982, 12)

In this long passage, which is characteristic of Rowe's method in all his writing, heavy demands are placed upon the reader. The writing does not describe the

buildings, it is not a substitute for seeing them; one has already to have fixed in one's mind both a visual impression of the works, and of their abstractions as plans in order to be able to read it. Rowe is not prepared to use language as a potentially illusory and deceptive equivalent for optical sensation. The passage is not about the thing seen so much as about the act of seeing itself, about the space between visual sensation and mental perception. It was precisely in this space between 'the impression upon the eye' and the transcendental aesthetic attributes that the substance of Kant's aesthetics was located. The interest of Rowe's writing is in its almost exclusive confinement to this area – he neither duplicates visual impression, nor attempts to describe the transcendental idea itself, well knowing that both were beyond the reach of language.

To the eighteenth-century architect or critic, to Boullée, for whom 'to describe one's pleasures was to cease living under their influence', language could be properly only applied to objects. The modernist 'revolution' reversed this, declaring description of things an improper use of language, and turning what formerly had been forbidden territory into critical language's principal reserve. If on the one hand the legacy of Kantian aesthetics was, as Clement Greenberg put it in his classic essay 'Modernist Painting', that 'Each art had to determine, through the operations peculiar to itself, the effects peculiar and exclusive to itself' (755), then language had no place in a visual art; but on the other hand, it was also a legacy of Kantian aesthetics to allot to language a particular and narrowly defined area of competence between seeing and understanding. It was in this area that modernist critical language flourished.

(opposite) Villa Malcontenta (Foscari), Mira, Venice, A. Palladio (1550–60), with first floor plan.
(above) Villa Stein, Garches, garden facade, Le Corbusier, 1926–28, with first floor plan.
Colin Rowe's comparison of the Villa Stein and the Villa Malcontenta scrupulously avoided *description* of the buildings and entirely concentrated instead on the relation between what the eye sees and the mind (from the plans) knows.

2

The architect and his clients, photograph
by John Maltby for *Modern Woman*, July
1958. In a visual convention going back to
the Italian Renaissance, the architect is
identified by the drawing he holds. It is
architects' command of drawing that has
customarily distinguished them from the
other occupations involved in building.

I have no need whatsoever to draw my designs. Good architecture, how something is to be built, can be written. One can write the Parthenon.
Adolf Loos, 1924, 139

Architecture does not exist without drawing, in the same way that architecture does not exist without texts. Bernard Tschumi, 1980–81, 102

What can language do that drawing, the architect's other principal medium, does not? To ask about the differences between language and drawing relative to architecture makes certain things about each more distinct. We are fortunate that compared to the barren landscape that meets one on enquiry into the relationship of language to architecture, drawing's relationship with architecture is a valley of luxurious abundance. I have no hesitation in taking advantage of, in particular, Edward Robbins's *Why Architects Draw* (1994) and Robin Evans's *The Projective Cast* (1995), as well as Evans's previous articles, in reflecting on some of the differences between the two media.

Drawing and architecture are so bound up with each other that it is normally assumed – at least by architects – that, as Tschumi says, without drawing, there would be no architecture. To take one single example of a point of view that has been repeated over and over again in modern times, a remark by the Italian architect Carlo Scarpa (1906–78) will illustrate drawing's privileged status: 'My architecture is done with the architect's medium which is drawing and drawings only' (quoted in Teut). Even if this is so in the late twentieth century (which one might have cause to doubt) it has certainly not been true of all time. In previous periods of history, antiquity and the Middle Ages, drawings played little or no part in the production of buildings, and while one might then say that the practice that produced them was not therefore 'Architecture', this would be an excessively restrictive categorization. Only with the Italian Renaissance, in the fifteenth and sixteenth centuries, did drawings become a significant feature of building production with the newly emerged manifestation of the 'art' of architecture. The basis of the changes that took place in Italy at this time, and in the rest of Europe rather later, were the

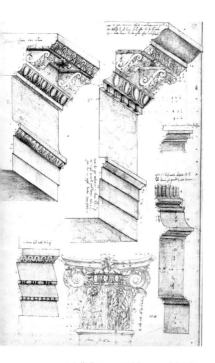

A. Palladio, measured drawing of details of the Porta dei Leoni, Verona. It was above all Palladio's acquisition of the skill of drawing, which he applied to both recording what he saw and inventing anew, that lifted him out of the manual trade of stonemason.

transfer of responsibility for a part of the production of some buildings to people independent of the building crafts, and trained in, particularly, the visual arts of painting and sculpture. Apart from a familiarity with ideas to which members of the building trades ordinarily had no access, and a freedom to think about buildings in terms outside the normal conventions of the building trades, the particular skill which such men displayed was the ability to draw, and to represent their ideas graphically, in such a way that they could both be discussed with patrons, and also translated into buildings. Many of the Renaissance treatises, from Filarete onwards, laid particular stress on the importance of drawing as the first skill to be acquired by anyone aspiring to be an architect. Sebastiano Serlio, whose *Tutte l'opere d'architettura e prospectiva* was the most popular of all sixteenth-century architecture books, purposefully remarked at the beginning of Book II 'perspective would be nothing without architecture and the architect nothing without perspective' (37), and drew attention to the fact that the great architects of his day, Bramante, Raphael, Peruzzi and Giulio Romano, had all started life as painters. And as the historian John Onians points out, Serlio's decision to begin his treatise not with the principles of architecture, its parts, techniques and materials, but with the principles of architectural drawing, was unprecedented, and set a pattern followed in many subsequent architecture books (Onians, 264). In the new division of labour that took place during the fifteenth and sixteenth centuries, what above all set the new *genus* of architects apart from the building trades was their command of drawing; it both made possible the separation of their occupation from building, and because of drawing's connection with geometry in the newly discovered science of perspective, gave architecture a means to associate itself with abstract thought, and thereby give it the status of intellectual, rather than manual labour. At the same time, though, within the new division of labour, drawing was the only part of the process of building production over which architects retained absolute and exclusive control; it was (and continues to be) the principal material object that architects themselves produced. During succeeding centuries the importance of drawing, which still in the sixteenth century had sufficient novelty for the authors of treatises to draw special attention to it, became taken for granted. Thus, for example, in the early nineteenth century, the French theorist J. N. L. Durand wrote, 'Drawing is the natural language of architecture'. And he went on to stress the particular qualities required of architectural drawing:

all language, to fulfil its object, must be in perfect harmony with the ideas of which it is to be the expression. Architecture, being essentially simple, enemy of everything without use [*inutile*], of all affectation, the type of drawing used must be free of every kind of difficulty, pretention and superfluity; then it will contribute singularly to the speed and ease of studying it and to the development of ideas; in the contrary case, it will only make the hand clumsy, the imagination lazy, and often even the judgment false. (vol. 1, 32)

What we find here is the belief that drawing can be a neutral medium, through which ideas pass as undisturbed as light through glass. Such was, until recently at least, the most common view of drawing within architectural practice.

But if drawing came to be accepted as the true medium of architecture, its *alter ego*, it is also the case that architects have been circumspect about it, for reasons which are made clear in the following remark by Le Corbusier in 1930:

I should like to give you the *hatred of rendering*.... Architecture is in space, in extent, in depth, in height: it is volumes and circulation. Architecture is made *inside one's head*. The sheet of paper is useful only to fix the design, to transmit it to one's client and one's contractor. (230)

Le Corbusier's objection to rendering belongs to a long-standing neo-Platonic tradition that sees *idea*, what is made inside one's head, as the measure by which everything made from it is judged. Plato's contempt for art, expounded in Book X of *The Republic*, on the grounds that the representation is always inferior to the idea of what it represents, is well known. Renaissance neo-Platonists inverted Plato's objections, and claimed that the particular quality of art was that it depicted an otherwise unknowable Idea. Applied to architecture, the results are expressed in Alberti's well known claim that 'It is quite possible to project whole forms in the mind without any recourse to the material' (7); and as a statement of the objectives of architecture, we might quote the seventeenth-century art theorist Giovanni Pietro Bellori: 'we say that the Architect must conceive a noble Idea and establish it in his mind, so that it can serve as law and reason for him' (Panofsky, 171). From this and many similar views derives the academic orthodoxy that was repeated by Le Corbusier. Whatever other effects this notion that art is the outward expression of a mental idea might be said to have had, its consequences for architectural drawing were both momentous, and contradictory: on the one hand, drawing was entrusted with the vital responsibility of carrying the idea from the architect's mind to the executed building, but on the other hand, it suffered from the disability that it is always assumed to be less than the idea, that it degrades the idea. In practice, this tension has generally been resolved by overestimating the truthfulness of orthogonal projection and exaggerating the mendaciousness of perspectival projection. Alberti was the first to do this:

The difference between the drawings of the painter and those of the architect is this: the former takes pains to emphasize the relief of objects in paintings with shading and diminishing lines and angles; the architect rejects

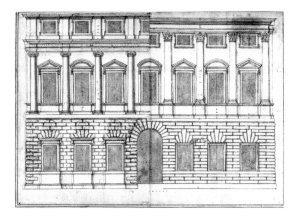

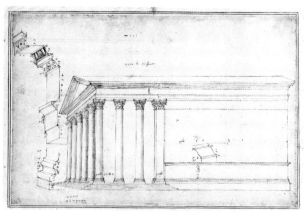

(above) A. Palladio, alternative designs
for Palazzo Porto Festa, Vicenza, c. 1549.
The orthogonal projection, in which every
point is seen as if from a position
perpendicular to it, was adopted by
architects as the preferred means of
representing buildings. But although
favoured over perspectival projections, it
is in its own way no less artificial and
deceptive.
(above right) A. Palladio, perspective
drawing of Temple of Antonius Pius and
Faustina. The 'untruthfulness' of
perspectival drawings – which Palladio
rarely used – has generally been
exaggerated by architects since the
Renaissance so as to reinforce the notion
that orthogonal drawings are pure
representations of the architect's 'idea'.

shading, but takes his projections from the ground plan and, without
altering the lines and by maintaining the true angles, reveals the extent
and shape of each elevation and side. (34)

And Le Corbusier's objection, which, it will be recalled, was against 'shading',
rendered drawings, not all drawings, falls within the same tradition. Yet,
as Evans pointed out, the differences between the two types of drawing,
orthogonal and perspective, are not so very great (1995, 110); by conventionally
ignoring the fictions of orthogonal projection, and overemphasizing those of
perspective, architects made the contradiction of drawing seem to disappear.

For a variety of reasons, then, we can say that Scarpa's claim that 'drawing
is the architect's only medium' is less than straightfoward; it is certainly not a
timeless, universal truth, but rather a statement about the circumstances in
which architects find themselves, and about the legacy of the neo-Platonic
tradition. It might be useful at this point to sum up the 'conventional' view of
the process of architecture in a diagram whose wrongness will be immediately
apparent, but which will nonetheless provide us with an opportunity to discuss
the relationship between the various activities that make up the whole practice
of architecture.

Idea → Drawing → Building → Experience → Language

The procedure summarized by this diagram starts with the client telling the
architect what is wanted; the architect turns those wants into an idea for a
work, which he or she then draws; the drawing is eventually translated into a
building, which people inhabit or encounter, and they articulate their experience
by talking, or writing about it (or possibly drawing or photographing it).
Another version of the same diagram might present it as circular, to indicate

that in the final stage the subject realizes in his or her own mind the idea born in the mind of the architect. A general and obvious fault of this whole scheme is that language is present not just in the final stage, but at every preceding stage too: the client *tells* the architect what is wanted; the architect does not only draw the building, he or she *describes* it, variously, to the client, to other architects, to regulatory authorities, to the contractor, to the tradesmen, to the press; and even the encounter with a work of architecture, its occupation, is itself rarely a wholly non-verbal affair ('No, that's the fire exit – the main entrance is over here…').

If we turn to examine the diagram stage by stage, the first, 'Idea → Drawing', is, as will already be apparent, flawed by its neo-Platonic, idealist assumptions. To suppose that ideas exist prior to their representation in drawings or language calls for a greater trust in metaphysics than most of us would, in other circumstances, normally be prepared to allow. Just as Merleau-Ponty, discussing writing, remarked 'The writer's thought does not control his language from without', and again, 'My own words take me by surprise and teach me what I think' (quoted in Derrida, 1978, 11), the same may be said of drawing. The drawing, as Evans insisted, is not so much a projection of an idea, it creates a particular reality of its own.

Erno Goldfinger at his office in Piccadilly, early 1960s. 'The architect's medium… is drawings and drawings only' – yet Goldfinger is talking on the telephone.

Evans concentrated his attention particularly on the stages 'Idea → Drawing' and 'Drawing → Building', and his work was above all a critique of the convention of thinking of these processes 'as an attempt at maximum preservation in which both meaning and likeness are transported from idea through drawing to building with minimum loss' (1986, 14). Yet, he acknowledged, 'pictures and words are always *less* than what they refer to' (1995, xxi). His solution to this dilemma was to argue that buildings and pictures of them should not be judged by the same standards – that pictures succeed better at being pictures than at being substitute buildings, and vice versa – and what he sought to do was consider architectural drawing within its own terms. Rather than treat it as an always less than adequate carrier, one should recognize that 'What comes out is not always the same as what goes in' (1986, 14). Indeed, in thinking about the relationship between drawings and objects, Plato, whose views on the relationship between ideas and pictures have been such an encumbrance to Western thought, had far more useful things to say, things that we might consider in this context. In the Dialogue of the Sophist, Plato asks, 'Do we not make one house by the art of building, and another by the art of drawing, which is a sort of dream?', and he continues, 'Other products of human imitation are also twofold and go in pairs, there is the thing, and the image' (266). Seen in these terms, we are encouraged to see drawings not so much as deficient versions of things, but as equal, though different realities. Could we not, then, think of verbal remarks about architecture in similar terms? If the drawing of the house 'is a sort of dream', compared to the somatic house, what is the house that is spoken of?

In the conventional view of the first half of the architectural process, language is normally considered a secondary effect: first comes the drawing, then one talks about it and what it contains. For several reasons, this seems less than convincing. In the first place, to many architects drawing and talking are not so distinct: for example, Peter Cook –

> I like drawing and talking. You have your pen out and say, 'Well it could be this or it could be that and, by the way, if you know such and such a building' to your client or student and ask 'Have you been in the Palm House at Kew?' Then you draw a little bit of a reminder and you progress from that into something else... (Cook and Parry, 42)

Nor, it seems in many cases, do architects regard drawings alone as adequate projections of their schemes: not only is talking about the drawings, whether to a client, or to some other audience, part of the convention of architecture, but some architects have gone in for writing, sometimes profusely, even sometimes on their drawings, to give in words what a visual image alone cannot describe. Philip Webb, for example, generally disparaging about architectural drawings – 'the ability to make picturesque sketches was a fatal gift to the architect' (Lethaby, 1935, 137) – on his own drawings wrote copious instructions about intended effects and finishes; or Balthassar Neumann, whose drawings contain long descriptions of intended effects of light and colour.

That architecture might be projected not in drawings at all, but entirely in words, has always been a possibility. In the late 1960s the Italian group Archizoom presented a scheme as a verbal description:

> Listen, I really think it's going to be something quite extraordinary. Very spacious, bright, really well arranged, with no hidden corners, you know. There will be fine lighting, really brilliant, that will clearly show up all those disordered objects.
>
> The fact is, everything will be simple, with no mysteries and nothing soul-disturbing, you know. Wonderful! Really very beautiful – very beautiful – very beautiful, and very large. Quite extraordinary! It will be cool in there too, with an immense silence.
>
> My God, how can I describe to you the wonderful colours! You see many things are quite hard to describe, especially because they'll be used in such a new way. ...You see, there'll be a lot of marvellous things, and yet it will look almost empty, it will be so big and so beautiful... How fine it will be... just spending the whole day doing nothing, without working or anything... You know, just great... (Ambasz, 234)

Philip Webb, in common with many architects, included verbal instructions on his drawings. This drawing for oak carving at Clouds, 1884, carries an extended discourse on the relationship of drawings, words and the resulting work: 'this sketch has been made thus particularly to indicate the effect intended: the carving will be seen at its *greatest* distance from the eye of *28 feet* and at its *nearest* 18 feet, so that the carving itself must be done very vigorously and even *rudely* done but not coarsely. The soft gradations shown on this drawing, except as an aid to the effect desired from the distance, will not be necessary, indeed the labour of doing it would be worse than wasted, but in a *drawing* there was no other way of indicating the *effect* to be produced in the carving… The carver will necessarily use his judgement to get the effect in *his* ways of the intention of the drawing.

To get the effect, as *little* laborious work should be done as possible: sharp gougings and trenchant channelling, after the faceting is rightly set out, should be employed, and the chisel marks only softened down, but *none* of the veining and other indications on the drawing to be lost sight of. In *repeating* the pattern *no* absolute match is wanted, so long as the general size, form and character are maintained.'

This description, it will be noticed, contains no particulars – no mention of what the space was *for*, whether 'house', 'office', 'library' or 'bar', and nothing about its physical delineation. The result, as Archizoom intended, was as many different versions of the project as there were subjects listening to the words and prepared to try and construct it, whether in their minds, or physically, in the world. Archizoom's experiment was not unique; the English architect William Alsop made a project in words, 'The Other Room' (see Alsop 1977), and the French architect Jean Nouvel's Diploma project was, apparently, entirely written. A verbal projection of a work of architecture – and such it seems were not so uncommon in the Middle Ages – presumes an unusual degree of trust in the builder; either, as was the case in the Middle Ages, the conventions were so well defined that the result will be as predicted, or as in the case of Morphosis's CDLT House (1989), the project must be treated as an experiment with an unknown outcome. Here, no working drawings were produced, and the builder worked from sketches produced each day; 'at the end of each day the contractor left lights pointed at areas on which he had been working but that needed resolution'. Significantly, though, the architects added, 'the builder had degrees in literature and musical composition, so it was possible to talk ideas with him' (Mayne, 152–63): in effect the 'ideas' could travel from the architect's head to the builder's hand without need for the conveyance of drawings. Works of architecture produced from verbal projections are not therefore impossible,

Interior of Hall at Clouds, Wiltshire, photographed in the 1890s. The oak carving for which the full-size drawing (above) was prepared runs just above the windows of the gallery.

but their outcome may be different to those produced from drawings.

If one objection to the assumed subordination of language to drawing in the process of architectural creation is that it oversimplifies this process, another is more historical. A common view of the relation between language and design – to use a more inclusive term for this process than just the physical preparation of drawings – is that design comes first, and is talked about afterwards. Or, to put the same point in more general terms, design precedes its verbalization. Such a view is explored by Paul-Alan Johnson in his *Theory of Architecture*. He writes:

> In our search for ways of talking about architecture, words often are unable to keep pace with changes occuring in current practice…. Could it be that the notion of theory guiding practice… is a misunderstanding arising from an assumed constancy, and therefore precedence, in the words used in design-talk, and that, in fact, the words are lagging behind design? Could this retardation in fact be a constraint that theory applies to practice, a natural conservatism, and that in the usual formulation, theory does not guide practice, but practice paces theory? (45–46)

Johnson's view that design, or practice, is what leads, and that 'theory' (by which he presumably means critical, verbal engagement with it) is its effect, is a more orthodox view of the architecture–language relationship than he supposes.

CDLT House, Silverlake, California, Morphosis/Michael Rotondi, 1989. Built without drawings, and with only verbal instructions to the builder.

And yet it is one that is not wholly in accord with the facts: it may indeed be the case that a term, or a category is coined to describe a quality in a new design, but for the most part the process is the reverse, as architects and critics draw upon pre-existing critical categories and vocabularies to describe what they want others to see in the work. The outstanding instance that contradicts Johnson's assertion is 'space', said to be twentieth-century architecture's most distinctive feature (see 'Space', Part II). Yet as a critical category, 'space' was developed before a recognizably 'spatial' architecture was brought into existence, and before architects started to describe their own work in spatial terms. While not suggesting that the prior existence of 'space' within the critical vocabulary of architecture was what led architects to realize spatial properties in their architecture, there is no doubt that in talking about what they were doing, they were able to draw upon an established vocabulary and turn it to their advantage. As this, and similar cases suggest, it would be wrong to regard language as merely an after-effect of design: it more generally exists already, but is pulled into design to do something for it that the somnabulist world of the drawing is not able on its own to provide.

This brings us to the question, in what does language succeed and drawing fail? Some suggestions as to how we might think about this question were made by Roland Barthes in his analysis of the system of fashion. He wrote:

> to combat the tyranny of visual perception and to tie meaning to other modes of perception or sensation is obviously one of the functions of language. In the order of forms, speech brings into existence values which images can account for only poorly: speech is more adept than images at making ensembles and movements signify (we are not saying: at making them more perceptible): the word places its force of abstraction and synthesis at the disposal of the semantic system of clothing. (1990, 119)

If, as Barthes suggested, language's power relative to images lies in 'abstraction and synthesis', and in the ability to draw out the meaning of 'ensembles and movements', what are its competencies within architecture? There are, I believe, five regions of difference between language and drawings that we might look at.

1. Given a choice between words and drawings, architects will generally choose drawing. The reasons are obvious – drawings are exact, and language is vague: as the architect Thom Mayne puts it, 'Drawings and models… allow a degree of precision often elusive in verbal discourse' (9). Yet to conclude from this that drawings or models are therefore a more perfect medium within architecture, and that language is an imperfect medium, is simply to surrender to the tyranny of visual perception. What language itself allows is ambiguity, and a freedom from the relentless exactitude of drawing; where drawing demands finite

Frank O. Gehry, Sketch for the Weatherhead School of Management of Case Western Reserve University, 1997. As a way of presenting to public view the intended effect of completed buildings, the architectural sketch (of which Gehry has been a particularly active propagator) has become increasingly common in the twentieth century, and may be seen as an attempt to make drawing more like language in its uncertainty.

precision – either there is a line or there isn't – language allows architects to deal with everything that they find difficult, or choose not to be precise about – nuances, moods, atmosphere. Where drawings pretend to project a reality, language is about keeping reality at bay. Language permits signification, it encourages one thing to be 'seen as' another, it stimulates the sense of potential ambiguity that lies at the basis of meaning, in a way that drawings can only do prosaically. It is for these reasons above all that the demands for a 'plain language of architecture' seem so out of place: language does not deal in directness, it deals in metaphor and ambiguity. There is only one kind of drawing that displays some of language's qualities of indistinctness and ambiguity – the sketch; and we might perhaps see in the greater value attached to the architectural sketch in the course of the twentieth century an attempt to render drawings more language-like.

2. The most fundamental distinction between language and images (whether drawings or photographs) is that, as Saussure put it, 'in language there are only differences' (120). All that language can signify – and what it excels at signifying – are differences; but in drawings, although the technique consists of a system of difference (line/no line), the overall finished result does not itself immediately draw attention to its unlikeness to some other representation.

Whereas in language, the entire significance of the appellations 'heavy' or 'complex' belongs in the opposition to 'light' or 'simple', a drawing has no immediately recognizable opposite. The drawing invokes primarily the thing it represents, and while someone practised in drawing might reflect on how other drawings, in other styles, or other projections, might cause one to see the thing represented differently, this is a secondary level of signification, and it is certainly not precise. On the other hand, everything that the word 'complex' invokes is contained within its not being 'simple'.

In short, language is very much better at signifying differences than drawing or images of any kind. That this is its routine occupation within architecture must be wholly familiar to anyone involved in architecture or its criticism.

3. A recognized feature of language is the distinction between the *object language*, and the *metalanguage*, between what words themselves signify, and the field of meaning that gives one the power to communicate in a given language. In normal conversation we are constantly checking, by remarks like 'you know what I mean', 'Do you follow?', to make sure that other people are using the same metalanguage. One of the features of the particular type of verbal memory loss called 'aphasic disorder' is that the sufferer is deprived of the metalanguage, so that words cease to have the 'capacity to assume additional, shifted meanings associated by similarity with their primary meaning' (Jakobson, 249). The world of architectural drawing is rather like that of the aphasic: although in certain regions of art – Picasso's collages and cubist reliefs, for example – there is a good deal of play between object language and metalanguage, in architectural drawing this has, traditionally at least, been discouraged. Where spoken and written language, as a matter of course, appeals constantly to the metalanguage, allowing it to be both ambiguous and precise, architectural drawings generally aim to stick to the 'object language' and to restrict 'additional, shifted meanings'.

4. It is in the nature of language that words have to be spoken or written in a linear sequence. A drawing, on the other hand, presents its image all at once. In this respect, buildings are more like language than they are like drawings, for they cannot be experienced all at once – they have to be explored by moving through and around them in a sequence; and this sequential motion is much more easily represented by language than it is by drawings. When people talk, as they often do, about 'reading' a drawing, what they are generally doing is projecting imagined bodily movement around a drawn plan or section, and describing what they would encounter; they are performing a language-like act of interpretation of an image. The 'all-at-once' impression that drawings are so much better at conveying than language is a property that has been heavily exploited; a long-standing ambition within architectural drawing has been

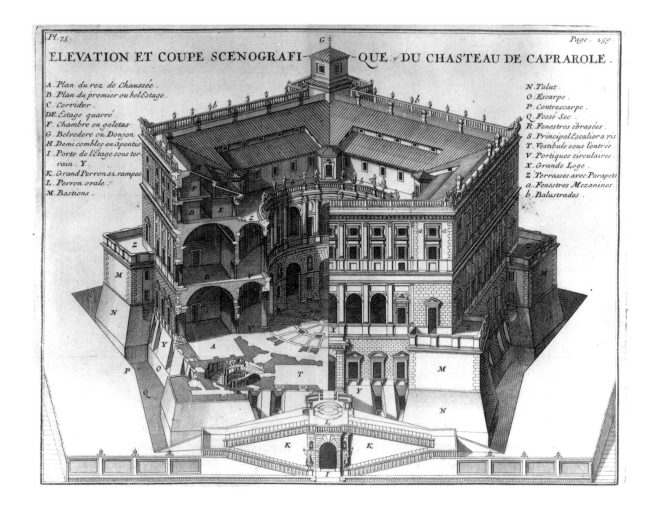

Pl. 73.

Page. 259.

ELEVATION ET COUPE SCENOGRAFI-QUE DU CHASTEAU DE CAPRAROLE.

A. Plan du rez de Chaussée.
B. Plan du premier ou bel Estage.
C. Corridor.
DE. Estage quarré.
F. Chambre en goletas.
G. Belvedere ou Donjon.
H. Demi combles en apentis.
I. Porte de l'Estage sous terrain. Y.
K. Grand Perron a 2. rampes.
L. Perron ovale.
M. Bastions.

N. Talut.
O. Escarpe.
P. Contrescarpe.
Q. Fossé Sec.
R. Fenestres ebrasées.
S. Principal Escalier a ris.
T. Vestibule sous l'entrée.
V. Portiques circulaires.
X. Grande Loge.
Z. Terrasses avec Parapets.
a. Fenestres Mezanines.
b. Balustrades.

Cut-away aerial perspective of Vignola's Villa Farnese, Caprarola, published 1617. Drawings offer the chance to show simultaneously the inside and outside of buildings – impossible to see in life – and from the earliest development of architectural drawing techniques, this has been one of their regular uses.

through a single image to present simultaneously every aspect of a building, inside and outside, front and back etc. In this particular contest, language is a non-starter – but this does not lessen the worth of language.

5. Received wisdom has it that drawings are easier to understand than language – 'a picture speaks a thousand words'. In what senses is this true? What demands do drawings and language respectively place upon understanding? The conventional systems of architectural drawing, relying upon either orthogonal or perspectival projection, place certain quite particular demands upon the viewing subject. Orthogonal drawings, projected from an infinity of points perpendicular to the surface of the paper, require viewers to imagine themselves atomized into a thousand beings suspended in space before the building; and perspectival drawings, conversely, expect the viewer to suppose they are

one-eyed and motionless in one spot. Both are fictions, neither has much correspondence to reality. More particularly, both projections, like all drawings, presuppose that one is *outside* the object: subject and object are conveniently separated by the surface of the paper. The drawing itself becomes a simulacrum of perception, and its exteriority to us requires us to suppose that perception, as well as the thing perceived lies outside the mind. Language places no such demands upon us: the words themselves carry no illusions, but act directly upon the mind; language allows perception to happen where it belongs, within the mind. In this respect at least, language does not demand the various intellectual contortions that are necessary (however little conscious we are of them) for us to understand a drawing.

The Viennese architect Adolf Loos did not explain what he meant by saying that 'Good architecture can be written'. Like many of Loos's remarks, it is both provocative and enigmatic – but not absurd.

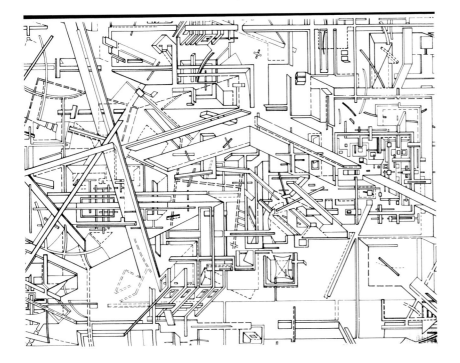

Daniel Libeskind, 'The Burrow Laws' (detail), *Micromegas*, 1979. Conventional drawing techniques created a separation between the viewing subject and the object represented, but experiments with non-orthogonal drawings have tried to make the act of perception integral with the object perceived: they are more like language in their operation.

3

The mythical origins of the Corinthian
order. From a sixteenth-century
manuscript copy of Francesco di Giorgio's
treatise on architecture, originally written
1478–81.

In language there are only differences. Saussure, 120

Language, itself a system of difference, is good at describing differences in a way that drawings and photographs are not. Much of the interest of critical vocabulary goes into the choice of particular metaphors to structure thought and experience. How does one say 'this', but not 'that'? How many different ways are there of saying 'this' but not 'that'? And why have some metaphors succeeded better than others?

In the history of architecture, the first consciously developed, fully articulated scheme of linguistic oppositions for critical purposes appeared with the publication in 1575 of Book VII of Sebastiano Serlio's Treatise on Architecture. John Onians has pointed out that in several respects Serlio, through his attention to architecture as an *art*, showed a 'modern' approach to the practice, quite unlike his predecessors. In particular was the prominence Serlio gave to 'judgment': 'It is certain that the finest quality of the architect is that he is not let down in his judgment [*giudicio*], as many are' (196). To aid right judgment, Serlio put forward in Book VII a system of six oppositions, in which he distinguished

> between an architecture which is solid [*soda*], simple [*semplice*],
> plain [*schietta*], sweet [*dolce*], and soft [*morbida*] and one which
> is weak [*debole*], flimsy [*gracile*], delicate [*delicata*], affected [*affettata*],
> harsh [*cruda*], in other words obscure [*oscura*] and confused [*confusa*],
> as I will make understood in the four following illustrations.
> (Onians, 266)

Serlio proceeded to apply his critical system to a discussion of the orders, in the course of which he introduces three further terms, *secca*, or dry, *robusta*, robust, and *tenera*, soft. From this exposition, and Onians's interpretation of it, one can set out Serlio's scheme thus:

soda (solid)	*debole* (weak) = presence/absence of structural strength
semplice (simple)	*gracile* (flimsy)
schietta (plain)	*delicata* (delicate) = refer to detail
dolce (sweet)	*affettata* (affected)
morbida (soft)	*cruda* (harsh); *secca* (dry) = degree of unity, and softness of transitions

All the qualities on the right-hand side fall under the general categorization of *oscura* and *confusa*; a further opposition, *robusta* (robust) to *delicata* (delicate) and *tenera* (soft), falls outside the general scheme of the first group.

According to Onians, Serlio took his terms from rhetoric, but as he points out, Serlio was careful to tie the metaphors to a visual demonstration and give them a specifically architectural meaning. In Serlio's relatively elaborate system we see a model of what all language does in relation to architecture: it distinguishes between 'this' and 'not this'. But Serlio's scheme was unusual in the care with which he balanced his oppositions, in each case giving as much weight to the negative as to the positive value. In most metaphors of difference, only one side of the opposition receives much attention, the other being merely roughly indicated, or frequently not named at all, subsisting simply as inexplicit otherness.

Among Serlio's various metaphors for structuring difference, one that was absent was gender, the distinction between male and female. As in most other arts, from the Renaissance onwards, there was within architecture a tradition of discriminating between works according to the characteristics of the sexes; the convention of describing architectural works as 'masculine' or 'feminine' was – until its abrupt disappearance with the advent of modernism – one of the most commonly used schemes of difference. It is to this tradition, and its sudden demise, that we shall now turn to investigate a distinction-making metaphor in action.

The gendering of architecture within the classical tradition begins with the mythical origins of the orders, according to which, as Bernini, in the seventeenth century, put it, 'the variety of the orders proceeded from the difference between the bodies of man and woman' (Fréart de Chantelou, 9). Bernini was of course referring to Vitruvius's account of the different orders, of how the Greeks 'proceeded to the invention of columns in two manners; one [Doric], manlike in appearance, bare unadorned; the other [Ionic] feminine.... But the third order, which is called Corinthian, imitates the slight figure of a maiden' (Book IV, chapter 1, §7–8). Vitruvius's gendering of the orders became a commonplace of the Italian Renaissance, and wherever classical architecture was adopted.[1] Thus, for instance, Hawksmoor wrote in 1735 to Lord Carlisle about the Mausoleum at Castle Howard, 'I esteem'd the Dorick more suitable to the Masculin strength we wanted'. Sometimes the classification was elaborated: Sir Henry Wotton, for example, in 1624 wrote

Mausoleum, Castle Howard, Yorkshire, N. Hawksmoor, 1729–36. 'Dorick more suitable to the Masculine strength we wanted', Hawksmoor wrote.

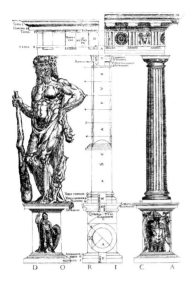

The *Dorique Order* is the gravest that hath been received into civill use, preserving, in comparison of those that follow, a more *Masculine Aspect*... The *Ionique Order* doth represent a kinde of Feminine slenderness, yet saith *Vitruvius*, not like a light Housewife, but in a decent dressing, hath much of the *Matrone*.... The *Corinthian*, is a *Columne*, laciviously decked like a Curtezane... (35–37)

'The variety of the orders proceeded from the difference between the bodies of man and woman.' The Doric, Ionic and Corinthian orders from John Shute, *The First and chief Groundes of Architecture*, 1563.

Wotton distinguished not just between masculine and feminine, but also between kinds of femininity, between the decency of the matron and the lasciviousness of the courtesan. We see suggested here the rich potential for the extension of the language of gender from the mere classifications of sexual difference, to descriptions of sexual orientation and even sexual perversion. From Wotton's day onwards, sexual deviancy has been a no less valuable source of metaphors than straightforward gender distinctions.

The gendering of the orders was a convention that lasted as long as the classical tradition, used by architects and critics alike; when Hegel wrote of the 'simple, serious, and unadorned masculinity exemplified in the temples at Paestum and Corinth' (vol. 2, 678), this was no more than the customary appellation for a Doric building. More interesting for our purposes is the characterization of other elements of architecture, and of whole buildings, in terms of sexual difference and deviancy. That this was going on at least as early as the start of the seventeenth century is confirmed by the note Inigo Jones's made in his sketchbook in 1614 – 'in architecture ye outward ornamentes oft

Somerset House, London, river front,
Sir William Chambers, 1776–1801.
'Bold and masculine'.

[ought] to be Sollid, proporsionable according to the rulles, masculine and
unaffected' (Harris and Higgott, 56). The context of this statement was a
criticism of the capricious, licentious ornaments devised by Michelangelo and
his followers, which Jones believed to be appropriate for interiors and garden
buildings, but, just 'as outwardly every wyse man carrieth a graviti in Publicke
Places', inappropriate for the outsides of buildings. 'Masculine' in this instance
implied decorum, and although Jones may well have picked up the term from
Vasari (who had used it in the sense conventional throughout the arts of
apparent physical strength, 'masculine, solid and simple'),[2] Jones gave to it
the more interesting inflection of 'behaviour becoming to a man'. As applied
to buildings, their ornaments, and even gardens, 'masculine' continued a
customary term in the critical vocabulary throughout the eighteenth century,
and into the nineteenth: in 1825, the architect Thomas Hardwick wrote of
his former master Sir William Chambers, 'The exteriors of his buildings are
marked and distinguished by a bold and masculine style, neither ponderous
on the one hand, nor too meagre on the other' (Chambers, 1825, L). On the
face of it, Hardwick might not appear to have been saying much by describing
Chambers's style as 'masculine', but anyone familiar with French eighteenth-
century architecture – as both Chambers and Hardwick were – would have
known differently.

From the mid-eighteenth century in France, 'masculine' (the usual word was
mâle) was used frequently, particularly in the attack upon rococo: J.-F. Blondel,
for example, contrasted rococo with 'that masculine simplicity' of the buildings

he approved of (1752, 116). And Laugier: 'in a church there must be nothing that is not simple, masculine [*mâle*], grave and serious' (1755, 156).

The more systematically minded of critics went to some trouble to define this term 'masculine' – and none more thoroughly than J.-F. Blondel, whose Academy in Paris Chambers had attended. In his *Cours d'Architecture*, published in 1771, but written in the 1750s, Blondel distinguished between three terms: the 'male' [*mâle*], the 'firm' [*ferme*] and the 'virile' [*virile*], as follows:

> A male [*mâle*] architecture can be understood as one which, without being heavy, retains in its composition the firmness suited to the grandeur of the location and to the type of building. It is simple in its general forms, and without too much ornamental detail; it has rectilinear plans, right angles, and projections which cast deep shade. A male [*mâle*] architecture is suited to public markets, fairs, hospitals and above all, military buildings, where care must be taken to avoid small compositions – the weak and the great not going together. Often, thinking to create a male [*mâle*] architecture, it is made heavy, massive and gross – the word is mistaken for the thing. (vol. 1, 411)

Cortile della Cavallerizza, Mantua, Giulio Romano,1538–39. Inigo Jones disapproved of Giulio Romano's licentious inventions: 'as outwardly every wyse man carryeth a graviti in Publicke Places...' external ornaments ought to be 'masculine and unaffected'.

Porte Saint-Denis, Paris, F. Blondel, 1672:
one of the eighteenth-century architect
J.-F. Blondel's examples of 'masculine'
architecture.

Blondel's examples include the work of Michelangelo, and in France, the
Palais de Luxembourg, the stables and orangery at Versailles, and the
Porte Saint-Denis.

> A firm architecture differs from a male [*mâle*] architecture by its masses;
> firm architecture has less weight, but nevertheless in its composition and
> division presents resolute forms with plane surfaces and right angles;
> everywhere it shows a certainty and an articulation, imposing and striking
> to the eye of intelligent persons. (vol. 1, 412)

Examples include the châteaux at Maisons, Vincennes and Richelieu.

> Although it may seem that a virile architecture differs little from the two
> previous characters, this term is used for works where the Doric order
> predominates. Maleness or firmness in architecture often need be expressed
> only with rustication or solidity, and do not require the presence of this
> order. (vol. 1, 413)

When Blondel turns to the feminine character, as with the virile, he identifies
it primarily with the use of a particular order:

> We term feminine architecture whose expression is drawn from the
> proportions of the Ionic order. The character expressed by the Ionic is more
> naive, gentler and less robust than that of the Doric order, and for that
> reason it must be used appropriately and with discretion in the decoration
> of buildings. It would be a misuse of feminine architecture were a perfectly
> correct but far less appropriate Ionic order to be applied to a building rather
> than the virile treatment which its particular purpose would seem to require.
> Again, we would deem it a wrong use of feminine architecture were the
> projecting parts of the façade of a building solid in style, to be composed of
> curvilinear rather then rectilinear members. Yet another misapplication of
> the feminine would have the effect of imparting uncertainty to the masses
> as well as the details of a building, whereas the intention had been that they
> should arouse admiration. This style should therefore be eschewed in all
> military monuments, buildings raised to the glory of heroes, and in the
> dwellings of princes. On the other hand the feminine can be applied approp-
> riately to the exterior decoration of a pretty country villa, a petit Trianon,
> in the interiors of a queen's or empress's apartments, and in baths, fountains,
> and other buildings dedicated to deities of the sea or the land. (419–20)

Within Blondel's scheme of criticism, masculine was unquestionably superior to
feminine architecture; masculine architecture was resolute, expressed its purpose

clearly, with no more decoration than was absolutely necessary, and conveyed structural solidity and permanence; while feminine architecture, meant to charm, was permitted a degree of equivocation and ambiguity. The *salon de la princesse* (1735–39) at the Hôtel Soubise in Paris is an example of what Blondel would have considered 'feminine architecture': created as a setting for the elderly Prince de Rohan's young bride, Boffrand's interior, with its illusions of depth beyond the walls, conveyed an appropriate degree of uncertainty. Yet although Blondel assumed that masculine architecture was invariably superior to feminine – an assumption that runs through the entire history of the language of gender distinction in architecture – Blondel was nonetheless unusual in acknowledging 'feminine architecture' as a specific category in its own right, with its own value and uses.

Blondel's definitions of masculine architecture were followed for the rest of the eighteenth century in France. An idea of how the distinction could be

Salon de la Princesse, Hôtel Soubise, Paris, G. Boffrand, 1735–39. This room, for the Princesse de Rohan, where wall merges imperceptibly into ceiling, and mirrors suggest ambiguous depth beyond the walls, created just that degree of equivocation and uncertainty that J.-F. Blondel considered the qualities of a 'feminine architecture'.

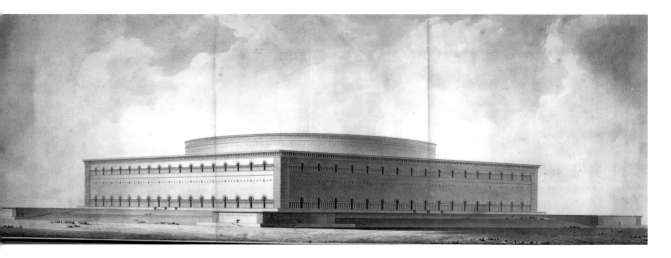

E.-L. Boullée, design for a Town Hall:
'It is smooth masses which produce
masculine effects.'

applied within architectural practice can be had from Boullée, for example, writing in the 1790s about his design for a town hall – a design which by Blondel's criteria was pre-eminently masculine:

> While reflecting on methods of creating a proud and masculine form of decoration, and on the need for many openings, you may imagine that I was brought up short and thrown into the greatest confusion; a house open to all must necessarily appear as a kind of beehive; and without question, a Town Hall is human beehive; now anyone who knows about architecture, knows how a multiplicity of openings spread across a façade produces what is described as skinniness [*maigreur*]. In decoration it is smooth masses which produce masculine effects... (131)

The language of gender was so much a part of the classical tradition of architecture that one might have expected it to have died out with that tradition. On the contrary, though, with the Gothic revival, it not only continued, but in both Britain and the USA had more invested in it than ever before. To many Gothicists, the very essence of Gothic architecture was, as William Burgess put it in 1861, 'boldness, breadth, strength, sternness and virility' (403). And when *The Ecclesiologist* reviewed Butterfield's All Saints, Margaret Street, London, on its completion in 1859, it could give no higher praise than 'our general admiration for the manly and austere design' (vol. XX, June 1859, 184–89). A little later, in 1884, Robert Kerr felt it necessary to caution against the 'sometimes too masculine manners of the Gothic revival' (307). On the other hand, amongst Gothicists, 'feminine' invariably denoted disapproval. For example, the architect George Gilbert Scott wrote in 1850 that the merits of the geometrical Decorated style 'as compared with the flowing style consist chiefly in its retention of the masculine and rigorous character of earlier days. The flowing tracery, though to some eyes more perfect, is too soft and feminine in its beauty to be admitted as the main characteristic of a perfect style' (100). The critic Beresford Hope distinguished between varieties of Gothic by comparing the 'overpowering and masculine qualities of early French Gothic, ... to Decorated's feminine "hectic flush" ' (19–20). And Robert Kerr expressed his national preferences in what was becoming a familiar formula: 'vastly as I admire all French art, I can never divest my mind of the feeling that I am admiring something whose charms are feminine. I say, therefore, that England, the very home of rough-and-ready muscularity, will probably never follow the precise formulas of French taste' (296). And in the eyes of Kerr's contemporary, the American architect and critic Henry van Brunt, so far removed was French architecture from the standards he admired that it verged on the deviant – 'refinement is often pressed to the verge of effeminacy' (161). In America, though, the language of gender filled a rather different need. From the 1830s, the failure of America to develop a distinctive national style in the arts was a recurrent concern amongst America architects and critics. The philosopher Ralph Waldo Emerson, reflecting in 1836 on what he saw as the superiority of European art, noted of the work of American artists, writers and architects, that it was 'in all, feminine, no character' (vol. IV, 108). Whether or not consciously following Emerson, architects and critics in the latter part of the nineteenth century repeatedly presented the issue of the relation of American to European culture in gendered terms: only when American art became 'masculine' would it have proved its worth. The architecture of H. H. Richardson was widely regarded as having achieved this state: his work was described by van Brunt, for example, as having a 'large, manly vigor' (176). But this was nothing to Louis Sullivan's 1901 eulogy of Richardson's Marshall Field Warehouse in Chicago (see ill. p. 52), in what must be the greatest celebration of architectural masculinity of all time:

All Saints, Margaret Street, London, William Butterfield, 1849–59: 'manly and austere design', wrote the *Ecclesiologist*.

> Here is a *man* for you to look at. A man that walks on two legs instead of four, has active muscles, heart, lungs and other viscera; a man that lives and breathes, that has red blood; a real man, a manly man; a virile force – broad, vigorous and with a whelm of energy – an entire male. (1976, 29–30)

Sullivan's own architecture in its turn became praised for its masculinity, though not in terms of a generalized ideal, but as a direct expression of the gender of the occupants. This is the the critic L. P. Smith in the *Architectural Record* in 1904 on the Guaranty Building in Buffalo: 'It is an American office building dominated by men... the elements of activity, ambition and directness of purpose are all shown in its architectural forms'. Interestingly, though, Smith

Marshall Field Warehouse, Chicago, H. H. Richardson, 1885–87 (demolished 1930). 'Here is a *man* for you to look at' – Richardson's Marshall Field Warehouse evoked one of the most outspoken evocations of architectural masculinity of all time.

also saw in the decoration at the street level of the Carson Pirie Scott Store in Chicago as 'appealing in its quality to femininity', to the femininity of its predominantly female customers.

But the terminology of sexual difference stopped abruptly with Sullivan. By 1924, the year of Sullivan's death, gender had ceased to be the organizing metaphor for the whole variety of hierarchical distinctions, 'strong/weak', 'plain/delicate', 'purposeful/equivocal' and so on, which Blondel had outlined, and which had structured the thought of architects and critics for three centuries. No modernist spoke about architecture in terms of gender – nor even gave a reason for not doing so – and even amongst critics who did not align themselves with modernism, the metaphor was abandoned as abruptly. From the 1920s until recently, with a few rare exceptions, the language of sexual

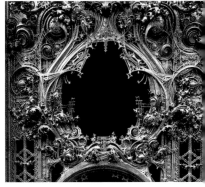

difference only occurs used anachronistically by critics and historians to describe features of past architecture in the terminology of its own time. Thus, for example, the description by Nairn and Pevsner in the Surrey volume of the *Buildings of England* of Lutyens's Tigbourne Court (see ill. p. 54) built between 1899 and 1901: 'The texture is the most intricate and carefully worked out of all Lutyens's buildings and gives Tigbourne an extraordinarily feminine – not effeminate – appearance: Bargate stone, galletted throughout, with brick quoins and thin horizontal bands of tiles running across the whole house' (487). (One may remark here a rare case of 'feminine' used to describe a positive quality, and not a deficiency of 'masculinity'.) The question we are left with is why sexual difference disappeared from the everyday vocabulary of architecture – and disappeared so suddenly?

(above left) Carson Pirie Scott Store, Chicago, L. Sullivan, 1899–1901 and 1903–4. 'Appealing in its quality to femininity'.

(above) Carson Pirie Scott Store, detail of decoration at street level.

Tigbourne Court, Surrey, E. Lutyens, 1899–1901, entrance front, and detail of stonework: 'an extraordinarily feminine – not effeminate – appearance'.

Of the likely reasons, the most immediate lies in the constraints placed upon language by modernism. 'Masculine' and 'feminine' had belonged to a critical vocabulary shared by all the arts, and were therefore incapable of describing the specificity of architecture. Moreover, they shared the fate of all human 'character' descriptions, that they referred in the most obvious way to objects outside architecture, and so entirely failed to describe the particularity and uniqueness of architecture's own medium. And furthermore, if the business of language within modernism was to deal solely with the act of perception itself, there was no means (until recently) to talk of this in terms of sexual proclivity, nor would it have seemed likely that a set of terms so deeply embedded in the values of bourgeois culture would have been capable of describing this process with any objectivity. If, in every way, gender metaphors ran counter to modernism, what probably finished them off, and made them unacceptable even to critics out of sympathy with modernism, was the explicitly masculine, not to say homo-erotic, orientation of culture in the totalitarian regimes of inter-war Europe. This is evident from the iconography of the works themselves, but was also explicit within the discourse of artists within those countries. For example, in Italy the 1931 Manifesto of Rationalist Architecture proclaimed, 'The architecture of the age of Mussolini must answer to the character of masculinity, of strength, of pride in the Revolution' (Patetta, 192). Under these circumstances, it was unacceptable for anyone with liberal, anti-fascist tendencies to use the terminology of sexual difference at all, and after 1945, throughout Europe they all but disappeared. Of the few exceptions, one in particular is worth quoting, on account of the attention it aroused. The occasion was the Festival of Britain exhibition in London in 1951, about which the otherwise impeccably modernist architect Lionel Brett wrote, 'It is easy to see that this style of the fifties will be thought flimsy and effeminate by the next generation, but we should lose no sleep on that account'. To invoke the obsolete language of gender terminology to describe the work of his contemporaries was not only to suggest that it failed to be 'modern' and was politically suspect, but worse, by calling it not 'feminine' but 'effeminate', indicated that it had failed even in the essential requirement of manhood, to be manly. If the 'normal' state of architecture was masculine, nothing could be worse than to have surrendered to 'effeminacy'.

Yet although 'masculine' and 'feminine', 'manly' and 'effeminate' and all the other various sexual distinctions apparently disappeared from the vocabulary of architecture, does this mean that architecture no longer has a gender? Do we only have neuter architecture now? Does a particular system of mental distinction, in use for the best part of two millennia, cease simply because the

(above) Senate Building, University of Rome, M. Piacentini, 1932: 'The architecture of the age of Mussolini must answer to the character of masculinity.'
(left) Sea and Ships Pavilion and the Dome of Discovery, Festival of Britain, South Bank, London, 1951: 'flimsy and effeminate... but we should lose no sleep on that account.'

Clustered pilasters on the apse of St Peter's, Rome, Michelangelo, 1546–64: forms 'unfulfilled to the point of discomfort' according to Wölfflin.

metaphors in which it was presented have become unsuitable? Or could the same distinction have been displaced elsewhere, so that it now subsists in some other vocabulary? Some reflection on the language of architectural discourse might suggest that we have indeed not entirely renounced the organizing structure provided by gender, even if it appears in another guise.

The first case of its possible displacement is to what may be called the language of 'form'. As a key term in the critical vocabulary of modernism, 'form' (see 'Form', Part II) derived from the German tradition of philsophical idealism developed by Kant and Hegel. For Hegel, the form of the work of art was the external, material shape by which the idea was made known to the senses. This theory of art relied upon a direct correspondence between the form and the internal, underlying idea or theme; the work of art whose external appearance failed to communicate the idea had failed in the most elementary requirement of art. During the latter part of the nineteenth century a considerable amount of intellectual effort went into considering the precise nature of art's means to communicate the idea, and the particular aspects of the idea which each art was best equipped to reveal. An influential line of argument was that the forms of art could and should represent movement: in the words of the aesthetic philosopher Robert Vischer, 'art finds its highest goal in depicting a moving conflict of forces' (121). Interpreted for architecture, the interest and uniqueness of architecture was perceived to lie in the particular manner in which it represented the static forces of the building's resistance to gravity.

(above left) Laocoön, first century BC, and detail. Expression in static form of combined muscular and psychic effort. (above) Venus de Medici, first century BC. Dismissed by Winckelmann as no more than a delectable natural object, comparable to a rose opening before the rising sun, or a firm and not quite fully ripe fruit. The ideal female figure lacked correspondence between its outward form and internal muscular structure.

Heinrich Wölfflin's analysis of Roman mannerist architecture rested primarily on the way static forms communicated frustrated movement: 'the baroque [by which he meant mannerism] never offers us perfection and fulfilment, or the static calm of "being", only the unrest of change and the tension of transience. This again produces a sense of movement'; and 'the ideal of tenseness was promoted by forms which were *unfulfilled to the point of discomfort*', as an example of which he gives clustered pilasters (1984, 62–63). The notion that architecture represents implied movement within forms that are not themselves in motion has been a conventional part of modernist thinking, and still seems to be widely taken for granted.

This entire notion of form as the static representation of a conflict of internal forces relies upon an ideal of the male anatomy, for it is in the male body that the closest correspondence of external form to muscular effort is to be found. Wölfflin's understanding of 'form' owed much to the reading of classical figure sculpture in German art historical scholarship originated by Winckelmann.[3] In antique sculptures of the male figure, the quality that was especially admired was the representation in static form of the combined concentration of muscular and psychic effort. Nowhere could this be seen better than in the Hellenistic sculpture of the Trojan priest Laocoön's struggle with the two snakes sent by the gods to kill him. The ideal female anatomy, on the other hand, lacked this correspondence between its internal muscular structure and its outward, visible form, so the female figure could never realize this quality of frozen energy – and conventionally, classical sculptures of the female nude showed a motionless figure, frequently at rest. It would have been impossible for Wölfflin to conceive his theory of movement in terms of the female body, for it was simply the wrong shape.

Wölfflin's theory of form, which he had developed in his doctoral thesis, was based on the empathetic projection of the sense of one's own body into architectural form. As he put it, 'Physical forms possess a character only because we ourselves possess a body' (1886, 151). It is through the 'most intimate experience of our own body' and its projection 'onto inanimate nature' that aesthetic perception occurs (159). What seems to be clear though is that Wölfflin is not talking about bodies in general, but about *his* body, the male body, as the one that gives form its meaning.

'Form' as used by most modernists was male, a masculine ideal. If this sounds far-fetched, one should look at what some critics of modern architecture have said about forms. Take, for example, Vincent Scully on Le Corbusier's Chandigarh:

> the High Court is a great, hollowed-out, concrete mass. Its glass skin is again masked, on the entrance side, by a *brise-soleil* which keeps the scale integral and pushes upward and out with threatening power. Up through this projection, continued further upward by the hung vaults of the canopy, rise the great piers as purely upward-thrusting forces. Between these, men enter, and ramps of almost Piranesian violence rise behind them. Their physical power can be grasped if we compare them with Paul Rudolph's entrance for his second High School in Sarasota, Florida, which was, as the architect freely admits, inspired by them. The American design has become thin, planar, and linear. It is tautly stretched as a parasol against the sun, and cannot be read as analogous to the confident human body, assuming position in a place, as Le Corbusier's demands to be. (48)

Entrance, High Court, Chandigarh, India, Le Corbusier, 1955. 'Piers as purely upward thrusting forces'.
© FLC L3(4)1-61

Were one to substitute female ideal beauty for the male ideal, the whole analysis would fall flat. Seemingly neuter, 'form' is, in the way it has been conceived and discussed in the twentieth century, a largely masculine ideal. A significant and unusual exception to the implicit masculine identity of much modernist criticism was Frank Lloyd Wright's quite regular description of certain of his buildings as feminine objects: for instance, in 1943 he referred to the Johnson Wax administration building at Racine as the 'daughter of the Larkin building', and 'more feminine' than the 'masculine Larkin building' (*Collected Writings*, vol. 4, 182). In his willingness to see his buildings as female in relation to his own masculinity, Wright, as in so many other respects, went against the grain of modernist convention.

Neil Denari, COR-TEX, details study, drawing, 1993. Hard exterior, but soft in its responsiveness.

The second area of architecture where we might detect signs of gender distinction is in the critical reception of so-called Machine Architecture developed in California. Characterized by hard, metallic exteriors and soft insides, the word that recurs in the discussion of this architecture is 'dangerous', 'dangerous and inherently unpredictable' – and this dangerousness seems to be one cause of its fascination. The work of Neil Denari presents a subtle version of this genre: Denari attempted to discard the early twentieth-century machine aesthetic characterized by repetition and rigidity – taken to be essentially masculine features – and replace it by a machine aesthetic which is soft, intelligent, responsive and infinitely pliable – in a sense, feminine. Curiously, though, critics have been reluctant to accept this intepretation. For example, Lebbeus Woods writes of Denari's work:

Historical architecture is too loaded with known associations for him (or so it would seem), whereas the machine is ubiquitous, unaesthetic, amoral, neutral, cool, philosophical. The machine is beyond politics and topicality. It is the inevitable instrument of an intellect seeking to master natural and anonymous forces and at the same time submit to them, as a lover and willing accomplice, yet also as a human being... (43–44)

This sounds just like a description of male sexuality – cool, mastering nature so as to be able to submit to its seductions. Part of the fascination exercized by the work of Denari and other Californian 'machine architects' would seem to be to do with its so easily being seen in terms of male conquest of the 'natural and anonymous forces' of the feminine: a description of the relationship between intellect and matter so thoroughly Aristotelian as to make every Western artist since antiquity feel at home.

Even if the language of gender is no longer a part of everyday critical vocabulary, gender distinctions still apparently structure our thought processes.[4] The absence of the metaphor may not mean that the distinction has altogether ceased to exist.

What would happen if the relationship between 'masculine' and 'feminine' were reversed? Conventionally, the best architecture was always masculine. The characteristics of masculine architecture were there for all to see: they fulfilled an ideal. Feminine architecture, on the other hand, was not only always inferior, but for most writers, with the significant exceptions of Blondel and Frank Lloyd Wright, it lacked any specific qualities, positive or negative, of its own. Commonly feminine architecture was no more than the inexplicit otherness of the esteemed qualities of masculine architecture. None of this should surprise us, for as others have pointed out, the feminine is simply an invention of male discourse, not a category in its own right; 'Male discourse invents the feminine for its own purposes' (Bergren, 12). But even when people stopped referring to architecture as masculine or feminine, they still seem to have taken it for granted that the best architecture is always masculine. Is this irreversible? An interesting remark by Michael Sorkin suggests that it need not be. Reviewing Richard Rogers's Patscenter building at Princeton in 1985, he wrote,

> the ensemble does participate deliberately in an historical machine culture, overwhelmingly masculine. One has read in the pages of *Architectural Review* theories of 'British high-tech' which pin its prominence on the early childhood training of its progenitors, their pre-pubescent bedrooms glutted with Meccano toys and scale replicas of Sopwith Camels. More directly relevant may be the sartorial history of men managing machines, from the resplendently haberdashered admiral on the bridge of his gigantic dreadnought... to the nattily turned out Marlboro man on the flight deck of the 747. The point is simply this; it's a history of the machine that stands outside the history of architecture and which brings with it special prejudices about the social environment. (134–35)

Sorkin's view of high-tech architecture is that it suits men, but women look out of place in it. From the point of view of the history of 'masculinity' in architectural thought, Sorkin's article could be the first time a mainstream critic used 'masculine' not to signify a superior ideal, but rather to draw attention to small-minded misogyny. By reversing the polarity of the opposition, a new set of possibilities become available.

The differences between man and woman provided architects and critics with a ready-made system of distinction. Even if most critics failed to articulate the properties of the feminine, the biological and cultural differences between the sexes offered a means of structuring perception in a scheme where each pole had its own readily identifiable attributes. In fact, the majority of terms used within the critical vocabulary of classical architecture conformed to this characteristic of a strong binary polarity within which each side of the opposition had recognizable qualities of its own: 'solid/light', 'hard/soft', 'natural/artifical', and many other oppositions followed this pattern of binary pairing. What is, by contrast, striking about the critical terms favoured by modernism – 'form', 'space', 'order' – is the indefiniteness of their opposites. Even if the modernists' attachment to 'form' was undoubtedly predicated on a horror of 'formlessness', what constituted 'formlessness' – or 'aspatiality', or 'disorder' – remained unarticulated and inexplicit. 'Form', 'space' and 'order' were generally presented as absolutes, concepts that embraced the entirety of their categories, that subsumed their 'other'. This is a feature that contributed much to the impenetrability of modernist language and part of any enquiry into critical terminology must involve consideration of their opposites.

Patscenter, Princeton, New Jersey, R. Rogers, 1982–83. The American critic Michael Sorkin commented – unflatteringly – on the 'overwhelming masculinity' of the machine culture evoked by High-Tech architecture.

1 See Rykwert, *The Dancing Column*, 1996, especially 29–34 and 97–115 for more detail on the history and development of the myth.

2 See Higgott, '"Varying with Reason": Inigo Jones's theory of design', 1992, 56.

3 See Potts, *Flesh and the Ideal*, 1994, especially chapter IV, 113–44.

4 A further instance of the power of the distinction was suggested by Robin Evans. He proposed that part of the interest of Le Corbusier's chapel at Ronchamp – 'dedicated to women, masterpiece of the subjective, reputed destroyer of the right angle and straight line' – is that its distinctly feminine forms were the outcome of an assertively masculine process of creation. See Evans, *The Projective Cast*, 1995, 287 and 320.

4

House at Penshurst, Kent, dated 1610.
'How very unsatisfactory every modern
building really is… compared with the
productions of any village mason or
parish priest at an age when men sought
only to express what they felt strongly,
and sought to do it only in their own
natural mother tongue, untrammelled by
the fetters of a dead or unfamiliar foreign
form of speech' (James Fergusson, 1862).
The now commonplace notion of an
architectural 'vernacular' – of which
Fergusson was an early and vigorous
exponent – rests, like several other figures
of architectural speech, upon an analogy
with language.

Most urgent seems to me at the moment the need to restore the integrity and the necessary optimism of our discipline by renewing the full implications of the linguistic analogy. Joseph Rykwert, 1971, 59

There are numerous ways to equate architecture with language. Yet such equations often amount to a reduction and to an exclusion.
Bernard Tschumi, 1977, 94

Of all the metaphors found in architecture, there have been few put to such a variety of uses, and certainly none so contentious, as those derived from language. A significant proportion of the words discussed in Part II have, in their architectural usage, had connotations with the field of linguistics and this alone would make an enquiry into the general phenomenon of language metaphors worthwhile.[1] But what makes such an enquiry particularly necessary is that in the last twenty years or so comparisons between architecture and language have been the cause of so much argument: there has been nothing like a linguistic analogy for stirring up a fight in architectural circles. In the present general reaction against seeing any aspect of architecture in terms of verbal language, it may sometimes be overlooked how extraordinarily productive an analogy it has been in the past; and a tendency to bundle all linguistic analogies together, as if they were all the same, all subject to the same faults, has obscured the fact that there are whole expanses of architecture that would have forever remained unthought had it not been suggested that, in one way or another, one might see architecture as like language. Even in what is otherwise one of the best historical discussions of linguistic metaphors, an article by the French historian Jacques Guillerme, he treats them all as differing manifestations of the single 'architecture-language syntagm', and all therefore as equally defective.[2]

To assume that all language analogies are fundamentally the same imposes an unnecessary restriction upon our freedom to think about this topic. One of the most striking features about language metaphors is their astonishing variety and range, as diverse as the concepts of and about language itself. The 'linguistic analogy' is not a monolith: it consists of a great many different applications, and one may legitimately argue about the relative merits and values of these different metaphors. We talk as a matter of course about 'reading' a plan, and there may indeed be no better way of describing the particular process of perception involved in this activity; but to talk of 'reading' a plan is a very long way from claiming that a work of architecture is a linguistic sign. As a step towards a more reasonable approach to the question of language analogies in architecture, we can usefully discriminate between the various metaphorical equivalents language offers to architecture.

Before doing so, a few general distinctions will be useful. First of all, there is all the difference in the world between saying that architecture is *like* a language, and saying that it *is* a language. Or, to put the same point slightly differently, it is one thing to say that architecture has certain things in common with language, for example that it can mediate things apart from what is contained within its own materiality; but it is quite another thing to say that architecture fully conforms to the various syntactical or grammatical rules that are found in spoken languages. Secondly, we should distinguish between analogies concerned with the *semantic* aspects of language, with meaning; and analogies relating to the *syntactic* aspect of language, with language as a grammatical and structural system. And thirdly, we may distinguish between those metaphors which compare architecture to *literature*, to developed compositions within a given language; and those metaphors which treat architecture as analogous to *language*, in the sense of the general linguistic phenomenon.

A further task will be to distinguish historical changes in language metaphors: when eighteenth-century architects and critics drew comparisons between architecture and language, their motives and the ideas they hoped to express were utterly different to those of an architect or critic in the 1960s. We cannot assume that simply because they invoked language, they were speaking about the same thing, for what was understood by 'language' in the 1780s was not necessarily what was meant in the 1960s. Even the title of Sir John Summerson's best-selling book *The Classical Language of Architecture* is misleading, for it suggests, wrongly, that 'language' was a defining theme of the classical tradition, when in fact no sixteenth-, seventeenth- or eighteenth-century architect ever contemplated describing their art, in its entirety, as a language. Even more than notions of architecture have changed, so have conceptions of language. No social product has given rise to more continuous speculation and more various theories than has language, and in this has been much of its fascination to architects. Language has for the last two hundred years been an ever-open quarry, to which, as new strata become exposed, architects and critics have returned repeatedly to find fresh metaphors.

Those who have used linguistic metaphors have often been well aware of their unsatisfactory nature. What, therefore, has been their appeal? What has been achieved by their use, despite their acknowledged shortcomings? There is no doubt that part of the reason for the pervasiveness of language metaphors since the 1950s has been an effect of the general imperialism of language in the twentieth century, and of the claims of linguistic theory to explain not just verbal language itself, but all cultural productions. Every other art practice, literature, painting, cinema, as well as architecture, has succumbed to linguistic interpretation. But this does not wholly explain the appeal of linguistic analogies, for these appeared in architecture well before linguistics made its claim to be able to provide a general theory of culture. To an extent, therefore, the reasons for the appeal of linguistic metaphors must be understood in terms specific to architecture. Architecture offers its own particular history of drawing upon language, one which does not entirely correspond to the history of other art practices.

Language metaphors, as they have been used in architecture, fall into six general categories. They will be presented here in the chronological order of their appearance. There has been, of course, nothing to stop the use of more than one type of metaphor at a time; indeed a certain amount of switching between metaphors has been routine.

1. Against invention

The first use of language as a metaphor was as an argument against invention and innovation. Fréart de Chambray, in his *Parallèle d'Architecture* of 1650, objected to the composite order as follows: 'an architect should no more employ his industry and study in finding out new Orders… than should an orator, to acquire the reputation of being eloquent, invent and coin new words that were yet never spoken' (104). This conservative argument against innovation of all kinds recurred repeatedly in various forms throughout the succeeding two and a half centuries. For example, in 1820, the English critic James Elmes, in his essay 'On the Analogy between Language and Architecture', objected to the Gothic revival on the grounds that it was an attempt to bring a dead language back into use. More famously, John Ruskin used the same analogy in *The Seven Lamps of Architecture* (1848) against the development of new styles:

> We want no new style of architecture. …But we want *some* style. …it does
> not matter… whether we have an old or a new architecture, but it matters
> everything whether we have an architecture truly so called or not; that is,
> whether an architecture whose laws might be taught at our schools from
> Cornwall to Northumberland, as we teach English spelling and English
> grammar, or an architecture which is to be invented fresh every time we
> build a workhouse or a parish school.

But Ruskin went on to use the analogy in a more positive sense to clarify the extent to which an architect was free to invent:

> There seems to me to be a wonderful misunderstanding among the majority of architects of the present day as to the very nature and meaning of Originality, and of all wherein it consists. Originality in expression does not depend on invention of new words. …A man who has the gift will take up any style that is going, the style of his day and will work in that. …I do not say that he will not take liberties with his materials, or with his rules. … But… those liberties will be like the liberties that a great speaker takes with the language, not a defiance of the rules for the sake of singularity. (chapter VII, §iv)

Half a century later we find the metaphor still in use, by the architect Reginald Blomfield, in a warning against Art Nouveau's 'futile attempts of originality':

> The forms of architecture are, at this period of the world's history, very old, in much the same sense in which the words of a language may be said to be very old. Nobody has yet asserted that the possibilities of the English language, for example, are exhausted, and it is so with architecture. (1908, 151)

Modernism, whose *raison d'être* lay in innovation, routed this particular analogy, though it was to reappear in the conservative postmodernist tendencies of the 1980s.

Hector Guimard, interior of his own residence, 122 avenue Mozart, Paris, c. 1910. 'Futile attempts of originality': Reginald Blomfield condemned Jugendstil architecture's new forms as absurd as attempts to invent a new spoken language.

2. To describe what made architecture an art

Throughout the seventeenth and eighteenth centuries, a recurring need in architectural circles was to establish that architecture was a liberal and not a mechanical art. The measure of a liberal art was provided by music, and particularly by poetry: the degree to which other arts approximated to these legitimated their claims to liberal status. In the pictorial arts, the theory of *ut pictura poesis*, developed in the seventeenth century, derived from the Roman author Horace's text *The Art of Poetry*, proposed that just as poetry could in its different genres (tragedy, comedy, pastoral, epic etc.) evoke particular moods and emotions, so too might pictures. In mid-eighteenth-century France, the same argument was extended to architecture by Germain Boffrand, in his *Livre d'Architecture* (1745), and the idea that architecture had the power of expressing different moods and characters (see 'Character', pp. 121–31) became an important one in the latter part of the century. The success of the *ut pictura poesis* analogy for architecture rested on two things in particular: on its grasp of the correct disposition of parts, an understanding, as Horace said of poetry, 'of the power of words used in the right places and in the right relationships' (87); and the ability to show that it was capable of different 'styles', comparable to the different genres of poetry. The primary use of language metaphors in the eighteenth century was to show that architecture conformed to Horace's conception of poetry.

(i) *As an account of the relationships of the part to the whole.* The proper relation of the parts of buildings to the whole has been a long-running concern throughout the history of architecture: it was present in medieval architecture, and was recodified for classical architecture in the fifteenth century by Alberti, but with the development of the *ut architectura poesis* theme, it was reformulated in literary and linguistic terms. As Boffrand put it in his *Livre d'Architecture*, 'The sections of mouldings and the other parts which make up a building, are, in architecture, what words are in a discourse' (18). This idea of particular elements of buildings as words, which must be combined properly so as to achieve the correct expressive effect, became commonplace in later eighteenth-century writing. The Italian architect Francesco Milizia, in his *Principii d'architettura civile* of 1781, closely following French thought, wrote, 'the materials in architecture are like words in discourse which separately have little or no effect and can be disposed in a despicable manner; but combined with art and expressed with a motive and agile energy are capable of unlimited effects' (Guillerme, 22). And in remarkably similar terms, the English architect Sir William Chambers, who had attended Blondel's Academy in Paris, put it as follows:

> materials in architecture, are like words in phraseology; having separately but little power; and they may be so arranged, as to excite ridicule, disgust, or even contempt; yet when combined with skill, expressed with energy, they actuate the mind with unbounded sway. An able writer can move even in a rustic language, and the masterly disposition of a skilful artist, will dignify the meanest materials. (75–76)

This analogy between architectural and verbal composition was undermined by the theory of the *fragment*, developed in the early nineteenth century, a theory which drew attention to the *unlikeness* of architecture and language. Drawing upon the analogy with biology, where the French scientist Cuvier had in 1812 boasted that from careful study of a single bone one 'might reconstruct the the whole animal to which the bone had belonged' (60–61), it was argued (most famously by Viollet-le-Duc) that likewise in architecture entire ancient buildings might be reconstructed from a few stone fragments.[3] A parallel, though different argument emerged out of German Romantic thought: Goethe claimed that every

Fragment of Temple of Apollo Didymaeus from *Ionian Antiquities*, vol. 1, 1769. The cult of the fragment – from which the missing work, and indeed the spirit of entire civilizations might be recreated – pointed to an *unlikeness* between language and works of architecture.

fragment of a great work was so suffused with the inner life of the object that it was possible to feel the spirit of the whole without necessarily knowing the object. Under no circumstances would it be possible either to reconstruct an entire work of literature, or to even to grasp its organic spirit, from a single word or even sentence, in the way that was claimed for architecture and sculpture. Whereas Milizia had claimed that 'words in discourse separately have little or no effect', both theories of the fragment claimed that individual elements of architecture carried potentially as much effect as the work as a whole. The force of this particular argument about the unlikeness of architecture and literature would appear to have contributed to a loss of interest in analogies between architecture and classical literary theory.

(ii) *to characterize 'style' in architecture.* J.-F. Blondel's *Cours d'Architecture*, the largest and most important work of architectural criticism of the eighteenth century, is in part an extended application of the *ut pictura poesis* analogy to architecture. Blondel's book is full of comments about the relationship of architecture to the classical theory of poetry, principally in order to demonstrate the range of expressive genres and characters available in architecture, but also to show that 'style' was just as much a property of architecture as it was of poetry: 'architecture is like literature; the simple style is preferable to an inflated style, since one only weakens a great idea by trying to raise it up with pompous words' (vol. 4, lvi). Or, 'Architecture is like poetry; all ornament which is only ornament is excessive. Architecture, by the beauty of its proportions and the choice of its arrangement is sufficient unto itself' (quoted in Collins 1965, 180). The same conception of style recurs amongst later eighteenth-century authors: for example, C. F. Viel, *Principes de l'ordonnance et de composition des bâtiments*, 1797:

> However the word style is used in literature, one makes equal use of it in our present subject. It consists, in relation to literature, in that arrangement of words, that disposition of phrases which render diction pure and elegant… this word and its different qualities are applied with as much truth to the other arts and singularly architecture. (96)

Also often employed were distinctions between prose and poetry, usually to underline the distance between architecture and building. For example, C.-N. Ledoux, *L'Architecture considerée sous le rapport de l'art, des moeurs et de la législation* (1804): 'architecture is to masonry what poetry is to literature; it is the dramatic enthusiasm of the craft'. This distinction between architecture and building continued to be common, even into the twentieth century, amongst the successors of the French classical tradition. According to Peter Collins (1959, 199), in the 1920s Auguste Perret saw architecture's relation to building as common speech was to poetry. Modernists, generally anxious to underline architecture's singularity and avoid dependence upon other art practices, eschewed this analogy; it is significant that Perret's pupil, Le Corbusier, made no use of it in *Towards a New Architecture* when he discussed the difference between architecture and construction.

It should be emphasized that no eighteenth-century critic ever claimed that architecture was itself a linguistic phenomenon: there was no attempt to derive a general theory of architecture from language. Indeed, without a general theory of language – and no such theory was available until towards the end of the eighteenth century – would there have been any future in such an attempt? The sole purpose of the literary analogies employed by eighteenth-century French critics was to draw attention to the affective powers of architecture, and legitimate its status as a liberal art.[4]

3. To describe the historical origins of architecture
The question of how architecture originated had been a preoccupation of architectural writers from Vitruvius onwards. Whether it originated in Greece, Rome, Egypt, or with the first cave-dwellers, was hardly resolved by Laugier's entirely speculative theory of its origin in nature, put forward in 1755. The issue

continued to concern architectural thinkers throughout the latter part of the eighteenth century, culminating in the brilliant solution to the problem suggested by Quatremère de Quincy in his prize-winning essay *De l'Architecture Egyptienne* (written in 1785, but not published until 1803, by which time it had been substantially revised).[5] Quatremère argued that architecture did not originate in any one place, but like language, was a development of the human faculties, occurring wherever mankind existed:

> Architecture did not have for its inventor a single and particular people. It is necessarily a universal consequence of the needs of man, and of the pleasures that in the state of society are mixed with needs. The invention of architecture must be put on a parallel with that of language, that is to say, neither one nor the other can be attributed to a particular man, but are the attributes of mankind in general (12).

Quatremère went on to say that just as the discovery that two different languages could share a common syntax had not led people to conclude that one language necessarily developed from the other, so one should not make the same supposition about architecture.

It was not until around 1850 that Quatremère's clever account of the origin of architecture was turned to advantage, when the German architect Gottfried Semper began to develop a systematic general theory of architecture. Semper's efforts, which culminated in the two volumes of *Der Stil* (1860–63), the first comprehensive theory of architecture to discount entirely its origination in the classical orders, were based upon the belief that he was looking at a phenomenon analogous to language. As he explained in the introduction to *Der Stil*,

> Art has its particular language, residing in formal types and symbols which transform themselves in the most diverse ways with the movement of culture through history, so that in the way in which it makes itself intelligible, an immense variety prevails, as in the case of language. Just as in the most recent research into linguistics, the aim has been to uncover the common components of different linguistic forms to follow the transformation of words through the passage of centuries, taking them back to one or more starting points where they meet in a common *Urform*... a similar enterprise is justified in the case of the field of artistic inquiry. (vol. 1, 1)

There were many implications in Semper's analogical theory, but one of the most important was the conclusion that the forms of architecture, like those of language, were capable of infinite development – an argument which removed from the classical tradition its claim to be the ultimate and exclusive

The First Hut, from Viollet-le-Duc, *The Habitations of Man*, 1876. Quatremère de Quincy argued that architecture originated in no one place but was, like language, a universal attribute of mankind.

embodiment of architectural expression, as well as controverting the original language analogy's resistance to innovation.[6]

Semper's mention of the influence upon his thinking of 'recent research in linguistics' – mostly likely a reference to the German philologist Franz Bopp's *Comparative Grammar* of 1833–52, and to Wilhelm von Humboldt's *On Language* published in 1836 – should alert us to realization that only with the development of a general theory of language could language become a significant model for thinking about architecture. As there are several correspondences between Humboldt's theory of language and some of the most original aspects of Semper's thought, it is worth discussing Humboldt's book briefly. According to Humboldt, language manifested a constant and unifying factor, which he called its 'form', a concept linked closely to Goethe's theory of the *Urformen*, the organic organizing principles underlying all natural organisms – and Semper uses the same term.[7] For Humboldt, language was not a 'product', but an 'activity', 'the ever-repeated mental labour of making the articulated sound capable of expressing thought' (49); and the fixed element in language was its underlying laws of generation, from which genetic principles could be produced an indefinite range of speech possibilities corresponding to the range of human thought. According to Humboldt, 'the constant and uniform element in this element of mental labour of elevating articulated sound to an expression of thought, when viewed in its fullest possible comprehension and systematically presented, constitutes the *form* of language' (50): were we to substitute 'worked material' for 'articulated sound', we would have a reasonable summary of Semper's theory of architectural form. And just as Humboldt considered the origins of language to be an uninteresting and irrelevant question, so metaphorical transfer of his theory to architecture made the archeological pursuit of the historical origin of styles a much less interesting subject than the search for underlying generic principles of architectural form. The indirect effects of Humboldt and the other early nineteenth-century linguistic philosophers in releasing architectural thought, and ultimately architecture, from the constraints of classical theory and the conventions imposed by the authority of ancient Greek and Roman building, is not to be underestimated.

4. To discuss architecture as a medium of communication

Interest in language as an analogy for discussion of the semantic aspect of architecture does not occur before about 1800. Although some late eighteenth-century architecture later became known as '*architecture parlante*', this expression, coined in 1852 by Léon Vaudoyer, was not intended to mark approval, but rather to draw attention to the poverty of Ledoux's architecture.[8] No late eighteenth-century architect or critic ever claimed that their art carried the range of expression possible within a language; Piranesi referred in his

Prima parte de architetture (1743) to the monuments of ancient Rome as 'speaking ruins' (*parlanti ruini*, 1972, 115), but this seems to have been an uncharacteristic rhetorical flourish that was not repeated. In general, in so far as eighteenth-century architects drew analogies with language, their measure of comparison was solely with the poetic genres. The English critic James Elmes's essay of 1820 'On the Analogy between Language and the Arts', makes no attempt to discuss architecture as a means of communication, although Elmes was well aware that this was a property of language. Elmes, not a great or original thinker, was still in 1820 unaware of the ideas about the expressive power of the plastic arts then just being developed in Germany and France.

(i) *Architecture as text*. For the history of the idea that works of architecture are there to be 'read', as if they were works of literature, we must return to Quatremère de Quincy. In the same work (*De l'Architecture Egyptienne*, 1803) as he had put forward the idea that the development of architecture corresponded to that of language, he also made the surprising observation that the monuments of ancient Egypt were 'public libraries'. The purpose of their exorbitant solidity and massive smooth surfaces was not some aesthetic effect, but to carry inscriptions, for they were

> in the most literal sense, the public records of the people; this function of being historians, which religion and government imposed upon them, this educational faculty with which they were invested, without doubt made it a sacred obligation to render eternal these monuments which were, not in a metaphorical sense, the depositories of the customs, beliefs, exploits, glory and ultimately of the philosophical and political history and the nation. (59)

The ideas in this curious passage from a relatively obscure architectural treatise were to reappear (whether by direct influence or not is unknown) in one of the most popular works of fiction written in the first half of the nineteenth century, Victor Hugo's *Notre Dame de Paris*, first published in 1831. In the second, 1832 edition, Hugo included an additional chapter entitled 'Ceci tuera cela' – 'This will kill that' – in which he put forward the idea that until it was displaced by the printed book, Gothic architecture had been the most complete and permanent record of human thought and history.[9] As Hugo put it, 'from the origin of things up to and including the fifteenth century of the Christian era, architecture was the great book of mankind, man's chief form of expression in the various stages of his development, either as force or as intelligence' (189). By the phrase 'This will kill that', Hugo meant 'that as human ideas changed their form they would change their mode of expression, that the crucial idea of each generation would no longer be written in the same material, so that the book of stone, so solid and durable, would give way to the book of paper'

(189). Hugo developed his analogy, suggesting that in the Middle Ages even dissident ideas were articulated through architecture, for 'thought was free only in this one mode, and so it was written out in full only in the books known as buildings' (193). 'Whoever', he continued, 'was then born a poet became an architect'. Summarizing his argument, Hugo wrote, 'that up until the fifteenth century architecture was the principal register of mankind, that during that period all ideas of any complexity which arose in the world became a building;

Amiens Cathedral, west front, begun 1220. According to the novelist Victor Hugo, prior to the fifteenth century 'architecture was the great book of mankind, man's chief form of expression'. Hugo's view of Gothic cathedrals was passionately endorsed by the English critic John Ruskin, and applied most particularly in his account of Amiens.

every popular idea, just like every religious law had its monuments; that the human race, in fact, inscribed in stone every one of its important thoughts' (195). The influence of this chapter, one of the most remarkable of all nineteenth-century statements about architecture, cannot, given the novel's great popularity (there were four different English editions between 1833 and 1839), be fairly calculated. What is clear, though, is that Hugo's concern about architecture's loss of meaning in his own time, and his evocation of a past in which architecture had been meaningful, resonated widely with the feelings of others, as did his analogy of architecture with the book.

Most famous amongst those to employ the same metaphor was John Ruskin. For example, in the final paragraph of the famous chapter of volume 2 of *The Stones of Venice* entitled 'The Nature of Gothic', Ruskin announced, 'Thenceforward the criticism of the building is to be conducted precisely on the same principles as that of a book', by which he meant that both existed in order to be read. Hugo's idea that buildings were books was taken up and elaborated upon more poetically by William Morris, in remarks such as, 'the only work of art which surpasses a complete Mediaeval book is a complete Mediaeval building' (1892, 321). For Morris, the two requirements of all living art were that it should adorn a surface and tell a story. The story told by architecture was historical: 'the untouched surface of ancient architecture bears witness to the development of man's ideas, to the continuity of history... not only telling us what were the aspirations of men passed away, but also what we may hope for in time to come' (1884, 296). For Morris, this was the reason to oppose the restoration of old buildings, and for his insistence that repairs should always be visible as new work, for 'the way of working the stone was the language of the story when stories were told in building' (1889b, 154).

The analogy between architecture and books, suggesting that architecture conveyed a narrative, was to be vigorously criticized, and rejected, in the early twentieth century. A good and perhaps the most developed example of the critique was that by Geoffrey Scott in chapter 2 of *The Architecture of Humanism* (1914). The basis of his criticism of what he called 'The Romantic Fallacy' (which included virtually all nineteenth-century architecture) was that 'Architecture, in fact, becomes primarily symbolic. It ceases to be an immediate and direct source of enjoyment, and becomes a mediate and indirect one' (1980, 54). Scott's book was paradoxical in its combination of advanced German aesthetic theory with very conservative architectural tastes; but in this statement, though, we find as clear an expression as any by a modern architect upon modernist thinking about semantics. Within orthodox modernism, works of architecture were not there to be 'read' as narratives to external events – they were there to be themselves.[10] It is against this position, or in its defence, that much of the later twentieth-century dispute over the 'linguistic analogy' has to be understood.

(ii) *Architecture as spoken language*. Complementary to, and indeed necessary to the notion that works of architecture were there to be read as books are read, is the idea of architecture's existence as a widely understood vernacular language, for otherwise built works would be incomprehensible to those who encountered them. This idea certainly underlay Hugo's description of Notre Dame, both Ruskin and Morris elaborated upon it, and it was an argument employed by many nineteenth century writers. James Fergusson, in *A History of the Modern Styles*, 1862, wrote:

> where Art is a true art, it is as naturally practised and as easily understood, as a vernacular literature; of which it is indeed an essential and most expressive part; and so it was in Greece and Rome, and so too, in the Middle Ages. But with us it is little more than a dead corpse.... It expresses truthfully neither our wants nor our feelings, and we ought not therefore to be surprised how very unsatisfactory every modern building is, even when executed by the most talented architects... (34–35)

These laments have occurred regularly over the last century and a half, whether it is in appeals to the urban domestic architecture of the eighteenth century, 'the anonymous products of a uniform architectural language such as we need today more than anything else' (Richards, 1956, 19), or to the commercial vernacular of 1970s America as described by Venturi and Scott Brown in *Learning from Las Vegas* (1972).

This particularly forceful and persistent view of architecture as a vernacular language was made possible by developments in the study of language itself that arose out of the Romantic movement in late eighteenth-century Germany. In the new theory of language developed initially by J. G. von Herder, but followed by Fichte, Goethe, and to some extent Humboldt also, language constituted the purest and most vital expression of the collective being of a people, its *Volksgeist*. For Herder the significance of languages lay in their uniqueness; the way, for example, that in a given language certain things could be said that could be neither said nor thought in any other language confirmed the existence of a common spirit amongst the speakers of that language. For the Romantics and their successors, language was the ultimate manifestation of a nation's soul. As the Swiss historian Jacob Burkhardt was later to put it, 'Languages are the most direct and specific revelation of the spirit of the nations, their ideal image, the most perdurable material in which they enclose the content of their spiritual life' (56). Within this theory of language, language was not simply a medium through which one speaker communicates ideas to another, it is also a medium that communicates the entire collective being of all those to whom that language belongs. It was this model of language that was to have such lasting impact upon architecture.

The 'Golden Nugget' Gambling Hall, Las Vegas, post-1964, as illustrated in Venturi and Scott Brown, *Learning from Las Vegas* (1972). Venturi and Scott-Brown's celebration of everyday American commercial architecture as a contemporary vernacular drew attention to its symbolic richness, which they saw as comparable to that of older architectural traditions: in the second edition of their book, this picture faced that of Amiens cathedral (illustrated here on p. 73).

The origins of these ideas were contained in Herder's prize-winning essay, *A Treatise Upon the Origin of Language*, written in 1770. Herder's essay was an extended attack upon Rousseau's theory of the 'natural' origins of language; rather than the result of a divine gift, or of a philosophical system, Herder argued that the origin of language lay in man's ability to reflect and to reason. Language for Herder was not a system developed out of the mere utterance of feeling, rather 'language is the natural result of the first act of reason' (part II, 31). 'It was the intelligence of the soul itself, an intelligence necessary to man as man' (30). While at work on his essay in Strasbourg, Herder made friends with the young Goethe, and inspired him to write his own remarkable essay 'On German Architecture' (1772). Goethe cleverly adapted Herder's idea that language originated in the human capacity for reflection to say that similarly architecture was the outcome of the human will to self-expression in plastic form: 'For in man is a plastic nature, which at once, when his existence is secure, proves active. As soon as man has nothing to worry him or to make him fear, the demi-god gropes around for matter to breathe his spirit into' (159). For Goethe, architecture was like language in that it provided immediate expression of man's intellect and spirit. At the same time, again following Herder, Goethe saw that architecture, like language, was not simply a medium of individual expression, but more importantly expressed the entire collective identity of particular peoples, the *Volksgeist*.

Without the model of language provided by the German Romantics, the notion of an architectural 'vernacular', so powerful throughout nineteenth- and twentieth-century architecture, would have had little force. Of those who contributed to the diffusion of this idea, one of the most important was John Ruskin: his remark in *The Seven Lamps of Architecture* (1849), that 'the architecture of a nation is great only when it is as universally established as its language' – a remark whose origins in German Romantic thought will be plain enough – has been a legitimation for successive quests for an architectural vernacular in almost every country of the world.

It is worth pointing out that, powerful though the idea of architecture was as a language-like medium of individual and collective communication, there were those who cautioned against pressing the analogy too far. The German philosopher G. W. F. Hegel in his *Aesthetics* stressed particularly the *sensuous* nature of art: whereas language communicates purely through a sign, the word, it was the particular and distinctive feature of art that its communication of idea relied upon a corresponding sensory experience (vol. 2, 635). While being like a language, for Hegel, the essential nature of all art, architecture included, depended upon its *not* being a language. And the English philosopher-critic, James Fergusson, contemporary of Ruskin, though later a proponent of the architectural 'vernacular', in his first book, *An Historical Enquiry into the True Principles of Beauty in Art* of 1849, went out of his way to stress the inappropriateness of language as analogy for architecture as a medium of communication: 'Architecture can repeat no narrative, illustrate no book – it imitates nothing, illustrates nothing; it tells no tale, and barely manages to express an emotion of joy or sorrow with the same distinctness with which they can be expressed by the unphonetic brutes' (121–22). Indeed, this same argument has been one of the most substantial objections to analogies with the semantic aspects of language, and one that was reiterated in the 1970s: for not only is architecture, if it is a medium of communication, a clumsy and unreliable one, but there is no way that individuals can speak to each other through it, any more than they can carry on a dialogue with the originator of the architectural 'message' through the same medium. It allows only a one-way communication.

Interest in the semantic possibilities of architecture declined sharply with modernism: early modernist architects and critics almost entirely abandoned all analogies with language. Although the release from traditional architectural models had been made possible in part by Semper's linguistic analogy, by the 1920s, the desire to indicate the autonomy of architecture made any suggestion of the literary or linguistic nature of architecture unwelcome. This embargo upon linguistic analogies was only lifted after the Second World War, initially in Italy. The peculiar and contradictory circumstances of post-war Italy – a strong Communist party with a share in government until 1948, the urge to create a new popular national culture to replace that established by fascism, and the wish to rehabilitate the work of modernist artists and architects who had worked under the fascist regime – led to an interest in the semantics of works of architecture. In particular, the problem of turning architecture from being part of the identity of the fascist state, into a democratic and popular art, contributed to a preoccupation with the meaning of works of architecture that emerges, for example, in the pages of the magazine *Casabella* during this period. For Marxist critics and architects, one of the main problems of contemporary culture was the inherent impossibility of developing a proletarian or indeed any culture outside the hegemony exercized by the dominant bourgeois order. The Italian critical and philosophical tradition was dominated by the idealist view of art, by which the merits of a work depended upon its ability to render an idea as sensuous; the effect of bourgeois culture had been to deprive art of its idea-mediating purpose by turning it into a medium which simply gratified the desire of individuals to appear different, or cocooned them from the reality of their own condition. Art had, in other words, lost the very quality that made it art. What was perceived as the crisis of art, and of architecture, was that it was no longer capable of saying anything of significance about the material or ideological relationships of contemporary society; it was, in the words of the best-known contributor to this debate, the historian and critic Manfredo Tafuri, a 'semantic' crisis, in which architecture had effectively been reduced to silence.

At the same time as the political and cultural question of architecture's meaningfulness was under debate, introduced into that debate was the science of semiotics, derived from the work of Saussure in Switzerland and Peirce in the USA. The extraordinary interest that developed in semiotics (discussed in more detail in subsection 6 below) in Italy during the 1950s and 1960s is partly to be understood in relation to the underlying problems about architectural meaning. While semiotics, itself a modernist science in that it attached no value whatsoever to history, was attractive to modernist architects and critics struggling with questions of meaning, it was also vigorously resisted by Marxist critics – most notably by Manfredo Tafuri. While Tafuri had no doubt that architecture was a language, he was adamant that the scientific study of language could not itself solve the crisis of 'the loss of public meaning in architecture'. In chapter 5 of *Theories and History of Architecture* (1968), he argued why, if the problem of modern architecture was a linguistic one, he did not believe that the scientific study of languages had anything to offer. For Tafuri, in modern architecture 'the semantic crisis that exploded in the late eighteenth and early nineteenth century still weighs on its development' (173); the post-war attraction for semiotics was a symptom of the desire to avoid the kind of scientific historical analysis Marxist historians had attempted. In a particularly obscure sentence, he explains 'The emergence, within architectural criticism, of the *language problem*, is then a precise answer to the *language crisis* of modern architecture' (174). By this he meant that the development of architectural semiotics and other attempts to subject architecture to analysis by methods for the study of languages are to be explained as a response to the general semantic crisis of architecture. While Tafuri was critical of 'semiology's frantic search for meanings', he recognized that it was nonetheless a response, even if a partial and inappropriate one, to the need to expose how architecture and urbanism had been reduced to 'dangerous persuasion techniques, or, in the best of cases, to the broadcasting of superfluous, rhetorical and exhortative messages' (174). It was therefore right to be critical of semiotic research, because it obscured the reality of the material conditions affecting architecture, but wrong not to recognize 'all those difficulties as elements of the language itself' (175) – and by 'language' here he meant 'architecture'. Tafuri believed furiously and passionately that architecture was a language (to the extent that it is often unclear whether he is talking about architecture or the linguistic form itself) but the principal problem was to keep it clear of the sciences of language, and develop historical critiques. Tafuri's persistence in calling architecture a language may seem hard to understand from the standpoint of northern Europe in the 1990s; it can only be explained by the cultural circumstances of post-war Italy, and by the overwhelming blankness and emptiness that orthodox modernism presented to the world at that period. For many critics, among them Joseph Rykwert, quoted at the beginning of this chapter, and the first English-speaking critic to make extensive use of the semantic analogy of language in its new post-war version, the significance of seeing architecture as language was to open up its discussion from the impossibly narrow limits imposed by modernism.

5. Analogies with grammar

In 1802, the French architect J. N. L. Durand, in *Précis des leçons d'architecture*, a textbook for engineers at the Ecole Polytechnique, suggested that the process of learning architecture could be like that of learning a language.

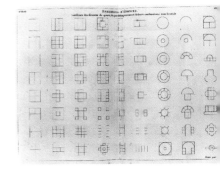

> When we are familiar with these various objects [supports, walls, openings, foundations, floors, vaults, roofs and terraces], which are to architecture what words are to discourse, notes to music, and without which it will be impossible to go further, we may see first how to combine them, that is to say how to dispose each in relation to the others, horizontally as much as vertically; secondly how by means of these combinations, one arrives at the formation of different parts of buildings, such as porticoes, porches, vestibules, staircases... thirdly how to combine these in their turn in the composition of whole buildings... After all we have said, one may understand how the study of architecture may be reduced to a small number of general and fertile ideas, to an inconsiderable number of elements, but sufficient for the construction of all kinds of buildings, and to a few simple combinations, of which the results are as rich and as varied as those resulting from the combination of the elements of language; one may realize, I have said, how such a study must be at once productive and succinct; how it is right to give to pupils the means of composing all kinds of buildings, even those they have never heard of, and at the same time, to get rid of the obstacles that the shortness of time available to them might seem to make stand in their way. (1819 ed., 29–30)

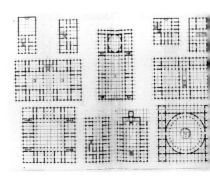

In other words, Durand proposed that by presenting architecture in terms of a grammar, it could easily and rapidly be taught. This particular analogy, that a set of principles and elements, like the grammar of a spoken language, can be extracted from architecture, has had a currency since Durand's time, and owes its appeal to the institution of systems of education outside the apprenticeship system. For educators, the attraction of being able to teach architecture in the same way as a language through a set of grammatical principles, is obvious; there have been many successors to Durand's method – in recent times one might cite Francis Ching's *Architecture: Form, Space and Order* (1979), or Christopher Alexander's *A Pattern Language* (1977). Throughout the nineteenth century and until the early twentieth century, the grammar analogy appears to have been used fairly regularly in ordinary architectural parlance: for example

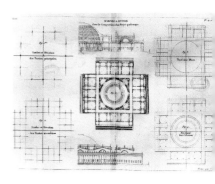

J. N. L. Durand, stages of architectural composition, *Précis des leçons d'architecture*, 1809 and 1817. Durand's method for teaching architecture presented it as a 'grammar'; simple shapes when combined together provided the means to create complex compositions.

Louis Sullivan famously referred to 'the pier, the lintel, the arch... the three, the only three letters, from which has expanded the Architectural Art as a great and superb language' ('What is Architecture?', 1906; Twombly ed., 175). And in the 1920s, the French architect-engineer Auguste Perret was fond of saying that

> the elements of architecture – columns, beams, arches, walls, apertures, vaults and slabs – were comparable to a vocabulary, which could be combined together in an infinite variety of patterns according to practical requirements and emotional needs. Like spoken words, these elements might be modified or even completely transformed by changing social conditions. (Collins, 1959, 198–99)

The main objection to this particular linguistic analogy has been that if learning the principles of architecture is as easy as learning a language, then anybody can do it. Unsurprisingly, both Durand and Alexander had anti-professional motives in advancing the view of architecture as grammar. Modernism did not on the whole favour 'grammars' of architecture; attempts to develop systems of architectural morphology, such as those pioneered by Leslie Martin and Lionel March, generally justified themselves by reference to analogies with the underlying 'structure' of language. A recent example of the attempt to present such a grammar is Willam J. Mitchell's *Logic of Architecture: Design, Computation and Cognition* (1990).

6. Semiotic and structuralist applications to architecture

We come here to by far the most contentious part of linguistic analogies. Strictly speaking, semiotics and structuralism propose language not as a metaphor for architecture, but rather that architecture *is* a language. However, even amongst semioticians, and certainly amongst architects, this distinction has been so blurred that it is not inappropriate to consider semiotics in the general context of linguistic metaphors. The reasons for the sharp rise of interest in the linguistic analogy have already been mentioned – dissatisfaction with the blankness of orthodox modernism and the limited discussion permitted around it, and the peculiar circumstances in post-war Italy. Coincident with these concerns was the emergence of semiotics and structuralism, sciences whose claims to the linguistic analysis of all human culture offered a more promising basis for discussion of architecture as a language than had ever been available before. As the Italian critic Gillo Dorfles, in one of the first of the exceedingly numerous Italian studies of architectural semiotics, wrote in 1959:[11]

> The problems of architecture, if considered in the same ways as other arts, as a 'language', are the basis for a whole new current of thought, which allows it to be treated in terms of information and communication theory;

and that the meaning can be treated as a process which connects objects, events and beings with 'signs', which evoke just these very objects and beings. The cognitive process lies in our ability to assign a meaning to the things around us, and this is possible because the 'signs' are links between our own consciousness and the phenomenological world. So signs are the first and immediate tools of every communication. I am sure of one thing: architecture, like every other art, must be considered as an organic whole and, to a certain extent, institutionalized ensemble of signs, which can be partially identified with other linguistic structures. (39)

Semiotics, the science of signs, originated more or less simultaneously in the period just before the First World War in two independent versions by Ferdinand de Saussure in Switzerland and by Charles Peirce in the United States, was concerned not with what things mean, but with how meaning occurs; their fundamental proposition was that all human activities conformed to a linguistic model of signification.[12] For semioticians, artefacts in general and architecture in particular presented a specific and important test case for the general applicability of the semiotic model, for unlike verbal language, in which communication was the primary purpose, in artefacts and in architecture the primary purpose was to serve a function. How far artefacts with functional purposes could conform to linguistic models of communication was a question addressed, amongst others, by the linguistic philosopher Umberto Eco.[13] It is important to recognize that a significant part of the interest in the semiotics of architecture came initially not from architects, but from semioticians anxious to test the validity of the theory; it was the coincidence of this concern with that of architects' concern with meaning that explains the surge of interest in this subject during the late 1950s and 1960s. For the majority of architects who showed an interest in semiotics and structuralism the technicalities of semiotic systems and their extension to non-verbal codes were unimportant: their significance was to make architects think about the limits to their power to determine meaning. As the Dutch architect Herman Hertzberger, who was strongly attracted to the semiotic analogy, put it: 'what matters with forms, just as with words and sentences, is how they are read, and the images they evoke in the eyes of "readers" ' (1977, 127). Though of no great profundity, this was a thought that would have been impossible without semiotics.

During the later 1960s, attention shifted from architecture to cities as more promising material for semiotic analysis. One of the most famous examples of this tranfer of the linguistic model to the urban scale was Aldo Rossi's *The Architecture of the City*, providing him with the means to argue that buildings were capable of infinite modifications of use and signification while still themselves remaining unchanged. He wrote: 'The significance of permanent elements in the study of the city can be compared to that which fixed structures

Aerial view of Antifeatro Romano, Lucca. The persistence in cities of certain forms – the oval of the amphitheatre – and their transformation over time to other purposes – residential buildings – suggested to Aldo Rossi an analogy between urban and linguistic forms.

have in linguistics; this is especially evident as the study of the city presents analogies with that of linguistics, above all in terms of the complexity of its processes of transformation and permanence' (22–23). But again, the shift in interest towards the city as a linguistic system was partly initiated by the semioticians themselves for their own theoretical purposes. Roland Barthes wrote, 'He who moves about the city... is a kind of reader'; but his reason for drawing attention to this was to illustrate the impossibility of arriving at a certain or definitive reading of anything. Barthes's interest in the city corresponded to the beginning of his post-structuralist phase in which he acknowledges the elusiveness and ultimate unattainability of any definitive signifieds. In the same essay, on the city, he remarks on how 'in any cultural or even psychological complex, we are faced with endless chains of metaphors whose signified is always retreating or becomes itself a signifier' (1967b, 170). This was particularly evident in cities, producing what he described as their 'erotic dimension', their infinitely metaphorical nature. Barthes's interest in the semiotic possibilities of the city appears to have come, at least in part, from the psycho-geographical explorations of the Situationists, and their technique of the *dérive* (literally 'drift'; used to describe a subjective rearrangement of the parts of a city as one moved about in it) to dislocate normative representations of the city and reconstitute its experience subjectively – though the Situationists' entirely non-literary mode of encountering the urban was also to be used by Henri Lefebvre and others as a way of resisting the incursions of linguistic models into the analysis of social phenomena.[14]

Also in the late 1960s, there was an interest in the potential application of new syntactic theories of language. The American architect Peter Eisenman relates that in 1966

> I began looking into other disciplines where problems of form had been presented within some critical framework. This took me into linguistics, and more particularly to the work of Noam Chomsky in syntax. From this analogy it was possible to make several analogies between architecture and language, and more specifically to construct a crude hypothesis about the syntactic aspects of architectural form. (1971, 38)

Briefly, Eisenman's interest was how the conventional forms of construction found in architecture – columns, walls etc. – could be combined so as to give rise to new meanings. The 'hypothesis' was that forms in architecture presented themselves both in a 'surface' aspect – texture, colour, shape – recognized by the senses, and also in a 'deep' aspect as relationships of frontality, obliqueness, recession, etc., recognized only in the mind. This distinction, Eisenman suggested, was analogous to the distinction made by Chomsky between the deep and surface structures of language – and he wished to indicate that it was possible to think of modifications at the 'deep' or syntactical level, without being concerned with the immediate, surface aspects of form presented to the senses. Given that it was a long-term ambition of Eisenman's to demonstrate the independence and self-sufficiency of architecture as a discipline, it was slightly ironic that he resorted to an analogy with language to describe the specificity of architecture. Shortly after writing this article analysing works by the Italian architect Giuseppe Terragni, Eisenman abandoned his interest in language theories as metaphors, and in his subsequent writings he avoided explicit linguistic analogies, though he continued to be interested in the possibilities of an underlying syntactical system for architecture.

By the mid-1970s, both architects and intellectuals in general were beginning to react against the linguistic model. The extremeness of this reaction has to be understood in relation to the imperialism of the structuralist and semiotic claims for the absolute and total priority of language in all social practices, a thesis in whose daring lay a part of its fascination. Criticisms of the linguistic model of architecture focussed on three things in particular. Firstly, it was argued that the attention to what the work signified or symbolized drained attention away from the work itself, reduced it to the status of a mere carrier of an idea that lay elsehwere, and denied the possibility that that work itself might constitute the limits of its own aesthetic, and be a source of pleasure in itself. This, broadly speaking, was the argument developed by Bernard Tschumi.[15] Secondly, semiology, as a theory of semantics, was called into question by positing alternative theories of linguistic meaning, in particular that of the philosopher Gottlob Frege.[16] Thirdly, as argued by Henri Lefebvre in particular, semiology entirely failed to take into account the production of spatial objects, nor adequately to describe how meanings might be constituted out of lived experience.[17] For example, Lefebvre wrote of Gothic churches: 'This space was *produced* before being read; nor was it produced in order to be read and grasped, but rather in order to be *lived* by people with bodies and lives in their own particular urban context' (143).

In architectural circles, it is now as customary to condemn linguistic analogies as it was thirty years ago to invoke them. A particularly thoughtful discussion of the inappropriateness of language metaphors towards understanding the kinds of meanings architecture makes possible is contained in chapter 5 of Richard Hill's *Designs and their Consequences* (1999) – but this is far from the only instance. The force of the reaction against linguistic analogies has been to make all comparisons between language and architecture suspect, and to place an interdiction upon *all* linguistic or literary metaphors. Yet this reaction seems excessive. Even if architecture is not a language, it does not lessen the value of language as a metaphor for talking about architecture. There is no reason why a metaphor should be required to reproduce every detail of the object to which it is compared: metaphors are never more than partial descriptions of the phenomena they seek to describe, they are always incomplete. Indeed, were they to succeed in total reproduction, they would cease to be metaphors, which subsist through likenesses drawn between inherently unlike things. The all-or-nothing attitude characteristic of many recent discussions about the architecture-language analogy conceals the fact that for certain aspects of architecture, language provides a workable, and indeed possibly the best, metaphor. In the 'reading' of a plan or a facade, in the existence of an architectural 'vernacular', in the 'articulation' of architectural elements, even in our capacity to think of architecture free of the conventions laid down by ancient Greece and Rome, we are indebted to language – yet to subscribe to any of these metaphors does not necessarily demand allegiance to a full-blown system of architectural linguistic semantics. And there seems no reason to suppose that, when the current witch-hunt against linguistic analogies is past, language will not continue to be as productive a source of ideas to architecture as it ever was.

1 See in particular 'Flexibility', 'Form', 'Order', 'Structure', and 'Type'.

2 'The Idea of Architectural Language: a Critical Enquiry', *Oppositions*, no. 10, 1977, 21–26.

3 See Steadman, *Evolution of Designs*, chapter 4.

4 See Collins, *Changing Ideals in Modern Architecture*, 1965, chapter 17; and Collins, 'The Linguistic Analogy', 1980.

5 See Sylvia Lavin, *Quatremère de Quincy*, 1992, 56–59.

6 See Podro, *Critical Historians of Art*, 1982, 44–55.

7 On Humboldt's linguistic theory, see Chomsky, *Cartesian Linguistics*, 1966, especially 19–28.

8 See Vidler, *Claude-Nicolas Ledoux*, 1990, ix.

9 On the strange history of this novel, see the introduction by John Sturrock to his translation, Penguin Books, 1978; and Neil Levine, 'The book and the building: Hugo's theory of architecture and Labrouste's Bibliothèque Ste-Geneviève', in R. Middleton (ed.), *The Beaux Arts and Nineteenth Century French Architecture*, London, 1982, 138–73.

10 For further discussion of this question, see the entry on 'Transparency' in Part II.

11 Scruton, *The Aesthetics of Architecture*, 1979, 283, note 1, lists some of the main books from this period dealing with the linguistic properties of architecture.

12 See also Iversen, 'Saussure versus Peirce: Models for a Semiotics of Visual Art', 1986.

13 See particularly his 'Function and Sign: the Semiotics of Architecture', in Leach (ed.) *Rethinking Architecture*, 1997.

14 On the Situationists, see T. F. McDonough, 'Situationist Space', *October*, no. 67, 1994.

15 For a philosophical discussion of this issue, see Munro, 'Semiotics, Aesthetics and Architecture', 1987.

16 See Scruton, *The Aesthetics of Architecture*, 1979, chapter 7, 'The Language of Architecture'.

17 See especially Lefebvre, *The Production of Space*, 130–47.

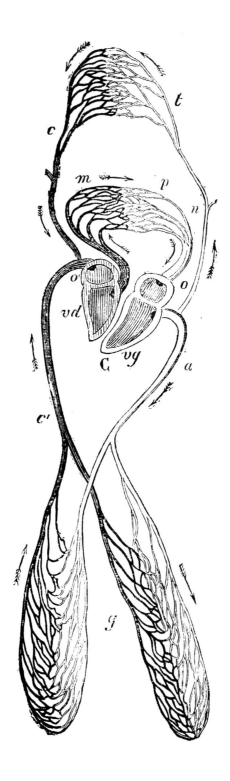

5

The human circulation system, from
Pierre Larousse, *Grand Dictionnaire
Universel du XIXme Siècle*, 1869.
The introduction in the nineteenth
century of the architectural term
'circulation' was a direct borrowing from
anatomy.

Many of the metaphors in the architectural lexicon come from science. Architecture is hardly alone in its debt to the language of science – and the reasons for this may indeed be obvious, in so far as science has become the dominant discourse of our times – but we should not assume that just because a term comes from science it will make a good metaphor. Rather, we should enquire what the conditions are that allow some metaphors to be successful, and others to fail.

As the first case for investigation, let us take 'circulation' – the conventional word for the means of movement, particularly human movement, within or around a building. This term – unquestionably a metaphor, drawn from physiology, as the early instances of its use will confirm – has become virtually indispensable to the way we have come to think and talk about architecture: indeed, one may recall Le Corbusier's 'outrageous fundamental proposition: *architecture is circulation*' (1930, 47). Yet although 'circulation' might now appear to have acquired the status of an objective architectural category, to have become a 'thing', the modern sense of the term was unknown before the second half of the nineteenth century. The first instance I have been able to find of 'circulation' as a description for the means for human movement within a building was in the second volume of Viollet-le-Duc's *Lectures*, published in 1872, and although Viollet may well not have been the very first to use the word thus, it seems fairly certain that no one had tried it out before about 1850.

The fact that 'circulation', now apparently so indispensable to the architectural vocabulary, only became so after the 1850s at once raises two questions: the first is why it entered the lexicon then, and neither earlier, nor later; and the second is whether when talking about 'circulation' architects were simply renaming something previously known by another word, or whether they were articulating a genuinely new and previously non-existent concept. As a description for the movement of blood around the body, 'circulation' was first coined in 1628 by Sir William Harvey; its potential as a metaphor to describe flow in other substances was seized upon almost at once by other disciplines, notably economics, where it was in general use by the second half of the seventeenth century. Yet in architecture, despite its availability, it was not taken up for two and a half centuries. Why not?

In answer, we should bear in mind that in French, which is the language in which the metaphor was first applied to architecture, *circulation* also means vehicular traffic. That particular sense of the word appears to have been introduced, also as a metaphor, rather earlier, in the late eighteenth century. One of the first instances of that usage is in Pierre Patte's *Mémoires sur les Objets les Plus Importans de l'Architecture* of 1769, where he refers to 'la libre circulation des voitures' (11), but apparently this sense did not become widespread in French until the 1820s.[1] When French architects and critics started after the 1850s to refer to the 'circulation' of buildings, they drew inevitably upon this earlier meaning, giving their use of the word a double signification.

To discover whether the concept of 'circulation' had existed previously, but by another name, we might look to the earlier architectural writers who might be expected to testify to some awareness of it. Of the various suitable witnesses, one of the most eligible must surely be J. N. L. Durand, whose *Précis des Leçons d'Architecture* was first published in 1802. Durand in fact uses the word 'circulation' only once, and in the most insignificant context: 'an isolated support should generally be cylindrical, the form which best facilitates circulation' (vol. 2, 9). In common with earlier writers, Durand concentrated his, and his students', attention upon the *distribution*, that is to say the arrangement of volumes so as to preserve the axes of the plan, the *communications* between rooms and parts of a building, and the *dégagements*, or service communications. For Durand, *distribution* was the most important business of architecture, and there is no evidence that he ever considered the system of human movement around a building independently, or thought of it as having any particular significance for the design. If we go back a little further, to the eighteenth century, there is evidence that a series of interconnecting rooms might permit people to 'circulate' – Boullée remarked of Versailles 'the public can circulate [*circuler*] easily throughout the first part of the palace' (142) – but there is no evidence that architects ever thought of this arrangement as constituting a system of 'circulation'. Although modern historians have described the interconnecting entertainment rooms of eighteenth-century aristocratic town and country houses as forming a 'circuit', there is no evidence that anyone at the time ever used this word, or thought about it in this way: contemporary accounts describe each room along the route in turn, but do not make the leap to describe the entire route as a system of its own that could be considered apart from the individual rooms and staircases constituting the experience. To call this arrangement a 'circuit' is to superimpose a modern concept upon it.[2] And if we go back even earlier, while we can certainly find physiological metaphors to describe the relationship of different parts of buildings, they do not suggest that human movement was considered a separate component of the architecture. Thus, in 1615, in a distinctly pre-Harveian metaphor, the Venetian architect Vincenzo Scammozzi described staircases:

> Of all the parts without doubt the stairs are the most necessary in buildings, like the veins and arteries in the human body; because just as these serve naturally to administer the blood to every part of the body, so do the principal stairs and the secret stairs reach to the most intimate parts of the building. (312)

If none of these examples suggest that architects before 1850 had an equivalent to the modern concept of 'circulation', the point may be reinforced by looking at the very distinctive way the metaphor was used in the 1850s and 1860s. One of the very first and most interesting post-1850 instances was in the French critic César Daly's analysis of Barry's Reform Club in London, a work which Daly regarded as prefiguring the architecture of the future: 'This building', Daly wrote in 1857, 'is no inert mass of stone, brick and iron; it is almost a living body with its own nervous and cardiovascular circulation systems' [*presque un corps vivant avec son système de circulation sanguine et nerveuse*]' (346–47). Daly was referring not so much to the means for human movement, but to the largely invisible heating, ventilation and systems of mechanical communication buried within the walls. In Daly's demonstratively physiological metaphor, what

Library and exterior of Reform Club, London, C. Barry, 1839. The comfort of the Reform Club, where members could sit in large rooms untroubled by cold or draughts, was made possible by extensive systems of warmed air. These, and the hidden service passages and stairs, inspired the French critic César Daly to describe the Reform Club, in a consciously physiological metaphor, as 'almost a living body with its own nervous and cardiovascular circulation systems'.

he suggested was that each of these services were systems of their own, and could be considered quite apart from the materiality of the building they served: it is this that sets his use of the metaphor apart from those earlier conceptions of architectural arrangement. Similarly, Viollet-le-Duc's use of the circulation metaphor in his remarks on domestic architecture in the *Lectures* is interesting in this light, as it is also for his use of the term 'function' within the same passage:

> There is in every building, I may say, one principal organ, – one dominant part, – and certain secondary orders or members, and the necessary appliances for supplying all these parts, by a system of circulation. Each of these organs has its own function; but it ought to be connected with the whole body in proportion to its requirements. (vol. 2, 277)

For Viollet, 'circulation' was a very fresh metaphor, and like Daly, he pointedly drew attention to its physiological origins. Also, like Daly, his purpose, in using the metaphor was to stress the extent to which the circulation might be considered as a system of its own, independently of the other organs of the house. Daly and Viollet were, it seems, expressing in 'circulation' something not found in all those earlier terms for describing the arrangement of buildings. '*Distribution*', '*communication*', '*dégagements*', are all tied to the materiality of architecture: you have to have a building in view, or at least in mind, to understand what they mean. With 'circulation', though, you do not, for what it describes refers not to the physicality of the building, but to the possibility of flow within or about it. What is special about 'circulation' is that it describes not just an arrangement of parts, but, as Daly stressed in his description of the Reform Club, a complete, self-contained system which can be considered independently of the inert, physical substance of the building. This is indeed the way in which 'circulation' was soon adopted by architects and architectural theorists. By 1871, the architect of the Paris Opéra, Charles Garnier, was using 'circulation', without any particular self-consciousness of its metaphorical nature: the stair, he wrote, 'is one of the most important arrangements [*dispositions*] in theatres because it is indispensable to the ease of arranging the exits [*dégagements*] and the circulation, but more because it produces an artistic motif' (57). Yet, interestingly, elsewhere in the same book, Garnier did not entirely give himself up to the abstraction of the noun, and in the following passage, 'circulate' retains an active sense, embodied in a specific group of people: 'if the walls of the stair well are full of openings, everyone circulating [*circulant*] at each level can at their fancy divert themselves by the sight of the great vessel, and by the incessant circulation of the crowd going up or down the flights' (85). 'Circulation' rapidly became accepted within French academic circles as a fixed and orthodox category, and so for example, Julien Guadet's

Staircase, Opéra, Paris, C. Garnier, 1854–70. 'The incessant circulation of the crowd going up and down' was, for the architect Charles Garnier, a major theme of the building.

Eléments et Théories d'Architecture, the classic manual of the French Beaux-Arts training, first published in 1902, had a whole chapter on 'Les Circulations', treating it as an independent element within architectural composition. From here, it was but a short step to Le Corbusier's 'outrageous proposition'.

If the significance of 'circulation' was to allow an aspect of architecture to be considered as a discrete system, its introduction must be seen as a symptom of the desire to bring scientific method into architecture. For architecture to approximate to a scientific practice it was necessary to be able to isolate and abstract specific features or properties from the complex phenomenal reality of the built work, and to subject those abstractions to independent analysis. The concept covered by 'circulation' fulfilled this criterion relatively well, and it is perhaps no surprise therefore that it has remained a favourite topic for architectural research.[3] But while we may say in general terms that the effect of introducing 'circulation' was to allow architecture to proceed in a scientific manner, what exactly did those who coined the metaphor hope to express by it? It is in the nature of metaphors that they allow one to be precise about some things, while remaining vague about others: 'circulation' was precise about presenting an aspect of architecture as a discrete system, but vague about what flowed around that system – for Daly it was warm air, and mechanical services, for Viollet and Garnier it was people. As a further instance of the possibilities of what sort of flow 'circulation' could describe, we might look at what another writer, the German art historian Paul Frankl, had to say about 'flow' in his *Principles of Architectural History*, first published in 1914. Frankl insisted not only that human movement in buildings was blood-like in character, but that knowledge of the system as a whole was necessary to understand a work of architecture:

> To understand a secular building we must get to know it as a whole by walking through it from end to end, from cellar to roof, through all its outstretching wings. The entrance, the vestibule or passage leading to courtyard or stair, the connections between several courtyards, the stairs themselves and the corridors leading away from them at each level, like the veins of our bodies – these are the pulsating arteries of a building. They are the passages that form the fixed circulation [*Zirkulation*] leading to individual rooms, to individual chambers, cells or loges. The organism of the house reaches as far as these arteries guide the circulation. (79–80)

However, physical movement, whether of people, of things, or of energy – be it electrical currents or sound waves – is not the only sort of motion to be found in architecture. As well as the actual physical movement of matter or energy, there is also the perceived bodily movement through which we experience architecture. Indeed Merleau-Ponty argued that our ability to extend in imagination the body's power of movement lies at the origin of all knowledge: 'motility in its pure state possesses the basic power of giving a meaning' (142). And more specifically, Edmund Husserl, in an article written a few years before Frankl's book, had argued that knowledge of space came about through the sense of movement present in the unmoving subject: 'All spatiality is constituted through movement, the movement of the object itself and the movement of the "I" ' (quoted in Mallgrave and Ikonomou, 84, footnote 222). Frankl, in the *Principles of Architectural History*, was just as aware of movement as the agency of perception as he was of it as a functional property of architecture. There is in certain buildings, as he puts it, a 'great flood of movement that urges us round and through the building' (148). In other words, there is, so to speak, movement there in the building before anyone has arrived, and it is not the people who move, but space itself that goes round and round. Frankl was aware that he was dealing with two categories of circulation – one to do with the experience of spatiality, the other to do with routes of human activity – and generally, but not always, he used the term 'flow' to distinguish perceived spatial movement from the physical paths taken by people. (On 157, he distinguishes between 'circulation' as purposive movement of people between places, and the sense of movement implied by the spatial forms.) We should not forget that 'circulation' may refer to a more than one kind of movement in architecture.

At this point, we might reflect that perhaps 'circulation' is not the most appropriate metaphor for human movement in buildings. When Sir William Harvey originally applied the term 'circulation' to the flow of blood, he did so to draw attention to the fact that blood did not simply *move* in the body, but that a single fixed volume of fluid (not as had previously been thought, two sorts of fluid) travelled around the body, and always returned to the same point, the heart.[4] This does not correspond to what normally goes on in buildings: it is not always the same group of people who move about in a building, not all of them generally pass into all parts of it, nor (except perhaps for the guests at social gatherings in eighteenth-century town houses) do they go round and round it always returning to the same point. On the other hand, it is quite a good description for the sort of spatial movement that Frankl was concerned with. The lack of correspondence between the circulation of the blood in the body and the movement of people in buildings does not seem to have stood in the way of the success of 'circulation' as a metaphor, so it must have some other attraction. The most likely explanation for its appeal is to be found in the feature common to the use made of it by Daly, Viollet and Frankl, all of whom invite the reader to think of the building as a sealed system, without orifices, and self-sufficient – in other words a body, but a body perceived in the most clinical and unmetaphysical terms. For those many architects and building owners who persist, against all the evidence to the contrary, in seeing buildings as strictly bounded, self-contained entities, a metaphor reinforcing this delusion

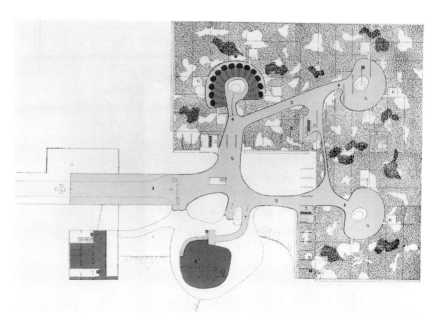

Le Corbusier, design for Olivetti electronic calculator plant at Rho-Milan, 1957, 4th and 5th floor plans, from *L'Oeuvre complète 1957–65*. The arrangements for human movement in Le Corbusier's project more closely resemble a *respiration* system than a *circulation* system.

could not fail to be attractive.[5] It is quite possible, though, to think of other physiological metaphors that could express human movement in buildings with a rather closer correspondence to what goes on in them – think of 'respiration', 'breathing' – and interestingly the arrangement of Le Corbusier's Olivetti project of 1957 is much more like a respiratory system than a circulation system. But 'respiration' has not caught on, for the reason, one suspects, that it would make buildings into open systems, with indistinct boundaries – a prospect altogether too messy and too disturbing for most architects and building owners to want to be troubled with.

'Circulation' has without question been a very successful metaphor – indeed, one might say, far too successful. What started as an innocent analogy is now perceived as a fixed category: architectural textbooks from late modernism took it for granted that 'circulation' was a factor in the design of buildings, and still today critics talk about it as if it were an absolute, objective property of architecture.[6] So deeply ingrained has this essentially modernist category become that for most of us it requires a positive act of mental effort to think about architecture *without* 'circulation'. When we ask to what we may attribute the success of this particular metaphor, it is clear that it is not do with any exactness of correspondence between the flow of substances around bodies and around buildings. Instead, I suggest, its success is due to two more structural reasons: firstly, it made architecture amenable to scientific method, and secondly it satisfies a wish to see buildings as enclosed, self-contained systems against all the evidence to the contrary. It allows people to talk about what is untrue as if it were true, and not be troubled by the contradiction.

The second set of scientific metaphors to which we might turn our attention come from mechanics, both fluid and static: terms like compression, stress, tension, torsion, shear, equilibrium, centrifugal, centripetal and so on. It is the use of these words to describe not the actual stability of buildings, but their formal and spatial properties, that we should enquire into, for there is without question something surprising in the choice of terms from the most material of sciences, mechanics, for the least material aspects of architecture, its spatiality.

These mechanical metaphors originated in German aesthetics, where there was a tradition, going back to Hegel and Schopenhauer in the early to mid-nineteenth century, of seeing architecture as the expression of its resistance to the force of gravity: 'properly speaking', wrote Schopenhauer, 'the conflict between gravity and rigidity is the sole aesthetic material of architecture' (vol. 1, 277). Later in the century this theme was developed by several writers, and so, for example, the German aesthetic philosopher Robert Vischer proposed that 'art finds its highest goal in depicting a moving conflict of forces' (121). Undoubtedly the most imaginative exponent of the idea was Heinrich Wölfflin, who, in his doctoral thesis, 'Prolegomena to a Psychology of Architecture' (1886), developed a theory of the empathetic experience of architecture, a theory which he then applied in *Renaissance and Baroque* (1888) to the architecture of a particular place and time. Wölfflin's account of architecture in *Renaissance and Baroque* rests largely on 'movement', that is to say the implied movement arising from 'the opposition between matter and the force of form' (1886, 189) within things that are not themselves in motion. Although this could just as well be a description of the science of statics, we should not assume that is why these metaphors hold our interest. Wölfflin was not interested in the actual forces present in the building, but in how the architecture gave the observer the sensation of feeling the compression of the columns, the thrust of the vaults and so on. It is the way the architecture communicates these experiences to the viewer, rather than the way the forces are actually transmitted through the structure of the building, that mattered to him. In these descriptions, Wölfflin undoubtedly benefitted from the use of the same set of metaphors – tension, stress, etc. – as had already been appropriated by psychology to describe emotions; and indeed Wölfflin often exploited the coincidence, in remarks like 'The baroque never offers us... the static calm of "being", only the unrest of change and the tension of transience' (1888, 62). It would seem that the success of mechanics as a source of metaphors for the aesthetic experience of architecture had less to do with any direct correspondence it might have with the tectonic aspects of architecture, than with the availability of these same metaphors to describe states of feeling and emotion in the human subject.

Wölfflin's successor Frankl took over the same set of metaphors, and his *Principles of Architectural History* extended them to the description of

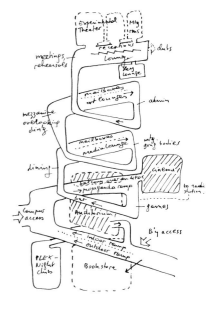

Bernard Tschumi, circulation diagram, Lerner Center, Columbia University, New York, 1994. For modern architects, it is commonplace to represent the 'circulation' as a thing in itself, independent from the building's substance.

Monastery of Sainte-Marie de la Tourette, Evreux, Le Corbusier, 1959. North facade, showing flank wall of chapel. In Colin Rowe's remarkable analysis, this side of La Tourette becomes a vortex of rotating and spinning forces.

architectural space. By the 1950s, these metaphors from mechanics seem to have become sufficiently familiar for the critic Colin Rowe to be able to assume that when he referred to 'the spatial mechanics' of Le Corbusier's monastery of La Tourette, his readers would know what he meant (1982, 186). Rowe's own writing made full play of these metaphors. There is a wonderful description of the effect of the north side of the chapel at La Tourette, the first view the visitor has of the building, a description that shows us more than any image possibly could.

> Le Corbusier has... built into this frontal plane a depth which by no means exists in reality. The oblique cut of his parapet should now be noticed. It is a line so slightly out of the horizontal that the eye has an instinctive tendency to 'correct' and translate it for what average experience suggests that it

should be. For, being eager to see it as the normal termination of a vertical plane, the eye is consequently willing to read it, not as the diagonal which physically it happens to be, but as the element in a perspective recession which psychologically it seems. Le Corbusier has established a 'false right angle'; and this *fausse équerre*, which in itself infers depth, may also be seen as sporadically collaborating with the slope of the ground further to sponsor an intermittent illusion that the building is revolving.

Something of the vital animation of surface, the small but sudden tremor of mobility, in the area between bastion and belfry certainly derives from the torsion to which the wall is thus subjected; but, if this phenomenal warping of surface may be distinctly assisted by the real flexions of the bastion wall itself, then at this point it should also be observed how the three *canons à lumière* now introduce a counteractive stress.

For the spectacle of the building as seen on arrival is finally predicated on a basis, not of one spiral, but of two. One the one hand there are the pseudoorthogonals which, by the complement they provide to the genuine recession of the monastery's west facade, serve to stimulate an illusion of rotating and spinning. But, on the other, are those three, twisting, writhing, and even agonized light sources – they illuminate the Chapel of the Holy Sacrament – which cause a quite independent and equally powerful moment of convolution. A pictorial opportunism lies behind the one tendency. A sculptural opportunism lies behind the other. There is a spiral in two dimensions. There is a contradictory spiral in three. A corkscrew is in competition with a restlessly deflective plane. Their equivocal interplay makes the building. And, since the coiled, columnar vortex, implied by the space rising above the chapel, is a volume which, like all vortices, has the cyclonic power to suck the less energetic material in towards its axis of excitement, so the three *canons à lumière* conspire with the elements guaranteeing hallucination to act as a kind of tether securing a tensile equilibrium. (1982, 191–92)

In this remarkable description, where the metaphor moves from static mechanics, to fluid mechanics and back again to statics, the whole effect comes about through Rowe allowing himself to see 'voids… act as solids' (1982, 192). It should be said that the La Tourette article is the most phenomenological of Rowe's criticism; in it, he is almost entirely concerned with the sensations experienced by the viewer as a result of the various optical illusions, but despite the great range of the metaphors, their success would seem to come from the ambiguity of reference to both psychology and to statics.

When, however, we turn to another exponent of spatial mechanics, Colin Rowe's one-time student Peter Eisenman, we find them used rather differently. Whereas for Rowe the metaphors referred to what he could see, Eisenman, in the article on Terragni published in 1971, explicitly used them to describe what he could *not* see. Eisenman distinguished between the sensual qualities of objects – surface, texture colour and shape – and a 'deep aspect concerned with conceptual relationships which are not sensually perceived; such as frontality, obliqueness, recession, elongation, compression and shear, which are understood in the mind' (38–39). An example of his application of these terms, which he does not acknowledge to be metaphors, but sees as literal descriptions of the relationships of parts of buildings, is his analysis of the north facade of the Casa Giuliani Frigerio. Referring to the forward projection of the left hand part of the facade, he writes

> This volumetric extension seems purposely conceived as an element which does not carry across the entire facade, in order to create a condition of shear. This condition allows a dual reading: either the facade has been extended, in an additive manner, or the outer edge has been eroded to reveal an internal 'solid' volume. (47)

The 'shear' of which Eisenman writes is not a sensation experienced by the observer, nor is Eisenman interested in that possibility. On the contrary, it is something that belongs in the structure of the architecture, and it really needs Eisenman's analytical diagrams to understand it. The absence of any psychological dimension to his use of these terms, his entirely formalist interpretation of them, may have something to do with why Eisenman soon abandoned this kind of analysis.

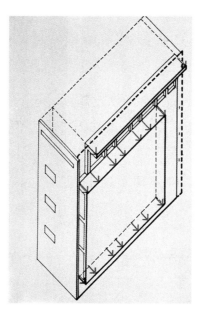
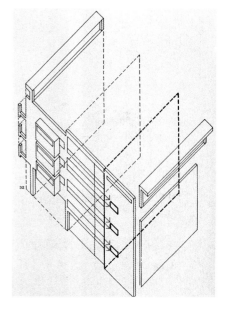

Peter Eisenman, isometric diagrams of Casa Giuliani Frigerio. Eisenman's drawings explain his analysis of the static forces implied in the facade.

(opposite) Casa Giuliani Frigerio, Como, Italy, Giuseppe Terragni, 1939–40. The composition of the facade created, according to Peter Eisenman, 'a condition of shear'.

To draw this discussion together, what has been suggested so far is that the success of the most common scientific metaphors is not just to do with their being scientific, but because they reinforce certain other perceptions of architecture, perceptions which may be rooted in social or psychological desires. The question we might now reflect on is what these, and the abundance of other scientific metaphors, can tell us about the relationship between architecture and science. On the face of it, the adoption of words like 'function', 'structure', 'circulation' or 'transformation' by architecture would seem simply to be symptoms of a trend towards the scientization of the practice, a general characteristic of modernism. However, if we consider the matter in terms of what is known not about architecture, but about metaphors, it turns out to be slightly less straightforward. Although, as has been suggested, part of the attraction of these metaphors may have lain in their making architecture *seem* like a science, and so amenable to scientific procedures of analysis, what they really do is – paradoxically – to confirm the opposite, that architecture is *not* a science, and indeed is not particularly like a science. Successful metaphors rely on the unlikeness of things, not upon their likenesses. The characteristic of an effective metaphor is that it borrows an image from one schema of ideas, and applies it to another, previously unrelated schema. As the philosopher Nelson Goodman wrote – in what is itself a wonderful metaphor – a metaphor is 'an expedition abroad', from one realm of thought to another; or, he says, it may be regarded as a 'calculated category mistake' (73). But to be able make that category mistake, there has to be a category distinction in place to begin with. To call a work of architecture 'functional' – which is unquestionably a metaphor – relies on an initial assumption that architectural objects are *not* natural organisms, *nor* mathematical equations, even though it may express a wish to see them as one or other of those things. The success of the word 'functional' relies upon a commonly accepted agreement that architecture is different from both biology and mathematics. And furthermore, since the scientific metaphors employed in architecture are drawn from such a diversity of scientific fields, from natural sciences as well as physical sciences and mathematics, the cumulative effect is to suggest the unlikeness of architecture to science in general.

The most obvious thing we can say about these scientific metaphors in historical terms is that they belong exclusively to the modern era. Although the science of mechanics and the circulation of the blood have been known about since the seventeenth century, and were therefore potentially available as metaphors, nobody seems to have been interested in applying them to architecture until a century and a half ago. Why not? In other practices they were – 'circulation' was taken up by economists almost as soon as Harvey had discovered it in the body; and terms like 'stress' and 'tension' from mechanics featured in early nineteenth-century psychology, so why not in architecture?

There appear to be two alternative sorts of answers to this question: either, as has already been suggested was the case with 'circulation', these metaphors expressed something that had not needed to be said before; or there was some obstacle to their use as architectural metaphors. Let us concentrate for a moment on the second possibility, that there may have been some structural reason why they could not be applied to architecture.

If indeed, as Alberto Pérez-Gomez suggests in his *Architecture and the Crisis of Modern Science*, there was no conceptual distinction between science and architecture prior to the late eighteenth century, it is not surprising that no one was interested in scientific metaphors – for they would have been entirely ineffective. Only when science became a field of knowledge separate from architecture would there have been any appeal in seeing architecture as if it was a science. Metaphors are experiments with the possible likenesses of unlike things. Each one of the countless scientific metaphors in twentieth-century architecture is a little experiment, an attempt to find a relationship between architecture and one or another branch of science, but they all rely on our belief that really, at the bottom, architectural practice is not scientific. Were this epistemological separation ever to end, and some kind of a reparation between architecture and science to occur, one sure sign that it had happened would be for every scientific metaphor to shrivel up and be discarded, and for no new ones to be invented. But until that happens, every scientific metaphor in architecture will continue to take its sustenance from our intransigent conviction – however misguided – that architecture cannot reach where science may.

1 See *Trésor de la Langue Française*, vol. 2, 1977, 'Circulation'.

2 See Girouard, *Life in the English Country House*, 1978, 194–201, for a case of pre-modern architecture described in modernist notation.

3 See for example the studies of hospital ward layouts, Nuffield Provincial Hospitals Trust, *Studies in the Function and Design of Hospitals*, 1955, 9–11; the early development of 'Space Syntax' (see Hillier and Hanson, *The Social Logic of Space*, 1984) was also based upon the modelling of potential human movement within defined spaces.

4 Harvey, 'Movement of the Heart and Blood', 1635, trans. 1963, 58. Harvey took the concept 'circulation' from Aristotle's description of the cycle of water vapour and rain in the atmosphere: 'We have as much right to call this movement of the blood circular as Aristotle had to say that the air and rain emulate the movement of the heavenly bodies'.

5 Critics of the tight boundary conception of buildings include Groák, *The Idea of Building*, 1992, especially 21–39; and Andrea Kahn, 'Overlooking', 1996.

6 For a textbook reference to 'circulation' see Broadbent, *Design in Architecture*, 1973, 393–99; for an example of contemporary critical use, consider Curtis, *Lasdun*, 1994, 196: 'Circulation is always a driving force…'.

6

'The most vital force in our time seems
to be the awakening spirit of
democracy... and it may be that the living
art we hope for will be the outcome of
this spirit' (Barry Parker, 1910). 'Living'
was the term Parker favoured to describe
the qualities of his housing schemes, such
as this at Litchfield Square, Hampstead
Garden Suburb, London, designed by
Parker with Raymond Unwin in 1908.
(From Unwin, *Town Planning in Practice*,
1909)

Both shores had a line of very pretty houses, low and not large, standing back a little way from the river; they were mostly built of red brick and roofed with tiles, and looked, above all, comfortable, and as if they were, so to say, alive and sympathetic with the life of the dwellers in them.
William Morris, *News from Nowhere*, 1890, 9

For a practice with such strong claims to realize, and to improve, mankind's social existence, architectural modernism was surprisingly inarticulate when it came to describing the specific social qualities aimed for in its works. If, as Walter Gropius claimed, 'relating their work to the life of the people' and seeing 'the individual unit as part of a greater whole' (1954, 178) were major concerns of the modern architect, even the most able critics often found themselves falling back upon language no more exact than William Morris's to characterize the results. Rich though architectural vocabulary is in terms for the perception of the physical properties of architecture – 'depth', 'plasticity', 'transparency', 'articulation', 'texture' and so on – attempts to define its social qualities immediately reveal the poverty of the language. Even as fluent a critic as Lewis Mumford, committed to a social view of architecture, struggled visibly with the limitations of language to express himself. The list of terms most regularly used to describe the social properties of architecture – 'functional', 'organic', 'flexibility', 'reality', 'urbanity', 'living', 'alive', 'homely', 'the user' – includes some of the most overworked and unsatisfactory words in the architectural lexicon, and the others are hardly the freshest of metaphors. 'Functional', 'flexibility' and 'the user' are discussed in detail in Part II, and this chapter is more of a general enquiry into modern architecture's difficulties in expressing verbally the social qualities claimed for its works.

The description of the social had been less of a problem in the nineteenth century, mainly because architects and critics had had fewer aspirations for a 'social' architecture. Apart from the limited discussions that took place round concepts of utility, *convenance* and 'fitness' (see 'Function', pp. 188–92), the principal nineteenth-century critical theme connecting architecture to social relationships concerned the quality of the labour that went into making works of architecture. On this matter, at least, British architects and critics talked and wrote with assurance. Once John Ruskin had formulated in *The Seven Lamps of Architecture* (1849) the notion of 'living architecture', he and his successors found little difficulty in distinguishing degrees of social quality between buildings. As Ruskin put it,

> I believe the right question to ask, respecting all ornament, is simply this: Was it done with enjoyment – was the carver happy while he was about it? It may be the hardest work possible, and the harder because so much pleasure was taken in it; but it must have been happy too, or it will not be living. (ch. 5, §24)

Ruskin's term 'living' to describe his doctrine of 'the value of the appearance of labour upon architecture' was derived, it would appear, from Schiller's *Letters on the Aesthetic Education of Man*, in which the concepts of 'life' and 'life-force' had been central to his explanation of how man achieved aesthetic fulfilment from works of art. But Schiller had not considered 'living' as carrying any *social* connotations: this was Ruskin's originality. To Ruskin's term 'living', William Morris added 'organic', but the meaning was much the same: architecture was the embodiment of work, and the extent to which it expressed the vitality and freedom of those who had built it was the measure of its social quality.

The view that the 'social' quality of architecture lay in its production, in the particular quality of the productive relations occurring between the workers involved in its execution, certainly continued into the modernist era. In Le Corbusier's celebrated chapter 'Architecture or Revolution' at the end of *Towards a New Architecture*, the principal argument (closely following Henry Ford) was that architecture's potential for the redemption of society lay in taking advantage of the new techniques of mass production, as much as through the design of buildings themselves. Likewise, for the architects of the German *Neues Bauen* in the early 1920s, architecture as a social issue was to be approached through the re-organization of building production. For example, Mies van der Rohe wrote in his 1924 article 'Industrialized Building': 'I hold that the industrialization of building constitutes the core problem of our time. If we are successful in carrying out this industrialization, then the social, economic, technical and even artistic questions will solve themselves' (248). Despite the emphasis upon modern industrial methods, such statements belonged to a nineteenth-century view of the socialization of architecture as rooted in the relations of production. Nor did experiments with the organization of production as a means of giving architecture social value come to an end in the 1920s: for a more recent example one might refer to the houses designed in Britain by Walter Segal between 1963 and 1985 for construction

San Michele, Lucca, detail of facade engraved from drawing by John Ruskin. The variety and inventiveness of the carving in the 'crazy front of Lucca' fulfilled Ruskin's notion of a 'living' architecture: one where 'the value of the appearance of labour' freely given was instantly apparent.

with the occupants' own labour.[1]

However, where architectural modernism diverged from nineteenth-century ideas about the social content of architecture was in looking for social expression in its *use*, as well as in its production. Through what went on in works of architecture, through their use, the ideal raised by European modernism was that architecture might give expression to the collectivity of social existence, and, more instrumentally, improve the conditions of social life. In theoretical terms, this ideal presented two significant difficulties. The first was how to conceptualize the 'society' architecture was alleged to represent. The second was to find a means of incorporating 'use' within the aesthetics of architecture.

Within architectural discourse, the two most regularly occurring conceptions of 'society' have been those contained in the notion of 'community', and in the dichotomy between 'public' and 'private'. The appeal of these to architects over other models of society can be explained by the ease with which they can be given spatial equivalents, thus holding out the prospect for architects and urbanists to evaluate, and even quantify, buildings and spaces in social terms. Other concepts of society – as a nexus of economic relationships, as a dialectic between individuality and collectivity (as in the work of the German social theorist Georg Simmel), or as a structure of myths – were less attractive for architects because they conceived society not as a thing, but as a dynamic, and so were harder to translate into built or spatial equivalents. Of the two favoured models, 'community' was the older, and was the one that dominated architectural thinking until the 1950s. As a modern concept of social formation, 'community' is generally attributed to the German social theorist Ferdinand Tönnies, whose book *Gemeinschaft und Gesellschaft* was first published in 1887, and translated into English as *Community and Association* in 1940; and it has been suggested that it was principally Tönnies who provided European modernists with the notion of society as consisting of communities.[2] The conception of society as formed out of a division between public and private spheres has a long history, but its entry into architecture only occurred after the Second World War, and was greatly stimulated by the publication of Hannah Arendt's *The Human Condition* in 1958. Arendt's views on the demise of the 'public' in political and social existence had obvious equivalence in spatial terms, and she herself noted the decline of architecture since the eighteenth century as a symptom of this process (36).

The second difficulty under which architectural modernists laboured in their wish to make architecture an art that represented the 'social' was the longstanding exclusion of anything to do with use from the category of the aesthetic. Ever since Kant in *The Critique of Judgment* of 1794 first established the modern concept of the aesthetic as a distinct class of human perception, the purpose and utility of things were declared to lie outside aesthetic judgment –

On-site assembly of prefabricated building components, Praunheim, Frankfurt, 1926. For German architects of the *Neues Bauen* in the 1920s, the *social* issue of architecture lay primarily in the reorganization of building production along the lines introduced by Henry Ford.

and this was one of the major differences between Kant and earlier British aesthetic philosophers like Lord Kames, who had accommodated utility within their conception of beauty. According to Kant, all questions of ends merely interfere with the perception of free beauty: he explains, 'In respect of an object with a definite internal end, a judgment of taste would only be pure where the person judging either has no concept of this end, or else makes abstraction from it in his judgment' (74). As regards architecture, which is unquestionably purposeful, the conclusion Kant drew is that either it can never attain the realm of the aesthetic, or that it can only be beautiful in so far as it has no purpose. As he puts it, 'In architecture the chief point is a certain *use* of the artistic object to which, as the condition, the aesthetic ideas are limited' (186). Kant found landscape gardening, whose utility was nil, more congenial an art than architecture.

The majority of German aesthetic philosophers succeeding Kant accepted the embargo upon 'use' as constituent of aesthetic judgment. The problem of how architecture could therefore be an art was one that exercized successive philosophers – and the general agreement, as expressed by F. W. Schelling in his *Philosophy of Art*, delivered as lectures in 1801 and 1804, was that architecture 'is beautiful only when it becomes independent of need' (167). Although Hegel, in his lectures on aesthetics, was more accommodating, and suggested that the aesthetic of architecture lay precisely in the relation between its purpose and its inherent meaningfulness independent of its purpose (vol. 2, 633), almost all nineteenth-century architectural theorists within the German tradition treated use as lying outside the aesthetic. The only significant exception was Gottfried Semper – and even he was only interested in needs as a precondition of production, not in relation to the finished results. The same was true of the British tradition of architectural writing, dominated by Ruskin, who like Schelling, discounted purpose or need as having any part in the aesthetic judgment of architecture. Even though Ruskin had a developed concept of the 'social' in architecture in relation to its production, Ruskin had nothing whatsoever to say about the occupation or social use of works of architecture as an element of their aesthetic. Within writing on the aesthetics of architecture prior to the 1920s, perhaps the only significant attempt to consider utility as an element of architecture was in Paul Frankl's *Principle of Architectural History* of 1914. In this book, Frankl's fourth aesthetic category for the historical analysis of architecture was what he called 'Purposive Intention' (*Zweckgesinnung*), by which, he wrote,

> I mean that architecture forms the fixed arena for actions of specific duration, that it provides the path for a definite sequence of events. Just as these have their logical development, so the sequence of spaces, and so too the principal and secondary passages existing within each space, have their logic. (157)

Although Frankl's desire to interpret works of architecture as 'moulded theatres of human activity' (159) was original, and suggestive, he had, as he himself acknowledged, little to work on, and in the end his analysis was rather schematic and idealist.

The result of this long-running embargo upon purpose and use in the aesthetics of architecture was that when, in the 1920s, architects – particularly those in Germany – found themselves wanting to present architectural modernism not as an art dedicated to traditional aesthetic ends, but to social ends, they found the vocabulary of architecture singularly lacking in words to describe what they hoped to achieve. The problem, as perceived by adherents of the new architecture or *Neues Bauen* in the early 1920s, was how architecture, previously dedicated to expressing the individuality of members of society, was now to represent society as a collectivity, and yet remain an art. A good statement of this commonly perceived difficulty comes from the Berlin architect Arthur Korn, writing in 1923:

> the impersonal utilitarian building is only habitable if behind the satisfied
> need there stands the symbolic art form that feels the organism and asks:
> ...How does the whole acquire significance in relation to the smallest part
> and in what way does the whole become a cell of the larger community?

One answer – the conventional one – was to conceive of individual objects and buildings as representative of a social collectivity in relation to technique, to the means of their production. In the early 1920s, this was how most architects and critics saw the solution: this was how Korn himself described it, it was the principle underlying the Bauhaus, and it is how another German critic, Adolf Behne, put it in an article of 1922 entitled 'Art, Craft, Technology'. Behne wrote 'a technology guided by awareness and responsibility will, through collectively interconnected work that leads, above all else, to a realization of deep mutual dependence and conditionality of relativity, set in motion and articulate the mass. Thus will community crystallize out of the mass' (338).

So far, architects and critics had not succeeded in articulating the social in terms other than the expression of productive labour. The attempt to extend the expression of the social collectivity into the uses of buildings, and to regard this as part of their aesthetic – just as Frankl had – depended to a large extent on two words in particular, *Sachlichkeit* and *Zweckmässigkeit* (or *Zweckcharakter*) – all usually translated into English as 'function'. These words already had connotations of use and of occupation in the German architectural vocabulary, but prior to the 1920s, they had invariably (with the possible exception of Frankl) been treated as *outside* the category of the aesthetic. What is interesting is the way in which in the course of 1920s they were re-inflected to become *aesthetic* terms with social denotations – even though this was resisted by some, amongst them Mies van der Rohe. Particularly interesting in this context are the writings of Adolf Behne, an enthusiastic supporter of the *Neues Bauen*. In his 1926 book *The Modern Functional Building*, we see him consciously compressing the two previously separate categories – 'When the parts of a building are arranged according to a sense of their use, when aesthetic space becomes living space... the building throws off the fetters of the old, fossilized static order'; and he continues, 'through this suitability to function, a building achieves a much broader and better unity: it becomes more organic' (119–20). (Behne's use of 'organic' to signify the unification of utility with aesthetic is characteristic of the new inflection that this word, too, was given in the 1920s). Not only did Behne make of *sachlich* a term for the expression of collective social purpose – he writes in a later, 1927 article 'To work *sachlich* means therefore to work socially in each discipline. To build *sachlich* means to build socially' (quoted in Bletter, 53) – but Behne saw the aesthetic as arising from this collective social purpose: 'For here, in the social sphere after all, must lie the primeval elements of the aesthetic' (1926, 137). By the end of the 1920s, these ideas were quite commonly shared amongst members of the *Neues Bauen*. Bruno Taut, in his book *Modern Architecture (Die Neue Baukunst)* of 1929, when summing up the features of the new architecture, declared 'Beauty originates from the direct relationship between building and purpose [*Zweck*]'; and he went on

> If everything is founded on sound efficiency, this efficiency itself, or rather its utility [*Brauchbarkeit*] will form its own aesthetic law... The architect who achieves this task becomes the creator of an ethical and social character; the people who use the building for any purpose, will, through the structure of the house, be brought to a better behaviour in their mutual dealings and relationship with each other. Thus architecture becomes the creator of new social observances [*gesellschaftlicher Formen*]. (1929, 8–9)

Taut's statement is interesting not only for his acceptance of purpose and utility as aesthetic properties, but because he went further, and asserted that not only did architecture express the social collectivity, but that furthermore it had the power to shape social relations. However, in his efforts to describe this perceived social property, Taut failed to find any word for it.

With the collapse of the Weimar republic, and the demise of the *Neues Bauen*, experiments with the socialization of architecture came to an end in Germany. Those German architects who emigrated to Britain or the United States not only found the political climate in those countries hostile to their reformist approach to architecture, but were also frustrated by the English language's lack of vocabulary to convey the socialized aesthetics that they had been developing in Germany in the 1920s. The English word 'functional' was wholly unable to communicate the accumulated nuances of '*Zweck*' and '*sachlich*', and it is no surprise that they preferred not to use the word at all. Walter Gropius, in his 1935 book *The New Architecture and the Bauhaus*, written for an English audience, declared 'catch phrases like "functionalism" (*die neue Sachlichkeit*) … have had the effect of deflecting appreciation of the New Architecture' (23) – and for a time he effectively disowned the term.

If we now turn our attention to some of the ways that people in countries other than Germany have tried to articulate the social content of architecture, we might start with the concept of 'reality'. Developed primarily as a theory of literature in the 1930s, it has always been contentious how far 'realism' might apply in architecture and urbanism. According to the Hungarian literary theorist Georg Lukács, writing in 1938, the realist's 'goal is to penetrate the laws governing objective reality and to uncover the deeper, hidden, mediated, not immediately perceptible network of relationships that go to make up society' (38). Or, in what was to become the official socialist realist policy of the Soviet Union, realism 'means knowing life so as to be able to depict it truthfully in works of art, not to depict it in a dead scholastic way, not simply as "objective reality", but to depict reality in its revolutionary development' (Zhdanov, 1934, 411). These arguments lent themselves most obviously to representational arts – literature, painting and cinema – yet even if no 'realist' theory of architecture emerged out of the debates that took place in the 1930s, it is nonetheless possible to find architects and critics talking about architecture and cities from early in the century in terms which correspond to the realist agenda, even if they did not themselves use the words 'realist' or 'reality'. A particularly good instance of this is in the English architect and town planner Raymond Unwin's *Town Planning in Practice* of 1909. Advocating the merits of co-operative residential development (see ill. p.102), he wrote:

> it seems possible to hope that with co-operation there may be
> introduced into our town suburbs and villages that sense of being
> the outward expression of an orderly community of people, having
> intimate relations one with the other, which undoubtedly is given in
> old English villages, and which has been the cause of much of the beauty
> we find there. (381–82)

In describing the property of architecture as 'the outward expression of an orderly community of people', architects and architectural critics have not generally used the word 'realist'. This may well be to do with 'real' and 'realist' having carried quite other meanings in the architectural vocabulary, primarily to do with structural reality – for this was the sense in which the term was generally used in late nineteenth-century Germany (see 'Function', pp. 180–81), and in France and Britain too. When the English architect W. R. Lethaby wrote

'Only by being intensely real can we get back wonder into a building once more' (1911, 239), he meant following the principles of constructional rationality. The only well known case of a work of architecture following an explicitly 'realist' programme, in the sense defined by Lukács, was in the housing estates built by the Italian housing authority INA-Casa in the years 1949–54. One scheme in particular, the Quartiere Tiburtino on the outskirts of Rome, designed by Ludovico Quaroni and Mario Ridolfi, was described by its architects and has been discussed by critics as 'realist'.[3] Designed for rural immigrants to Rome, and intended to boost employment by using existing building labour skills, the scheme had nothing of architectural modernism's rational approach to city planning with grids and rectilinear blocks; instead the layout was informal, and the buildings were a bizarre mix of types – three-, four- and five-storey terraces, and some seven-storey towers – with varied building masses, pitched tile roofs and other elements that had more in common with the rural villages from which the inhabitants came than with conventional ideas of urban architecture. The impression of the whole was as the outcome of discontinuous, incremental development. Although the Tiburtino scheme gave rise to a controversy in Italy as to what a 'realist' architecture should be, nowhere else outside Italy was the term 'realism' itself taken up in architectural circles. In Italy, the word continued in currency – so, for example, in 1977 Rossi described his research of the early 1960s, 'I was looking for an everyday and ancient realism', but in fact by then Rossi's interest in realism was less concerned with the representation of society than with the 'collective memory' of the city. Amongst the members of Team X, the international group that broke away from the Congrès International d'Architecture Moderne (CIAM) in 1956, one comes across realist sentiments, but nothing that could be called a developed theory of realism. For instance the British architects Alison and Peter Smithson wrote in 1957,

> Our functionalism means accepting the realities of the situation, with all their contradictions and confusions, and in trying to do something with them. In consequence, we have to create an architecture and a town planning which – through built form – can make meaningful the change, the growth, the flow, the *vitality* of community. (333)

But, despite a passing reference to 'realities', the Smithsons' concern was not to develop a realist account of architecture, but rather to resist the doctrinaire and abstract model of the city found in early modernism, and to replace it by a more flexible one formed around 'community' and 'association'. Despite the widespread and well understood use of 'realism' and 'reality' in other modern art practices, it never – except in post-war Italy – became part of the vocabulary of modernist architecture.[4]

INA-Casa, Quartiere Tiburtino, Rome,
Ludovico Quaroni and Mario Ridolfi,
1949–54. The calculated irregularity,
reminiscent of the villages from which
the inhabitants largely came, contributed
to the Tiburtino's reputation as a
'realist' scheme.

There are two other words that are interesting in relation to the efforts of English-speaking architects and critics to find a description for architecture's social qualities during the modernist era. These are 'monumental' and 'urbanity'. 'Monumental' was a heavily contested term in the modernist vocabulary, and formed the subject of extensive debate in Britain and the United States in the late 1940s.⁵ Without rehearsing all the various senses in which the word was used, there is one particular inflection which it was given by the American critic Lewis Mumford that is worth drawing attention to. In pre-war modernist criticism, 'monumental' was generally derogatory. For example, it was the word the Czech critic Karel Teige used to draw attention to everything he thought was unsatisfactory about Le Corbusier's Mundaneum project (see ill. p. 166), and the normative modernist view, as expressed by the German critic Walter Behrendt, was that 'a democratic society whose structure, based on the concept of organic order, is of dynamic character has no use, and therefore no desire for the monument' (1938, 182). In the late 1940s, though, Mumford, tried to turn 'monumental' from a negative into a positive descriptive of social value. As he wrote in 1949, 'It is by its social intention and not by its abstract form that the monument reveals itself'. The examples he gave were Dudok's Hilversum Town Hall and the Römerstadt Siedlung at Frankfurt, where, he explained, 'In essence the monument is a declaration of love and admiration attached to the highest purposes men hold in common' (1949, 179).

Town Hall, Hilversum, Netherlands, W. Dudok, 1924–31. Lewis Mumford regarded the 'monumentality' of Dudok's Town Hall as social in its ends – a 'declaration of the love and admiration... men hold in common'.

But Mumford's attempt to reverse the meaning of 'monumental' was hardly successful, and other critics of the time, like Bruno Zevi, persisted in using it pejoratively. Even Mumford himself seems soon to have abandoned his brief attempt to make it into a positive term, for by the time he reviewed Le Corbusier's Marseilles Unité d'Habitation in 1957, he had reverted to its more customary sense: he criticized the work because 'Le Corbusier betrayed the human contents to produce a monumental effect' (81). Nonetheless, Mumford's short-lived experiment with 'monumentality' is instructive as an attempt to break out of the confined vocabulary available for signifying the social in architecture.

The other term, also a re-inflection by Mumford in the 1950s, was 'urbanity'. In addition to its traditional meaning of being urbane, courteous and well mannered (and it was in this sense, for the demeanour of buildings, that Trystan Edwards used it in his 1924 book *Manners in Architecture*), since around 1900 it had been common to use this word to signify the condition of life in a city. But this second sense had always been relatively neutral, not a qualitative evaluation; in Mumford's hands, though, the two meanings were merged, giving 'urbanity' a positive value, denoting all that was commendable about the social life of cities. In his 1953 essay on the British New Towns, he commented on their wide streets, 'Such openness not merely reduces urbanity, but it also reduces social amenity' (40); and in another essay the same year on

(above) Unité d'Habitation, Marseilles, Le Corbusier, 1951. By 1957, when he wrote about the Unité, Mumford no longer regarded 'monumentality' as having any social value.

(left) Elizabeth Square, Lansbury Estate, Poplar, London, LCC Architects, 1951. Praised by Lewis Mumford: 'Here is urbanity without social stultification'. Notice the similarity of the layout to Litchfield Square, illustrated on p. 102.

the Lansbury estate in East London, he remarked 'Here is space without social dispersion, urbanity without social stultification, variety without empty caprice …' (30). Although not immediately apparent from these quotations alone, read in the context of Mumford's other writings, it is evident that by 'urbanity' he meant the realization of a civilized collective urban life, and of personal self-fulfilment, which together he saw as the true ends of cities. Following Mumford's example, other architects and critics started to use 'urbanity' in the same sense. A good example is Serge Chermayeff and Christopher Alexander's *Community and Privacy* (1963), one of the first pieces of architectural writing in which the post-Arendt preoccupation with the public/private spheres model of society became explicit. 'Urbanity' is a recurring term in the book; they introduce it with a quotation by E. F. Sekler, 'Every lack of differentiation in its [the city's] physical pattern means a negation of choice, and thus a negation of true urbanity. An inhuman anonymity then results…' (50). 'Some people', Chermayeff and Alexander continued, 'are old enough to have enjoyed the life of urbanity that existed in the well defined cities of the past'; this urbanity, they explain, derived from an 'interaction between the inhabitants, the social purpose, and the manner of building [which] gave each city its identity' (51). It is unambiguous from these statements that 'urbanity' is the result of the merging of the social with the physical. It is the term that comes closest of any that we have considered so far to describing that dream of architectural modernism, the moment of fusion when the physical becomes social, and the social becomes physical.

In his subsequent writing, Christopher Alexander remained committed to the social nature of built space, and his research in the 1960s was dedicated to finding ways of configuring social forms and relationships spatially. In his books of the 1970s, he abandoned his interest in mathematical techniques, and reverted to a humanism that was closer to that of Mumford's 1950s writing. In particular, what emerged in *A Pattern Language* (1977) was his commitment to the view that the value of architecture is in its capacity to enable individuals to realize their collective existence as social beings. The vocabulary Alexander used to describe this is interesting. 'Towns and buildings', he writes, 'will not be able to become alive, unless they are made by all the people in society, and unless these people share a common pattern language' (x). 'Alive' and 'living' are recurring terms in Alexander's trilogy – and they do not mean the same as Ruskin's use of them. Rather they are descriptions of the way people respond to certain places. Over and over again, he contrasts what is 'alive' with what is 'dead': 'The stair is itself a space, a volume, a part of the building; and unless this space is made to live, it will be a dead spot' (638); or 'the courtyards built in modern buildings are often dead' (562). 'Dead' architecture to Alexander means places where people do not congregate; in 'living' architecture, people linger, and random encounters occur. The purpose of *A Pattern Language* was to identify the tectonic and spatial features that were 'alive': thus, for example, 'people will always gravitate to those rooms which have light on two sides, and leave the rooms which are lit only from one side unused and empty' (747). Although Alexander's terminology has a poetic appeal (his other favourite classification is 'warm/cold'), perhaps the reason for his choice of these relatively vague terms is to be understood in relation to his wish to de-professionalize architecture, to free it from the control of experts, and to empower every individual with the means to make architecture; one strategy for this desired liberation was a noticeable avoidance, as far as possible, of the words conventionally used by architects.

In this respect, Alexander can be contrasted with the Dutch architect Herman Hertzberger who was Alexander's contemporary, and shared a similarly humanist view of architecture, but who took a rather different solution towards the problem of verbalizing architecture's social content. Briefly summarized, Hertzberger's view of the social nature of architecture is that just as mankind is distinguished by its use of language, so too does mankind have the facility to adapt and give meaning to spaces. Like language, this is not something that can be controlled by any one individual, but is negotiated socially. In these circumstances, architects can only create the opportunities for individual and social usage of built space, but not determine the outcome. Ultimately, like his teacher Aldo van Eyck, Hertzberger was strongly influenced by phenomenology, and there is an assumption that architecture is a means to revealing what it is to be in the world as a social being. Thus Hertzberger writes 'architecture is also capable of showing that which is not actually visible, and of eliciting associations you were not aware of before', and when successful, 'an architectural environment will moreover "visualize" these embedded realities and will thus tell the users something "about the world" ' (1991, 230). A single passage, describing two of his own buildings, the Apollo Schools (1980–83) in Amsterdam (see ill. p. 116), will illustrate Hertzberger's characteristic use of language:

> Every kind of step or ledge by a school entrance becomes a place to sit for the children, especially where there is an inviting column to offer protection and to lean against. Realizing this generates form. Here again we see that form generates itself, and that it is less a matter of inventing than of listening attentively to what men and objects want to be. (1991, 186)

Hertzberger's descriptive language is borrowed in part from linguistic theory – hence his liking for 'structure' – but in all other respects it is heavily reliant on the conventional modernist vocabulary: 'form', 'function', 'flexibility', 'space', 'environment', 'articulation' and 'users' are recurrent words. Hertzberger's choice of these words, given their flaccidity, may seem surprising; but it is

nonetheless understandable, for in a sense he had no choice, this was the
available language of architecture, and there was no other. Just as Hertzberger
aimed to give the existing tectonic language of modern architecture a social
inflection, so too he wanted to make its verbal vocabulary more expressive
of social values.

Between the poetic vagueness of Alexander's 'alive', and Hertzberger's
resolute adherence to existing modernist terms, the only other alternative to
those wanting to articulate the social content of architecture was to invent a
new set of terms. To some extent this was attempted by Alexander in the 1960s,
particularly in his *Notes on the Synthesis of Form* (1964), but abandoned by
him in his reaction against the rule of experts. It has, however, been the solution
of another architectural theorist, Bill Hillier, who is wholly committed to the
view of buildings as social objects. 'Buildings are', he writes, 'among the most
powerful means that a society has to constitute itself in space-time, and through
this to project itself into the future' (1996, 403–4). In *The Social Logic of Space*
(1984), he and Julienne Hanson developed a terminology to describe built space
in such a way as to correlate it with social activity. If the terms they introduced,
like 'convexity', 'axiality' and 'integration', need to be explained before they can
be understood, at least they do not involve bundling another layer of meaning
onto the already overloaded existing vocabulary, and avoid the risk of confusion
through ambiguity.

In general, in the attempts to describe the 'social' aspects of architecture,
language has let architecture down. Language's particular strength – the creation
of differences – has been of limited value in this domain; while the task of
making evident a relationship between two such utterly disparate phenomena
as social practice on the one hand and physical space on the other has proved
to be largely beyond the capacity of language.

1 See *Architects' Journal*, vol. 187, 4 May 1988 (special issue on Walter Segal); and McKean, *Learning from
Segal*, 1989.

2 See F. Dal Co, *Figures of Architecture and Thought*, 1990, 23–26; and M. Tafuri and F. Dal Co, *Modern
Architecture*, 1979, 100.

3 For discussion of this scheme in English, see Tafuri, *History of Italian Architecture 1944–1985*, 1989, 16–18; and
P. Rowe, *Civic Realism*, 1997, 106–16.

4 See Huet, 'Formalisme – Réalisme', *Architecture d'Aujourd'hui*, vol. 190, April 1977, 35–36, who confirms this
opinion. The recent book by Peter Rowe, *Civic Realism* (1997), is a unique attempt to develop 'realism' as an
architectural concept.

5 See G. R. and C. C. Collins, 'Monumentality: a Critical Matter in Modern Architecture', *Harvard Architectural
Review*, no. IV, Spring 1984, 14–35.

Apollo School, Amsterdam, H. Hertzberger,
1980–83. 'We see that form generates
itself, and it is less a matter of inventing
than of listening attentively to what men
and objects want to be'.

Part Two

A dictionary begins when it no longer gives the meaning of words, but their tasks.

Georges Bataille, 'L'Informe', 1929

Character

Character is a large word, full of significance; no
metaphoric river can more than hint at its meaning.
Louis Sullivan, *Kindergarten Chats*, 33

Introduced into architectural discourse in the eighteenth
century, the term 'character' has been central to efforts
to demonstrate a relationship between built works of
architecture and ulterior meaning. References to
'character' almost always raise issues of 'meaning', and
this must be taken into account in analysis of the term.
In particular it has been through the word 'character'
that the successive debates over what has sometimes been
called the 'crisis of representation' have been conducted.
The multiple uses of 'character' within architecture over
the last two and a half centuries are, to a large extent, the
outcome of the uncertainty as to whether or not buildings
carry 'meaning', and if they do, how it is to be discerned.

Although generally identified as a product of the
classical tradition, which is where it was principally
developed, 'character' is a term by no means restricted to
classicism, and it has been used widely in the twentieth
century. Despite the attempt by the critic Colin Rowe
(in his essay 'Composition and Character' written in
1953–54) to expunge it from the modernist vocabulary,
there is plenty of evidence for its unapologetic use
throughout the modernist era. Examples range from the
proto-modernist Otto Wagner, who directed his students
to attend to 'a clear, easy, and immediately apprehensible
expression of the building's character' (89); to David
Medd, a British mid-century schools architect – 'colour is
perhaps the single most important factor in determining
the character of a building' (1949, 251); to the American
late-modern urbanist, Kevin Lynch – 'If Boston districts
could be given structural clarity as well as distinctive
character, they would be greatly strengthened' (1960, 22);
and to the British critic Robert Maxwell writing in 1988:
'There seems no doubt that the building [Mississauga City
Hall] has communicated a character, and that it has

succeeded in this by means of a skilful rhetoric' (1993,
85). If Rowe's claims – that 'the present day has imposed
critical taboos on characterization', and that the word
was 'somewhat suspect' (62) – are not borne out by the
evidence, his essay was nonetheless important in that
it conformed to a particular, high modernist view,
elaborated in his other writings, that the meaning of
architecture lay solely in the immanence of its perception,
and that architecture could represent nothing beyond its
own immediate presence.

Over the last twenty years, interest in 'character'
has increased. This is a symptom of the decline of
semiotic theories of meaning, and the growing favour
for phenomenologically based analyses of meaning. The
present-day use of 'character' belongs very much within a
view that meaning is to be understood as the outcome of
the occupation of a particular physical place by an active
human subject. The best-known instance of this kind of
discussion occurs in the writings of Christian Norberg-
Schulz who, following Heidegger, posited the two
fundamentals of architecture as 'space' and 'character'.
Space, or whatever is enclosed, is where man is; while
character, denoted by adjectives, is what satisfies man's
need 'to *identify* himself with the environment, to know
how he is in a certain place' (1976, 7). 'Character' is both
'a general comprehending atmosphere, and on the other
[hand] the concrete form and substance of the space-
defining elements. Any real *presence* is intimately linked
with a character' (5–6). According to Norberg-Schulz,
'we have to emphasize that *all places have character*, and
that character is the basic mode in which the world is
"given"' (6). A more comprehensive discussion of the
problem of architecture's meaningfulness, also informed
by phenomenology, occurs in an article by Dalibor Vesely,
who sees the development of the concept of 'character'
since the eighteenth century as a primary symptom of the
collapse of a general system of transcendental meaning
in architecture: 'The ambition to subsume the traditional

City Hall, Mississauga, Canada, E. Jones and M. Kirkland, 1982–86: 'no doubt that the building has communicated a character'. 'Character' has remained in constant use throughout the modern era, despite Colin Rowe's attempt to expunge it from the modernist vocabulary.

metaphysics and poetics of architecture into the aesthetics of *character* created a temporary illusion of order, but in the long run proved to be a basis of relativism, arbitrariness and confusion' (1987, 26). Vesely's argument is that 'character' allowed architecture to become perceived as 'representational', as a cypher for the thing represented, producing a duplication of reality. 'The belief that the building before us is representing by referring to something not present disregards the simple fact that the only possible way that we can experience the reference is through the situation of which not only the building but also we ourselves are part' (24–25). As developed in architectural discourse, Vesely's contention is that 'character' encouraged people to take for granted a distinction between the work as built and a symbolic meaning. 'Character', a product of the eighteenth-century separation of aesthetic and scientific knowledge of the world, induced 'a tendency to move towards the surface of a building, an interior or a garden, towards the experience of appearances' (26). Yet, if as Vesely suggests, 'character' has been partially responsible for depriving architecture of meaningfulness, it is nonetheless 'the prime, if not the only, link still preserved with the more authentic tradition of representation' (25) that allegedly

existed before the eighteenth century. Therefore, while Vesely sees 'character' as unsatisfactory and harmful in its effects upon architecture, he nonetheless believes it to be worth holding on to.

Vesely's critique of 'character' should be borne in mind when we turn to the history and various uses of the term. It is generally agreed that 'character' was introduced into architecture by the French architect and writer Germain Boffrand, in his *Livre d'Architecture* (1745).[1] Drawing an analogy from Horace's *Ars Poetica* he wrote:

Although architecture may seem only to be concerned with what is material, it is capable of different *genres*, which make up, so to say, its forms of speech, and which are animated by the different characters that it can make felt. Just as on a stage set a Temple or a Palace indicates whether the scene is pastoral or tragic, so a building by its composition expresses that it is for a particular use, or that it is a private house. Different buildings, by their arrangement, by their construction, and by the way they are decorated, should tell the spectator their purpose; and if they do not, they offend against the rules of expression and are not as they ought to be. (16)

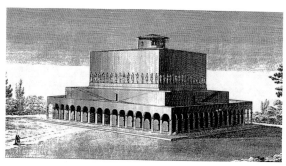

'Character' according to Blondel 'announces the building to be what it is'. For Ledoux, in common with other eighteenth-century French architects, the task was to give each *genre* an appropriate character. From top to bottom: Superintendents' house, Source de La Loue; Woodcutter's Workshop; Panarèthéon (House of Good Conduct), from Ledoux, *L'architecture*, 1804.

Summarizing his argument, Boffrand wrote:

> A man who does not know these different characters, and who cannot make them felt in his work is not an architect ... A banqueting hall and a ballroom must not be made in the same way as a church ... in every one of the modes, or orders, of architecture one can find the signifying characters which are most particularly suited to each sort of building. (26)

Boffrand's idea of character was, as he made clear, borrowed from poetry and drama – yet this translation to architecture was not without difficulties, for the characteristic genres of poetry and drama – epic, pastoral, comedy, tragedy – did not readily fit architecture, and much of the subsequent discussion of the topic in the eighteenth century was taken up with attempts to find characters more appropriate to architecture. It was of course precisely this dependence of 'character' upon a critical vocabulary developed in other art practices that made it so unattractive to Colin Rowe and other modernist critics.

The most systematic development of Boffrand's idea was by J.-F. Blondel. In an essay of 1766, reprinted in the *Cours d'Architecture*, he wrote:

> All the different sorts of architectural production should bear the imprint of the particular purpose of each building, all should have a character determining their general form, and announcing the building to be what it is. It is not enough for the distinctive character to be indicated only by the attributes of the sculpture ... It is the fine arrangement [*disposition*] of the general masses, the choice of forms, and an underlying style which gives to each building a bearing which suits only those of its sort. (vol. 2, 229–30)

Blondel went on to distinguish sixty-four different building *genres* (or 'types' – see 'Type', p. 304–5) discussing the form and decoration appropriate to each. Earlier, in chapter four of volume one of the *Cours*, Blondel had described the range of characters which were possible in architecture – in all he listed no fewer than thirty-eight – among them sublime, noble, free, male, firm, virile, light, elegant, delicate, pastoral, naïf, feminine, mysterious, grand, bold, terrifying, dwarf, frivolous, licentious, ambiguous, vague, barbaric, flat, trifling and impoverished (on 'male' and 'feminine', see chapter 4). Fascinating though his expositions of the architectural expression of each character are, when he came to the description of the sixty-four building *genres*, he made little use of them, which is indicative of the difficulty of fitting these essentially literary figures to the determinate forms of architecture.

More fruitful than Blondel's literal borrowing from literary modes was that of Blondel's contemporary, the architect J.-D. LeRoy, who suggested that the themes expressed by architecture might instead be drawn from the experience of nature. LeRoy, in his *Histoire de la Disposition et des formes différents que les chrétiens ont données à leurs temples depuis le règne de Constantin le Grand à nos jours* (1764), wrote – and this is the English translation made by Sir John Soane, whose attachment to 'character' we shall turn to shortly –

> All grand spectacles impose on man: the immensity of the sky, the vast extent of the earth or of the sea, which we discover from the tops of mountains or from the middle of the ocean, seem to raise our minds and to enlarge our ideas. Our great works make likewise on us impressions of the same nature. We feel at their sight strong sensations, very superior to those which are only agreeable and which are the only ones which small edifices can give us. (50; Soane's translation quoted in Watkin, 1996, 201)

It is the attempt to perceive in architecture an analogous range of sensations to those experienced in front of nature that was to become the main preoccupation of late eighteenth-century discussions of character. This theme was introduced first in two British books on aesthetics, Lord Kames's *Elements of Criticism* (1762), and Thomas Whately's *Observations on Modern Gardening* (1770), both of which were translated shortly after publication, the former into German, the latter into French, and had considerable influence on continental thought. Kames's was the first English use of 'character' in relation to architecture in the new sense introduced in France by Boffrand: 'every building ought to have a character or expression suited to its destination' (vol. 2, 386). Kames placed considerable stress upon the expression of utility as part of the pleasure of architecture, and was critical of literal, emblematic devices – such as the temples of Ancient and of Modern Virtue at Stowe – to create 'the certain agreeable emotions or feelings' that were the foundation of the art (vol. 2, 432, 384). Whately put forward a more exact classification of 'character' into three kinds – emblematic, imitative, and original. The shortcoming of emblematic characters – such as

Foundations of Castel S. Angelo, Rome, etching by G.-B. Piranesi, *Antichità Romana, 1756*. LeRoy, familiar with Piranesi's engravings and Burke's *Essay on the Sublime*, pointed out that the works of man were no less capable of stimulating emotions of horror, wonder and delight than were spectacles of nature; in the late eighteenth century, 'character' acquired a secondary meaning as a description of the property of works of architecture giving rise to such emotions.

allegorical garden ornaments, with mythological or other significance – was that 'they make no immediate impression; for they must be examined, compared, perhaps explained before the whole design of them is well understood'; far better that the allusions be 'not sought for, not laboured, and have the force of a metaphor, free from the detail of an allegory' (158). Likewise imitative character, because of the consciousness of resemblance, 'checks that train of thought which the appearance naturally suggests' (159). Whately argued that

> the art of gardening aspires to more than imitation: it can create *original* characters, and give expressions to the several scenes superior to any they can receive from allusions. Certain properties, and certain dispositions, of the objects of nature, are adapted to excite particular ideas and sensations: ... all are very well known: they require no discernment, examination, or

discussion, but are obvious at a glance; and instantaneously distinguished by our feelings. (160–61)

The merit of 'original character' is that 'we soon lose sight of the means by which the character is formed' (163).

It was this idea, that architecture might achieve a direct appeal to the spirit without mental reflection, that fascinated late eighteenth-century French architects, in particular Le Camus de Mézières, Boullée and Ledoux, and which dominated discussions of character in the latter part of the century. Here, it seemed, there was a real possibility that architecture might create 'characters' that, while analogous to nature in their effect, were entirely specific to architecture. In *Le Génie de l'architecture* (1780) Le Camus de Mézières made use of analogies from both painting and theatre to explain his notion of character, but ultimately saw architecture as capable

Elysian Fields, Stowe, Buckinghamshire, W. Kent, *c.* 1735. Whately suggested that landscape gardening had the power to create 'original characters', whose direct appeal to the emotions was unencumbered by allegory or intellectual reflection.

Humphry Repton's proposed changes to West Wycombe Park, Buckinghamshire, 1794–95. 'Unity of character' for practitioners of the picturesque like Repton meant 'it seemed as if some great artist had designed both the building and the landscape, they so peculiarly suit and embellish each other'. From Repton, *Observations*, 1805.

of producing its own specific characters. Within the house, 'Each room must have its own particular character. The analogy, the relation of proportions, decides our sensations; each room makes us want the next; and this engages our minds and holds them in suspense' (88). It was from Le Camus de Mézières that Boullée developed his notion of the Poetry of Architecture: here, Boullée described character in terms of the moods of the seasons – the magnificent splendour of summer, the smiling variety of autumn, the sombre gloom of winter – each of which could be expressed in architecture by means of their particular qualities of light and shade (see ill. p. 230). 'This type of architecture based on shadows', he claimed, 'is my own artistic discovery' (90).

To the two main eighteenth-century senses of 'character' described so far – the expression of the building's particular purpose, and the evocation of specific moods – we should add a third, the sense of character as expression of locality, of place. Fundamental to the practice of picturesque landscape and architecture, this particular meaning follows from Alexander Pope's well-

known lines in his 'Epistle to Lord Burlington' of 1731:

> To build, to plant, whatever you intend,
> To rear the Column, or the Arch to bend,
> To swell the Terras, or sink the Grot;
> In all, let *Nature* never be forgot.
> Consult the *Genius* of the *Place* in all.

For practitioners of the picturesque, like Humphry Repton, 'unity of character' was 'amongst the first principles of good taste' (1795, 95). And as Repton's contemporary Uvedale Price explained, 'union of character' was found where 'it seemed as if some great artist had designed both the building and the landscape, they so peculiarly suit, and embellish each other' (1810, vol. 2, 177).

Of the architects mentioned so far, probably the most enthusiastic exponent of 'character' was the English architect Sir John Soane. Soane's extensive reading of French architectural thought, and his familiarity with the principles of the picturesque, gave him a particularly broad grasp of the various senses of the concept, and in his Royal Academy lectures it was (together with 'simplicity') one of his two most heavily used critical terms, conferred upon everything of which he approved – for example of Vanbrugh, he writes 'His works are full of character, and his outlines rich and varied' (563). Soane used 'character' in all the ways so far considered. It appears in the sense used by the picturesque, to describe the relatedness of the architecture to its natural setting: 'The surrounding scenery having determined the architectural character of the villa …' (588). Secondly, following Boffrand and Blondel, Soane used 'character' to describe the architectural expression of the building's purpose. In a long and eloquent passage in Lecture XI, he pressed this sense:

> Too much attention cannot be given to produce a distinct character in every building, not only in the great features, but in the minor details likewise: even a Moulding, however diminutive, contributes to increase or lessen the character of the assemblage of which it forms a part.

Interior, St Martin's-in-the-Fields, London, James Gibbs, 1722–26. Criticized by Soane for inappropriate character: 'who that looks at the interior of St Martin's… but is inclined to imagine himself in a private box in an Italian theatre than in a place of devotion'.

(opposite) Joseph Gandy, view under the Dome of Sir John Soane's Museum, 1811. Soane's own house in Lincoln's Inn Fields was a complex essay in the various notions of 'character' current at the end of the eighteenth century: not only did the building advertise itself as 'the house of an architect', but within Soane experimented with effects of light and dark to create different moods or 'characters' appropriate to the stages of a narrative, or of a theatrical drama.

Character is so important that all its most delicate and refined modifications must be well understood and practised with all the fine feelings and nice discrimination of the artist. He who is satisfied with heaping stone upon stone, may be a useful builder, and increase his fortune. He may raise a convenient house for his employer, but such a man will never be an artist, he will not advance the interests or credit of the art, nor give it importance in public estimation. He will neither add to its powers to move the soul, or to speak to the feelings of mankind.

Notwithstanding all that has been urged to the contrary, be assured my young friends, that architecture in the hands of men of genius may be made to assume whatever character is required of it. But to attain this object, to produce this variety, it is essential that every building should be conformable to the uses it is intended for, and that it should express clearly its destination and its character, marked in the most decided and indisputable manner. The cathedral and the church; the palace of the sovereign, and the dignified prelate; the hotel of the nobleman; the hall of justice; the mansion of the chief magistrate; the house of the rich individual; the gay theatre, and the gloomy prison; nay even the warehouse and the shop, require a different style of architecture in their external appearance, and the same distinctive marks must be continued in the internal arrangements as well as in the decorations. Who that looks at the interior of St Martin's church, and observes its sash-windows and projecting balconies at the east end, but is inclined rather to imagine himself in a private box in an Italian theatre than in a place of devotion?

Without distinctness of character, buildings may be convenient and answer the purposes for which they were raised, but they will never be pointed out as examples for imitation, nor add to the splendour of the possessor, improve the national taste, or increase the national glory. (648)

Thirdly, in a reference to Le Camus de Mézières and Ledoux, Soane described 'character' in terms of the mood created by light:

> The 'lumière mystérieuse', so successfully practised by the French artists, is a most powerful agent in the hands of a man of genius, and its power cannot be too fully understood, nor too highly appreciated. It is, however, little attended to in our architecture, and for this obvious reason, that we do not sufficiently feel

the importance of character in our buildings, to which the mode of admitting light contributes in no small degree. (598)

Turning from Soane, immersed in English and French theory, we must now consider the other generic theory of 'character' developed in the eighteenth century, that of the German Romantics. Principally identified with Goethe, the theory of 'expressive character' was developed in reaction to the various French theories, and in part emerged out of Goethe's theories of animal and plant morphology – themselves developed in reaction to French methods of biological description. The earliest and most passionate statement by Goethe of this new theory was in his essay 'On German Architecture' (1772), in which his contemplation of Strasbourg cathedral (see ill. p. 300) led him to see its character as the expression of the soul of its mason, Erwin von Steinbach. Goethe deduced from this that the truth (see p. 299–301) of all art and architecture lay in the degree to which it expressed the character of its maker: 'Now this characteristic art is the only true art. If, out of ardent, united, individual, independent feeling, it quickens, unconcerned, yea, unconscious of all that is strange, then born whether of rough savageness or of civilized sensibility, it is whole and living' (159). This notion of 'character' as the outward expression of an inner force, whether of the individuality of the artist, or of his culture, places art in a correspondence to nature. As developed by the German Romantics, this theory of character was used most particularly in relation to the national identity of art. Thus, for example, in an essay of 1816 Goethe wrote: 'just as we bring out the character of the individual which consists in not being controlled by circumstances but controlling and conquering them, so we rightly recognize in every people or group a character which manifests itself in an artist or other remarkable man' (Gage, 146).

Although the older senses of 'character', particularly that of manifesting the building's purpose, continued in normal usage during the nineteenth century, it was to be 'expressive character' that became the most active and interesting sense in which 'character' was to be used, and it was to be this theory of 'character' which prevailed, particularly in Germany and in the English-speaking world. For instance, Jacob Burckhardt's writings all rest upon the principle that national distinctions in architecture are the outcome of the expression of the specific, historically developed characters of particular peoples; and in the United States, discussions about the development of an American architecture took place largely in terms of 'char-

acter' – one may recall Emerson's indictment of American culture, 'in all, feminine, no character' (1910, vol. 4, 108).

Yet despite the widespread adoption of the notion of 'expressive character', of works of art as the outward expression of their makers' spirit, it did not go uncriticized. Even John Ruskin, whose enthusiasm for the German Romantic idea that architecture's meaning lay in its power to communicate the soul of its builders informed all his architectural writings, was nonetheless aware of its problems as a theory of architectural expression – for how was the viewing subject to be certain of understanding what they perceived in the way intended by the makers? Ruskin identified this problem in volume one of *The Stones of Venice*:

> A building which recorded the Bible history by means of a series of sculptural pictures, would be perfectly useless to a person unacquainted with the Bible beforehand .... So, again, the power of exciting emotion must vary or vanish, as the spectator becomes thoughtless or cold; and the building may be often blamed for what is the fault of its critic, or endowed with a charm which is of its spectator's creation. It is not, therefore, possible to make expressional character any fair criterion of excellence in buildings, until we can fully place ourselves in the position of those to whom their expression was originally addressed, and until we are certain that we understand every symbol, and are capable of being touched by every association which its builders employed as letters of their language. (chapter 2, §2)

It was precisely so as to put the nineteenth-century spectator 'in the position of those to whom their expression was originally addressed' that Ruskin wrote the chapter on 'The Nature of Gothic' in volume two of *The Stones of Venice*. In this chapter, the most exhaustive analysis of 'expressive character' attempted by any nineteenth-century writer, Ruskin set out to show exactly how the immanent properties of Gothic architecture communicated themselves to their audience. Drawing an analogy with the double character of rocks and minerals, their external crystalline form, and their internal atomic structure, so,

> Exactly in the same manner, we shall find that Gothic architecture has external forms, and internal elements. Its elements are certain mental tendencies of the builders, legibly expressed in it; as fancifulness, love of variety, love of richness, and such others. Its

John Ruskin, sketch of island of basalt, from his Early Geological Notebook. Ruskin gave precision to the notion of 'expressive character' in architecture by an analogy with the crystalline structure of rocks and minerals in geology: the internal elements – in architecture, the mental tendencies of the builders – correspond to the outward shape of the rock, or building.

external forms are pointed arches, vaulted roofs, &c. And unless both the elements and the forms are there, we have no right to call the style Gothic. ... We must therefore inquire into each of these characters successively; and determine first, what is the Mental Expression, and secondly, what the Material Form, of Gothic architecture, properly so called. (§4)

Ruskin proceeded to list six properties of the material form of Gothic architecture (Savageness, Changefulness, Naturalism, Grotesqueness, Rigidity, Redundance), and then to show the correspondence of each of these to specific mental tendencies of the builders. Ruskin's particularly ambitious system of relating the visible characteristics of Gothic architecture to the mental and social life of its builders took the theory of 'expressive character' a step beyond the looseness of all previous uses of the concept.

The other nineteenth-century theorist to show ambivalence towards 'character' was Viollet-le-Duc. Although he, in common with many other architects and critics, lamented the lack of character of the works of his own time ('Will this age, which is so fertile in discoveries ... transmit to posterity only imitations or hybrid works, without character' [Lectures, vol. 1, 446]), Viollet was fiercely opposed to the whole system of elucidating the meaning of architecture in terms of character types. As he wrote in the entry on 'Construction' in the Dictionnaire Raisonné,

A building can in no way whatsoever be 'fanatical', 'oppressive', or 'tyrannical'; these are epithets that simply do not apply to a unitary assemblage of stones, lumber and iron. A building is either a good building or a bad one, well thought out, or devoid of any rational justification. (1990, 116)

As far as Viollet was concerned, the only meaning a building could have was in the integrity of its structure, and the system of 'characters' was superfluous. This reaction against 'character' was to become even more explicit amongst Viollet-le-Duc's American followers. Leopolod Eidlitz stated: 'The character of his [the architect's] work must refer solely to construction, and construction to the idea which is to be expressed and to the material which is at his command for the purpose' (1881, 486). And in a similar vein Henry van Brunt, in his essay 'The Growth of Characteristic Architectural Style in the United States' (1893), writes:

> the most distinctive character of our best work in architecture is its hospitality to new materials and new methods of construction, its perfect willingness to attempt to confer architectural character upon the science of the engineer, and to adapt itself without prejudice to the exactions of practical use and occupation. (321–22)

Louis Sullivan's ambivalence towards 'character', noted in the quotation at the beginning of this entry, presumably derived from the difficulty of reconciling his own passionate enthusiasm for the 'expressive character' of German Romantic thought with the structural rationalists' hostility towards 'character'.

The relative decline of 'character', in all its senses, in the early twentieth century would appear to have been primarily due to the influence of structural rationalism. Wherever structural rationalism took hold, 'character' was ridiculed. For example, W. R. Lethaby ended his rationalist 1910 lecture 'The Architecture of Adventure' by saying:

> The method of design to a modern mind can only be understood in the scientific, or in the engineer's sense, as a definite analysis of possibilities – not as a vague poetic dealing with poetic matters, with derivative ideas of what looks domestic, or what looks farmlike, or looks ecclesiastical – the dealing with a multitude of flavours – that is what architects have been doing in the last hundred years. (95)

Yet, suspicious though architects and critics became of 'character' in the modernist era, they never, as we have seen, found it possible to dispense with altogether.

1 On the history of 'character' see Szambien, *Symétrie Goût Caractère*, 1986, chapter 9, 174–99; Egbert, *The Beaux-Arts Tradition in French Architecture*, 1980, chapter 6; Watkin, *Sir John Soane*, 1996, chapter 4, 184–255; Vidler, *Claude-Nicolas Ledoux*, 1990, chapter 2, 19–73; and for a slightly different view, see Rykwert, *The Dancing Column*, 1996, 43–56.

E.-E. Viollet-le-Duc, design for a French Street Villa. Viollet-le-Duc and his followers outlawed 'character', as irrelevant to the methodical pursuit of reasoned construction that they considered to be the principal business of architecture. From Viollet-le-Duc, *Entretiens sur l'Architecture*, vol. 2, 1872.

Context

The task of the architectural project is to reveal, through the transformation of form, the essence of the surrounding context. V. Gregotti, 1982 introduction to French edition of Gregotti 1966, 12

Introduced into the architectural vocabulary in the 1960s, 'context', 'contextual' and 'contextualism' were part of the first substantial critique of modernist practice, and might on that account be classed as postmodernist terms. But whether they were the last modernist terms, or the first postmodernist ones matters very little; they are included here partly on chronological grounds, as belonging to the period of late modernism, and partly because they were wholly directed towards the discourse of modernism, but most particularly because they illustrate so well the imperialism effected by the act of translation from one language to another.

The story begins in Milan in the 1950s, when in the editorials written by Ernesto Rogers for the magazine *Casabella Continuità* in the middle of the decade there appeared the first serious critique of the work of the first generation of modernist architects. Rogers criticized their tendency to treat every scheme as a unique abstract problem, their indifference to location, and their desire to make of every work a prodigy. Rather, Rogers argued, consider architecture as a dialogue with its surroundings, both in the immediate physical sense, but also as a historical continuum. The terms used by Rogers were '*le preesistenze ambientali*' (surrounding pre-existences), or '*ambiente*', and although both have since been translated into English as 'context' this is misleading, for Rogers used neither this word, nor its Italian equivalent *contesto* – which entered general use in Italy in the 1970s as a translation of the English word 'context' only after that had become current in the USA. It is worth investigating what Rogers meant by *preesistenze ambientali*, for it differed in several respects from the Anglo-Saxon 'context' with which it has subsequently become

confused. Compared to previous arguments for the responsiveness of architecture to location – such as the *genius loci* of the English picturesque, or the English critic Trystan Edwards's objections to the 'selfish' modern commercial building (1946, 2) – what distinguished Rogers's concept was the absolute importance of the historical continuity manifested by the city and existing in the minds of its occupants. As Rogers wrote in one of his editorials, 'to consider *l'ambiente* means to consider history' (1955, 203). For Rogers, the two concepts of *preesistenze ambientali* and 'history' (see pp. 196–205) were indissolubly linked: '*to understand history is essential for the formation of the architect*, since he must be able to insert his own work into the *preesistenze ambientali* and to take it, dialectically, into account' (1961, 96). Rogers's idea of *ambiente* as a historical process came from a variety of sources, but one in particular which he cited specifically was an essay by the poet T. S. Eliot, 'Tradition and the Individual Talent' (1917). It is worth quoting from this essay, for it helps make clear the interconnectedness of continuity, history and *ambiente* in Rogers's mind. Eliot wrote, 'the historical sense involves a perception, not only of the pastness of the past, but of its presence' –

> The existing monuments form an ideal order among themselves, which is modified by the introduction of the new (the really new) work of art among them. The existing order is complete before the new work arrives; for order to persist after the supervention of novelty, the *whole* order must be, if ever so slightly, altered; and so the relations, proportions, values of each work of art towards the whole are readjusted; and this is conformity between the old and the new. Whoever has approved this idea of order, of the form of European, of English literature will not find it preposterous that the past should be altered by the present as much as the present is directed by the past. (1917, 26–27)

Shop, office and apartments, 2–4 Corso Francia, Turin, Italy, Banfi, Belgiojoso, Peresutti and Rogers, 1959. The 'ambiente' revealed through this project included the Italian historical tradition of mixed-use buildings shaped to fit existing plots; covered arcades over the pavement; and the marking of the city boundary by monumental towers – all reinterpreted in the idiom of modern architecture.

It is this sense that all work impacts upon present consciousness of the historical past that was so essential to Rogers's notion of 'ambiente'.

Two examples will suffice to show how Rogers used *preesistenze ambientali* in his critique of orthodox modern architecture: 'One might accuse of formalism an architect who does not absorb into his work the particular and characteristic contents suggested by the *ambiente*' (1955, 201); or,

> Let us resist the affected cosmopolitanism which in the name of a still shallowly felt universal style raises the same architecture in New York, Tokyo, or Rio; identical architecture in both the country and the town. Let us seek rather to blend our works into the *preesistenze ambientali*, both the natural surroundings, and those created historically by human genius. (1956, 3)

The scheme which first brought these ideas to international notice – as well as contributing to Rogers's own formulation of them – was the controversy in 1954 over Frank Lloyd Wright's Masieri Memorial in Venice. His project, which would have occupied a prominent location on the Grand Canal, provoked passionate argument inside Italy and abroad about the suitedness of modern architecture to historic sites, and about the degree to which Wright's design did or did not take sufficient account of its surroundings. That the scheme was not built had less to do with the merits of the design than with the political objections at the time to an American building in Italy.[1]

Rogers's *ambiente* became a topic of general discussion amongst the circle of Milan architects associated with *Casabella*, and featured significantly in their writings; particularly worth remarking on are Vittorio Gregotti's *Il Territorio dell'Architettura* (1966), and above all Aldo Rossi's *The Architecture of the City* (1966) whose subsequent fame has eclipsed all other Italian architectural criticism of that era, but which can only satisfactorily be understood in relation to it. *The*

Architecture of the City is in part an extended disquisition upon the concept of *ambiente*. For readers of the American edition of the book, where the word *ambiente* was translated throughout as 'context', this nuance is rendered invisible, and it is made to seem that Rossi was party to the same debate as Colin Rowe and others at Cornell University where, as we shall see, 'contextualism' was invented. Nothing could have been further from the truth: the word Rossi used throughout was *ambiente*, never *contesto* or 'context', and his objections to 'context' were in fact objections to Rogers's *ambiente* (or its perversion by others), and unrelated to any New England conversations. The paradox presented to readers of the English-language edition, of how someone could be so critical of 'context' and yet put forward such a persuasive argument for it, is purely an effect of the translation and does not arise in the Italian original. Rossi's objections that 'context seems strangely bound up with illusion, with illusionism. As such it has nothing to do with the architecture of the city' (123), or 'As for the term *context*, we find that it is mostly an impediment to research' (126), were, we must remember, objections to *l'ambiente*, not 'context'. Rossi's criticism of Rogers's *l'ambiente* was that it was insufficiently concrete: and what Rossi wanted to

show was that it could be made concrete if one studied architectural forms themselves, independently of their functions, for in these forms was the only tangible point of contact between the economic processes of cities, on the one hand, documented through the verifiable histories of land development and partition, and on the other hand the vagueness of the 'collective historical consciousness' of the city that was Rogers's *preesistenze ambientali*.

If we turn now to the history of the English-language word 'context', its first significant appearance within the vocabulary of architecture seems to have been in Christopher Alexander's *Notes on the Synthesis of Form* of 1964, though its presence in this particular text seems to have had little to do with its subsequent usage. Alexander used 'context' as a synonym for 'environment': introducing the book, he wrote 'every design problem begins with an effort to achieve fitness between two entities: the form in question, and its context. The form is the solution to the problem; the context defines the problem' (15). This mechanistic relationship is softened later in the book – the aim of design, he writes, is not to meet the requirements in the best possible way, but 'to prevent misfit between the form and the context' (99). Nonetheless, the purpose of the book was to devise a scheme for ordering the variables that constituted 'context' so as to develop a method of design free from all the preconceptions that, in Alexander's opinion, had hampered previous efforts to achieve truly functional design. Alexander's choice of 'context' instead of the more customary 'environment' may have been due to his desire to include cultural variables, but otherwise his strictly functionalist use of the term had little to do with its subsequent history.

The introduction of 'contextualism' and 'contextualist' into the architectural vocabulary occurred in 1966 in the Urban Design studio that the English critic Colin Rowe had started teaching at Cornell University in 1963 (Rowe, 1996, vol. 3, 2; Schumacher, 1971, 86). It seems likely that the terms were borrowed from the literary New Criticism movement – even though their sense there was entirely different, and negative, rather than positive, as was the case in architecture. Rowe's Cornell studio developed a critique of modernist architecture that had a good deal in common with Ernesto Rogers's. They shared a distaste for 'prodigy' architecture, and for the modernist supposition that the particularity of a building's programme justified in every case a unique solution; and

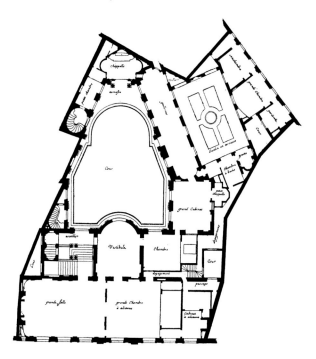

First floor plan, Hôtel de Beauvais, Paris, Antoine Le Pautre, 1652–55. Le Pautre's preservation of the internal symmetries and room relationships while adapting the standard arrangement of the Parisian *hôtel* to an irregular plot was one of Rowe's favoured examples of satisfactory relation of building to context.

many of the examples they chose to illustrate their ideas were the same. But there were also significant differences. Whereas Rogers was concerned with how the dialectical processes of history were manifested through architecture, Rowe was uninterested in this speculative understanding of the historical environment, and concentrated on the formal properties of works of architecture. And whereas Rogers thought of the environment as formed by objects, 'monuments', Rowe was more interested in the relationships between objects and the spaces they occupied. Indicative of Rowe's approach were his preferred exemplars, like Antoine Le Pautre's Hôtel de Beauvais (1652–55) in Paris, where the model French town house was compressed and deformed to fit the irregular site without losing the distinctive features of the type; Rowe compared this to Le Corbusier's Villa Savoie, an isolated primary solid, indifferent to the boundless spatial field it occupies (Rowe, 1978, 78). In the first published statement of the Cornell studio's 'contextualism' (which appeared, significantly, in *Casabella*), an ex-student, Thomas Schumacher, wrote: 'It is precisely the ways in which idealized forms can be adjusted to a context or used as "collage" that contextualism seeks to explain, and it is the systems of geometric organization which can be abstracted from any given context that contextualism seeks to divine as design tools' (1971, 84). In general, Rogers's and Rossi's interest in *ambiente* was distinguished by 'history', whereas the Cornell studio's concern with 'context' was formal, marked in particular by its study of figure/ground relationships.[2] And where the Italians were polemical, marked by an underlying commitment to the 'modern', Rowe's aim was compromise, between the modernist, and the pre-modernist city. Rowe has since summed up the studio's approach: 'If not conservative, its general tone was radical middle of

the road. … Its ideal was a mediation between the city of Modern architecture – a void with objects – and the historical city – a solid with voids' (1996, vol. 3, 2).

In the final testament of Cornell contextualism, Rowe and Koetter's book *Collage City* (1978), the authors made practically no reference to 'context' or 'contextualism'. By this time, though, 'context' had become well established in the architectural vocabulary. Kenneth Frampton in 1976 reviewed James Stirling's 1975 competition entry for the Düsseldorf Museum in terms of its 'contextual' content, and it was not long before Stirling himself began to talk about his own work, including schemes designed before the word had gained currency, in terms of 'context'; for example, commenting in 1984 on the 1971 design for an art gallery at St Andrews University, Stirling wrote 'It was both *formal* and *contextual*' (1998, 153).

Rowe and Koetter were already avoiding the words 'context' and 'contextual' by the late 1970s, yet it was around this time, as if to stiffen up the idea and give it broader credibility, that the Italian *ambiente* was taken over and subsumed into the American 'context'. However, it was not to be long before reservations about the concept itself started to be voiced. Commenting in 1985 on a scheme to extend Frank Lloyd Wright's Guggenheim Museum in New York, the American critic Michael Sorkin wrote, 'A consequence of the profession's present preoccupation with "context" is a kind of collective confidence about the possibility of adding on. There's an implicit argument that architects, duly skilled and sensitized, should be able to intervene anywhere' (148). Sorkin went on to explain why he thought this wrong. By the late 1980s, there was no doubt that many architects were uncomfortable about 'context', and were increasingly prepared to say so; in his 'diary' of the design for the French national library competition in 1989, Rem Koolhaas wrote in exasperation, 'But can such a container still have a relationship with the city? Should it? Is it important? Or is "fuck context" becoming the theme?' (1995, 640).

1 See Levine, *The Architecture of Frank Lloyd Wright*, 1996, 374–83.
2 For a useful comparison of European and American notions of context, see Shane, 'Contextualism', *Architectural Design*, vol. 46, November 1976, 676–79.

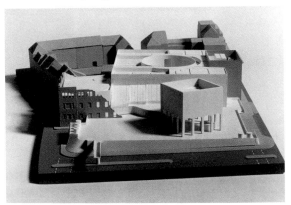

Model, competition entry for Düsseldorf Museum, James Stirling and Michael Wilford, 1975. As Kenneth Frampton observed, its 'evident dependence on a broad cultural context stands in considerable contrast to much of his work' (1976).

Design

When in 1932 the English architect Howard Robertson, Principal of the Architectural Association School of Architecture, revised his book *Principles of Architectural Composition* (1924), he renamed it *Modern Architectural Design*. This simple change of title at once tells a great deal, though not quite everything, about the inflation of the word 'design' in the mid-twentieth century, a word which after 1945 was in danger of altogether subsuming 'architecture' itself. Architects came to be referred to as 'designers', the discipline taught in schools of architecture became known as 'design', and a great many books about architecture featured 'design' in their titles. The pervasiveness of the word did not go unresisted; to Alison and Peter Smithson, for example, ' "design" was a dirty word' (201), and they preferred the term 'ordering' (though that too had its own connotations).

Why is 'design' a confusing word? As a verb, it describes the activity of preparing instructions for making an object or a building. As a noun, it has two distinct meanings. First of all, it is those instructions themselves, particularly in the form of drawings: the word comes from the Italian *disegno* (drawing), and in English by the seventeenth century, 'design' was routinely used for the drawings of the architect – Sir Roger Pratt talks of 'drafts and designs' (34) as synonymous. Secondly, as a noun, it may also refer to the work executed from the instructions, as one may say referring to an object, 'I like the design': this sense has also been common since the seventeenth century – John Evelyn, visiting Chambord in 1644, recorded in his Diary, 'That which made me desirous of seeing this Palace, was the extravagance of the designe, especially the Stayre-case mention'd by the Architect Palladio' (80). In both cases, whether drawing or executed work, in the neo-Platonic climate of the Italian Renaissance, 'design' was widely taken, so Vasari (1568) put it, as 'nothing but a visual expression of the concept which one has in the intellect';[1] this direct equivalence between the 'artistic idea' and its representation, so

necessary to the understanding of the modern usage, was already in place in English by the early seventeenth century – Sir Henry Wotton explained in *The Elements of Architecture* (1624) that Vitruvius's term *dispositio* means nothing 'more than a neate and full expression of the first *Idea* or *Designment* thereof' (118). When modernism appropriated 'design' in the 1930s, it was able to capitalize upon these already existing meanings. 'Design' fulfilled modernism's need for a term that enabled one to distinguish between a work of architecture in its materiality, as an object of experience, and a work of architecture as the representation of an underlying 'form' or idea. If 'form' was to be a primary category of architecture, then 'design' was its necessary accomplice, for 'design' is the activity which realizes form, and brings it into the world: as Louis Kahn put it, 'Design calls into being what realization – form – tells us' (288). 'Design', with its inherent confusion between 'visual expression of a concept in the intellect' and a drawing, between what emanates from the architect's mind and a built work, was grist to modernism's mill. If, as Paul-Alan Johnson remarks, 'architecture is the last stronghold of Platonism' (244), 'design' is the principal concept that has made this possible, for it is what has allowed works of architecture to appear, paradoxically, as both pure 'idea' and at the same time as solid material objects; it takes its place in the modernist triad with 'space' and 'form'.

At one level, we might regard the growth in the popularity of 'design' from the 1930s as no more than a substitution for the term 'composition' – as the change in the title of Howard Robertson's book suggests. These two words had coexisted throughout the nineteenth century, and had been used synonymously and interchangeably, as Soane did in his lectures (559). But by 1930, objections had been raised against 'composition' by certain modernist practitioners and critics, and an alternative was needed:[2] 'design', with its other connotations, was a more than adequate replacement. Frank Lloyd Wright, for example, famously declared in 1931 'Composition is dead that creation may live'; and the Czech critic Karel Teige, in 1929, indicted Le Corbusier's 'Mundaneum' project: 'Composition; with this word it is possible to summarize all the architectural faults of the Mundaneum' (90). But 'design', while undoubtedly filling the void left by the extirpation of the suspect term 'composition', was no mere substitute.

The pervasiveness of 'design' is to do with the polarities it set up: 'design' provided a means of creating an opposition between 'building' and all that that implied on the one hand, and everything in architecture that was non-material on the other hand. This opposition was made clear by Geoffrey Scott in his *The Architecture of Humanism* of 1914: 'The relation of construction to design is the fundamental problem of architectural aesthetics' (100). In other words, 'design' concerns what is *not* construction. This polarity was not new – for example, in 1726 Leoni had translated the important distinction made by Alberti at the beginning of *De Re Aedificatoria* as 'the whole art of building consists in the design, and in the structure' (1). Though as Rykwert, Leach and Tavernor point out (422–23) in their recent translation, 'design' – at least with its late twentieth-century connotations – is hardly what Alberti meant, and they retain the Latin original *lineamenti*. Leoni's choice of words for Alberti's distinction suggests that 'design/structure' was an accepted and well-understood trope in the eighteenth century, as a way of describing two aspects of a single activity – architecture. This convention continued throughout the nineteenth century, but in the early twentieth century this distinction, hitherto belonging only in speech and thought, was to become manifested as two discrete activities.

The attraction of 'design' was that for an occupation aspiring to join the liberal arts, but actually concerned with the materiality of building and encumbered with associations of manual work and commerce, the word indicated that part of its product which was the pure work of mind. This had undoubtedly been the appeal of 'design' to sixteenth-century Italian architects, but the need to distinguish between the manual and intellectual content became all the more necessary in the early twentieth century for one reason in particular: the change in the training of architects. Until the beginning of the twentieth century, architects in all countries except France (and even there, too, to a large degree) learnt the business by working, as articled pupils or apprentices, in the workplace of practising architects. In the early part of the twentieth century, training was transferred almost

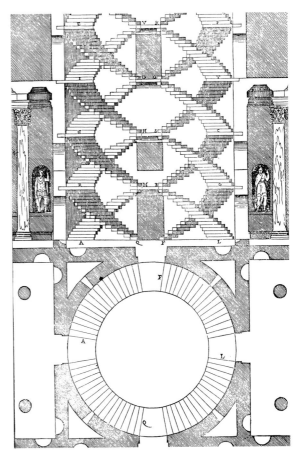

Double spiral staircase, Château de Chambord, France, c. 1530, from A. Palladio, *Quattro Libri*, 1570. Having seen Palladio's illustration, John Evelyn wanted to see Chambord for 'the extravagance of the designe, especially the stayre-case'.

everywhere to the academy, to universities and to schools of architecture – a change that corresponded to that taking place in the majority of other occupations. In architecture, its effect was that what architects learnt in their training ceased to be 'practice', and became 'principles', in other words a wholly dematerialized and cerebral version of the art; and what students 'produced' from their training was not 'architecture', but drawings – commonly referred to as 'designs'. The separation between architecture as a mental product – which was taught – and architecture as a practice engaged with the material world, now emerged for the first time as a visible fact of life. Hitherto, the opposition of 'design' and 'structure' had been no more than a way of thinking about two aspects of one activity – architecture – and it had been inconceivable that either could exist without the other. Now, with the separation of education from practice, 'design', rather than being a convenient way of conceptualizing a particular feature of architecture, came to be seen as a pure and self-sufficient activity within itself. Education made real a division that had existed previously only in discourse; and the appropriation within education of the term 'design' with its long and seemingly respectable pedigree, helped to make this quite arbitrary and artificial separation between training and practice seem normal and commonsensical. In short, the category 'design' allowed architecture to be *taught*, rather than learnt by experience.

The sense in which 'design' became perceived as a mental activity disengaged from the world is strikingly clear from the pronouncements of architectural educators: in the remarks of Richard Llewelyn Davies, the instigator of reforms in British architectural education in the 1960s, it is noticeable how 'design' is presented as an activity which is an end in itself: 'Design work in the studio is our strong point. ... In the studio, the student is continuously reminded of the one-ness of architectural design ...' (13). It is no surprise that architects, anxious to validate the intellectual component of their work, willingly embraced this separation and reification of 'design'. However, it has to be said that in the long run it has been to their disadvantage, for the development of what is called 'design and build' – in which architects are employed by building contractors to supply designs – has taken at their word architects' claim to specialization in the mental activity of 'design', and accordingly relegated them to this as their sole sphere of competence.

The turning of 'design' from being a category within architecture into an activity of its own was substantially assisted by arguments of philosophers. Just as Plato and neo-Platonism enabled Renaissance architects to distinguish between an object and its 'design', the philosophy of Kant encouraged people to think of 'design' as a pure property in its own right. In *The Critique of Judgment* (1790), Kant had written 'In painting, sculpture, and in fact in all the formative arts, in architecture and horticulture, so far as fine arts, the *design* is what is essential' (67). By 'design' Kant was referring in part to the long-standing trope of drawing (or design) *versus* colour, but also to it as the manifestation of 'form', in which sense it provided the basis for all pure judgments of taste.

If philosophy tended to support the existence of 'design' as a thing in itself, this point of view did not go uncontested. A major theme of nineteenth-century political economy was the separation between mental and manual labour, a theme taken up in its implications for architecture by John Ruskin. Ruskin's argument, developed in 'The Nature of Gothic', valued Gothic architecture because of the freedom enjoyed by the medieval craftsman to direct his own work; while recognizing the need for some division of labour in architecture between those who directed and those who executed the work, what he deplored in the architecture of his own time was the degraded and dishonourable status of those who worked with their hands, relative to their medieval forebears. Ruskin did not take issue with the distinction in architecture between those who conceived the work and those who executed it; what he objected to was regarding the one as an honourable, the other as a dishonourable occupation. As he put it, 'in each several profession, no master should be too proud to do its hardest work. The painter should grind his own colours; the architect work in the mason's yard with his men' (§21). Ruskin hardly ever used the word 'design' in relation to architecture; in fact, 'design' (by which he generally meant the specific sense of 'drawing') was an activity that Ruskin valued highly because it was the moment when human creativity demonstrated its power to transform nature into art: 'A looking-glass does not design – it receives and communicates indiscriminately all that passes before it. ... design properly so called, is human invention, consulting human capacity' (*The Two Paths*, 35–36). If Ruskin was silent on 'design' in architecture, his English successors, William Morris and the architects Philip Webb and W. R. Lethaby, looked to the implications of what he had said, and treated 'design' with suspicion, for in it they saw both the cause and the symptom of the social degradation of manual work.

Design Studio, Crown Hall, IIT, Chicago, late 1950s. It was above all the institutionalization of architecture in schools of architecture, separating training from practice, that led to 'design' becoming an end in itself.

Lethaby, in 1892, emphasized the historical change the activity had undergone, and contrasted its past with its present status: 'Design was not the abstract exercize of a faculty plus a pair of compasses ... It was insight as to the capabilities of material for expression when submitted to certain forms of handiwork. ... The crafts ... are even now being destroyed by a system in which design is divorced from work' (153). And Philip Webb, in a letter to Lethaby, made a revealing correction that sums up all the objections when he crossed out the word 'design' and substituted 'invention' (Lethaby, *Webb*, 136). If one asks why, despite evident resistance to the word, it should have become so widespread, it should be born in mind that Webb and Lethaby were also opposed to the model of architectural education introduced in the early twentieth century, and that their objections to 'design' ultimately carried no more weight than their objections to the institutionalization of architectural education.[3]

We have so far considered 'design' in relation to architecture, but specifically in Britain the word also has another sense, relative to commodities and consumer goods, implied in the phrase 'good design'. When, in 1937, Nikolaus Pevsner wrote that 'to fight against the shoddy design of those goods by which most of our fellow-men are surrounded becomes a moral duty', and was 'an integral part of *the* social question of our time' (11), he was not (despite the tone) presenting a new argument, but simply bringing up to date a debate about 'design' that had already been going on for over two hundred years.

In Britain, from the early eighteenth century onwards, it became common to judge a nation's cultural wealth not by its monuments and architecture, but by its 'many thousands of large and rich shops ... stocked with all sorts of goods' (Souligné, 1709, 154).[4] However, while the existence of all these goods might be a sign of an advanced civilization, as *possessions* owned by individuals they also signified luxury – and luxury, as Voltaire observed, is a paradox, everywhere desired, but universally condemned as a vice. The threats presented by articles of luxury were that they made people covetous, and so threatened public order; and that if they fell into the wrong hands, they devalued social distinctions. Satirizing the pursuit of luxury, Swift made Gulliver say of early eighteenth-century England, 'When I am at home and dressed as I ought to be, I carry on my body the workmanship of an hundred tradesmen; the building and furniture of my house employ as many more, and five times the number to adorn my wife' (288). If Swift

thought it absurd that one woman's dress should need a thousand men's labour, others of his contemporaries were arguing exactly the opposite. In *The Fable of the Bees* (1714) Bernard Mandeville argued, as had others before, that the pursuit of luxury was advantageous to society as a whole because of the wealth it caused to circulate; in addition, though, he also suggested that vain lust for material goods need not be the threat to public morality it was generally assumed to be, but that, if regulated by good taste, the pursuit of such objects would divert the selfish passions into a socially acceptable and harmless form of rivalry. This important and original observation opened up the possibility that, if they were suitably contrived (or 'well designed'), consumer goods need not be vulgar and offensive luxuries that threatened public order. This argument lay at the heart of subsequent debates about 'good design', particularly as they developed in mid-nineteenth century Britain.[5] Nikolaus Pevsner's mission against 'shoddy design' belongs within the same tradition (though Pevsner had learnt the argument in Germany through the Deutsche Werkbund, where it had been subtly inflected to become also a mild critique of capitalism).[6]

The other sense of 'design', which also originated in the early eighteenth century, was as a means of economic competition. The success of French luxury goods was largely seen as due to their superiority in design. In 1735, Bishop Berkeley in *The Querist* recommended setting up a school of design in Ireland to train textile designers, asking 'Whether France and Flanders could have drawn so much money from England for figured lace, silks and tapestry, if they had not had academies for designing' (§65). And he went on, 'Whether those who may slight this affair as notional have sufficiently considered the extensive use of the art of design, and its influence in most trades and manufactures...' (§68). By the mid-eighteenth century, the sense of 'design' as a form of added value seems to have been generally understood; the architect Sir William Chambers commented that for articles of consumption, 'Design is of universal benefit, and stamps additional value on the most trifling performances, the importance of which, to a commercial people, is obvious; it requires no illustration' (75). This principle underlies the many attempts by governments – whether in Britain in the 1840s, or in Germany in the 1900s, or again in Britain in the 1980s – to improve standards of design as a way of securing economic competitiveness.

All the ambiguities surrounding the word 'design' are contained in the present-day 'designer sunglasses',

Living room and dining room, 1 Kensington Palace Gardens, London, before and after alterations by Wells Coates, 1932. A familiar theme of modernist discourse in Britain and Germany was the contrast of 'bad' (i.e., cluttered and ornamental) versus 'good design' (i.e., simple, undecorated) – 'bad design' signalled the imminent collapse of civilization and resistance to it was seen, therefore, as a 'moral duty'.

or 'designer T-shirt': tinged with contempt for things so obviously luxurious, the expression at the same time concedes a socially acceptable interest in such objects, even a desire to possess them because of the opportunity they present for the exercize of taste; but the epithet also acknowledges that the attentions of a designer have justified a price far in excess of that of their humbler, 'design-free' counterparts.

1 Panofsky, *Idea*, pp.60–62, discusses this passage in the context of Renaissance art theory.

2 Rowe, 'Character and Composition', in *The Mathematics of the Ideal Villa and Other Essays*, 1982, pp.59–87.

3 See Swenarton, *Artisans and Architects*, chapter 4, and Crinson and Lubbock, *Architecture: Art or Profession*, pp.65–86, on the contested models of education.

4 This argument is developed at length by Jules Lubbock in *The Tyranny of Taste*, 1995, from which the quotation is taken.

5 See Lubbock, *The Tyranny of Taste*, 1995, chapter 3.

6 See Schwarz, *The Werkbund*, 1996, pp.13–73.

Flexibility

In our time the demand for 'flexible' structures has come to the fore. C. Norberg-Schulz, 1963, 152

Flexibility is, of course, in its own way a type of Functionalism. P. Collins, 1965, 234

An important modernist term, particularly in the period after about 1950, 'flexibility' offered hope of redeeming functionalism from determinist excess by introducing time, and the unknown. Against the presumption that all parts of a building should be destined for specific uses, a recognition that not all uses could be foreseen at the moment of design made 'flexibility' a desirable architectural property. As Alan Colquhoun has put it,

> The philosophy behind the notion of flexibility is that the requirements of modern life are so complex and changeable that any attempt on the part of the designer to anticipate them results in a building which is unsuited to its function and represents, as it were, a 'false consciousness' of the society in which he operates. (1977, 116)

Although, as we shall see, particular elements of flexibility had been acknowledged in works of architecture produced earlier, as a general architectural principle, the word 'flexibility' entered currency around the early 1950s. One of the earliest statements is by Walter Gropius, who, in 1954, set out his convictions thus: '(1) that the architect should conceive buildings not as monuments but as receptacles for the flow of life which they have to serve, and (2) that his conception should be flexible enough to create a background fit to absorb the dynamic features of our modern life' (1954, 178). By the 1960s, 'flexibility' had become an axiom of architectural criticism: Louis Kahn's 1961 Richards Laboratories at Philadelphia were criticized (and gained notoriety) because 'the buildings, not mindful enough of the

demands for flexibility on the part of the scientists, do not work very well' (Stern, 1969, 11). And James Stirling, describing in 1965 his own Leicester University Engineering Building completed five years earlier, stated it had been 'essential to propose a generalized solution that can take change and has inherent flexibility' (1998, 99).

The first of the controversies over 'flexibility' was whether flexibility was better achieved by making the work of architecture incomplete and unfinished in certain respects, leaving it to the future to decide, or whether the architect should design a building that was complete, though nonetheless flexible. A case for the incomplete solution was put by the English architect John Weeks, on the grounds that for many large institutions, such as airports or hospitals, it was impossible to predict the changes that might be required before the buildings became physically obsolete, and so the only viable solution was an indeterminate architecture, in which certain elements were left unfinished (Weeks, 1963). Forceful opposition to this came from the Dutch architects associated with Team X. (For some inexplicable reason, Dutch contributions to the concept of 'flexibility' exceed those of all other nations.) Writing in 1962, Aldo van Eyck attacked 'Flexibility and False Neutrality': 'Flexibility as such should not be overemphasized or turned into yet another absolute, a new abstract whim. ... We must beware of the glove that fits all hands, and therefore becomes no hand' (1962, 93). And in the same issue of *Forum*, Herman Hertzberger strongly criticized the results of 'flexibility':

> Flexibility signifies – since there is no single solution that is preferable to all others – the absolute denial of a fixed, clearcut standpoint. The flexible plan starts out from the certainty that the correct solution does not exist, because the problem requiring solution is in a permanent state of flux, i.e. it is always temporary. Flexibility is always inherent in relativity, but in

actual fact it only has to do with uncertainty; with not daring to commit oneself, and therefore with refusing to accept the responsibility that is inevitably bound up with each and every action that one takes. (1962, 117)

In Hertzberger's view 'flexibility' could only ever represent 'the set of all unsuitable solutions to a problem', an argument he amplified in a subsequent article: 'flexibility does not necessarily contribute to a better functioning of things (for flexibility can never produce the best imaginable results for any given situation)' (1967). Hertzberger's main objection was that architecture which tried to anticipate all future possibilities while choosing none of them produced boring results, with which subjects could not identify. Instead he wanted single, distinctive permanent forms, that were 'polyvalent' – 'a form that without changing itself, can be used for every purpose and which, with minimal flexibility, allows an optimal solution'. But Hertzberger's attack upon 'flexibility' was also an attack upon functionalism, and upon the tendency of functionalism to render human use into abstract 'activities':

even if living and working or eating and sleeping could justifiably be termed activities, that still does not mean that they make specific demands on the space in which they are to take place – it is the people who make specific demands because they wish to

interpret one and the same function in their own specific ways. (1962, 117)

As we shall see, this desire to oppose 'the collective coagulation of individual freedom' imposed by functionalism connected with another, altogether different sense of 'flexibility'.

By the late 1970s, 'flexibility' was losing some of its appeal as an architectural quality: for example James Stirling, earlier an adherent of flexibility, was reported as saying *apropos* his design for the Stuttgart Staatsgalerie (1977–82), that 'he was sick and tired of the boring, meaningless, non-committed, faceless flexibility and open-endedness of the present architecture' (Stirling 1984, 252).

The *purpose* of 'flexibility' within modernist architectural discourse was as a way of dealing with the contradiction that arose between the expectation, so well articulated by Gropius, that the architect's ultimate concern in designing buildings was with their human use and occupation, and the reality that the architect's involvement in a building ceased at the very moment that occupation began. The incorporation of 'flexibility' into the design allowed architects the illusion of projecting their control over the building into the future, beyond the period of their actual responsibility for it.

It is possible to identify three distinct strategies of 'flexibility' in architecture.

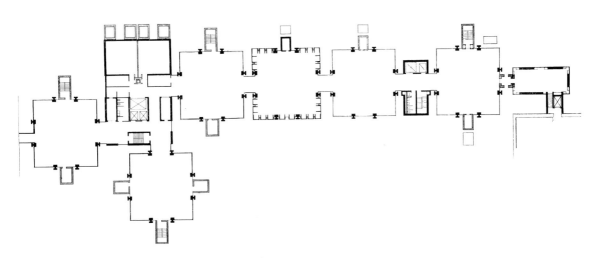

Plan, Richards Laboratories, University of Pennsylvania, Philadelphia, Louis Kahn, 1957–61. 'Not mindful enough of the demands for flexibility on the part of the scientists' – the Richards laboratories were widely criticized for lacking 'flexibility'.

Central courtyard, Staatsgalerie, Stuttgart, James Stirling and Michael Wilford, 1979–83. Stirling said the Staatsgalerie came from his being 'sick and tired of the boring, meaningless, non-committed, faceless flexibility and open-endedness of the present architecture'.

1. *Redundancy.* This is explained well by the architect Rem Koolhaas in *S,M,L,XL* (1995) in relation to the Koepel at Arnhem, a circular Panopticon-type nineteenth-century prison building.

> Perhaps the most important and least recognized difference between traditional … and contemporary architecture is revealed in the way a hypermonumental, space-wasting building like the Arnhem panopticon proves flexible, while modern architecture is based on a deterministic coincidence between form and program, its purpose no longer an abstraction like 'moral improvement' but a literal inventory of all the details of everyday life. Flexibility is not the exhaustive anticipation of all possible changes. … Flexibility is the creation of margin –

excess capacity that enables different and even opposite interpretations and uses. (239–40)

The spatial redundancy identified by Koolhaas in the Arnhem prison is a characteristic of many pre-modern buildings: it was a feature of, for example, baroque palaces, where rooms were not dedicated to specific uses. However, though this type of flexibility may now be discernible in these older buildings, it was not described as such in their own time.

2. *Flexibility by Technical Means.* The exemplary modernist case of this type of flexibility – and apparently the first instance in which the quality of 'flexibility' was so designated – was Rietveld's 1924 Schröder House at Utrecht, where the open upper floor was installed with

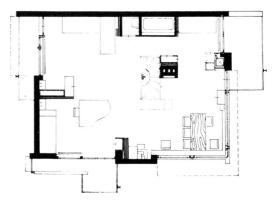

Interior, Koepel Prison, Arnhem, 1882. Koolhaas points out that the 'flexibility' of pre-twentieth century buildings like the Koepel lay in their wasteful surplus of space.

moveable partitions. In the words of the Dutch critic J. G. Wattjes, writing in 1925: 'A system of portable screens has replaced the usual fixed dividing walls, thus providing a great degree of flexibility in the interior spatial division … the intention is that the interior can be altered daily according to the changing needs of the different times of day or night' (quoted in Bonta, 192). There have been many subsequent modernist buildings in which there have been attempts to attain flexibility through making elements of the building – walls, windows, even floors – moveable; a particularly ambitious and noteworthy example was Beaudouin, Lods, Bodiansky and Prouvé's Maison du Peuple of 1939 at Clichy in Paris (see ill. p. 146), where morning use of the building as a market hall could be converted to afternoon and evening use as a theatre and cinema

Plans and interior of first floor, Schröder House, Utrecht, Netherlands, G. Rietveld, 1924. The sliding partitions of the Schröder House could turn the open plan of the upper floor into various combinations of smaller compartments: it has often been regarded as the prototype for the 'flexible' modern interior created by technical means.

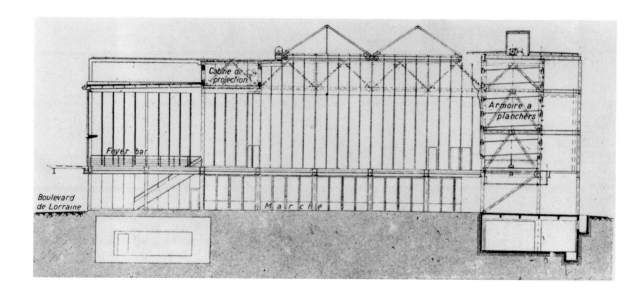

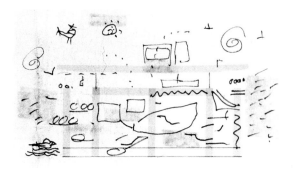

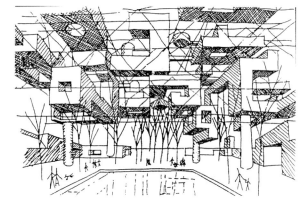

(top) Section of Maison du Peuple, Clichy, Paris, Beaudouin, Lods, Bodiansky and Prouvé, 1939. One of the most ambitious of 'flexible' buildings, the Maison de Peuple for the socialist commune of Clichy could be turned from an open market hall in the mornings into a theatre and cinema in the afternoons and evenings, by means of moveable floors, roof and walls.

(above left) Cedric Price, Fun Palace, 'story board' sketch, 1964.

(above right) Yona Friedman, Spatial City, drawing, 1958–60. Friedman envisaged that modern constructive techniques would allow 'buildings' and 'urban space' to be separated, so that space, unencumbered by buildings, could become the endlessly flexible medium of a free society.

by means of moveable floors, roof and walls.[1] In the post-war period, flexibility through technology shifted away from the ingenious systems of sliding or folding elements (though these continued to feature in many later modernist buildings), and concentrated instead upon the development of lightweight building structures, and of mechanical services, which allowed climatic control of spaces without the need for traditional architectural elements at all. Particularly influential were the systems developed in the United States the 1950s by Anton Ehrenkrantz and Konrad Wachsmann for buildings in which all services were carried in the roof space. Intended so as to offer freedom in the layout

Inter-Action Centre, Kentish Town, London, C. Price and E. Berman, 1972–77.
Perhaps the closest built example to the ideal of a totally 'flexible' architecture –
in which flexibility of the structure and flexibility of use become indistinguishable.

and arrangement of school and factory buildings, these systems were seized upon by certain European architects, Yona Friedman in France, Constant Nieuwenhuys (known as Constant) in the Netherlands, and Cedric Price in Britain, as holding the potential for something very much more, offering not merely flexibility within buildings, but releasing buildings from their traditional fixity, and making possible a city within which all buildings could be mobile. Friedman's demand that 'New constructions serving for individual shelters must 1. touch a minimum surface on the ground; 2. be demountable and moveable; 3. be transformable at will by the individual' (1957, 294) envisaged a city carried

in a service structure, within which everything would be mobile and flexible.

Cedric Price's Fun Palace (1964; see ills. above and p. 170) was 'a flexible education and entertainment centre' where an open framework of steel lattice towers and a high-level truss roof both provided support for short-life enclosures within, and carried all the services and heating which could be directed anywhere within the overall enclosure.[2] The Fun Palace was not built, but a smaller project of 1972–77, Cedric Price's Inter-Action Centre at Kentish Town in North London, was the closest built example to this ideal of a totally 'flexible' architecture, achieved through technical means; though it should be added that the Inter-Action Centre was also the result of a somewhat unusual and anarchic design process, where the supporting steel frame was erected before anyone knew what it was to contain, and was left for a year awaiting further building while the various parties involved argued over what they wanted put within it.[3] The Centre Beaubourg in Paris, though claims were made for its 'flexibility', was not truly so; and the fact that its 'flexibility' was no more than emblematic has been born out by the need for its recent lengthy closure for repairs.

It was a feature of all the attempts to attain 'flexibility' by technical means for the 'flexibility' to be invariably perceived as a property of the building. This assumption that 'flexibility' is achieved through the building, and that it is the business of the architect to embed it in the design, has been a general feature of the normal architectural use of the concept – and is what sets it apart from the third sense of 'flexibility', which sees it not as a characteristic of buildings, but of use.

3. *As a political strategy.* The critique of capitalism developed by the Situationist International in the late 1950s centred particularly upon capitalism's tendency to commodify all aspects of everyday life. Domestic life, leisure and space had all in turn become removed from the realm of individual freedom by being separated into their functional components and turned into commodities with an exchange value. Part of the object of the Situationist International was to resist this process, and to recover, through 'the free realm of playful activity', all those aspects of life that had been brought under capitalist regulation. In relation to cities and urban space, the particular strategy developed was the *détournement* – the (mis)appropriation of existing buildings and spaces with already determined uses. Some of these ideas are to be found, more developed, in Henri Lefebvre's *The Production of Space* (1974). For Lefebvre, the capitalist domination of space, both by imposing functional categories upon it physically, and by imposing an abstract schema through which the mind perceived space, was one of capitalism's most invasive acts. 'Functionalism stresses function to the point where, because each function has a specially assigned place within dominated space, the very possibility of multifunctionality is eliminated' (369). Against the 'asphyxiation' of everything by abstract space, Lefebvre envisaged a new sort of spatial practice which would 'restore unity to what abstract space breaks up – to the functions, elements and moments of social practice' (52). Lefebvre had in mind actions like the early Christians' co-opting of the originally secular

Roman basilicas for their worship, and which in time became the model for Christian churches (369): in this case, the act preceded the form which became in time associated with the purpose. For Lefebvre, resistance to 'dominated space' can only be effected by appropriation, by the assertion of the freedom of use, through the user's realization of the space's flexibility and multifunctionality; but, he writes regretfully, 'The true space of pleasure, which would be an appropriated space par excellence, does not yet exist' (167).

In Lefebvre's idea that through use, through positive acts of appropriation, the functionalist domination of space can be broken, 'flexibility' acquires its political connotation. As far as Lefebvre was concerned, architects and architecture, complicit in the practice of abstract, dominant space, had no part whatsoever to play in the realization of flexibility: 'use' was a political act to be directed *against* architecture. But the architects Constant, Yona Friedman, and to some extent Hertzberger too, envisaged architecture as enabling an active fulfilment of diversified use. Although both Constant and Friedman were interested in the technical means of achieving flexibility, it must be stressed that the ultimate aim of flexibility was to disturb the established property relations and functional classifications set up by capitalism. This is evident in, for example, Constant's article 'The Great Game to Come' (1959): 'We believe that all static, unchanging elements must be avoided and that the variable or changing character of architectural elements is the precondition for a flexible relationship with the events that will take place within them' (63). The stress is upon the events to take place, for which the mobile architectural elements are merely the precondition. Within this scheme, 'flexibility' is not a property of buildings but of spaces; and it is a property which they acquire through the uses to which they are put.

If 'flexibility' has been a confusing word, it is surely on account of having had to perform two contradictory roles – on the one hand it has served to extend functionalism and so make it viable, but on the other hand it has been employed to resist functionalism. This distinction has not often been acknowledged in architects' use of the term.

---

1 See Ellis, 'Prouvé's People's Palace', *Architectural Review*, vol. 177, May 1985, 40–48.
2 See *Architectural Review*, vol. 137, January 1965, 74–75.
3 See Alsop, 'Speculations on Cedric Price Architects' Inter-Action Centre', *Architectural Design*, nos 7–8, 1977, 483–86.

Form

The architect must be a form-artist; only the art of form leads the way to a new architecture. August Endell, 1897

The paradigm of the architect passed down to us through the modern period is that of the form-giver, the creator of hierarchical and symbolic structures characterized, on the one hand, by their unity of parts and, on the other, by the transparency of form to meaning.
Bernard Tschumi, 1987, 207

In the ninety years between the optimistic enthusiasm of August Endell and the cynical scepticism of Bernard Tschumi unrolls the history of 'form', the most important, but also the most difficult concept within the architecture of this century. In a single sentence, Tschumi warns us of several of the problems we shall encounter with it: of its indispensability to modernist discourse; of the supposition that 'form' is what architects create; of the belief that 'form' exists to transmit meaning.

Form is one of the triad of terms ('space' and 'design' are the other two) through which architectural modernism exists. In its dependency on 'form' architecture is not alone – in every other art practice, and in culture in general, 'form' has become an indispensable category, without which whole territories of analysis would remain unknown and be unapproachable. Yet architecture lays claim to particular privilege in matters of 'form', because of its work in physically shaping the material objects and spaces that surround us – a claim that takes us straight away to the central problem of 'form', one that underlies its entire significance within Western thought. There is in 'form' an inherent ambiguity, between its meaning 'shape' on the one hand, and on the other 'idea' or 'essence': one describes the property of things as they are known to the senses, the other as they are known to the mind. In its appropriation of 'form', architecture has, according to one's point of view, either fallen victim to, or taken mischievous advantage of this

inherent confusion. Much of what we shall have to say about 'form' concerns the working out, in the practice of an art concerned with making material objects, of the ambiguity between the two senses of the term. The German language (which is where the modern concept of form was principally developed) has a slight advantage over English for thinking about this problem, for where English has only the single word, 'form', German has two, '*Gestalt*' and '*Form*': *Gestalt* generally refers to objects as they are perceived by the senses, whereas *Form* usually implies some degree of abstraction from the concrete particular.[1]

Until the end of the nineteenth century, almost nowhere except within the world of German philosophical aesthetics was 'form' used in architecture in any other sense than to mean simply 'shape' or 'mass', or in other words, than as a description of the sensory properties of buildings. It was the appropriation of its other 'ideal' sense to architecture that the German architect August Endell announced so excitedly in 1897, and whose adventures in the world of architecture we shall be following here. When in the English-speaking world 'form' started to be used in its enlarged, modernist sense around 1930, people frequently had difficulty in accommodating the new concept within their previous understanding of the term: for example, in one of the first English books to attempt to describe the principles of the new architecture, *Modern Architectural Design* (1932), the author, Howard Robertson, wrote: 'The major *aesthetic* task therefore is to deal interestingly and appropriately with form. It is this preoccupation with basic, what one might call "naked" form, which distinguishes modern architectural design' (20). Robertson knew that form was important, but without quite understanding why, or what it could mean apart from 'shape'. It is still the case that people frequently use 'form' when they mean no more than 'shape', and a useful mental test of the meaning intended is to try substituting 'shape' or 'mass'.

In addition to the 'form/shape' confusion, there is another more complex problem in understanding 'form' in the vocabulary of architecture in the twentieth century. This problem is that for much of the time, what 'form' itself has been taken to mean has been rather less important that what it does *not* mean. It can be argued that the real significance of 'form' has been its use as an oppositional category to define other values: 'form', this flabby container, has, as we shall see, accommodated itself to an astonishing variety of sometimes quite contradictory concepts, but it has also been used as a defining category against a succession of other values. To anticipate the discussion that follows, it has been opposed variously to: decoration; mass culture; social values; technological experimentation and development; and functionality.

To talk about architecture without using the word 'form' may now seem inconceivable, but let us be clear about one thing: *'form' is merely a device for thought –* it is neither a thing, nor a substance. And as a device within everyday architectural speech, its availability is of relatively recent origin, for it has only entered currency within the last century. To those who say that the apparently commonsensical consensus that surrounds its use hardly merits bringing it in for questioning, we can only reply that its very normality is precisely what should make us suspicious of it. Like a virus that invades a cell and becomes part of it, 'form' has entered criticism so completely, overcoming all resistance, to the extent that now we can hardly speak about architecture without it. As the historian David Summers has warned in relation to visual art, 'Form is far from the neutral taxonomic and developmental category it might be thought to be';[2] the same goes for architecture.

'Form' in Antiquity: Plato and Aristotle

What made 'form' such a pliable and versatile concept, so convenient to the purposes of twentieth-century architecture? Part of the explanation for this lies in its long history within Western philosophy, during which it served as the solution to a wide variety of philosophical problems. It is worth looking briefly at the philosophical uses of 'form' before it was appropriated by architecture, both in order to find some of the causes for its attraction, but also because in its various original purposes are revealed the sources of some the confusions in its modern architectural currency.

The principal originator of the concept of 'form' in antiquity was Plato. For Plato, 'forms' provided the

solution to a complex of problems – the nature of substances, the process of physical change, and the perception of things.[3] Against Pythagoras's earlier theory that all things could in essence be described as numbers or ratios of numbers, Plato proposed that geometrical figures, triangles and solids underlay the substance of the world. Plato's argument is developed in the Dialogue of *Timaeus*. There Plato first of all distinguishes between 'that which always is and never becomes' and 'that which is always becoming but never is'. The first is 'apprehensible by intelligence with the aid of reasoning, being eternally the same', the second is the object of sensation; what is unchanging and known only to the mind is the 'form', contrasted with the thing, known to sense. This distinction, fundamental to Plato's thinking, is repeated throughout his philosophy: 'particulars are objects of sight but not of intelligence, while the Forms are the objects of intelligence but not of sight' (*Republic*, §507). In making any thing, argues Plato, the maker follows the 'form', not things already existing (§§27–28). Elsewhere, in the Dialogue of *Cratylus*, he gives as an example a carpenter making a shuttle: 'And suppose the shuttle be broken in the making, will he make another, looking like the broken one? Or will he look to the form according to which he made the other?'. The answer, of course, is to the latter; and Plato continues 'Might not that justly be called the true or ideal shuttle?' (*Dialogues*, vol. 3, §389). From this, it is readily apparent that as far as Plato was concerned, forms were always superior to things made in their resemblance. Returning to *Timaeus*, Plato develops the distinction between the form and the thing as follows:

> there exist, first, the unchanging form, uncreated and indestructible, admitting no modification and entering no combination, imperceptible to sight or the other senses, the object of thought: second, that which bears the same name as the form and resembles it, but is sensible, has come into existence ... is apprehended by opinion with the aid of sensation. (§52)

Forms, as objects of thought, find their correspondence in things, which are bounded by surfaces, all of which according to Plato are composed of either one of two types of triangles (§53). In the *Republic*, Plato explains that philosophers, in pursuit of the intelligible forms, start with basic geometric figures, 'though they are not really thinking about them at all, but about the originals which they resemble'. And he continues, 'The figures they draw or model ... they treat as illustrations only, the real subjects of their investigation being invisible except to the eye of the mind' (§510). By presenting as a series of 'shapes' those features of objects that were the inherently invisible form of things, Plato set up that confusion over the two senses of form with which the modern use of the concept is still entangled, and in no field more than so than architecture.

In Plato's pupil Aristotle, we find a reluctance to make categorical distinctions between forms and things. In general, Aristotle refused to accept that forms had any absolute existence independently of the matter of the objects in which they were found: 'Each thing itself and its essence are one and the same' (*Metaphysics*, §1031b). Although Aristotle used 'form' in a variety of different senses, both referring to shape and to idea, his most inclusive definition, and the one that most comprehensively conveys his thought, is when he says 'By form I mean the essence of each thing and its primary substance' (§1032b). Aristotle's discussion of form has other interesting aspects: thus he conceives the form of things existing in what they are not, or in what they have not yet become. In other words, form may be conceived of as a lack (*Physics* Book II, chapter 1, §193b); and this attraction of two opposites he describes in terms of gender, 'what desires the form is matter, as the female desires the male' (*Physics*, Book I, chapter 9, §192a).

But one should not see Aristotle's notion of 'form' as merely arising out his critique of Plato, and a reluctance to accept the absolute priority to what is always 'imperceptible to the sight or the other senses'; Aristotle's ideas about 'form' arose from his consideration of a different question, the generative process of plants and animals. At the beginning of *On the Parts of Animals*, Aristotle argued that it was wrong to look for the origin of organic things in the process of their development, but that rather one must start by considering their characteristics in their completed, final state, and only then to deal with their evolution. Aristotle justified this by an analogy with building:

> the plan of the house, or the house, has this and that form; and because it has this and that form, therefore is its construction carried out in this or that manner. For the process of evolution is for the sake of the thing finally evolved, and not this for the sake of the process.

Plants and animals have their pre-existence not in an idea, but in an actual predecessor in time – 'for man is generated from man; and thus it is the possession of certain characters by the parent that determines the development of like characters in the child' (§640a). Elsewhere, Aristotle argues that same is true of all processes of material production, for everything must come from something: thus he says 'house comes from house', for no house can exist independent of the material object (*Metaphysics*, §1032b). And even in the case of works of art, which have spontaneous novelty, they have their pre-existing cause in the skills and abilities of a human, sentient artist, and in the identifiable conventions of that particular art. Although 'Art indeed consists in the conception of the result to be produced before its realization in the material' (*Parts of Animals*, §640a), Aristotle's sees this 'form' as like the genetic transmission between organic objects, not as an uncreated, indestructible pure object of thought. In the distinction between Plato's 'form' as an unknowable, pre-existing idea, and Aristotle's 'form' as the genetic material produced from the mind of the artist, we have a further cause for modern ambiguity.

Neo-Platonism and the Renaissance
Aristotle's metaphor of building to describe the relationship between form and matter was used by successive philosophers in later antiquity and the Middle Ages though, confusingly, it was most popular with neo-Platonists who adopted it in order to identify the causes and origins of beauty – which was not at all the purpose for which Aristotle had intended it. Thus the third-century AD Alexandrian philosopher Plotinus, in the *Ennead*, to show that beauty lies in the Ideal-Form, asks

> On what principle does the architect, when he finds the house standing before him correspondent with his inner ideal of a house, pronounce it beautiful? Is it not that the house before him, the stones apart, is the inner idea stamped upon the mass of exterior matter, the indivisible exhibited in diversity? (Hofstadter and Kuhns, 144)

Plotinus's fifteenth-century Florentine translator, the neo-Platonist Marsilio Ficino, outlines a similar argument to identify beauty as in the independence of form from matter:

> In the beginning, an architect conceives an idea of the building, like an Idea in the soul. Then he builds, as nearly as possible, the kind of house he has thought out. Who will deny that the house is a body, and that it is very much like the incorporeal idea of the builder in likeness to which it was made? Furthermore, it is

(opposite) Michelangelo, Tomb of Giuliano de'Medici, Medici Chapel, San Lorenzo, Florence, 1531–33. Sculpture, according to Vasari (following Michelangelo), was 'an art which lifts the superfluous from the material, and reduces it to that form which is drawn from the mind of the artist'.

(above) A. Palladio, Villa Godi, Lugo di Vicenza, 1532–42. 'Buildings are esteemed more for their form than their materials': Palladio, like most architects until the modern era, used 'form' as a synonym for 'shape'.

to be judged like the idea more because of a certain incorporeal plan than because of its matter. Therefore, subtract its matter, if you can. You can indeed subtract it in thought, but leave the plan; nothing material or corporeal will remain to you. (Hofstadter and Kuhns, 225)

These and similar conceptions of 'form' deriving from classical philosophy circulated amongst Renaissance humanists during the fifteenth and sixteenth centuries. However, their influence appears to have been insignificant in the day-to-day vocabulary of architecture, where 'form', in so far as it was used at all, was generally only a synonym for shape. Thus Vasari, in his life of Michelangelo, records 'The people of Rome … were anxious to give some useful, commodious and beautiful form to the Capitol' (1965, 388). The exceptions to this are those Renaissance humanists who were concerned to show that architecture conformed to ancient philosophers' conception of the world, and indeed provided an analogue for its processes. Alberti, in *De Re Aedificatore*, written in the mid-fifteenth century, managed to make use of several of the antique theories of 'form' already mentioned. His well known claim that 'within the form and figure of a building there resides some natural excellence that excites the mind and is immediately recognized by it' (302), is based upon the Pythagorean theory of numbers and arithmetic as the basis of everything. On the other hand, when he says that 'It is quite possible to project whole forms in the mind, without any recourse to the material' (7), this accords with neo-Platonist thought; and Erwin Panofsky interpreted Alberti's distinction between *materia*, the products of nature, and *lineamenti*, 'the products of thought', in the same terms. Panofsky, with a modernist's propensity to see everything in terms of 'form', translated *lineamenti* as 'form', but this is unconvincing, for Alberti's

definition of *lineamenti* has little in common with any notion of form, ancient or modern: Alberti describes *lineamenti* as 'the correct, infallible way of joining and fitting together those lines and angles which define and enclose the surfaces of the building' (7).[4]

The Aristotelian notion of form, as a property of all material things, seems to have featured little in Renaissance architectural thought, though it did appear in relation to sculpture – defined by Vasari as 'an art which lifts the superfluous from the material, and reduces it to that form which is drawn in the mind of the artist' (1878, vol. I, 148); and Michelangelo's view of sculpture as what encloses the artist's idea had, as Panofsky points out, a definite Aristotelian basis.[5] A rare case of a more Aristotelian view of 'form' used relative to architecture occurs when Daniele Barbaro, Palladio's patron, wrote as follows in his commentary on Vitruvius: 'Imprinted in every work raised up from reason and accomplished through drawing is evidence of the artist, of the form and quality that was in his mind; for the artist works first from the mind and symbolizes then the exterior matter after the interior state, especially in architecture' (11).

Post-Renaissance
In general, it can be said that while the notions of form developed in ancient philosophy were of interest to humanist scholars, they had little impact on the ordinary practice of architecture, or its vocabulary, until the twentieth century. Throughout the sixteenth, seventeenth and eighteenth centuries, and indeed until the twentieth century everywhere except in German-speaking countries, when architects and critics talked about 'form', they almost invariably meant only 'shape'. When Palladio stated that 'buildings are esteemed more for their form than for their materials' (Burns, 209), it does not appear, notwithstanding his association with Daniele Barbaro, that he had anything metaphysical in mind. Nor, for

example, when the French theorist Quatremère de Quincy wrote in 1788 that 'stone, in copying itself, or to put it better, in copying nothing, has offered no form to art', is it likely that he meant more than 'shape'. And when Sir John Soane, in his *Lectures*, said the student 'will learn to appreciate that succession and variety of forms' (591) found in the works of the sixteenth-century Italians, his use of the word was entirely characteristic of English nineteenth-century writers. And even when in 1825 Joseph Gwilt wrote in his introduction to his edition of Sir William Chambers's Treatise that 'Form alone fastens on the mind in works of architecture' (76) – although this might sound like a 1920s modernist – he was simply stressing that it was not materials themselves that mattered, but the way they were arranged. Nor, when Viollet-le-Duc announced at the beginning of his *Lectures* (1860) that his purpose was 'to inquire into the reason of every form – for every architectural form has its reason' (vol. 1, 7) should we imagine that he was talking about an abstract concept. Although Viollet referred repeatedly to 'form' in his Lectures, his purpose in doing so was to stress its dependence upon the structural principle employed:

> form is not the result of caprice … only the expression of structure … I cannot give you the rules by which the form [*forme*] is governed, inasmuch as it is the very nature of that form to adapt itself to all the requirements of the structure; give me a structure and I will find you the forms that naturally result from it, but if you change the structure, I must change the forms. (vol. I, 283–84)

The transformation of 'form' into an altogether more vital and dynamic concept started in Germany, in the 1790s, and until the early twentieth century remained almost entirely confined to German-speaking countries. Even there, for most of the nineteenth century, discussion of 'form' was largely restricted to philosophical aesthetics, only in the 1890s becoming widely used by artists and architects in its by then greatly expanded sense. The new interest in 'form' that developed in the 1790s had two distinct aspects, each in their own way important for the subsequent development of the concept. The first emerges from the philosophy of aesthetic perception developed by Kant; the second from the theories of nature and natural generation developed by Goethe.

Kant

The discipline of philosophical aesthetics in the late eighteenth century took off with the realization that the source of beauty lay not in objects themselves, but in the process by which they were perceived. In the development of this argument, 'form' was to be a key concept, no longer (as it had been throughout antiquity and the Renaissance) a property of things, but exclusively of the seeing of them. The single most important contributor to this new approach was Immanuel Kant, whose *Critique of Judgment* (1790) established 'form' as the basic category for the perception of art. Kant argued that the judgment of beauty belonged to a separate faculty of mind, unconnected to either knowledge (cognition) or emotions (desire). Our ability to make sense of the bewildering variety of sensations presented to us lay in the existence within the mind of constructs of space and of time, and of a faculty of 'form', which Kant described as 'that which so determines the manifold of appearance that it allows of being ordered in certain relations' (*Critique of Pure Reason*, 66). It is important to stress that for Kant, form was different to that aspect of things which is known through sensation – that is *matter*; and *form* is not *matter*. Aesthetic judgment, the perception of what the mind finds pleasing, occurs through its ability to recognize in the external world features that satisfy the internal concept of form. Kant stresses that aesthetic judgments are *only* related to 'form' – 'in a pure judgment of taste the delight in the object is connected with the mere estimate of its form' (*Critique of Judgment*, 146). Everything about an object that brings to mind either knowledge or desire is irrelevant to the pure aesthetic judgment, 'whose determining ground, is … simply finality of form' (65). And anything that gives rise to charm, or other association, that is to say all contingent properties like colour, or ornament, is superfluous: as Kant puts it, 'In painting, sculpture, and in fact in all the formative arts, in architecture and horticulture, so far as fine arts, the *design* is what is essential. Here it is not what gratifies in sensation, but merely what pleases by its form, that is the fundamental prerequisite for taste' (67). Kant also excludes from aesthetic judgment those aspects of an object that concern its usefulness, since these involve knowledge about what the object does or is, and so belong to cognition, and not to the aesthetic: 'the aesthetic judgment … brings to our notice no quality of the object, but only the final form in the determination of the powers of representation engaged upon it' (71). Not surprisingly, since it would have undermined his argument that 'forms' were a property of the beholders' mind, Kant was unspecific about the appearance forms might take in objects – though he did suggest that forms of the regular geometric kind favoured by neo-Platonists are not conducive to aesthetic judgments, for they are presentations of determinate concepts, whereas irregularity, because it is not suggestive of purpose, allows more freedom to the exercize of purely aesthetic judgments (86–88).

The significance of Kant's thought, in the history of 'form', was to establish that 'form' lies in the beholding, not in the thing beholden, and that in so far as the mind recognizes beauty in objects, it is because it sees within them a representation of that form, independent of content or meaning. Kant's contemporaries, the Romantic writers Goethe, Schiller and A. W. Schlegel, while they were enthusiastic about Kant's account of the relationship between the beholder and the object in creating aesthetic experience, felt that his abstract scheme failed to provide a satisfactory account of why we take pleasure in forms, and in the nature of that pleasure. Schiller, in his *On the Aesthetic Education of Man* (1794–95), developed the notion of 'living-forms' to describe what made works of art aesthetically satisfying. Schiller proposed a scheme in which human psychology could be accounted for through two drives – 'form-drive' and 'sense-drive', while a third drive, 'play-drive', allowed each of the two main drives to recognize their opposite, while retaining their integrity. The outward objects to which the play-drive corresponded were 'living-forms'. Schiller explained how these were manifested:

> the term beauty is neither extended to cover the whole realm of living things nor is it merely confined to this realm. A block of marble, though it is and remains lifeless, can nevertheless, thanks to the architect or sculptor, become living form [*lebende Gestalt*]; and a human being, though he may live and have form [*Gestalt*], is far from being on that account a living form. As long as we merely think about his form, it is lifeless, a mere abstraction; as long as we merely feel his life, it is formless, a mere impression. Only when his form [*Form*] lives in our feeling and his life takes on form in our understanding, does he become living form. (XV.3)

For Schiller, as for Goethe and Schlegel, the subject of all art was to articulate in such 'living forms' the life we feel within ourselves.

Goethe

Schiller's concept of 'living form' corresponded closely to the ideas that his friend Goethe was developing about natural science. In his research into the morphology of plants, undertaken from the late 1780s, Goethe wanted – in an essentially Aristotelian quest – to find an original plant, to whose *Urform* all other plants – even those not yet existing – could be related. Goethe's thinking focussed particularly in what he saw as the inadequacy of the methods of biological classification developed by Linnaeus and later Cuvier, methods which essentially categorized plants and animals according to their component parts, as if they were constructed in the same way as man-made artefacts. For Goethe, this system failed because it neither took account of the essential coherence and wholeness of specimens, nor of their quality as vital and living; as he remarked to Schiller, 'there ought to be another method of presenting nature, not in separate pieces, but as living actuality, striving from the whole to the parts' (Magnus, 69). Moreover, the Linnaean system treated natural form as essentially static, neglecting that in nature, as Goethe put it, 'nothing stands still'.[6] The alternative method of classification proposed by Goethe placed all specimens within a series from the simplest to the most complex; from the features common to all specimens, Goethe deduced the existence of an *Urpflanze* (an archetypal original plant), from whose form all other plants might be contrived. As he wrote to Herder in 1787,

> The archetypal plant [*Urpflanze*] will be the strangest growth the world has ever seen, and Nature herself shall envy me for it. With such a model, and with the key to it in one's hands, one will be able to contrive an infinite variety of plants. They will be strictly logical plants – in other words, even though they may not actually exist, they could exist. They will not be mere picturesque and imaginative projections. They will be imbued with inner truth and necessity. And the same law will be applicable to all that lives. (*Italian Journey*, 299)

Seen in these terms, the 'Urform' was a principle of all organic material, in accordance with which all generation took place. And Goethe was at pains to stress that in no sense could the form be considered apart from the inward spirit: as he wrote,

> Nature has neither core
> Nor shell,
> But everything at once does spell.

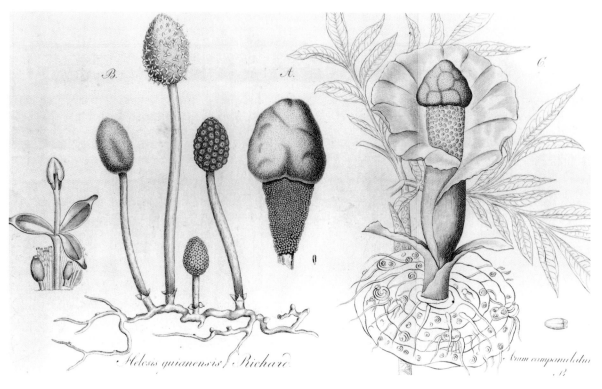

Archetypal plants, from J. W. von Goethe, *Zur Naturwissenschaft*, 1823, vol. 2.
Goethe speculated upon the existence of an archetypal, original plant, from
which the forms of all other plants might be deduced.

Look to thyself, and thou shalt see
Whether thou core or shell mayest be.
(Magnus, 238)

For Goethe and the other Romantics, exactly the same
principles of organic form found in nature applied
equally to art, and indeed to all products of human
culture. The very same concept of *Urform* was adapted
by Wilhelm von Humboldt to the study of language,
whence in turn it provided an analogy for architecture,
in the thinking of Gottfried Semper (see chapter 5, p. 71).
The significance of Goethe's theory was to provide a
theory of 'form' which acknowledged the ever-changing
features of nature – and of art – without positing the
existence of an absolute ideal category, known only
to thought. One of the clearest, and perhaps one the
most influential statements of the Romantics' conception
of 'organic form', occurs in Schlegel's *Lectures on
Dramatic Art* delivered in 1808–9, and translated into
English in 1846:

we must understand the exact meaning of the term
form, since most critics, and more especially those
who insist on a stiff regularity, interpret it merely in
a mechanical, and not in an organical sense. Form
is mechanical when, through external force, it is
imparted to any material merely as an accidental
addition without reference to its quality; as, for
example, when we give a particular shape to a soft
mass that it may retain the same after its induration.
Organical form, again, is innate; it unfolds itself
from within, and acquires its determination
contemporaneously with the perfect development
of the germ. We everywhere discover such forms in
nature throughout the whole range of living powers,
from the crystallization of salts and minerals to plants
and flowers, and from these again to the human body.
In the fine arts, as well as in the domain of nature –
the supreme artist, all genuine forms are organical,
that is determined by the quality of the work. In a
word, the form is nothing but a significant exterior,

the speaking physiognomy of each thing, which, as long as it is not disfigured by any destructive accident, gives a true evidence of its hidden essence. (340)

While the Romantics' notion of 'living form' preserved the Kantian idea that form was a property of the beholder as much as of the object, it also threatened the purity of Kant's conception, for form was in danger of becoming, as Schlegel said, a *sign* of something else, of an inner life force. While the Romantics were at pains to preserve the unity between the two concepts through their insistence that it was through the subject's sense of their own psychology that they were able to recognize the living form in the object, a tendency to separate the mental category from the property of objects became apparent in the development of idealist philosophy in early nineteenth-century Germany to which we shall now turn.

Philosophical Idealism

For idealist philosophers, of whom Hegel is the most famous, the appearance of things presented to the senses concealed an Idea that lay within, or beyond – an approach based upon Plato, even if it was also critical of him. The purpose of aesthetics was to reveal that underlying Idea: in art, 'every definite content determines a form [*Form*] suitable to it' (Hegel, *Aesthetics*, 13). The possible content signified by the form ranged from the character of individual artists, to the character of whole civilizations or epochs. Considered in terms of the practice of art, the idealist attitude towards 'form' is well summarized by a later idealist philosopher, Robert Vischer, in an essay of 1873: 'form', he argues, is the 'surrogate' of Idea, and it is the aim of the artist 'to emancipate this idea' (120).

It will already be apparent how very confusing a concept 'form' had become by the early nineteenth century in Germany: on the one hand, in Kant, exclusively a property of perception; on the other hand, in Goethe, a property of things, recognizable as a 'germ', or genetic principle; and in Hegel, a property above and before things, knowable only to the mind. It is hardly surprising that when architects first started to make use of 'form', all three different senses were easily mixed up. The first architectural writer in whose work 'form' was an important concept, Gottfried Semper, employed it in at least two senses. For Semper, 'the forms of art ... are the necessary outcome of a principle or idea that must have existed before them' (quoted in Ettlinger, 57); or as he put it elsewhere, form is 'the idea becoming visible' (*Der Stil*, trans. Mallgrave, 190) – both of which are purely idealist,

Hegelian statements of the notion of form. On the other hand, his description at the beginning of *Der Stil* of the project as a search for the common *Urform* that underlay the successive transformations of art (see p. 71 above), was clearly indebted to Goethe; as too was his statement in the Prolegomenon to show not 'the *making* of artistic form, but its *becoming*' (183).

Formalism

If 'form' was already a confusing concept in the early nineteenth century, what happened to it later in the century made it even more so. From the 1830s, German philosophical aesthetics was divided between two schools, one generally referred to as idealist, concerned with the signification of forms;[7] the other, formalist, concentrating upon the mode of perception of forms devoid of suprasensory meaning. Common to both, but with an utterly different meaning to each, lay the single term 'form'. Within the field of philosophy, formalism was the more dominant school for most of the century. The leading post-Kantian was J. F. Herbart, whose contribution to aesthetics was, as Mallgrave and Ikonomou put it, to argue that 'the meaning of a work of art is superfluous because each work consists, in essence, of a set of unique relations of form, composed by the artist with craft and intention' (10). Herbart defined aesthetics in terms of the psychological reception of the elementary relations of lines, tones, planes and colour, and much of his work was devoted to psychological aspects of this process; and indeed, his work contributed as much to the early development of psychology as it did to aesthetics. One of Herbart's better-known disciples was the Swiss pedagogue Friedrich Froebel, whose 'gifts' (see ill. p. 158), sets of progressively more complex colourless, geometrically shaped bricks, provided an object lesson in the process of Herbartian formalist aesthetics – the bricks are 'pure forms' from which the young child learns of what the world is made. The legend that the presentation of a set of Froebel bricks guided the young Frank Lloyd Wright's future choice of career provides an unexpectedly direct connection between Kant's aesthetics and modern architecture.[8]

Herbart's aesthetics were developed by other philosophers in the second half of the nineteenth century, principally by Robert Zimmermann, who developed an extensive 'science of form', which concentrated particularly on the relationships perceived between forms, rather than the forms themselves. Something of the potential for the application of formalist aesthetics to architecture was realized in an essay by the architect

Froebel Gift no. IV, c. 1890: 'Pure forms'. The philosopher Herbart's idea that forms exist independently of meaning was developed into a pedagogical system by the Swiss educationalist Friedrich Froebel, whose 'gifts' – sets of plain wooden bricks – provided the child with instruction by stages in the elements of which the world is supposedly made.

Adolf Göller, 'What is the Cause of the Perpetual Style Change in Architecture?' (1887), in which Göller proposed that 'Architecture ... is the true *art of visible pure form*' (198). Göller defined the beauty of form as 'an inherently pleasurable, meaningless play of lines or of light and shade' (195); 'form delights the spectator even without there being any content' (*Aesthetik*, 6). Unlike painting or sculpture, 'architecture offers us systems of abstract, geometrical lines without the images of concrete things that we encounter in life. In viewing architectural works, we therefore lack the latent ideas or memories that invariably and necessarily come to mind with painting and sculpture. It follows that architectural forms mean

nothing to natural reason' ('Style Change', 196). This surprising view, anticipating the development of abstract, non-objective art and suggesting that its origin lay in architecture, was possible because of Göller's rigid, Kantian exclusion from 'form' of anything that signified a content.

Göller's essay was unusual, and from the 1870s, what reanimated the potentially arid formalist approach to aesthetics was the recovery of the earlier, Romantic notion of 'living form' to create the more scientific concept of 'empathy'. The basis of this, that works of art hold interest for us because of our ability to see in them the sensations that we know from our own bodies, was first made explicit by the philosopher Hermann Lotze, in 1856: 'no form is so unyielding that our imagination cannot project its life into it' (I, 584). Taken up by the philosopher Robert Vischer, empathy was first related to architecture in an important and influential, though entirely speculative, essay of 1873, 'On the Optical Sense of Form'. Applied to architecture, empathy was to be fruitful in enriching the concept of 'form' in the 1890s. Although it was widely taken up, the two writers with most influence on its subsequent use (and not just in architecture, but in all the arts) were the art historian Heinrich Wölfflin and the sculptor Adolf Hildebrand. We shall now consider in more detail what these two had to say about 'form'.

Wölfflin

Wölfflin's doctoral thesis, 'Prolegomena to a Psychology of Architecture', was presented in 1886 (although not published until the 1930s), and states particularly clearly the conception of form contained in his later and well known books, *Renaissance and Baroque* (1889) and *Principles of Art History* (1915). The opening question of the 'Prolegomena' is how is it that forms of architecture can express a mood or emotion? Wölfflin's answer was in the principle of empathy – 'Physical forms express a character only because we ourselves possess a body' (151); for 'Our own bodily organization is the form through which we apprehend everything physical' (157–58). Having established a correspondence between the sense of our own body and of the work of architecture, Wölfflin turns to an account of architecture in which the conception of 'form' is clearly indebted to Goethe and the Romantics (the source he acknowledges is Schopenhauer):

> What holds us upright and prevents a formless collapse? It is the opposing force that we may call will, life, or whatever. I call it force of form [*Formkraft*]. *The opposition between matter and force of form*, which sets the entire organic world in motion, is the principal theme of architecture.... We assume that in everything there is a will that struggles to become form and has to overcome the resistance of a formless matter. (159)

He continues, emphasizing in a manner reminiscent of Aristotle, the coexistence of form and matter: 'form is not wrapped around matter as something extraneous but works its way out of matter as an immanent will. Matter and form are inseparable' (160). A number of interesting observations follow from this proposition. First of all, it allows him to see ornament not – as most modernists were to do – as what is antagonistic to form, but rather as 'the expression of excessive force of form' (179). Secondly, there are his comments on 'modern' (i.e., Renaissance and post-Renaissance) architecture: 'The modern spirit characteristically prefers the architectural form to work its way out of the material with some effort; it does not look for a conclusion so much as for a process of becoming: a gradual victory of form' (178). Thirdly, and perhaps most importantly, he acknowledged that if 'form' belongs primarily to the viewer's perception, then historical changes in architecture are to be understood primarily in terms of changes in the mode of vision – in other words, that vision has *its* history as well as architecture. This proposition, which follows naturally from Kant's aesthetics, was to present something of a problem in the subsequent modernist use of the concept of form, for it undermined the argument that new forms were the necessary outcome of new material conditions; and it also called into question the widespread supposition – for example in the teaching of the Bauhaus – that in dealing with form one was dealing with a timeless, universal category. This fundamental difficulty may be one of the reasons why, as we shall see, there was little interest in the further development of 'form' after the 1920s.

Hildebrand

Adolf Hildebrand's essay *The Problem of Form in the Fine Arts* (1893), although principally about sculpture, has some important things to say about architecture, and as it was widely read in avant-garde circles in the early part of the twentieth century, appears to have had some influence on architectural thinking. The book is directed against 'impressionism', against the view that the subject of art consists in the appearance of things. Hildebrand starts by distinguishing between 'form' and appearance: things present themselves in a multitude of changing appearances, none of which reveals the form, which can only be perceived by the mind. 'The idea of form is the sum total that we have extracted by comparing appearances' (227–28). The sense of form is gained by the kinaesthetic experience, the real or imagined movement necessary to interpret the appearance things present to the eye. Developing out of this argument, Hildebrand has one profoundly original observation, and one which shifted the entire conception of 'form' in architecture, and that is that the 'form' in architecture is *space*; in architecture, he says 'space itself, in the sense of inherent form, becomes effective form for the eye' (269). Although the concept of

Getty tomb, Graceland cemetery, Chicago, L. Sullivan, 1890. Forms, in Louis Sullivan's remarkably perceptive summary of their purpose in architectural discourse, 'stand for relationships between the immaterial and the material, between the subjective and the objective'.

'spatial form' had certainly been used before (see Wölfflin, 'Prolegomena', 154), it is to Hildebrand, as well as to the aesthetic philosopher August Schmarsow, that we owe the proposition that 'form' in architecture is to be identified primarily through the experience of space. Schmarsow presented a more developed version of this theme in a lecture given the same year as Hildebrand's book. In 'The Essence of Architectural Creation' (1893) Schmarsow argued that the particularity of architecture lies in the fact that the viewer's empathetic sense is directed not to its masses, but into its space. Schmarsow proposes a direct equivalence between architectural space and the body's form:

> The intuited form of space, which surrounds us wherever we may be and which we then always erect around ourselves and consider more necessary than the form of our own body, consists of the residues of sensory experience to which the muscular sensations of our body, the sensitivity of our skin, and the structure of our body all contribute. As soon as we have learned to experience ourselves and ourselves alone as the centre of this space, whose co-ordinates intersect in us, we have found the precious kernel ... on which the architectural creation is based. (286–87)

Schmarsow subsequently elaborated this argument, and as a contribution to the meaning of 'form' relative to architecture, it was fundamental to both Paul Frankl's *Principles of Architectural History* (1914), and to the aesthetics of modern architecture. For example, in 1921, H. Sorgel in *Architektur-Aesthetik* wrote, in what was by then a fairly unoriginal remark, 'The "problem of form" in architecture must be transposed into a "problem of space"' (Neumeyer, 171).

We might at this point take stock of what, by about 1900, 'form' had been used to mean. There are at least four sets of opposing ideas:
(i) 'form' as a property of the seeing of objects (Kant), or of the objects themselves;
(ii) 'form' as a 'germ', a generative principle contained within organic matter, or works of art (Goethe); or as an 'idea' preceding the thing (Hegel);
(iii) 'form' as the end of art, and entire subject of art, as Göller had proposed; or as merely the sign, through which an idea or force was revealed;
(iv) 'form' in works of architecture presented by their mass; or by their space.

Loaded down as it was with the burden of representing some of the major divisions of thought in nineteenth-century aesthetics, it is hardly surprising that the term lacked clarity when it started to be widely used in architectural vocabulary in the twentieth century. Indeed, as we shall see, in its ambiguity lay part of its appeal.

So far, we have considered the later development of 'form' only within the German-speaking world. Its entry, in its newly enlarged sense, into the English-language vocabulary of architecture occurred in the United States, where the Vienna-trained architect Leopold Eidlitz, in his book *The Nature and Function of Art* (1881), was the first to present an essentially Hegelian view of 'form' to an American audience. Eidlitz's attitude to form can be summed up in his statement, 'Forms in architectural art are the expressions of ideas in matter' (307). Eidlitz's book precedes the much better-known and quite unique discourse on 'form' by Louis Sullivan in *Kindergarten Chats*, numbers 12, 13 and 14 (1901). These essays, usually read for Sullivan's views on 'function', are even more interesting for what he says about 'form'. To quote a characteristic passage:

> Form in everything and anything, everywhere and at every instant. According to their nature, their function, some forms are definite, some indefinite; some are nebulous, others concrete and sharp; some symmetrical, others purely rhythmical. Some are abstract, others material. Some appeal to the eye, some to the ear, some to the touch, some to the sense of smell … But all, without fail, stand for relationships between the immaterial and the material, between the subjective and the objective – between the Infinite Spirit and the finite mind. (45)

Even from this passage, it will be clear that Sullivan was primarily inspired by the 'organic form' of the German Romantics, of Goethe and Schiller, and their view that in this lay the correspondence between nature and art. As an expression of their relevance to architecture, *Kindergarten Chats* cannot be equalled, at any date or in any other language.

'Form' within twentieth-century modernism
Architectural modernism adopted 'form' and made it its cardinal term for various reasons: (1) it was not a metaphor (if its biological derivation was overlooked); (2) it implied that the true substance of architecture lay beyond the immediately perceptible world of the senses; (3) it connected the mental apparatus of aesthetic perception with the material world; and (4) it gave to architects a description for that part of their work over which they held exclusive and unequivocal control. None of these factors describe what 'form' actually meant in modernist discourse, and to find this out, we must look at the various oppositions in which it was used.

Form as resistance to ornament. This is the first and probably most familiar use of 'form' within modernism, as a means of describing, and validating, that aspect of architecture which is *not* ornament. This sense is made clear for example by the German critic Adolf Behne, writing in the 1920s: 'The concept of "form" does not deal with accessories, decoration, taste or style … but with the consequences arising from a building's ability to be an enduring structure' (137). The main source of the anti-decoration concept of form lay in the polemics against Secession artists and designers in Vienna in the 1890s, evolved most famously by Adolf Loos. Although his essay 'Ornament and Crime' of 1908 is the best-known expression of this point of view, it is important to understand that Loos was able to reach the position advanced in this essay through the already existing propositions about 'form'. In an earlier article, 'The Principle of Cladding' (1898), Loos had written 'Every material possesses its own language of forms, and none may lay claim for itself to the forms of another material. For forms have been constituted out of the applicability and methods of production of materials' (66). Loos was here attacking the simulation of one material in another, characteristic of Secession work. The notion that each material has its own forms is directly derived from Semper, and one might find its origin in a sentence such as the following from *Der Stil*: 'Every material conditions its own particular manner of formation by the properties that distinguish it from other materials and that demand a technical treatment appropriate to it' (§61, 258). However, Loos's rendering of Semper's idea about the relation between form and materials is rather reductive, and suggests a literal determination of Form by Material that Semper had been keen to avoid; for Semper, all forms were the outcome of an idea or artistic motive, which was simply modified by the particular material in which it was worked. While Loos removed all mention of 'Idea', the underlying conception of form which he is employing nonetheless remains idealist, and allows him to argue that there is a 'form' which is inherent to material, and which is endangered, or destroyed by decoration. Loos set the

Interior, ZentralSparkasse, Mariahilf-Neubau, Vienna, Adolf Loos, 1914.

precedent for twentieth-century modernism's use of 'form' as resistance to those despicable tendencies, the ornamental and the decorative.

Form as antidote to mass culture. In a long speech entitled 'Where Do We Stand?' delivered at the 1911 Congress of the Deutsche Werkbund, the architect and critic Hermann Muthesius drew two specific oppositions, between 'form' and 'barbarism', and 'form' and 'Impressionism'. Muthesius spoke as follows:

> What we are pleased to call culture is unthinkable without a compromising respect for form; and formlessness is just another name for philistinism. Form is a higher intellectual need in the same way that cleanliness is a higher physical need, because the sight of crude forms will cause a really cultivated

person something resembling bodily pain and the same uncomfortable sensation that is produced by dirt and foul smells.

While this may sound not unlike Adolf Loos's objections to ornament, in fact Muthesius's object of attack was very different. As Frederic Schwartz has shown, in pre-1914 Germany, 'culture' was a central and much discussed concept in the developing discourse of resistance to the alienating effects of capitalism.[9] 'Form' therefore was, amongst other things, a guarantee against the soullessness of modern economic life. Muthesius returned to this later in the speech with his attack upon 'Impressionism':

> It is evident that the ephemeral is incompatible with the true essence of architecture ... The present impressionistic attitude towards art in a sense is unfavourable to its development. Impressionism is

conceivable in painting, literature, sculpture and to some extent perhaps even music, but in architecture it does not bear thinking about. The few individualistic attempts already tried out by some architects to illustrate what might be an impressionistic manner are simply horrifying.

While this is an explicit attack upon Art Nouveau, as Schwartz points out, the reference to 'Impressionism', in the context of the Werkbund, refers to a discourse about the relationship between art and the market, and described both a social condition and art's response to it. Impressionism describes both the effects of laissez-faire – social atomization, individualism, and the indifference of those who sell goods to their production or their quality – and also the characteristics of the goods themselves, which betrayed signs of over-stimulated, nervous activity. Evidently 'form', as far as Muthesius was concerned, was not simply the means of achieving modernity, but also had the power to resist its worst aspects.[10] Later in the speech, Muthesius continued: 'The recovery of a feeling for architectural form is the first condition in all the arts nowadays …. It is all a matter of restoring order and rigour in our modes of expression, and the outward sign can only be good form'. Seen in these terms, 'form' is what redeems modern industry from its own worst excesses, and restores it to culture. This conception of 'form' was to be important to modernists in Germany in the 1920s; an English manifestation was Herbert Read's *Art and Industry* (1934). That such ideas could be accommodated around the concept of form was made possible by the notion of 'form' set up by Hegel, and mediated to late nineteenth-century architects by Semper.

Muthesius's exhortations to 'form' as the main theme of architecture presented certain pedagogical problems which manifested themselves in the 1920s, for how was the student to learn the principles of what had no material existence, but was a purely metaphysical category? This task was the theme of the educational programme developed at the Bauhaus under Walter Gropius's direction, and Gropius's many pronouncements on the subject attempted to explain how a student was to learn what, by definition, could not be taught: as Gropius put it in 1923, 'The objective of all creative effort in the visual arts is to give form to space. But what is space, how can it be understood and given a form?' (120). When it came to learning the principles of form, Gropius explained, the student 'is given the mental equipment with which to shape his own ideas of form' (123). Quite how such an individualistic process would lead to the

Entrance, ZentralSparkasse, Mariahilf-Neubau, Vienna, Adolf Loos, 1914. 'Forms have been constituted out of the applicability and methods of production of materials.' For Loos, 'form' was primarily a means of resistance to the decorative and ornamental excess of his contemporaries.

AEG large machine factory, Voltastrasse, Berlin-Wedding, P. Behrens, 1912.
'Culture is unthinkable without a compromising respect for form; and formlessness
is just another name for philistinism': to Behrens and his Werkbund contemporaries,
'form' was an antidote to the superficiality and soullessness of the mass culture
created by capitalism.

creation of the property that was meant to convey the
supra-individual, collective nature of architecture,
Gropius did not explain, and he later resorted to a more
straightforwardly materialist explanation of where forms
were to come from: 'by resolute consideration of modern
production methods, constructions, and materials, forms
will evolve that are often unusual and surprising' (1926,
95). At the Bauhaus's Russian equivalent, the Vkhutemas,
concerned with the same problem, Moisei Ginzburg
adopted a more speculative view: Ginzburg referred to

> the basic danger of CANONIZATION of certain
> forms, of their becoming fixed elements of the
> architect's vocabulary. Constructivism is LEADING
> the BATTLE against this phenomenon, and studies
> these basic elements of architecture as something
> *CONTINUOUSLY CHANGING in connection
> with the changing preconditions of the form-making
> situation.* IT NEVER ADMITS therefore the FIXITY
> OF FORMS. *Form is an unknown, 'x', which is
> always evaluated anew by the architect.*

Interest in 'form' as the means of resisting the effects of mass culture and of urbanization have been recurrent throughout the twentieth century. For example, writing in 1960, the American urbanist Kevin Lynch, concerned with the lack of intelligibility of contemporary American cities, wrote 'we must learn to see hidden forms in the vast sprawl of our cities' (12). He took this up again when he considered the means of making the city's image more evident, in an argument which gains much of its effect from the confusion between form as invisible idea, and as physical shape: 'the objective here is to uncover the role of form itself. It is taken for granted that in actual design form should be used to reinforce meaning, and not to negate it' (46).

Form versus social values. In the early 1920s 'form', so highly valued within the Deutsche Werkbund, began to treated with great suspicion by certain German architects. Mies van der Rohe, then a member of the G group in Berlin, wrote as follows in 1923:

> We know no forms, only building problems.
> Form is not the goal but the result of our work.
> There is no form in and for itself. ... Form as
> goal is formalism; and that we reject. Nor do we
> strive for a style.
> Even the will to style is formalism. (Neumeyer, 242)

For so-called 'functionalist' architects, amongst whom Mies van der Rohe included himself in the early 1920s, the end was, as the critic Adolf Behne put it, to 'arrive at a negation of form' (123). What underlay this was a complete rejection of the nineteenth-century Kantian tradition in which utility was excluded from the aesthetic in architecture: as a product of philosophical aesthetics, 'form' had no place in the scheme of those architects who saw architecture as purely the application of technology to social ends. Indeed the rejection of form was one of the clearest and most explicit ways of affirming their attachment to the view of architecture as committed to social purpose. And from this point on to draw attention to an architect's concern with 'form' has always been a way of simultaneously signalling their neglect of social questions. This occurs particularly in the pejorative use of the word 'formalist', as in the Czech critic Karel Teige's 1929 attack on Le Corbusier's Mundaneum project, which 'in its obvious historicism ... shows the non-viability of architecture thought of as art. It shows the failure of Le Corbusier's aesthetic and formalistic theories ...' (89). In recent times, 'form' has regularly

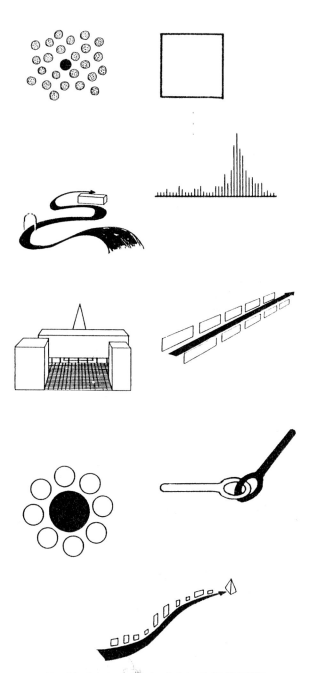

'Form Qualities of the City': nine diagrams from Kevin Lynch's *The Image of the City*, 1961. Reading from top left: 'singularity or figure-background clarity'; 'form simplicity'; 'motion awareness'; 'time series'; 'visual scope'; 'continuity'; 'dominance'; 'clarity of joint'; 'directional differentiation'. 'We must learn to see hidden forms in the vast sprawl of our cities': to Lynch and other urbanists, 'form' was the property that would overcome the alienation of modern cities – and it was the task of the urban designer to discover and reveal 'form'.

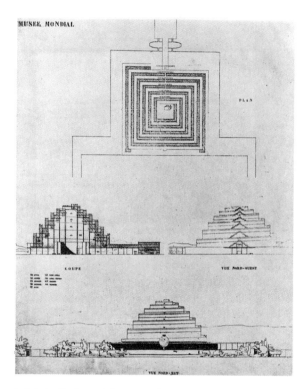

MUSEE MONDIAL

PLAN

COUPE

VUE NORD-OUEST

VUE NORD-EST

Le Corbusier, Mundaneum Project, 1928–29. The Mundaneum project attracted notoriety on account of its dominant pyramid form, which was taken to indicate the neglect of social content.

been used to imply a neglect of social concerns, as for example when Diane Ghirardo writes: 'Perhaps the fundamental continuity between Modernist and Postmodernist architects derives from the reassertion of the power of form, and hence the primacy of design, to the exclusion of other strategies for improving cities and living conditions' (27).

Even in the 1920s, the critic Adolf Behne tried in his book *The Modern Functional Building* to nullify this particular polarity, introducing the surprisingly novel idea that 'form is an eminently social matter'; in this attempt to rescue the concept of form from what he saw as the ultimate dissolution of form by the functionalists, Behne's argument that what he described as 'romantic functionalism' – in effect the application of a Schlegel-like notion that the form of each building is the working out of its particular inner purpose – would lead only to solutions that were entirely individual and specific to their own particular circumstances, and which, lacking any general significance, would lead ultimately to anarchy. But if each building were considered not individually, but as part of the collective sum total of all buildings, it must conform to certain generally valid principles. It was the consciousness of these general principles that Behne described as 'form'. As well as recalling the socially redemptive power of form contained in Muthesius's 1911 formulation, Behne's idea, particularly in its binary opposition between the pursuit of individuality and of a socialized whole, owed a good deal to the sociologist Georg Simmel, for whom the very possibility of the study of society had rested upon the coexistence of 'forms of socialization' with the actual social life experienced by individuals. Behne might have had in mind an essay like Simmel's 'Subjective Culture' of 1908, where Simmel had argued that while truly great works of art might be distinguished by the individual spirituality of their creator, such works were of little value from the point of view of *culture*, and that the more a work gained in cultural significance, the less apparent was the individuality of its creator. Behne proposed that 'form' in architecture corresponded to 'forms' in society. As he put it,

Form is nothing more than the consequence of establishing a relationship between human beings. For the isolated and unique figure in nature there is no problem of form. ... The problem of form arises when an overview is demanded. Form is the prerequisite under which an overview becomes possible. Form is an eminently social matter. Anyone

'Horseshoe Siedlung', Berlin-Britz, Martin Wagner and Bruno Taut, 1925–26. 'Form is an eminently social matter': the critic Adolf Behne attempted to reverse the prejudice against 'form' as inherently asocial by suggesting that 'form' was the means by which individuals would acquire consciousness of the collective nature of the society to which they belonged.

who recognizes the right of society recognizes the right of form. ... Anyone who sees a form in humanity, a pattern articulated in time and space, approaches the house with formal requirements, in which case 'formal' is not to be confused with 'decorative'. (137)

Behne's idea enjoyed some currency amongst the proponents of the New Architecture in Germany in the late 1920s: we find his contemporary, the architect Bruno Taut, making the same connection, in reverse, when he writes 'Architecture will thus become the creator of new social forms' (7). The idea reappears some time later, in 1955, used by the Smithsons, when writing about housing: 'Each form is an active force, it creates the community, it is life itself made manifest'. The notion that architectural forms are equivalent to social forms (whether they derive out of, or themselves constitute social forms, is left ambiguous in the Smithsons' text) was the single most important new sense of 'form' to emerge out of modernism – and is one that has been the most problematic and controversial.

Form versus Functionalism. At the time that Simmel was promoting sociology as a science of 'forms', similar things were happening in other disciplines outside the visual arts. The field within which 'form' was to have most significance, with the most far-reaching effects, was linguistics. In the nineteenth century the study of language had already benefitted from Goethe's theory of form that had influenced Humboldt's *On Language* (1836). In the early twentieth century, the importance of 'form' in lingusitics was to be asserted again by Ferdinand de Saussure, in lectures given in 1911, and later published as *Course in General Linguistics*, in which he famously formulated the principle *'that language is a form and not a substance'* (122). The significance of this proposition for the development of linguistics, and of structuralist thinking in anthropology and literary criticism, is well known; its influence upon architecture was not felt until later, in the 1960s, when it provided the means to attack functionalism, then regarded as the dominant and least satisfactory aspect of architectural modernism.

For a circle of Dutch architects, of whom Aldo van Eyck and Herman Hertzberger are the best known, and for the Italian architect Aldo Rossi, Saussure's proposition that language was a form, not a substance, was fundamental, as was the notion that the meanings of language were arbitrary. In resisting the reductiveness of functionalism, the notion that forms in architecture existed prior to, and independently of any specific purpose to which they might be put, or meaning that might be attached to them, was of particular significance. Rossi formulated this argument primarily in terms of 'types' – though the distinction between 'form' and 'type' was not particularly clear, and indeed he used the terms interchangeably. Thus for example, in the introduction to the Portuguese edition of *The Architecture of the City* in 1971, Rossi wrote 'the presence of *form*, of architecture, *predominates over questions of functional organization.* ... Form is absolutely indifferent to organization precisely when it exists as typological form' (174). The stress upon the fundamentally non-physical, and linguistic sense of 'form' is made clear by Herman Hertzberger in a recent interview: 'I am a little tired of people who try to link forms to signs, because then you get into the meanings of forms. I don't think forms have a meaning' (38).

In the American architect Peter Eisenman's twenty-year crusade against functionalism, 'form' has again been the instrument of attack. Against orthodox modernist thinking, exemplified by Le Corbusier's statement that 'A work can only affect us emotionally and touch our sensibility if its form has been dictated by a genuine purpose' (1925a), Eisenman has repeatedly asserted that there is no correlation between form and function, nor between form and meaning. As Eisenman put it, 'one way of producing an environment which can accept or give a more precise and richer meaning than at present, is to understand the nature of the structure of form itself, as opposed to the relationship of form to function or of

form to meaning' (1975, 15). Eisenman's single-minded pursuit of 'the structure of form' has a surprising similarity to Frank Lloyd Wright's views about form earlier in the century. Eisenman's belief that there exists 'an unarticulated universe of form which remains to be excavated' (1982, 40) is curiously similar to Frank Lloyd Wright's view that 'in the stony bonework of the Earth, ... there sleep forms and styles enough for all the ages, for all of Man' (1928, *Collected Writings*, vol. 1, 275). Although Wright believed that all the forms of architecture lay hidden in nature, whereas Eisenman believes that they are to be found within the processes of architecture, both share the view that forms are already in existence, only awaiting discovery by the artist. Both, in common with a great many other architects, seem to have lost sight of the fact that 'form' is no more than a device of thought, that can hardly have a determinate existence prior to thought.

Form versus meaning. In Hertzberger and in Eisenman we have already seen 'form' validated in order to expel questions of meaning from the architect's domain. A corresponding, but converse argument, that too much attention to form had destroyed interest in meaning, was put most famously by the American architect Robert Venturi. Introducing the second edition of his *Complexity and Contradiction in Architecture*, Venturi wrote that 'In the early '60's ... form was king in architectural thought, and most architects focused without question on aspects of form' (14). For Venturi, this meant that architects had neglected meaning and signification. His second book, *Learning from Las Vegas* (1972), written with Denise Scott Brown, 'a treatise on symbolism in architecture' (xiv), was intended to address this state of affairs. Against what they called 'Heroic and Original' modern architecture, in which 'the creation of architectural form was to be a logical process, free from images of past experience, determined solely by program and structure' (7), and whose 'total image derives from ... purely architectural qualities transmitted through abstract form' (129), the authors proposed 'Ugly and Ordinary' architecture. With its assortment of references to conventional roadside constructions, in 'Ugly and Ordinary' architecture, the 'elements act as symbols as well as expressive architectural abstractions'; as well as representing ordinariness symbolically and stylistically, they are enriching 'because they add a layer of literary meaning' (130). The modernist obsession with form, resulting in what Venturi and Scott Brown called 'ducks', denied attention to meaning.

(above) Central Fire Station, New Haven, Connecticut, Earl P. Carlin, 1959–62.

(right) Fire Station no. 4, Columbus, Indiana, Venturi and Rauch, 1965–67. Venturi, in his stand against modernist 'form', compared the New Haven fire station, 'whose image derives from... architectural qualities transmitted through abstract forms', to his own 'Ugly and Ordinary' Columbus fire house, whose image comes from the 'conventions of roadside architecture' – false facade, banality, familiarity of the components, and the sign.

Form versus 'reality'. Modern art, and particularly abstraction, had a direct relationship with theories of 'form' developed in late nineteenth-century Germany: Hildebrand's essay of 1893, and the writings of the historians Riegl, Worringer, and Wölfflin in Germany, or of the critics Clive Bell and Roger Fry in Britain, all contributed to the generally understood significance of

'form' as the pure substance of modernist art.
However, against this, there has always been some
resistance: in 1918–19 the Dadaists, Tristan Tzara
and others, were promoting chaos, disorder and lack
of form as the qualities of art; this interest continued
amongst the Surrealists, and was best expressed by
the French critic Georges Bataille, whose 'Critical
Dictionary' in 1929 included an entry on 'L'Informe',
the 'Formless', a category that celebrates meaninglessness,
'a term that serves to bring things down in the world…
What it designates has no rights in any sense and
gets itself squashed everywhere, like a spider or
an earthworm'. Against philosophy, which wants
everything to have form, 'affirming that the universe
resembles nothing and is only *formless* amounts to
saying that the universe is something like a spider
or spit'.

An anti-form movement emerged again in France in
the 1950s amongst the Situationists. Here its purpose
was not aesthetic, but an opposition to the process of
reification, of the tendency of capitalist culture to turn
ideas and relationships into things whose fixity obscures
reality, a process in which 'form' is variously both cause
and symptom. In a generally inexplicit way, the
Situationists were resistant to 'form'; in so far as there
could be a Situationist architecture at all, this presented
a paradox, and part of the interest of the work of the
Dutch artist/architect Constant Nieuwenhuys was to try
to conceive architecture which had no form, but which
dealt with 'reality' without distorting it or fixing it so
that it became an obstacle to the freedom to live out
one's life. The Situationists' general condemnation of
the world of appearances took, in architecture, the guise
of proposals for an architecture which was ephemeral,
transient, ludic, and lacking in any determinate form.
In his utopian city 'New Babylon', Constant proposed
a city not of static elements, but of 'ambience', in which
'the rapid change of the look of a space by ephemeral
elements' would count for more than any permanent
structure (Ockman, 315). There was a strong current
of interest in the inexplicit anti-form tendencies of the
Situationists during the 1960s and 1970s, manifested
particularly in the work of the Archigram group,
and in the earlier writings and work of the architect
Bernard Tschumi.

While the question of a 'formless' architecture will
no doubt continue to interest people, it nevertheless
depends upon the prior existence of a concept of
'form'; formless architecture is not one in which 'form'
is non-existent.

Form versus technical or environmental considerations.
The opposition between 'form' and 'structure' or
'technique' originated in the nineteenth century with
Viollet-le-Duc. As Viollet put it in his *Lectures*, 'all
architecture proceeds from structure, and the first
condition at which it should aim is to make the outward
form accord with that structure' (vol. 2, 3); the error of
the Renaissance was that 'Form was then the leading
consideration; principles were no longer regarded, and
structural system there was none' (vol. 2, 2). This
particular polarity of 'form' is a familiar one within
architectural modernism. An example occurs in the
writing of the historian and critic Reyner Banham in
the late 1950s and 1960s. Banham's resistance to 'form'
combined various tendencies – Situationist sentiments,
the aformalism of certain visual artists, and a strong
element of technological rationalism; one of his first
pieces with an anti-form theme was his 1955 article
'The New Brutalism', where the quality he singled out
in Alison and Peter Smithson's Golden Lane Competition
entry (see ill. p. 172) was 'its determination to create a
coherent visual image by non-formal means, emphasizing
visible circulation, identifiable units of habitation, and
fully validating the presence of human beings as part of
the total image'; while of the same architects' Sheffield
University Competition design, 'aformalism becomes as
positive a force in its composition as it does in a painting
by Burri or Pollock' (359). But Banham's hostility to
'form' was to be connected principally with an
enthusiasm for technological innovation: the lesson he
drew from the work of Buckminster Fuller in particular
was that a purely technical approach to issues of

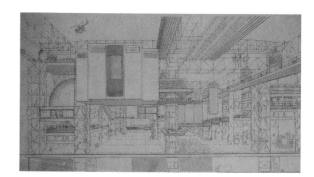

Cedric Price, Fun Palace, key drawing, 1964. 'Formless' architecture, of indeterminate
volume, and capable of endless change and rearrangement.

(opposite) Constant, 'New Babylon', drawing, 1961. Constant, a one-time member of
the Situationist International, in his 'New Babylon' developed between 1959 and
1966, investigated a city without 'form'.

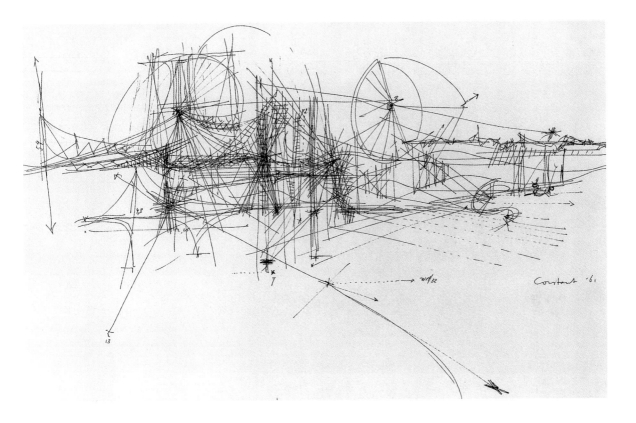

construction might lead to results that would be unrecognizable as architecture. Of Fuller's Dymaxion House he remarked – approvingly – 'the formal qualities ... are not remarkable' (1960, 326), and it was distinguished instead by the adaptation of aircraft construction techniques to building, and its innovative use of mechanical services. Banham's belief that the future of architecture lay with technology, with its inherent indifference to 'form', underlies his 1969 book *The Architecture of the Well-Tempered Environment* (see especially 21ff). Something of this approach appears in the work of Banham's friend Cedric Price, whose 'Fun Palace' project of 1964, described by its promoter Joan Littlewood as 'a University of the Streets', was a structure with an indeterminate form, capable of endless rearrangement. Price explained: 'The complex itself, having no doorways, enables one to choose one's own route and degree of involvement with the activities. Although the framework will remain a constant size, the total volume in use may vary, thus presenting a changing scene even to the frequent user'. The Fun Palace was a blend of Situationism, providing ever-changing opportunities for encountering and reproducing everyday life after one's individual desires, combined with an application of the most up-to-date technological systems, through which it was to be realized. A similar unlikely combination of Situationist liberation with a fascination for high technology occurred in the work of Archigram in the 1960s. However the most prominent essay in this idiom of ludic formlessness, the Centre Pompidou in Paris (1971–77), disappointed its critics by reverting to strongly architectural conventions of mass and volume, reminiscent of the American work of Mies van der Rohe.[11]

What will happen to 'form'? That it is not a permanent or timeless category of architectural discourse is clear. Developed in the nineteenth century as a solution to certain specific problems – in particular the nature of aesthetic perception, and the processes of natural morphology – 'form' was an extraordinarily productive concept both for these and many related fields. But

Competition entry, for Golden Lane, City of London, Alison and Peter Smithson, collage, 1952. Reyner Banham – an outspoken critic of 'form' – in 1955 singled out the Smithsons' Golden Lane project as creating 'a coherent visual image by non-formal means'.

whether it has been so successful an aid to thought about the different problems confronting architecture in the twentieth century is more doubtful. To take one in particular – the relationship of buildings to the social life in and around them – it might be said to have had disastrous consequences through its part in sustaining the belief in architectural determinism. The premise of this, the 'form-function' paradigm, in which it is alleged that the *form* of inanimate things directly influences human behaviour, is, as Bill Hillier points out, absurd, and a violation of common sense (1996, 379); and as he argues, the confusion and misconceptions surrounding this whole subject arise in part from the misapplication of 'form' to a problem for which it was not originally devised.

In a sense, 'form' is a concept that has outlived its usefulness. People talk *of* form all the time, but they rarely talk *about* it; as a term it has become frozen, no longer in active development, and with little curiosity as to what purposes it might serve. Ask this question, and it may lose some of its seeming naturalness and neutrality.

1 For discussion of the difference between these two words, see Schiller, *On the Aesthetic Education of Man*, edited and translated by Elizabeth M. Wilkinson and L. A. Willoughby, Oxford, Clarendon Press, 1967, 308–10.

2 David Summers, 'Form and Gender', in Bryson, Holly and Moxey (eds), *Visual Culture. Images and Interpretations*, Hanover, New Hampshire, 1994, 406.

3 See Popper, 'The Nature of Philosophical Problems', in *Conjectures and Refutations*, 1963, 66–96.

4 Panofsky, *Idea*, 1968, 209. See Alberti, *On the Art of Building in Ten Books*, 1988, 'Lineaments', 422–23.

5 See Panofsky, *Idea*, 1968, 115–21.

6 Fink, *Goethe's History of Science*, 1991, 88–89; see also Magnus, *Goethe as a Scientist*, 1906, especially chapters 4 and 5; and Chomsky, *Cartesian Linguistics*, 1966, 23–24.

7 See the Introduction to Mallgrave and Ikonomou, *Empathy, Form and Space*, 1994, 1–85, for a full account of this subject.

8 See Levine, *Frank Lloyd Wright*, 437, note 5, for references to this topic.

9 Schwartz, *The Werkbund*, 1996, 15–16.

10 Schwartz, *The Werkbund*, 1996, 91–95.

11 See, for example, Colquhoun, 'Plateau Beaubourg', in *Essays in Architectural Criticism*, 1981.

Formal

As the adjective of 'form', 'formal' has all the complications of 'form' – and some more. 'Formal' is regularly used with the intention of giving emphasis to the specifically 'architectural' properties in works of architecture; but as the nouns with which it is generally linked – 'order', 'design', 'structure', 'vocabulary' – are themselves so ambiguous, the confusion is compounded. For example, 'Boston is probably quite different from many American cities, where areas of formal order have little character' (Lynch, 1960, 22); or the press release for Frank Gehry's Vitra Museum: 'A consistent, albeit differentiated, formal vocabulary ties the various pieces together' (quoted in Maxwell, 1993, 109).

What makes 'formal' still more confusing is that as the opposite of 'informal' it also has the sense of 'ceremonious', or 'affected'. This has a longstanding use in architecture, and not only in relation to gardens. For example, Sir William Chambers warned that unless the architect was a master of drawing, 'his compositions will ever be feeble, formal and ungraceful' (94); and Sir John Soane, comparing Ancient gardens with modern: 'There can be no comparison between the stiff formal art, unnaturally applied, of the one, and the finest effects of nature, happily assisted by art, in the other' (627). In English, the use of 'formal' as the opposite of 'informal' is longer established than its other senses as the adjective of 'form', and there has always been a tendency for the meaning to revert by default to this original sense when no other is indicated – take a modern example, of Kahn's Yale University Art Gallery: 'the plan is very formal' (Banham, 1955, 357). Sometimes deliberate play is made of the 'formal/informal' contrast, while at the same time vesting 'formal' with a modern architectural sense; of Stirling and Wilford's Music Academy and Dance Theatre at Stuttgart: 'Thus both schemes are committed to the game of formality and informality, using the elements of axial stasis and diagonal movement to generate a dynamic balance' (Maxwell, 1993, 99).

'Formal' can sometimes be pejorative, in the sense of a limitation, deriving from the various negative senses of 'form'. For example, the Czech critic Karel Teige's 1929 attack upon Le Corbusier's Mundaneum project, which 'in its obvious historicism ... shows the non-viability of architecture thought of as art. It shows the failure of Le Corbusier's aesthetic and formalistic theories ...' (89). (Teige was probably taking advantage of Lukács's use of 'formalism' as a category within literary criticism, as what makes a work 'unrealistic'.) Lubetkin and Tecton's Highpoint II (1938) was criticized for setting 'formal values above use values' (Cox, 1938). Michael Sorkin comments on the difficulty of writing about city architecture, 'Appreciating it formally demands that the terms of the discussion be totally hemmed, that the question of effects be trivialized' (237).

When precision of meaning is desired (not, admittedly, always the case), 'architectonic' may be a better word than 'formal'; at least it does not mean so many so things.

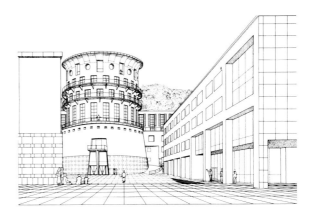

Perspective, Academy of Music, Stuttgart, James Stirling and Michael Wilford, 1987. 'Formality and informality.'

Function

'Function' (and in this category we shall include also 'Functional' and 'Functionalism') was without question an important concept in modern architecture, but it has above all been in the *critique* of modernism that it has come into its own. To a considerable extent, its definition, its meaning, even its naming, has come about through the activities of critics of architectural modernism since about 1960. As Bill Hillier has remarked, 'One scours the architectural manifestos of the twentieth century in vain for a thoroughgoing statement of the determinism from spatial form to function, or its inverse' (1996, 377–78). In so far as we have a 'theory' or theories of function, they are of recent making, and not of the period when 'functionalism' is alleged to have dominated modern architecture. Our immediate task, then, is to identify what 'function' meant *before* it was given its present coherence and intensity.

A 'function' describes the result of the action of one quantity upon another; relative to architecture, the question is what is acting upon what? From the first use of 'function' in the eighteenth century until the end of the nineteenth century, the quantity acted upon was almost always taken as the building's tectonic elements, its 'structure' (see pp. 276–85), a term with which 'function' has been closely associated; the quantities performing the action were principally the building's own mechanical forces. In other words, until the beginning of the twentieth century – with a few rare exceptions that will be discussed below – 'function' was a term primarily relating to the tectonics of building. During the twentieth century, a new use of 'function' became more widespread, one in which buildings themselves were described as acting upon people, or social material. It is this second meaning – and its converse, the action of society in determining the forms of buildings – that have attracted so much attention, but which are the more difficult to trace historically.

Considered historically, we can identify at least five different uses of 'function' prior to about 1930. What makes the concept complicated is that it is a metaphor, and a metaphor that borrows from at least two, and perhaps three different fields: from mathematics, from biology, and maybe from sociology. A further complication is that the English word 'function' as applied to architecture is a translation of terms originating in Italian, French and German; this is particularly problematic in relation to German, which has three words whose different nuances are lost by all being translated as 'function'.

1. *As a mathematical metaphor – a critique of the classical system of ornament.* The first use of 'function' relative to architecture was by the Venetian friar Carlo Lodolí in the 1740s.[1] Lodolí's motto, *'Devonsi unire e fabrica e ragione e sia funzion la rapresentazione'* – 'Unite building with reason and let function be the representation' – summarized an argument against the conventions of the classical system of ornament. Lodolí's main objection was to the imitation in stone of forms developed originally for timber construction; Francesco Algarotti, the author of one of the two surviving accounts of Lodolí's ideas, reported 'nothing, he insisted, should be represented which is not also true in function' (35). What Lodolí meant by 'function' is inferred from the other, more accurate, source of Lodolí's ideas, by Andrea Memmo. Memmo indicated that Lodolí wanted to develop forms of stone construction and decoration that derived from the mechanical forces acting upon the material. Evidence of the application of this idea is to be found in the surprising lintels and window-sills of the pilgrim hospice attached to S. Francesco della Vigna in Venice, apparently executed to Lodolí's instructions. According to Joseph Rykwert, Lodolí borrowed the term 'function' from mathematics, to which it had been introduced in the 1690s by Leibniz, to describe the compound of variables; Lodolí's notion of function is

(left) Carlo Lodolí, portrait; frontispiece to A. Memmo, *Elementi d'architettura Lodoliana*, vol. 1, 1834. 'Unite Building with Reason and Let Function be the Representation': the Venetian friar Lodoli was the first to use 'function' in relation to architecture, as part of his attack upon the classical system of ornament.

(above) Pilgrim's Hospice, S. Francesco della Vigna, Venice. In the only known work for which Lodoli was directly responsible, the window surrounds conform to his notion of 'function', the sills being thickest at the point they are most likely to crack.

the compound of mechanical force and material within any specific component of architecture. Lodolí's thinking was popularized by the late eighteenth-century Italian architectural writer Francesco Milizia, who misleadingly presented it simply as an argument against superfluous decoration: 'whatever is seen should always have a function' (*quanto è in rapresentazione, deve essere sempre in funzione* – 1781, vol. 1, xv); but Lodolí had not argued against decoration as such, but for a different system of decoration, based upon the inherent properties of materials. Since Milizia's books were translated into French from the 1790s, they may have provided a source for the term in French architectural circles; however, by this time the precision of Lodolí's mathematical metaphor was entirely lost, first of all misrepresented by Milizia, and now displaced by the arrival of a new analogue for 'function', drawn from the developing science of biology.

2. *As a biological metaphor, descriptive of the purposes of the parts of the construction relative to each other and to the whole.* In biology, a science created in France out of the work of Lamarck and Cuvier in particular, 'function' was a key concept. Whereas earlier natural historians had classified specimens according to the visual appearance of their organs, and their position in the body, in the new science of biology developed at the end of the eighteenth century, organs were analysed according to the functions they performed within the organism as a whole, and by their hierarchical relationship to other organs. 'Function' in this sense was closely related to 'structure' (see pp. 281–82), for it was the identification of 'functions' – of individual limbs and organs – which made it possible to deduce the structure.

Although developed by biologists in the 1790s, the term appears to have been little used by architects until rather later. 'The genius of modern times, which loves to

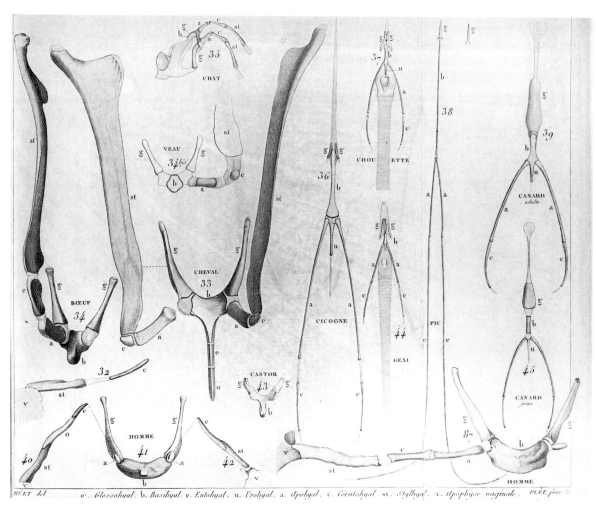

Comparative hyoids (cartilege connecting tongue to jaw) in various vertebrates, from Geoffroy Saint-Hilaire, *Philosophie Anatomique*, vol. 1, 1818. 'Function' became a major topic in early nineteenth-century biology. Geoffroy Saint-Hilaire's 'theory of analogues' suggested that, in evolutionary terms, the functions of specific organs were not fixed; he hypothesized that in all vertebrates there were organs which, though they might through the adaptation of species have developed different functions, were nonetheless related, analogously, to a single common origin.

assign every individual product or object a distinct function' was manifested most comprehensively in architectural discourse after the 1850s through the writings of Viollet-le-Duc, whose phrase this was (*Lectures*, vol.1, 449). For Viollet, 'function' was an important concept, fundamental to his whole theory of rational construction: for example, writing about walls, he says

> In every specimen of mason-work each piece taken separately in the case of dressed stone, or each section in concrete works, should clearly indicate its function. We ought to be able to analyse a building, as we take a puzzle to pieces, so that the place and function of each of the parts cannot be mistaken. (*Lectures*, vol. 2, 33)

And Viollet was – repeatedly – explicit about the biological origins of the metaphor.

It is in this sense, of the role played by each part within the structure, that 'function' was principally understood in the English-speaking world from the mid-nineteenth century; this may be to do with a familiarity with the careful analyses of the constructive systems of Gothic architecture by the English archeologists William Whewell and Robert Willis in the 1830s and 1840s, or to the influence of Viollet's books. To take a single example of the characteristic English-language use of 'function', we may cite the American critic Montgomery Schuyler's recollection of visiting the New York State Capitol at Albany around 1880 with Leopold Eidlitz, the architect of the alterations:

> Standing in the rotunda of the Court House one day, when his own vari-colored brick arches and columns had been inserted between the cast-iron panels of the older work, he said 'Is it possible for anybody to fail to see that this,' pointing to the new work, 'performs a function, and that that,' pointing to the old, 'does not?' (1908, 181)

3. *As a biological metaphor within the 'organic' theory of form.* A second, but quite different biological metaphor of 'function' derives from the organic notion of form developed by the German Romantics. This is the context of Louis Sullivan's famous remarks about form and function. Within German Romanticism, 'form' (see pp. 155–57) was either 'mechanical' or 'organic'. The distinction, first made by A. W. Schlegel, was paraphrased in English by Coleridge in 1818:

> The form is mechanic, when on any given material we impress a pre-determined form, not necessarily arising out of the properties of the material; as when to a mass of wet clay we give whatever shape we wish it to retain when hardened. The organic form, on the other hand, is innate; it shapes, as it develops itself from within, and the fullness of its development is one and the same with the perfection of its outward form. Such as the life is, such is the form. (229)

What constitutes the prime-mover within the organic theory of form – a question first posed by Aristotle – was left unanswered: but there is no doubt about the influence the theory had upon a wide variety of architects and writers, amongst them the American sculptor and art theorist Horatio Greenough, usually credited as the first

Aisle section, showing nave buttressing, Notre Dame-en-Vaux, Chalons-sur-Marne, from Viollet-le-Duc, *Dictionnaire Raisonné*, vol. IV. For Viollet-le-Duc – following the biologists' use of the term – the 'function' of each individual component, as a description of its relation to the constructional system of the whole, became a prime concern to the architect.

English speaker to apply 'function' to architecture. Greenough's essays on art and architecture, written in the 1840s, are all essentially to do with the development of organic form in the visual arts. 'Function' played a key part in this, but Greenough was never very exact about what it meant – his use of it shifted between the straightforward expression of the building's utilitarian purpose, and a much more transcendental notion of the outward expression of organic form, as, for example, when he writes as follows: 'Instead of forcing the functions of every sort of building into one general form, adopting an outward shape for the sake of the eye or of association, without reference to the inner distribution, let us begin from the heart as the nucleus, and work outward' (62). But in whatever sense he used it, Greenough's choice of the term 'function' was explicitly biological – 'as the first step in our search after the great principles of construction ... observe the skeletons and skins of animals' (58). And it is from these observations that he concludes 'If there be any principle of structure more plainly inculcated in the works of the Creator than all others, it is the principle of unflinching adaptation of forms to functions' (118). Twentieth-century commentators have tended to exaggerate the modernity of Greenough's ideas. We should remember that not only was Greenough's 'function' based upon the earlier Romantic notion of organic form, but it is also clear that Greenough was interested in 'function' less in terms of the satisfaction of human needs (about which he had no theory, and little to say), and more as a way of achieving that very eighteenth-century architectural aim, the expression of appropriate character: 'The unflinching adaptation of a building to its position and use gives, as a sure product of that adaptation, character and expression' (62). Greenough's originality was not to have anticipated twentieth-century functionalism (which he did not do, for he had no sense of the reciprocal action of society upon buildings and of buildings upon society), but rather in putting new life into the old concept of 'character' by linking it to use through the idea of 'function' – to present, as he put it, 'Character as the record of Function' (71).

If Greenough's conception of function was derived in part from the Romantics' organic theory of form, this was wholly true of the doctrine of 'suppressed functions' with which the mysterious John Edelmann so captivated the young Louis Sullivan (1924a, 207). Exactly where Sullivan – generally agreed to have coined the aphorism '*form follows function*' (1924a, 258) – acquired his ideas about function is uncertain, but his reliance upon German

thought is indisputable.[2] At no point did Sullivan's 'function' have anything to do with utility or the satisfaction of user needs; it was instead entirely based in metaphysics, the expression of organic essence. 'The Germ is the real thing: the seat of identity. Within its delicate mechanism lies the will to power: the function which is to seek and eventually to find its full expression in form' (1924b). When Sullivan talks about 'function', one could satisfactorily paraphrase his meaning as 'destiny'. This is clear from the long and famous discussion in *Kindergarten Chats* 12 and 13 that begins, 'generally speaking outer appearances resemble inner purposes. For instances, the form, oak tree, resembles and expresses the function or purpose, oak...' (43). Further proof of what Sullivan meant by 'function' comes from a remark of his partner, Dankmar Adler: 'Function and environment determine form' – implying that 'function' was not the same as 'environment'. 'Function', as far as Sullivan was concerned, was the inner spiritual force that determined 'organic' form; 'environment' is an external agency, a determinate of 'mechanical' form, in the terminology of the Romantics. During the twentieth century this distinction has been lost: the organic theory of form, with all its epistemological difficulties, has been largely forgotten, and 'function', to which it was once exclusively attached, has been transferred to the action of external agencies – 'environment' – upon form.

Sullivan was certainly also aware of the other biological sense of 'function' from Viollet-le-Duc, and, inevitably, Sullivan and others allowed the two to be confused. Interesting in this connection is the book by the American architect Leopold Eidlitz, *The Nature and Function of Art* (1881). Eidlitz had studied in Vienna, so was familiar with German thought, but moved to the United States in 1843 and became an enthusiastic disciple of Viollet-le-Duc. In his book, he attempted to reconcile Viollet's strictly mechanical, tectonic sense of 'function' with a German, idealist notion of function. Thus he writes:

All natural organisms are possessed of the mechanical ability to perform certain functions. This ability we find more or less clearly expressed in their forms as a whole or in their crystallization. In this way they convey to the mind an expression of these functions, and thus they tell the story of their being. The architect, in imitation of this natural condition of matter, so models his forms that they also tell the story of their functions; and these functions are always mechanical conditions of strength, elegance

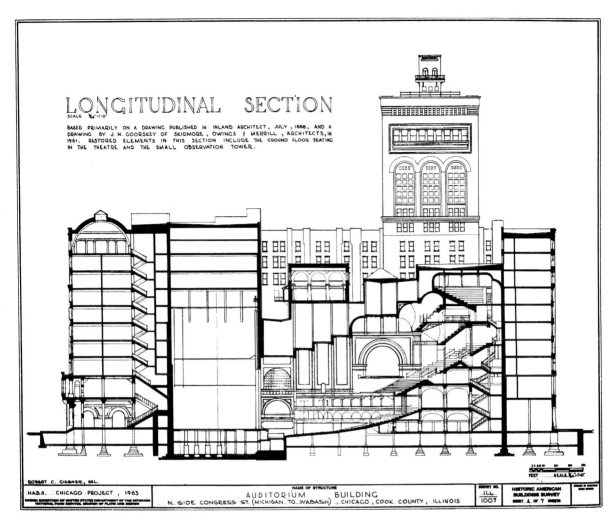

LONGITUDINAL SECTION
SCALE ¼"·I-0"
BASED PRIMARILY ON A DRAWING PUBLISHED IN INLAND ARCHITECT, JULY, 1888, AND A
DRAWING BY J. N. GOORSKEY OF SKIDMORE, OWINGS & MERRILL, ARCHITECTS, IN
1961. RESTORED ELEMENTS IN THIS SECTION INCLUDE THE GROUND FLOOR SEATING
IN THE THEATRE AND THE SMALL OBSERVATION TOWER.

ROBERT C. GILBNER, DEL.

HABS. CHICAGO PROJECT, 1963
UNDER DIRECTION OF UNITED STATES DEPARTMENT OF THE INTERIOR
NATIONAL PARK SERVICE, BRANCH OF PLANS AND DESIGN

NAME OF STRUCTURE
AUDITORIUM BUILDING
N. SIDE CONGRESS ST. (MICHIGAN TO WABASH), CHICAGO, COOK COUNTY, ILLINOIS

SURVEY NO.
1LL
1007

HISTORIC AMERICAN
BUILDINGS SURVEY
SHEET 4 OF 7 SHEETS

Longitudinal section, Auditorium building, Chicago, D. Adler and L. Sullivan, 1887–89.
'Form Follows Function': for Sullivan, who coined the phrase, 'function' meant
'inner purpose', the spiritual force directing the development of all living things –
including architecture.

and repose, in combinations of various quantities of these properties. The fundamental principle of the modelling of architectural forms is therefore mechanical. (223–24)

For Eidlitz, the expression of mechanical function provides the means to represent the building's innate function, 'the story of its being'.

4. *'Function' meaning 'Use'*. By the mid-nineteenth century, in both English and French, 'function' had a limited currency as meaning the activities designated for a particular building or part of a building. Two of the writers already discussed, Greenough and Viollet-le-Duc, both used 'function' in this sense. For example, Greenough wrote, 'to apportion the spaces for convenience, decide their size, and model their shapes for their functions – these acts organize a building' (21). Viollet-le-Duc says of domestic architecture – in an overtly biological analogy, discussed in another context

on p. 90 – 'There is in every building … one principal organ … and certain secondary organs or members, and the necessary appliances for supplying all these parts by a system of circulation. Each of these organs has its own function' (*Lectures*, vol. 2, 277). And George Gilbert Scott, in 1857, on the design of factories, advised 'making the parts which have the same functions uniform and alike' (212). As a description of the activities specific to a particular building or part of a building, 'function' occurs more rarely than one might expect before the twentieth century, although this has become a ubiquitous modern meaning.

5. *'Functional' as the translation of the German words 'sachlich', 'zweckmässig', 'funktionell'*. Where English has one word, 'functional', German, by 1900, had three.[3] While Germans often used the three interchangeably, they carry different nuances of meaning that give the concept a depth impossible to convey with the single English word.

Sachlichkeit
Sachlichkeit, literally meaning 'thingness', and without any equivalent in either English or French, was, according to Harry Mallgrave, first introduced into the vocabulary of architecture in 1896 by the German critic Richard Streiter.[4] Its significance lies in the context of a debate about 'realism' that preoccupied German and Austrian architects in the 1880s and 1890s. In German-speaking countries, 'realism' (*Realismus*) meant constructional rationalism, the expression of the mechanics of structure most clearly seen in modern engineering works. While these were valued for their successful disregard of historical style, they were also seen as lacking in the idea-bearing properties necessary to art, and were therefore considered defective as a model for 'modern' architecture. Something of the conflict of opinion architects felt towards 'realism' is conveyed by Otto Wagner in the Preface to his volume of *Sketches, Projects and Executed Buildings* (1890). After commending the effects of 'realism' in painting, where it had produced modern, open-air genre pictures, he continued:

> That such Realism in architecture can also bear quite peculiar fruit may be seen by several quite poignant examples, such as the Eiffel Tower, the Kursaal in Ostend, etc., etc. But whereas in such cases there is too much Realism, the bulk of our present day architecture shows too little. And especially in Vienna we see the attempt to lend an entirely foreign character to the ordinary dwelling and tenement

building via all kinds of additions, instead of bowing to the strict requirements of utility. (18)

The issue facing Wagner and his contemporaries was to bring the lessons of 'realism' in engineering to the material of architecture. Among the models to which architects and critics turned were American and British domestic architecture of the time, which seemed to exemplify a 'realist' approach to the home, creating conditions of physical comfort, while simultaneously successfully representing an idea – 'homeliness' – through, in particular, the expression of vernacular traditions. Various attempts were made to describe the qualities that made this architecture so successful – one term introduced was *bürgerlich* (respectable, middle-class), and in other cases the English words 'cheerfulness' and 'comfort' were used. In 1896, to express this property, the critic Richard Streiter coined the word '*Sachlichkeit*', which he used as follows:

> We Germans cannot and should not imitate many characteristics of English and American dwellings because they are not suited to our circumstances, but we could learn much from them, above all and most generally to take better account of the demands for practicality [*Zweckmässigkeit*], *Sachlickeit*, comfort and hygiene in our domestic furnishings. (1896)

In a second essay the same year, Streiter equated *Sachlichkeit* with realism – 'the most perfect fulfilment of the requirements of functionality [*Zweckmässigkeit*], comfort, health' (1896b). But he went on to say that *Sachlichkeit* itself was not enough to create art, one needed also to develop the character of the built work 'from the milieu, from the qualities of the available materials, and from the environmentally and historically conditioned atmosphere of the place' (1896b). In short, *Sachlichkeit* was a precondition of art, but could not itself be art. From this point on, the term was taken up and used widely by critics concerned with the realization of a programme of modern, realist architecture, and in particular by the Berlin architect and critic Hermann Muthesius, who in his short book of 1902, *Style-Architecture and Building-Art*, as Mallgrave puts it, codified the realist agenda. In the book, Muthesius uses the full range of the realist vocabulary – '*Realismus*', '*Zweckmässigkeit*', '*bürgerlich*', and '*Sachlichkeit*' all feature. Muthesius's purpose was to identify a German equivalent for the practicality of English and American domestic architecture, and this he identified in the non-

Sitting room, 185 Queen Anne's Gate, London, R. N. Shaw, 1896. *'Sachlichkeit'*. The German critic Herman Muthesius developed a whole new vocabulary of terms – 'homeliness', *bürgerlich, Sachlichkeit, and Zweckmässigkeit* – to describe the comfort, practicality and understatedness he perceived in late nineteenth-century English domestic architecture.

monumental architecture of the eighteenth-century German middle class: 'From high aristocratic art the middle class drew an art for its own needs – simple, *sachlich*, and reasonable…' (53); the error of the nineteenth century was the attempt 'to make monuments from everyday tasks. In virtually every earlier time, at least in those in which the practice of art still retained an indigenous quality, a distinction between a monumental building-art and a simple *bürgerlich* building-art was observed' (75). Muthesius proposes that in the present, 'style' should be banned:

> In our large bridges, steamships, railway cars, bicycles and the like… we see embodied truly modern ideas and new principles of design that demand our attention. Here we notice a rigorous, one might say scientific *Sachlichkeit*, an abstention from all superficial forms of decoration, a design strictly following the purpose that the work should serve. (79)

> [when the master builder] seeks only to do justice… to those demands presented by the site, the construction, the design of the rooms, by the ordering of the windows, doors, heating and lighting sources – then we would already be on the way to that strict *Sachlichkeit* that we have come to recognize as the basic feature of modern sensibility. (81)

For Muthesius, *Sachlichkeit* was the remedy for the stylistic excesses of nineteenth-century architecture, and if observed would lead to a genuine, German architecture. From these examples of the way in which Muthesius used *Sachlichkeit*, we can see that its connotations were many: anti-ornamental, non-aristocratic, based in the vernacular, found in everyday objects, rational, scientific, sober, practical, genuine, modern – all these and more. *Sachlichkeit* continued to be widely used, and not only in architectural circles; by the 1920s it was applied to all aspects of modernist culture, becoming in Weimar Germany virtually a synonym for 'modernism'. *Die neue Sachlichkeit* was a general description, often translated as 'the new objectivity', for non-expressionist modern art.[5]

Zweckmässigkeit

At the same time as using the newly coined term *Sachlichkeit*, Muthesius also employed the much more familiar word '*Zweckmässigkeit*'. The German word '*Zweck*', literally meaning 'purpose', was used by German-speakers both to signify the fulfilment of immediate material needs – utility, but also in the sense of inner organic purpose, or destiny – the sense of 'function' used by Sullivan. (For an example of its use in this sense, see Hugo Häring's 1925 article 'Approaches to Form'.)[6] What it generally does not mean is rational construction – the idea conveyed by '*Realismus*'. Although its sense as 'utility' was long established, what is particularly interesting is the attempt in the early part of the twentieth century to lend it *aesthetic* significance. Since Kant had specifically excluded purpose from the category of the aesthetic, this implied a major shift in the understanding of what constituted art. One indication of this change is in the historian Paul Frankl's book *Principles of Architectural History*, published in 1914. Frankl analysed the process of change in architecture through four categories: spatial form, corporeal form, visible form and 'purposive intention' (*Zweckgesinnung*). Frankl made it quite clear that his concern with 'purpose', *Zweck*, had nothing to do with construction. Rather it is a historical problem – the realization that while he can analyse space in aesthetic terms, without a sense of the use for which the space was intended, it remains meaningless.

> The church in Neubirnau on Lake Constance, 1746, for example, is particularly characteristic of the spatial, corporeal, and visible forms of the third phase, but because it is now empty, it resembles a blown egg. And every space that has lost its original

Theatre, Residenz, Munich, F. Cuvilliés, 1750–53. Frankl observed that, no longer occupied by the eighteenth-century court, and deprived of its 'purpose' – or 'function' – one element of the theatre's aesthetic was lost to the modern observer.

furnishings has the same plundered, lifeless effect. …When I speak of purpose in architecture, I mean that architecture forms the fixed arena for actions of specific duration, that it provides the path for a definite sequence of events. Just as these have their logical development, so the sequence of spaces, and so too the principal and secondary passages existing within each space, have their logic. (157)

The difficulty facing the historian is that he invariably missed the actions, the events that originally took place in the building, and so can never know this aspect of its space: 'It has frequently been said that the theatre of the Residenz in Munich, filled with the court society of 1753, was not the same then as it is today. People are part of architecture' (159). The lost experience of the historical original is even more acute in buildings whose use has changed – the convent that has become a prison – and 'even when an eighteenth-century palace retains some or all of its furnishing, and tourists are guided round its rooms, it is still a mummy' (159). 'Nevertheless', Frankl continues, 'a trace of this vanished life remains behind in a building to the extent that the purpose is incarnated in the form of a space' (160). It is this remark, conjoining

'purpose' with 'space', an *Anschluss* of the two categories whose separation Kant had so carefully policed, that anticipates what happened in the 1920s.

For the early 1920s circle of left-wing Berlin architects known as the G group, stress on *Zweckmässigkeit* was an important concern.[7] By so emphasizing it, they disturbed – intentionally – the whole previously existing conception of architectural aesthetics, so that what Kant had claimed lay outside art, its purpose, was now indeed its very subject. The interrelationship of architecture and use was now presented as the primary content of architecture, not just in opposition to the 'aesthetic', but taking its place, to constitute a wholly new meaning to that concept. As the German critic Adolf Behne put it, 'When the parts of a building are arranged according to a sense of their use, when aesthetic space becomes living space … the building throws off the fetters of the old, fossilized, static order' (119–20). It is in this context that we should understand Mies van der Rohe's surprisingly categorical remarks about *Zweckmässigkeit* in a lecture given in 1924, published as 'Building Art and the Will of the Epoch':

The claim that these [contemporary engineering works] are only functional structures [*Zweckbauten*]

Mies van der Rohe, office project, crayon drawing, 1923. 'The function [*Zweck*] of a building is its actual meaning'. Mies van der Rohe's stress upon 'function' in the early 1920s was calculated to overturn the whole previous tradition of architectural aesthetics.

is irrelevant. The purpose [*Zweck*] of a building is its actual meaning. The buildings of all epochs served purposes, and quite real ones. These purposes were, however, different in type and character. The purpose was always decisive for the building. It determined the sacred or profane form. (Neumeyer, 246)

In the later 1920s, Mies distanced himself from this point of view, and in an article of 1930, 'Build Beautifully and Practically! Stop This Cold Functionality [*Zweckmässigkeit*]', took a more moderate line, critical of the 'function-proclaiming' [*zweckbehaftet*] architecture of the present, and reverted to a point of view closer to Muthesius and Berlage, that while attention to purpose was a precondition of beauty, it was not itself the means to it (Neumeyer, 307). It is worth pointing out that Mies's turnabout is easily misunderstood when these remarks are translated by the English word 'function': his use of *Zweckmässigkeit*, not *Sachlichkeit*, makes it clear that he was referring to the expression of purpose, not to the rational expression of construction – upon which he never changed his mind. The reasons why Mies rejected *Zweckmässigkeit* are at least partly to be understood in relation to the way in which this, *Sachlichkeit* and *Funktion* developed in German architectural debate in the later 1920s.

It is a book already mentioned, Adolf Behne's *Der moderne Zweckbau* (The Modern Functional Building), published in 1926, that in particular elaborated the significance of the constellation of 'function' terms. Behne's title was slightly misleading, for it is just as much about *sachlich* building as about *Zweck* building. The book's aim was to discuss the whole range of points of view that could broadly speaking be considered *sachlich*, and part of its value was to give a very reasonable, polemic-free, critical account of the development of this tendency in the twenty years since the appearance of Muthesius's *Style-Architecture Building-Art*. What is particularly interesting about Behne's book is the extensiveness of the range of work that Behne considered *sachlich*, and his criteria for distinguishing between its different manifestations. Of pre-war architects, he refers particularly to Behrens and Berlage, but he was suspicious of their lingering attachment to heroic form (of Behrens's work for AEG he preferred the Assembly Hall in Humboldt-Hain, 'more sober, more *sachlich*' [109] than the better known Turbine Hall – see also ill. p. 164); before 1914, only Frank Lloyd Wright's houses displayed 'a positive *Sachlichkeit* ... directly based on life, by returning to the most elementary functions of the

inhabitants' (100). It is this criterion, the realization of the life of the building's inhabitants, that determined the quality of *sachlich* architecture, and in this Behne was putting forward something really quite different to previous views, and one that demanded a rather novel conception of the architect's role:

> The architect can only grasp and carry out his truly artistic work, that is, the creative work, when he addresses questions of his client's attitude to life, way of living, business methods ... For this reason 'being a client' is not just buying a piece of land, some bricks, and an architect. The client must be an activity, whose taking possession of the acquired space is so definite, clear, rich, and organic that it can be transformed into the relationships of masonry walls... (120)

Of post-war work that most successfully transformed the client's will into masonry, that treated architecture as 'shaped reality', Behne counted the work of Scharoun, of Häring, of Mendelsohn and Poelzig, work now usually described as 'Expressionist'. Indeed, one of his preferred examples was Mendelsohn's Luckenwalde Hat Factory (1921–23), in which 'there develops from the most expedient organization of the production process a tight, closely fitting, spatial form, a form intended to follow and be appropriate to the functions of the business, to the production sequence, like the parts of a machine' (116). But although sympathetic to the work of these architects, particularly in their tendency towards the negation of 'form', Behne was critical of the way the results exaggerated the individuality of each commission. This excess of individuality was, in Behne's view, contrary to the *sachlich* tendency of modernity. Behne – whose ideas about modernity, like those of many of his German contemporaries, were largely formed by the sociologist Georg Simmel – saw modernity as the working-out of the conflict of the principles of uniformity and universality with the individual and personal forms of life. He was critical of the German architects whom he characterized as 'romantic functionalists', because their work would not easily adapt to future changes of use, and so lacked the generality necessary to the social, as opposed to the individual condition. On the other hand, in Le Corbusier's work he recognized an architecture based on 'the primary awareness of belonging to human society' (131), evolved out of the general and the typical. 'His thinking moves from the whole to details', he 'makes the totality his starting point' (132). Like Simmel, Behne regarded it as impossible for

Cowshed, Gut Garkau, near Lübeck, Hugo Häring, 1922–25. 'Architecture becomes shaped reality.' The critic Adolf Behne approvingly compared the wholly *sachlich* curves of Häring's architecture to the romantic arbitrariness of art nouveau, but was nonetheless critical of its excessive individuality.

whatever evolved out of the personal or the individual to carry social significance, and to be truly functional, architecture had to realize instead what made a society, namely its collective nature.

> If every building is part of a built whole, then it recognizes from its aesthetic and formal requirements certain universally valid rules, rules that do not arise from its individual functional character [*Zweckcharakter*] but from the requirements of this whole. For here, in the social sphere after all, must lie the primeval elements of the aesthetic. (137)

Behne's idea that true functionalism was the making visible not of the building's individual purpose, but its purpose considered in relation to the general, collective purposes of society, was one that he elaborated on later. Writing in 1927, he says 'Each *Sache* [thing] is a nodal point, a crossing point of relations between human being and human being …. To work *sachlich* means therefore to work socially in each discipline. To build *sachlich* means to build socially' (quoted in Bletter, 53). Behne's identification of function with the social might sound like some post-1945 notions of functionalism; but as we can see from the thinking by which he arrived at this statement, it has nothing whatsoever to do with the mechanical-biological cause-effect notions of functionality on which those ideas are primarily based, but instead comes out of a German Romantic notion of the expression of essence and idea. While some of the views about function expressed by German-speakers in the late 1920s might seem straightforwardly mechanistic – for

example Hannes Meyer's often-quoted article 'Building' that begins 'All things in this world are a product of the formula: function [*Funktion*] times economy' (95) – the foregoing discussion makes it clear that even if Meyer conceived of the house as a biological apparatus, this was by no means a generally held point of view, and was no more than an extremist's polemic within the context of a larger debate about the extended meaning of 'function'.

6. *'Function' in the English-speaking world 1930–60.*
In English-speaking countries between about 1930 and 1960, 'functional' became a catch-all term for 'modern' architecture.[8] While émigré German architects, who must have found the flatness of the English word wholly inadequate to describe the range of thinking developed in Germany during the first three decades of the century, seem generally to have avoided using the word altogether, native British and Americans used it indiscriminately. For much of this period, it was the principal term through which the polemic about modern architecture was conducted, and so it was used equally by both supporters and opponents of the new architecture. A particularly good example of its ambiguous role is in Hitchcock and Johnson's *The International Style*, the book that accompanied the 1932 New York Museum of Modern Art exhibition. Hitchcock and Johnson's purpose, which was to win approval for modernism in the United States by cleansing it of its political content, characterized as 'functional' those aspects of European modernism they wished to discard – its scientific, sociological and political claims. But in order to present modern architecture as a purely stylistic phenomenon, they had to invent a fictitious category of 'functionalist' architecture to which they consigned all work with reformist or communist tendencies. In fact, their characterization of the 'functionalists' as those to whom 'all aesthetic principles of style are ... meaningless and unreal' (35) bore so little relation to what had been happening in Europe that they succeeded in finding only one architect, Hannes Meyer, who fitted the description. And their account of the 'functionalists'' way of working was a ludicrous caricature of Behne's carefully balanced argument: 'satisfying the particular client is one important function of architecture that the European functionalists usually avoid' (92).

Entrance lobby, penthouse apartment, Highpoint II, Lubetkin and Tecton, 1938. 'Technical functionalism cannot create definite architecture.' The liberation offered by 'functionalism' was shortlived: by the late 1930s most of the first generation of European modernists were anxious not to produce anything that could be described as 'functionalist'.

In the face of attempts like this to denigrate 'function', some modern architects and critics started from around 1940 to make considerable efforts to recuperate it. It was important for modernists to be able to show that their work was not dominated by 'form' and 'aesthetics', and yet to avoid being labelled crude functionalists. The result was attempts to refine the meaning of 'function', and slant it towards particular objects. One of the first indications of this comes from Alvar Aalto, who in an article of 1940 on what was to become a major theme of the decade, 'The Humanizing of Architecture', wrote 'Technical functionalism cannot create definite architecture'. Pressure from outside the modernist mainstream, from ex-Dadaists, Surrealists, and those who were later to become Situationists, for all of whom antagonism to functionalism was one of the main ways in which they defined their position, also forced modern architects to defend functionalism. For example, Frederick Kiesler, who in 1925 had demanded 'functional architecture. Building adequate to the elasticity of the functions of life', was by 1947 a New York Surrealist, and he declared '"Modern functionalism" in architecture is dead ... exhausted in the mystique hygiene + aestheticism' (150). But for every opponent of functionality, there were a hundred supporters, concerned to sharpen it. Thus Walter Gropius (who, when he came to England in 1935 had made a point of minimizing the importance of 'functionalism') in 1954 subtly revised the received account of the Bauhaus to make it sound more humanistic: 'Functionalism was not considered a rationalist process merely. It embraced the psychological problems as well' (97). And among the younger generation of architects, 'functional' was stretched even further away from its earlier meanings: 'the word "functional" must now include so-called irrational and symbolic values', declared Alison and Peter Smithson in 1957 (1982, 82). However, while 'function' was a contested term during this period, and these examples illustrate the attempts to extend its meaning or to give it greater precision, at no point did a comprehensive theory of function emerge. The identification of a theory of form-function relations only appears after 1960, ironically, as part of the general attack upon modernism.

7. *The Form–Function Paradigm*
Implicit in the polemic about 'functional' modernism was the assumption of a relationship between buildings and the members of society inhabiting them. As the issue has come to be understood since the 1960s, the problem was one of describing either the action of the social

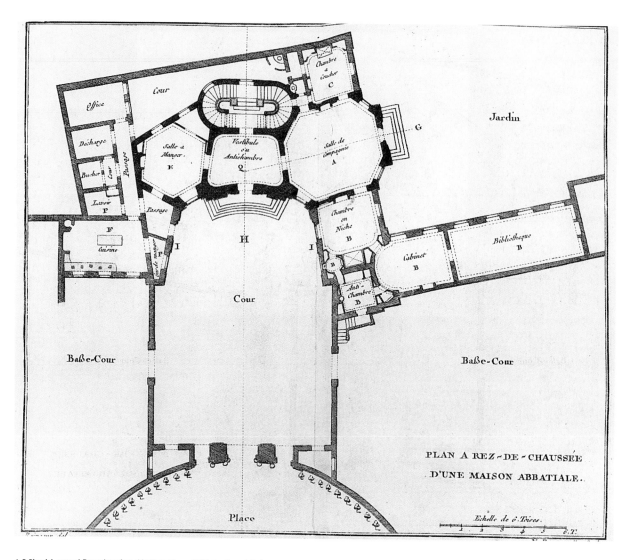

J.-F. Blondel, ground-floor plan of an abbot's residence, 1773. 'For the spirit of *convenance* to reign in a plan, every room must be situated according to its use and to the nature of the building...' Although Blondel's notion of *convenance* gave attention to use, it contained no theory about the relationship between buildings and their occupation.

environment upon the form of the building, or conversely, of the action of the buildings upon society. The difficulty in giving a historical account of this issue is that while such ideas certainly existed, and indeed were crucial to modernism, they were but poorly articulated, and rarely, if ever, referred to as 'functionalism' before the late 1920s. The historical question that we have to try and account for is the turning of 'function' from a description

of the action of a building's own mechanical forces upon its form, into a description of the action of the social environment upon buildings, and of the action of buildings upon society. Crucial to this transformation is the introduction of the concept of 'environment', which, it will be noticed, we have not been able to avoid even in describing the phenomenon we are seeking to understand.

As a first step, we might ask how far modern

Workers at Cadbury's, Bournville, Birmingham, resting in the garden adjacent to the factory, c. 1900. In the company towns created by progressive manufacturers in the late nineteenth and early twentieth centuries, there was an assumption that the improved environment would act upon the social and moral existence of the residents.

'functionalism' differs from earlier, classical theories about the relationship of people to buildings. There is no doubt that the suitability of buildings to their uses was important in the classical theory of architecture – it is part of what is covered by the Vitruvian term 'commodity'. This category underwent considerable refinement in eighteenth-century France, and the specific term developed to describe a satisfactory relationship between buildings and their occupants was 'convenance'. J.-F. Blondel writing in 1752 made convenance the first principle of architecture, explaining what he meant by it as follows: 'For the spirit of convenance to reign in a plan, each room must placed according to its use and to the nature of the building, and must have a form and a proportion relative to its purpose' (26). In English, convenance was usually translated as 'fitness': for example J. C. Loudon, a prolific English architectural writer and publisher of the 1830s, followed Blondel's classification fairly closely, rendering convenance as 'fitness for the end in view', and bienséance as 'expression of the end in view':

> An edifice may be useful, strong and durable, both in reality and in expression, without having any other beauties but those of use and truth; that is of fitness for the end in view, and of expression of the end in view; or, in familiar language, of being suitable to the use for which it was designed, and of appearing to be what it is. (1114)

The vagueness of both Blondel and Loudon as to what constitutes convenance or fitness is entirely characteristic of architectural theorists within the classical tradition who, while they considered a building's suitedness to its use as necessary, had nothing that could be called a theory about it. Moreover what Blondel, Loudon and every other writer in the classical tradition lacked was any account of the relationship between building and use – there was no suggestion that either one was in any way the outcome of the other; all that was required of the architect was to match the two together within an 'appropriate character'. Convenance became an increasingly undynamic concept that gradually collapsed into 'comfort'. (The significance of Horatio Greenough, it was suggested earlier, was his attempt to rescue convenance, or what he called 'adaptation to use', from stasis by linking it, through the German Romantic idea of 'function', to 'character'.) However, what all these classical categories lacked – and it is this lack that distinguishes them from subsequent modernist notions of 'function' – was any sense that the building fulfilled, in a mechanical sense, the requirements of the society within which it was produced. To argue this, it was necessary to have both a theory of society, and a theory of social causes and effects, and it is precisely the presence of such theories in modern functionalism that sets it apart from classical convenance.

The source of the theory of society that altered the understanding of the relation of buildings to use was, of course, biology. What biology gave to the study of society was, in addition to the notions of 'function' and of 'hierarchy', the concept of milieu, or 'environment'. What classical convenance lacked, and what modern functionalism contains, is this notion that human society exists through its interaction with the physical and social surroundings. Indeed, it cannot be stressed too strongly that without 'environment' modern functionalism would not exist (and conversely, whenever one meets the words 'environment', or the other coefficient in the functionalist equation, 'the user', one can be sure that functionalism is not far away). However, what is peculiarly difficult to establish is when, where and how this paradigm entered the discourse of architecture: we can confirm its absence in the eighteenth century, and we can be sure of its presence in the second half of the twentieth century, but what happened in between? This territory was explored by Michel Foucault in The Order of Things, and again more recently by Paul Rabinow in French Modern, but we are still very far from understanding how this ubiquitous concept, 'environment', became established within modern thought. The best we can do is to summarize some of the better-known points on the way.

Milieu or environment was a concept basic to the understanding of changes in plants and animals from Aristotle's time, but where Aristotle and his successors saw the relationship between the organism and its surroundings as harmonious and balanced, a decisive change was made in the late eighteenth century by Lamarck, who saw the relationship as basically unstable: an active organism seeks endlessly to attach itself to its milieu, which is indifferent to its survival, causing the organism to adapt. Adopted by social theorists such as Saint-Simon in the early nineteenth century, Lamarck's theory of the relationship of organisms to their environment became a highly popular model for the understanding of social process. It constitutes, for example, the theme of Honoré de Balzac's cycle of novels written in the 1830s and 1840s, La Comédie humaine; in the first, Le Père Goriot (1835), dedicated significantly to the Lamarckian naturalist Geoffroy Saint-Hilaire, the fortunes of the occupants of a Paris lodging house are described through their adaptation to their surroundings. But in the identification of its application to architecture and urbanism, we have to be more circumspect. While a writer like Viollet-le-Duc recognized the significance

The 'Penitentiary Panopticon', engraving, 1791, from drawing by Willey Reveley for Jeremy Bentham. The original model for the building as a device to regulate parts of society for the greater good of the whole.

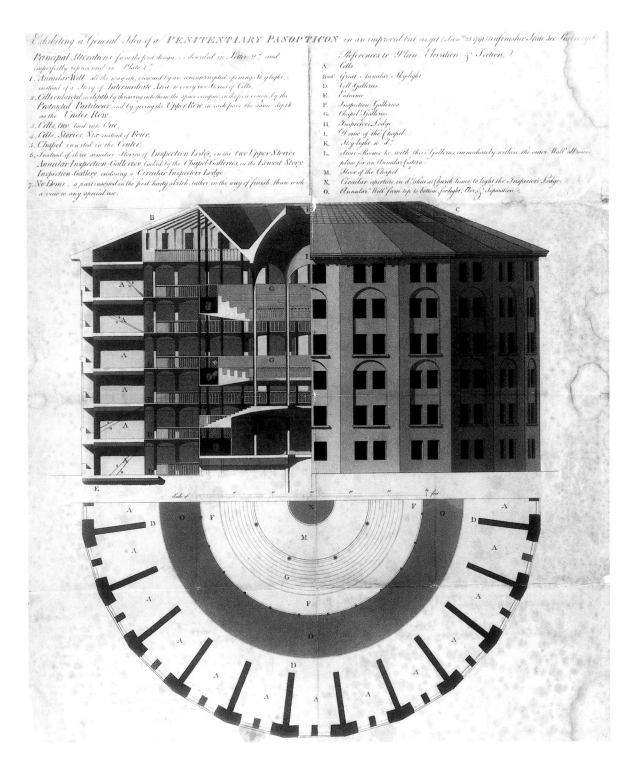

of social conditions (indeed, in Lecture X it was an important part of his argument in explaining why the same principles of construction, when applied in different times and places, produced different results) it was presented only in general terms and there was no reciprocal theory of the action of buildings upon society. Likewise, Leopold Eidlitz in 1881 insisted that 'what should be impressed on the mind of the architect is that architectural forms, like all art organisms, and like the organisms of nature, are the result of environments' (467); but again, we have here no more than a one-way process. On the other hand, by the end of the nineteenth century, in the English model villages built by reformist manufacturers for their employees (see ill. p. 189), and in the early productions of the garden city movement, there was a clear implication of the converse process, of buildings acting upon inhabitants. And in Tony Garnier's imaginary *Cité Industrielle* of 1901–4, there was a definite assumption about the relationship between the layout and buildings of the city and the way of life of the residents, consistent with the thinking of the *Musée Social* group. Rabinow, who discusses this era of French social and spatial thinking in some detail, comments that the rise of the 'social question' corresponds with the collapse of the liberal laissez-faire political economy, and the assumption by the state of responsibility for the welfare of its citizens (169); interest in *milieu*, and faith in 'functionalism' (even if it is not known as such), were part of this process, and came to the fore in the social democratic regimes of Weimar Germany, and then of post-war western Europe.

Another, rather different line of argument traces the influence of the eighteenth-century French Physiocrats, and of Scottish Political Economy. The early nineteenth-century Utilitarians, coming out of these traditions, believed in the need for the adjustment of the parts of the society for the greater good of the whole. Buildings had a part in this by bounding particular parts of the world – Bentham's Panopticon (see ill. p. 191) is the most famous example, but the same principle underlay the building of not only prisons, but also other institutional buildings, schools, hospitals and asylums. It was particularly in factories that the ideal of the harmonious action of many social units to the good of all was most comprehensively applied. But we should be careful not to assume, as there has been a tendency to do recently, that these institutions manifested an incipient modern functionalism. When the French architect L. P. Baltard commented in 1829 of English prisons that they 'function like a machine subject to the action of a single motor' (18), he was referring to the harmony of routine within the prison, not to its action

upon the inmates; and similarly it was 'the idea of a vast automaton, composed of mechanical and intellectual organs acting in uninterrupted concert' (13) that so excited Andrew Ure in 1835 about the cotton-mills of Manchester. In so far as either prisons or factories affected the moral state of those within them, early nineteenth-century contemporaries attributed this to the regimen operated in them, not to the buildings themselves; contrary to the implication of some recent historical writing, it is very hard indeed to find any evidence in the first half of the nineteenth century of a belief that behaviour could be modified by the form of a building. But this distinction is admittedly a fine one, and by the late nineteenth century, when progressive manufacturers started to extend the principle of organization within the factory to the lives of their employees outside the factory, by building model housing for them, the distinction had become imperceptible. At Bournville, for example, Cadbury's model village outside Birmingham, the expectation that the houses and their layout would of themselves bring about a change in the life and social development of the inhabitants was clear.

However, at no point did contemporaries refer to any of these developments as 'functional', nor is there a 'theory' known by any other name that can be attached to these practices. The invention of a historical narrative descriptive of the development of a practice of functionalism through these and other nineteenth-century examples has been the work of historians in the last thirty years. Similarly, the creation of anything like a theory of 'functionalism', synthesized from the disparate range of ideas and historical examples that we have discussed, only emerged in the 1960s when architects and critics started to react against modernism; modernist architects whose approach one might be tempted to describe as 'functionalist', like Sir Leslie Martin, were in general extremely careful to distance themselves from any implication of determinist thinking.

One of the first and most famous works to take issue with orthodox modernism was Aldo Rossi's highly influential book *The Architecture of the City*, first published in Italian in 1966. Rossi's critique of 'naive functionalism' is an important part of his argument that the architecture of a city consists of generic types in which its social memory is preserved; European cities consist of buildings that have largely outlasted their original purposes without any loss of meaning, making function an irrelevance for their continued existence. 'Naive functionalist classifications … presuppose that all urban artifacts are created to serve particular functions in a static way and

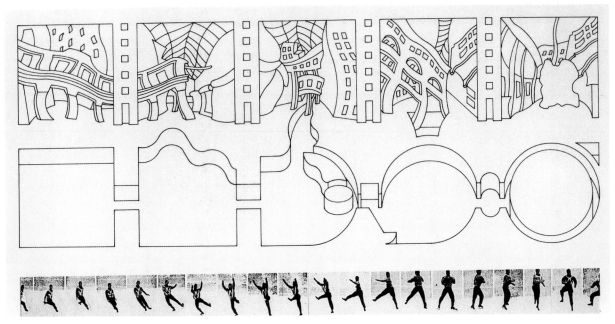

Bernard Tschumi, 'The Manhattan Transcripts', drawing, 1978. In 'The Manhattan Transcripts' there was an attempt to explore the relation of bodily and social movement to built space, *without* resorting to a notion of 'function'.

that their structure precisely coincides with the function they perform at a certain moment' (55). He continues,

> function alone is insufficient to explain the continuity of urban artifacts; if the origin of the typology of urban artifacts is simply function, this hardly accounts for the phenomenon of survival.... In reality, we frequently continue to appreciate elements whose function has been lost over time; the value of these artifacts often resides solely in their form, which is integral to the general form of the city. (60)

In fact, though, Rossi's own conception of 'functionalism' was vague: it gathers substance only in so far as it provided him with an antithesis for his notion of 'type', and thus enabled him to argue for the primacy of form.

Writing not long after Rossi, the French philosophers Henri Lefebvre and Jean Baudrillard both display a similar impulse to define 'functionalism', not so much from any interest in it for its own sake, but because it helped them to develop their arguments about modernity. For Lefebvre, in *The Production of Space*, 'functionalism' was one of the features of 'abstract space' (see p. 274), that flattened, homogenized, asphyxiating form of space

characteristic of modern capitalist societies. At one point, says Lefebvre, 'The science of space should ... be viewed as a *science of use*', but, he warns, 'It would be inexact and reductionist to define use solely in terms of function, as functionalism recommends'. 'Functionalism', he continues, 'stresses function to the point where, because each function has a specially assigned place within dominated space, the very possibility of multifunctionality is eliminated' (368–69). In place of the limitations imposed by a functional approach to use, Lefebvre was interested in the co-option of space (he gives the example of early Christianity's co-option of the Roman basilica), for it is through such processes that subjects themselves directly achieve the production of a lived, 'social space'. For Lefebvre (and he has this in common with Rossi), 'functionalism' impoverishes because it fixes use.

To Baudrillard, concerned with the tendency of capitalism to displace commodities by their sign, 'functionality is nothing other than a *system of interpretation*' (196–97): it is a wholly arbitrary (though seemingly rational) attempt to fix the meaning of objects according to their use and so protect them against the effects of fashion. 'When one ponders it, there is something unreal and almost surreal in the fact of reducing an object to its function: and it suffices to push this principle of functionality to the limit to make its absurdity emerge' (192–93). Baudrillard saw functionalism and surrealism as necessary opposites; functionalism pretended that form signified use, while 'surrealism plays upon the *distance* instituted by the functionalist calculus between the object and itself… Fusion of the skin of breasts and the folds of a dress, of toes and the leather of a shoe: surrealist imagery plays with this split by denying it' (193).

These examples will suffice to show that not just in architecture, but in a variety of disciplines, to give functionalism specific attributes was a necessary part of developing a critique of modernism, and of modernity in general. Historical study took a corresponding course. The extensive investigation of the histories of particular building types, schools, hospitals, prisons, town halls etc., from the late 1960s may be seen as part of a general attempt to find some basis for the form–function paradigm. But there are two books in particular from this period, Peter Collins's *Changing Ideals in Modern Architecture* (1965) and Philip Steadman's *The Evolution of Designs* (1979), that set out to find a pedigree for functionalist thinking in architecture, and in particular to identify the origin of the notion that environment acts upon form: both Collins and Steadman located this in Lamarck's theory of evolution. Yet although it may be perfectly true that some twentieth-century notions of function do correspond to Lamarckian ideas, there is disconcertingly little evidence, as we have already seen, that any nineteenth-century architect or architectural theorist (with the possible exceptions of Horatio Greenough and James Fergusson) ever understood 'function' to mean this, nor had any but the vaguest interest in architecture as part of the interaction between mankind and its environment. Though architectural writers were fond of the biological analogy in relation to theories of construction, there is only the most fragmentary evidence to suggest that they might have seen it as a means to develop an account of architecture as a social phenomenon. If Lamarck's theory of organism-environment is indeed the origin of the modern notion of functionalism, it seems more likely to have reached architecture via sociology than from any direct analogy with biology.

While in the period from the 1960s to the 1980s we see the assembly from the scattered fragments of earlier thinking of a more or less coherent account of functionalism – largely so as to denigrate it – in the period since there have been various attempts to

recuperate 'function'. These have come from people acting with widely different intentions. On the one hand, we have the architect Bernard Tschumi, who, introducing an anthology of his articles from the 1970s and 1980s, explained their general theme as follows: 'Opposing an over-rated notion of architectural form, they aim to reinstate the term *function* and, more particularly, to reinscribe the movement of bodies in space, together with the actions and events that take place within the social and political realm of architecture' (3–4). That Tschumi chose, in 1996, to present his earlier views in this manner was a not-so-oblique lunge at Peter Eisenman, who, for the previous twenty years, had been broadcasting pro-form, anti-function views. In fact, an examination of Tschumi's own earlier views shows him to have been a good deal more critical of 'function' than the 1996 remarks suggest. While he had consistently been interested in the realization of event, activity, movement and conflict, earlier he had regarded 'function' as inadequate to describe these. In 1983, he had written,

> By going beyond the conventional definition of 'function', the [Manhattan] Transcripts use their combined levels of investigation to address the notion of the program…. To discuss the idea of program today by no means implies a return to notions of function versus form, to cause and effect relationships between program and type or some new version of utopian positivism. On the contrary, it opens a field of research where spaces are finally confronted with what happens in them. (71–72)

Clearly in the thirteen years between these two texts, the connotations of 'function' had changed sufficiently for Tschumi to want to endorse its use.

Another apologist for 'function' is Bill Hillier, who has provided by far the most lucid investigation of the 'form–function paradigm' (the phrase is his) and its problems in *Space Is the Machine*. Hillier, though, is emphatic that it is not his purpose to dispose of 'functionalism', rather to understand what was wrong with the theory, in order to replace it with a better one. The popular perception of the failure of modern architecture quite correctly interpreted this in terms of failures of 'function'. 'The proper inference from this', writes Hillier,

> would seem to be that the functionalist theories used by the designers were wrong, but that functional

failure had confirmed the central importance of the form–function relation. There could, after all, be no functional failure if the relation between form and function were not powerful. The call should then follow for a new theory of function. Instead, there was an abandonment of functional theory in general, and an intellectual abandonment of the form–function problem at exactly the moment when functional failure had brought it dramatically to public attention. To understand this apparently perverse reaction – and also see that it was in a certain sense justified – we must understand exactly what it was that was rejected. (376)

Then, like all previous adventurers on this ground, Hillier has first to create speculatively, out of the few available scraps of evidence, the 'theory' that never was, but whose existence is necessary to know modernism. Some of the features of Hillier's account of 'form–function' theory I have already made use of in this entry, but it is worth summarizing his argument as a whole.

Hillier says that the error implicit in the form–function paradigm was the fallacious assumption that buildings can act mechanically upon the behaviour of individuals. 'How can a material object like a building impinge directly on human behaviour?' (379). Such a claim violates common sense – and it is worth recalling that no utilitarian or early nineteenth-century political economist ever claimed this. Yet nonetheless, also at a common sense level, there is a relationship of some sort between what goes on in buildings and their form. Hillier resolves this conundrum by the hypothesis that 'the relation between form and function at all levels of the built environment, from the dwelling to the city, passes through the variable of spatial configurations' (378). However, the modernist formulation of the paradigm, lacking any conception of spatial configuration, was – rightly – rejected as worthless.

The question of how such a fundamentally unsatisfactory theory of the relationship between people and buildings could ever have been given credence, Hillier attributes, as others had before, to the pervasiveness and persistence outside natural science of Lamarck's theory of evolution. Whereas in biology, Lamarck's theory of the interaction of organisms with their environments was quickly superseded by Darwin's theory of the evolution of organisms through a process of random mutations, in architecture and urbanism Lamarckianism survived. The inertia of environmental determinism, remarkable enough given its inability either to explain or to predict anything,

was, Hillier stresses, all the more remarkable in that it was founded upon a misleading and fallacious metaphor, in which the artificial environment is treated as if it were a natural environment.

> This blinds the enquirer to the most significant single fact about the built environment: that it is not simply a background to social behaviour – it is itself a social behaviour. Prior to being experienced by subjects, it is already imbued with patterns which reflect its origin in the behaviours through which it is created. (388–89)

It is, according to Hillier, the legacy of this particularly inapt metaphor in modern architecture that caused not only the form–function paradigm to be rejected, but temporarily at least caused the suspension of all interest in the relationship between buildings and their use in avant-garde architectural circles.

Looking back over the history of the concept 'function', it is clear that a practical need to talk about the relationship between buildings and the life within and around them has always existed. However, the manner of conceiving this relationship was one of the most distinctive differences between the classical tradition of architectural thought and the modernist one. If the means which modernism found to discuss this relationship was founded upon an inappropriate metaphor, which appears to be in the course of being discontinued, that does not mean that the need to discuss the relationship will also be terminated. The problem now appears to be to develop a satisfactory concept and appropriate terminology to replace 'function', or else to purge 'function' of its biological and environmental determinist connotations.

1 On Lodolí, see Rykwert, 'Lodolí on Function and Representation', 1976; and *The First Moderns*, 1980, chapter 8.

2 See Andrew, *Louis Sullivan*, 1985, 32–34, 62–67.

3 See R. H. Bletter, introduction to Behne, *The Modern Functional Building*, 1926 (trans. 1996), 47–49, for a short discussion of the relative meanings of these three words, and the difficulty of translating them.

4 See Mallgrave, 'From Realism to *Sachlichkeit*', in Mallgrave (ed.), *Otto Wagner*, 1993, 281–321.

5 See Willett, *The New Sobriety. Art and Politics in the Weimar Period*, 1978, especially 111–17, for the general meaning relative to the visual arts. And for its use in the architectural context, see Miller Lane, *Architecture and Politics in Germany*, 1968, 130–33.

6 On this article, and Häring's concept of 'functional', see Blundell-Jones, *Hugo Häring*, 1999, chapter 8, 77–89.

7 On the G group (G, standing for *Gestaltung*, was the name of their magazine), see Neumeyer, *The Artless Word*, 1991, 11–19.

8 See Benton, 'The Myth of Function' 1990, for a useful discussion of its meaning in England during the 1930s.

This [Futurist] architecture cannot be subject to any law of historical continuity. A. Sant' Elia and F. T. Marinetti, 1914, 35

History doesn't bother us very much now... I'm a traditionalist. I believe in history. P. Johnson, 1955

Ultimately, the history of architecture is the material of architecture. A. Rossi, 1982, 170

To produce meaningful architecture is not to parody history but to articulate it. D. Libeskind, 1994

When architects talk about history, it is always contentious – and frequently confusing. That 'history' became a 'problem' was primarily an effect of modernism, one of whose principal distinguishing features was widely assumed to be the elimination of everything to do with the past. However, in architecture 'history' was already an issue before the advent of modernism, and it is as well to understand its use in the nineteenth century before considering its significance in the twentieth.

'Historical architecture' in the nineteenth century
History was a nineteenth-century science: as such it not only generated a vast accumulation of knowledge about the past, but also developed various theories of the process of historical change to account for the differences between the present and the past. Art in general, and architecture specifically, had a particular place within the science of history, for not only did the experience of works of architecture allow one the illusion of passing through the veil that otherwise separated the past from the present, but the theory of art developed in the nineteenth century attributed to them an exceptional significance as historical evidence. For Hegel, the true content of art was to bring into consciousness all that the human mind was capable of, 'in forcing the human

being, educated or not, to go through the whole gamut of feelings which the human heart in its inmost and secret recesses can bear, experience and produce' (46). In this respect, art was quite unlike any other document or evidence from the past, for it admitted the observer into the very process of human consciousness itself. Thus when the Swiss art historian Jacob Burckhardt asked, in his lectures on history of 1868–71, 'In what ways does history speak through art?' (72), he took it for granted that part of the content of architecture was 'history', and not just in the sense of a record of past events, but as evidence of the human mind's capacity to reflect on its own existence.

For architects, the development of historical science in the nineteenth century could be a great benefit, for it provided them with the means to discover general principles common to the architecture of all times. Thus, Viollet-le-Duc, reflecting on the phenomenon, wrote in the article on 'Restoration' in his *Dictionnaire Raisonné*,

> Our era, and our era alone, since the beginning of recorded history, has assumed toward the past a quite exceptional attitude as far as history is concerned. Our age has wished to analyse the past, classify it, compare it, and write its complete history, following step by step the procession, the progress and the various transformations of humanity. A fact as novel as this new analytic attitude of our era cannot be dismissed, as some superficial observers have imagined, as merely some kind of temporary fashion, or whim, or weakness on our part. ...Europeans of our age have arrived at a stage in the development of human intelligence where, as they accelerate their forward pace, and perhaps precisely because they are already advancing so rapidly, they also feel a deep need to re-create the entire human past, almost as one might collect an extensive library as the basis for further future labours. ... How can anyone possibly

The Law Courts, Strand, London, G. E. Street, 1874–82. 'Historical architecture':
nineteenth-century architects were expected both to make use of the unprecedented
knowledge of past architecture available to them, and to create an architecture
that would be looked back upon by later ages as manifesting the qualities of
their own time.

hang back and continue to be blind to the meaning
of it all? (1990, 197–98)

As far as Viollet was concerned, what history offered
was the means to discredit old prejudices, and recover
forgotten principles.

But if history could be a source of strength to
architects, it also put them under an obligation; for two
reasons, 'history' became a problem. The first was that
the sheer accumulation of knowledge about previous
architecture hampered their scope for originality. As the
English architect George Gilbert Scott put it in 1857,

> The peculiar characteristic of the present day, as
> compared with former periods, is this, – that we
> are acquainted with the history of art. ... This is
> amazingly interesting to us as a matter of amusement
> and erudition, but I fear it is a hindrance rather than
> a help to us as artists. (259–60)

By the 1890s, many architects had become thoroughly
pessimistic about the chances of escaping from the burden
of an excess of historical knowledge; the American
architect Henry Van Brunt writing in 1893 made it clear
how detrimental was the expectation that architects
deploy the entire range of past architecture which history
had made known to them:

> In fact it seems sufficiently evident that, as long as we
> remember the past and what has been accomplished
> by the masters of architecture in all the ages, there
> can never again grow a distinctive style in the sense of
> what we call Greek, Roman, Christian, Mohammedan
> or Renaissance. (327)

Faced with an excess of archeological knowledge, one
of the main preoccupations of the second half of the
nineteenth century was how to avoid the inflationary
effect of the endless stylistic revivals, which could only
lead, as many architects saw, to the devaluation of the art.

The second problem 'history' presented to nineteenth-
century architects was the obligation it put them under to
create 'historical architecture'. That is to say, if previous
architecture gave access to human consciousness in the
past, then it could be assumed that the architecture
created in the nineteenth century would in turn reveal to
future generations the nature of the nineteenth-century
mind. It was this responsibility to the future that Ruskin
meant when he wrote under 'The Lamp of Memory' in
The Seven Lamps of Architecture of the duty 'to render

the architecture of the day, historical' (chapter 6 §2).
Many architects, fully aware of the responsibility they
carried, were deeply unhappy about the capacity of their
art to give an adequate account of the present, and this
issue was a major theme of architectural debate in the
second half of the century. One of the most interesting
statements of this problem appears in William Morris's
lecture 'Gothic Architecture' of 1889:

> Once for all, then, when the modern world finds that
> the eclecticism of the present is barren and fruitless,
> and that it needs and will have a style of architecture
> which, I must tell you once more, can only be as
> part of a change as wide and as deep as that which
> destroyed Feudalism; when it has come to that
> conclusion, the style of architecture will have to
> be historic in the true sense; it will not be able to
> dispense with tradition; it cannot begin at least with
> doing something quite different from anything that
> has been done before; yet whatever the form of it may
> be, the spirit of it will be sympathy with the needs
> and aspirations of its own time, not simulation of
> needs and aspirations passed away. Thus it will
> remember the history of the past, make history in
> the present, and teach history in the future. (492)

In Morris's lecture are contained both of the nineteenth-
century meanings of 'historical architecture': it could be
an architecture containing evidence of a comprehensive
knowledge of past architecture, whether in terms of
archeology or of its underlying principles; or it could
mean an architecture that would in the future be
recognized as manifesting the mind of the present.

'History' and modernism

The anti-historical attitude of the early twentieth-century
avant-garde is well known, and was to an extent an
inevitable outcome of the pressures placed upon architects
by the development of the science of history in the
nineteenth century. As Manfredo Tafuri puts it, 'In
founding anti-history and presenting their work not so
much as anti-historical, but rather as above the very
concept of historicity, the avant-gardes perform the only
legitimate act of the time' (1968, 30). Rejecting history
was their revenge on the past. Some of the groundwork
for the architects' revenge had been prepared by the
philosopher Friedrich Nietzsche, who in *The Birth of
Tragedy*, *The Uses and Disadvantages of History*, and
The Genealogy of Morals, had attacked the nineteenth-
century science of history. In fact Nietzsche did not deny

the significance of history as such, but saw the problem rather as the need to overcome history and forget it, to attain a supra-historical consciousness so as to live fully in the present;[1] but Nietzsche – and particularly his most widely read book, *The Birth of Tragedy* – could easily be interpreted as an exhortation to live without history. This is certainly the message that underlies one of the most famous anti-historical statements within modern architecture, the Futurist Architecture Manifesto of 1914, quoted at the beginning of this entry.

In the development of architectural modernism in Europe in the 1920s, opposition to architectural traditionalism, academicism, was one of the relatively few common principles on which most adherents of the new architecture could agree. At the founding meeting of *Congrès International d'Architecture Moderne* (CIAM) at La Sarraz in 1928, the first paragraph of the declaration stated that the signatories 'refuse to adopt for their works the design principles of earlier epochs and of bygone social structures'. In the educational programme set up under the direction of Walter Gropius at the Bauhaus in Germany, students were not taught the history of architecture – an unprecedented break with previous methods of architectural education. Gropius's later justification for this policy was that 'When the innocent beginner is introduced to the great achievements of the past he may be too easily discouraged from trying to create for himself' (1956, 62). And when Gropius emigrated to the USA in 1936, and was given the Chair of Architecture at Harvard, he took his anti-historicism with him, but pragmatically adapted it to the American context: capitalizing upon the myth that the strength of American culture lay in its absolute practicality and freedom from history – a myth propagated by people as diverse as Ralph Waldo Emerson and Henry Ford – Gropius justified his removal of architectural history from the core curriculum at Harvard by identifying the new architecture with New England pragmatism.[2]

On the evidence of the architecture produced by modern architects, and of events such as those just described, by the 1940s it was generally assumed that modernism was anti-historical. In fact, though, this was only a partial truth, for in another sense – the sense of William Morris – modern architecture was utterly 'historical', for it claimed to be an architecture wholly of the present, embodying the consciousness of the age, such as would be recognized in the future. It is precisely this point, to prove that modernism was a truly 'historical' architecture, that was the basis of the German historian Nikolaus Pevsner's polemical book, *Pioneers of the*

Modern Movement, published in 1936, and of Sigfried Giedion's *Space Time and Architecture* of 1941 (based upon lectures given, at Gropius's invitation, at Harvard in 1938–39). But since 'history' had by then become so pejorative a word, it would have been impossible for either of them to have described modern architecture as 'historical', even if this was what both intended. When Giedion said, 'We are looking for the reflection in architecture of the progress our own period has made towards consciousness of itself' (19), an earlier generation would immediately have recognized this objective as 'historical'. What critics like Giedion and Pevsner reviled most particularly was what they called 'historicism', a term made popular by Karl Popper's book *The Poverty of Historicism* (1957). Pevsner's own meaning of the word (entirely unrelated to Popper's) was directed against the practices of nineteenth-century architects, a dangerous return to which he saw amongst the architects of the present. As he explained in a lecture at the RIBA in London in 1961:

> Historicism is the trend to believe in the power of history to such a degree as to choke original action and replace it by action which is inspired by period precedent. … the phenomenon which interests me and which I mean by the return to historicism is the imitation of, or inspiration by, much more recent styles, styles which have never been revived. Of course, all reviving of styles of the past is a sign of weakness. (230)

'History' after modernism

Many of Pevsner's examples of 'historicism' were taken from Italy, and it is to post-war Italy that we must turn to understand 'history's' readmission to the discourse of architecture. When the editor of *Casabella Continuità*, Ernesto Rogers, wrote in 1955 'that the problem of historical continuity … is a fairly recent acquisition of architectural thought' (202), he was describing what was then a uniquely Italian phenomenon. There were several reasons for this. In the first place, pre-war Italian modernism had never been as categorically anti-history as Gropius and the majority of the CIAM membership; the *novecento* group had developed a style of architecture that was modern, but that also used traditional elements freely and explicitly, while even the more hardline modernists, the Rationalists, were surprisingly accommodating towards historical architecture.[3] And when post-war Italian modernists made use of self-evidently traditional forms and motifs, this was consistent

with their own understanding of modernism, though it scandalized the more doctrinaire Anglo-Saxon critics.[4] Secondly, the fact that all the pre-war Italian modernists had worked for the Fascist regime – and produced some outstanding work in the process – placed post-war Italian architects in a dilemma, for while they rejected Fascism, they did not want to deny the quality of the modernists' work. The solution to this evolved by Rogers was provided by the concept of *continuità*, where works of art carried significance not only by being of their time, but by speaking across time, and so transcending their immediate historical meaning. Thus Rogers wrote, 'No work is truly modern which is not genuinely rooted in tradition, while no ancient work has significance today unless it can resonate through our voice' (1954, 2). The quality of *continuità* relied upon the two related phenomena of 'history' and '*ambiente*' – or what has since become known as 'context' (see pp. 132–35). Rogers was unequivocal about the need for an architect to work with both: as he wrote in 1961, '*to understand history is essential for the formation of the architect*, since he must be able to insert his own work into the context [*preesistenze ambientali*] and to take it, dialectically, into account' (96). The importance Rogers attached to 'history' was not simply a response to the dilemma faced by architects in Italy: it was also a clearly elaborated critique of the work of the first generation of modernist architects (Gropius in particular), and of their assumption that every design problem should produce *sui generis* its own unique solution. Rogers's understanding of history was not naive; he knew his Croce, and did not fall into the error of confusing 'history' with 'the past'. 'History', a dialectic between past and present, could only be made in the present, and accordingly every new architectural work was also a historical act, that would, to a greater or lesser extent, cause all previously existing work to be re-interpreted. It is in this sense that Rogers saw architecture as 'history'.

Although Rogers, who can be held responsible for bringing 'history' into the discourse of modern architecture, made clear its importance to architects, it was far from clear what practical use the architect was to make of their knowledge. As a younger member of the *Casabella* circle, Vittorio Gregotti, wrote in 1966, 'history presents a curious instrument: its knowledge seems indispensable, yet once attained, it is not directly usable; it is a sort of corridor the full length of which one must

traverse in order to get out, but which teaches us nothing about the art of walking' (87). In two books, both by members of the Milan group, and both published in 1966, Gregotti's *Il Territorio dell'Architettura*, and Aldo Rossi's *The Architecture of the City*, their authors addressed this question of how historical knowledge might be turned to architectural use. Rossi's book, which was subsequently translated into German, French and Portuguese before finally appearing in English in 1982, is the better known, and has been primarily responsible for bringing 'history' to the attention of the English-speaking world. As an excursus on the subject of *continuità*, *The Architecture of the City* advanced upon the debate initiated by Rogers. Rossi's thesis was that functionalism (see p. 192) was inadequate as a theory of urban form, because buildings outlast their original functions and take on new ones without themselves undergoing change. Rather than a succession of changes of use, Rossi proposed that cities were constituted of 'permanences' – 'These persistencies are revealed through monuments, the physical signs of the past, as well as through the persistence of a city's basic layout and plans' (59). Historical study of the processes of urban land development and partition would reveal the permanencies of urban artefacts, and in this sense 'Cities become historical texts; in fact, to study urban phenomena without the use of history is unimaginable' (128). To a generation trained to believe that scientific methods were the only way to analyse cities, these suggestions, coming from a member of the architectural avant-garde were, to say the least, controversial.

If part of what Rossi meant by 'history' was the process of urban development manifested in the permanence of surviving artefacts, the other part was contained in the notion of 'collective memory', which he derived from French social geographers. Their concern had been to explain what made each place different: economic factors alone did not account for this, since the same conditions could apply to many places which were nevertheless different, so to explain the uniqueness of places they postulated that each place had its own 'being', a collective memory of which was expressed in its built form. Rossi adopted this idea: 'every city possesses a personal soul formed of old traditions and living feelings as well as unresolved aspirations' (162). The originality of Rossi's argument was to suggest that mediating between these two conceptions of the history of cities, as 'permanencies' and 'collective memory', there existed works of architecture which not only linked them, but also provided the only concrete evidence through which

Bottega d'Erasmo, Turin, Gabetti and Isola, 1953–56. 'All reviving of styles of the past is a sign of weakness': Nikolaus Pevsner singled out Gabetti and Isola's controversial Bottega d'Erasmo, for its 'historicism'.

Gordon Wu Hall, Princeton University, R. Venturi, 1984. (On the left of the picture is an older university building from the 1920s.) 'Guided... by precedent, thoughtfully considered': Venturi's 'history' was neither as radical, nor as ambitious as the sense given to it by the Italians.

to study and verify *continuità*. 'The value of history seen as collective memory, as the relationship of the collective to its place, is that it helps us to grasp the significance of the urban structure, its individuality, and its architecture which is the form of this individuality' (131). Ultimately Rossi's purpose was to make *continuità* a more rigorous concept; compared to the speculativeness and generality of Rogers, Rossi suggested how it could be researched, and actively contribute to new architecture.

If Rossi's *The Architecture of the City* was the book that on the European continent most particularly made 'history' a subject of serious attention for architects, in the United States and the English-speaking world, that role was provided by Robert Venturi's *Complexity and Contradiction in Architecture*. Published the same year, 1966, and like Rossi's book a critique of orthodox modernism, Venturi's book was otherwise utterly different, especially in what he meant by 'history'. While 'function' was Rossi's object of attack, Venturi's was 'form', specifically its oversimplification in modern architecture. Through an astonishing range of historical examples, Venturi argued the case for complex and ambiguous forms. He justified his presentation of an argument about contemporary architecture through historical examples by quoting T. S. Eliot: the implication was that if literary modernism could acknowledge its dependence upon tradition, so should architectural modernism – and by so doing its meaning would be much enriched. The sense in which Venturi used 'history' was far more modest, and indeed traditional, than Rossi's meaning of it: when Venturi wrote 'As an architect I try to be guided not by habit but by a conscious sense of the past – by precedent, thoughtfully considered' (13), this was an aim that would have been familiar to and approved of by most nineteenth-century architects. Venturi's 'history' consists of precedents, analysed from the point of view of modernist principles of composition. For postmodern architects, upon whom his influence was considerable, the principal lesson of Venturi's writings was that historical precedents enriched meaning, and for a significant number of postmodern architects this became 'history's' main attraction. The American postmodernist Robert Stern could not have summed this up more elegantly when he wrote in 1977, 'the history of buildings is the history of meaning in architecture' (275).

In 1955, any self-respecting modern architect – outside Italy – would have considered 'history' irrelevant; his or her work, if it was good, was above history. Philip Johnson, in a lecture given that year, nicely summarized:

The most important crutch in recent times is not valid now: the *Crutch of History*. In the old days you could always rely on books. You could say, 'What do you mean you don't like my tower? There it is in Wren'. Or, 'They did that on the Subtreasury Building – why can't I do it?' History doesn't bother us very much now. (190)

But by the early 1970s, everything had changed, and everyone wanted to show that their work had 'history'. In most cases, this meant saying that through the employment of recognizable motifs, it had a 'meaning'. What exactly architects understood by 'history' was often far from certain: when, for example, Aldo Rossi remarked of the early Modern Movement 'it seems to me that history is present in the best of its products' (1982, 14), one wonders what this mysterious ingredient was – yet in a way it does not really matter, for we know that all Rossi was trying to do was to make sure that the pioneer modernists, despite having disavowed history and tradition, could still be included in the canon of great architecture.

Listening to many an architect talk about 'history' in the last two decades, one could be forgiven for imagining that one was hearing an eighteenth-century architect talking about 'nature'. The same sense of an indefinite, given category which serves simply to situate the work and provide it with some of its characteristics, is common to both; and just as their predecessors in the eighteenth century took little interest in the processes through which nature might be constituted, so in general late twentieth-century architects showed a remarkable lack of curiosity about what had been going on within the discipline of history itself. For amongst historians during this century, the nineteenth-century notion of history as an exact science capable of definitive truths was challenged, and largely rejected. It became generally accepted that what history did was to create interpretations of past events that legitimated particular ideologies, and served the interests of particular groups of people, and much of historians' attention was turned to the examination of the processes by which history was made. Whereas amongst historians, 'history' was understood to be a product of the mind of the present, ordering and interpreting material from the past, amongst architects there lingered a belief that past works of architecture were themselves 'history'. How a work of architecture – made in the past – could ever *be* 'history' – made in the present – is a contradiction that not many architects bothered about. This confusion is nowhere better exemplified than in 'heritage': objects

and buildings preserved from the past are offered as 'history' itself, while the partiality and interestedness of the procedures that has rendered them as history is obscured under the satisfyingly concrete wholeness which they present to our eyes.

One of the few architects to have learnt the lessons of the twentieth-century philosophy of history, and to have applied them in his work, is Daniel Libeskind. Libeskind is well aware that history is not a given, fixed category, but exists only by virtue of being made, and remade in the present. As he wrote in 1994, 'An architect working in an open society has the responsibility to struggle with the conflicting interpretations of history expressed within the city. To produce meaningful architecture is not to parody history, but to articulate it; not to erase history, but to deal with it'. In a succession of commissions for museums (Berlin, Osnabrück, Victoria and Albert Museum London), projects whose very nature invites reflection on the processes of history, Libeskind has shown an acute understanding of the issue, particularly so in the Jewish Museum in Berlin, where he has tried to make the problematic nature of Jewish history in post-war Germany integral to the theme of the building. 'The museum', he said in a lecture at the Architectural Association in London in 1997, 'is intended to be not easy to organize, because history is not like that'. The museum shows that history is not over – and that it is we in the present who are ultimately accountable for it, even if the events we describe were performed by people in the past. In the understanding of 'history' revealed by the Jewish Museum, the essentially decorative view of history propagated by postmodernism has been left far behind.

1 On Nietzsche's ideas about history, see White, *Metahistory*, 1973, chapter 9.
2 See W. Nerdinger, 'From Bauhaus to Harvard: Walter Gropius and the Use of History' in G. Wright and J. Parks (eds), *The History of History in American Schools of Architecture*, 1990, 89–98.
3 See Doordan, *Building Modern Italy*, 1988, especially 74*ff*.
4 On the controversy created by the 'neo-Liberty' revival and the Torre Velasca in Milan, see Tafuri, *History of Italian Architecture, 1944–1985*, chapter 4.

Interior, Jewish Museum, Berlin, D. Libeskind, 1989–98. Libeskind's museums acknowledge that history, about the past, is made in the present – and emphasize the difficulties involved.

Memory

We may live without her [architecture], and worship
without her, but we cannot remember without her.
J. Ruskin, 1849, chapter VI, §II

And for a long time we have been speaking not of
history, but of memory. G. C. Argan, 1979, 37

...in the city, memory begins where history ends.
P. Eisenman, introduction to Rossi, 1982, 11

The creation of buildings for commemoration is one
of the oldest purposes of architecture. The expectation
that works of architecture can prolong collective social
memory of persons or events beyond the mental
recollections of individuals who knew or witnessed them
at first hand has been a regular feature of architecture
since antiquity, and we have many surviving examples
of what may be called 'intentional monuments', that is
works built to commemorate specific people or events.
Yet it has to be said that buildings have been an
unreliable means of prolonging memory; all too often the
object has survived, but who or what it commemorated
has been forgotten. For whom was the Roman
mausoleum at Glanum built? Even if the name is known,
it hardly matters, for we know nothing else about him.
And what did the arch at Orange commemorate?
A battle, a victory, certainly, but more than that nothing
is remembered. Despite the confidence placed in the
power of monuments to resist the fragility of human
memory, their record of success has been mediocre.

The modern interest in 'memory' and architecture
has been less concerned with intentional monuments than
with the part played by memory in the perception of all
works of architecture, whether intentional or not. The
notion that memory might be a necessary part of the
experience of buildings has reappeared in at least three
different forms since the eighteenth century, each time
serving a different purpose; it is one of the concepts most

symptomatic of general changes in architectural thought.
Never has this been more so than in its latest phase, when
after modernism's supposed annihilation of memory, the
1970s and 1980s saw a veritable flood of memory,
putting every corner of the city at risk of inundation.

'Memory' as part of the apprehension of architecture
is less straightforward than some recent discussions might
lead one to suppose. In the first place, it is far from
certain in what sense memory constitutes part of the
aesthetic of architecture, and indeed there is some doubt
as to whether it even belongs to it at all.[1] Secondly, the
difference between 'history' and 'memory' is not always
clear: in recent discussions the two often appear
synonymous. Thirdly, in each of its three historical
phases 'memory' has had a different meaning, and it
would be quite wrong to assume that Peter Eisenman in
the twentieth century is talking about the same thing as
John Ruskin in the nineteenth, or Horace Walpole in the
eighteenth. Fourthly, and finally, part of the reason for
the fascination of architects and urbanists with 'memory',
particularly in its postmodern phase, has to do with the
regularity with which since antiquity philosophers and
psychologists have used architecture and cities as
metaphors in their efforts to describe the phenomenon
of the mental process of memory. Even if the point of
these analogies has frequently been to draw attention
to the *unlikeness* of memory to a city, the temptation to
assume that memory and architecture are one of a kind
has proved irresistible. To take a single example of this,
Sigmund Freud in *Civilization and Its Discontents* used
Rome to illustrate the preservation of accumulated
material in the mind, but went on to stress how otherwise
unsuited this image was for a comparison with the mental
organism (6–8). This has not inhibited much talk about
Rome as an 'eternal city' and locus of memory.[2] But what
most particularly led to an assumed connection between
buildings and memory was the rediscovery by the
historian Frances Yates in her book *The Art of Memory*

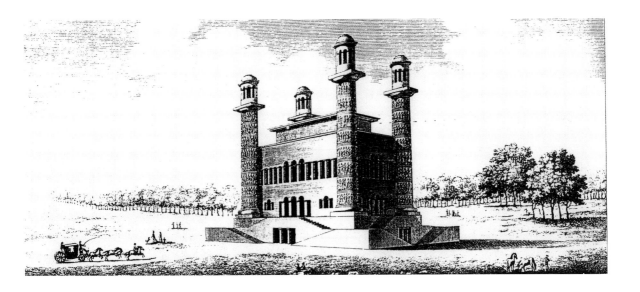

(above) C.-N. Ledoux, 'Temple de Mémoire'. Ledoux's 'Temple of Memory', designed for his ideal city, differentiated within a specific building a purpose that since the Renaissance has been regarded as generic to all architecture.

(below) Roman Mausoleum, Glanum, St Rémy, Provence, France, c. 30 BC. Whoever the mausoleum commemorated has long since been forgotten.

(1966) of the classical mnemonic technique of the memory palace or theatre as a means of memorizing long orations: by locating each part of the argument in a room or particular place within an imaginary building, the speaker could recall the discourse step by step. Although Frances Yates's book was widely read in architectural circles, and certainly influential, it was no more than the account of the history of a particular mnemonic technique, and itself hardly justified the more far-fetched claims made on its authority for architecture as itself an 'art of memory'. These and other complications need to be taken into account in thinking about 'memory' as a category of architecture.

Let us consider the three historical phases of 'memory'. Its first manifestation as an element in the aesthetic of architecture, and of the other arts, was an eighteenth-century development. Its appearance then is generally attributed to its seeming power to resist the fragmentation caused by the expansion of knowledge, and the perceived loss of the wholeness of culture and civilization. The cultivation of 'memory' as an aspect of the response to works of art held out the hope of some form of reparation.[3] Within the specific field of architecture, the particular value of 'memory' was that it established the liberty of the subject: whereas hitherto

Memory Palace, from Robert Fludd, Ars Memoriae, 1617. The rediscovery by Frances Yates of the memory palaces of mediaeval and Renaissance oratory contributed to a revival of interest in the relation between buildings and memory.

the qualities of architecture had been judged by rules of proportion and so on laid down by authority, the value accorded to memory gave every individual the freedom to derive their own pleasure from the work. In so far as the discovery of 'memory' had a philosophical origin, it has generally been identified with the account of mental processes put forward by John Locke in his *Essay on Human Understanding* (1690), and indeed the perceptual liberty it granted to the individual was consistent with the political freedoms Locke claimed for the citizen in his other writings. Locke's account of perception was popularized by Joseph Addison in a series of articles on 'The Pleasures of the Imagination' published in 1712 in the *Spectator* (nos 411–21). In the sixth of these articles, Addison proposed that pleasure derives not just from sight and the other senses, but from the contemplation

of what is imaginary – 'this secondary pleasure of the imagination proceeds from that action of the mind, which compares the ideas arising from the original objects, with the ideas that we receive from the statue, picture, description, or sound that represents them' (no. 416). The power of works of art, suggests Addison, derives from the association of ideas that they evoke. 'Our imagination … leads us unexpectedly into cities or theatres, plains or meadows' far removed from those presented to perception; and furthermore 'when the fancy thus reflects on the scenes that have past in it formerly, those, which were at first pleasant to behold, appear more so upon reflection, and that the memory heightens the delightfulness of the original' (no. 417). Addison himself said nothing about the association of ideas, and of memory, in relation to architecture. Apart from literature,

Temple of Liberty, Stowe, Buckinghamshire, England, James Gibbs, 1741. The building evoked specific – if dormant – memories of Anglo-Saxon liberty.

the art where his theory found its readiest application in eighteenth-century Britain was landscape gardening. Whereas in the first half of the century, the purpose of garden buildings, ruins and statues tended towards the evocation of specific memories and associations (those at Stowe, for instance, inspired thoughts of British history and constitutional liberty), a marked change took place in the latter part of the century, and there was a shift to an altogether less prescriptive form of association. This change was described by Thomas Whately in his *Observations on Modern Gardening* (1770) as a move away from an emblematic to an expressive mode of association, in which natural scenery, without any specific referent, would in every individual evoke particular trains of ideas which would themselves become the cause of aesthetic pleasure (see pp. 123–24).

In late eighteenth-century British aesthetics, the relation between three distinct levels of mental activity – the direct perception of objects, memory, and imagination – became a major theme. As Lord Kames in his *Elements of Criticism* put it, 'The world we inhabit is replete with things no less remarkable for their variety than their number: these ... furnish the mind with many perceptions; which, joined with ideas of memory, of imagination, and of reflection, form a complete train that has not a gap or interval' (vol. 1, 275). Following Kames, the argument developed by Archibald Alison and Richard Payne Knight was that the more extended and varied the train of associated thoughts, the richer the aesthetic sensation. As Alison explained in the *Essays on the Nature and Principles of Taste* (1790), 'the more that our ideas are increased, or our conceptions extended upon any subject,

James Russel, *British Connoisseurs in Rome*, oil painting c. 1750. The 'association of ideas' restricted aesthetic sensation to those sufficiently privileged to have acquired a stock of appropriate memories.

the greater the number of associations we connect with it, the stronger is the emotion of sublimity or beauty we receive from it' (vol. I, 37). Seen in these terms, memory offered a means to what Payne Knight in *An Analytical Enquiry into the Principles of Taste* (1805) called 'improved perception': it enhanced the range of ideas an object was capable of evoking. Payne Knight explained:

> As all the pleasures of the intellect arise from the association of ideas, the more the materials of association are multiplied, the more will the sphere of these pleasures be enlarged. To a mind richly stored, almost every object of nature or art, that presents

itself to the senses, either excites fresh trains and combinations of ideas, or vivifies or strengthens those which existed before. (143)

As a theory of aesthetic reception, the association of ideas had some fairly severe drawbacks, which at least partly explain its demise. In the first place, it relied heavily upon *individual* taste and judgment, and largely restricted aesthetic pleasure to those with the benefits of a liberal education, for only they enjoyed a sufficient stock of memories: as Alison explained in relation to classical architecture, 'The common people, undoubtedly, feel a very inferior Emotion of Beauty from such objects, to that which is felt by men of liberal education, because they have none of those Associations which modern education so early connects with them' (vol. II, 160). An account of the aesthetic which relied so heavily upon the accidents of a particular individual's experience lacked conviction as general theory. The second drawback of the association of ideas was that it located the aesthetic as lying entirely within the mental processes of the subject. The pleasures derive from the trains of thought evoked by the object – the ideas, as Payne Knight put it, 'associating themselves in our memories of their own accord' (136), not by the encounter with the object. Within the philosophy of aesthetics developed in Germany, principally by Kant, the aesthetic was concerned with what lay *between* the apprehension of the object and the emotions felt by the viewing subject. An account of the aesthetic that concerned itself solely with the interior of the mind, and regarded that as beyond conscious control, was of little interest to philosophers in this tradition, and it may be for this reason that 'memory' and 'association' occupied no place at all in Kant's philosophy, nor in German nineteenth-century philosophical aesthetics. And even in Britain, 'memory' and the association of ideas rapidly lost its appeal: as Coleridge, writing in 1817, remarked, 'The principle [of association] is too vague for practical guidance – Association in philosophy is like the term stimulus in medicine: explaining everything it explains nothing; and above all leaves itself unexplained' (vol. II, 222).

If the eighteenth-century conceptions of 'memory' and of 'association of ideas' may strike us, as they struck Coleridge, as defective, we should not forget that their principal purpose had been to undermine the authority of traditional rules of order, proportion and ornament. Once this end had been achieved, they had no further value, and we could afford to forget about them altogether were it not that they provided the basis for the second phase of

architectural 'memory', developed in the mid-nineteenth century by John Ruskin. It was Ruskin's achievement to take up the old, eighteenth-century theory of association, and to turn it into an altogether more durable and robust concept. 'The Lamp of Memory' was the sixth of *The Seven Lamps of Architecture* (1849), and here Ruskin wrote 'there are but two strong conquerors of the forgetfulness of men, Poetry and Architecture'. Of the two, architecture was superior, because it presented 'not only what men have thought and felt, but what their hands have handled, and their strength wrought, and their eyes beheld' (chapter VI, §ii). In other words, what architecture alone offered was the memory of human work, both manual and mental. The memories triggered by the sight of ancient architecture were not the generalized themes of ancient virtues and liberties, or of recollections of Claudian landscapes, but an exact sense of the nature of the work and conditions of labour under which the buildings had been executed. The differences between Ruskin's conception of 'memory' and that of his eighteenth-century predecessors are considerable. First of all, what is remembered is not an endless chain of mental imaginings, but is exact and determinate: work. Secondly, the memory is not individual, but social and collective: like its literature and its poetry, its architecture is one of the means by which a nation constitutes its identity through shared memories. And thirdly, 'memory' relates not just to the past, but is an obligation that the present has towards the future:

> when we build, let us think that we build for ever. Let it not be for present delight, not for present use alone; let it be such work as our descendants will thank us for, and let us think, as we lay stone upon stone, that a time is to come when those stones will be held sacred because our hands have touched them, and that men will say as they look upon the labour and wrought substance of them, 'See! this our fathers did for us.' (chapter VI, §x)

Ruskin's notion of 'memory' was closely related to his conception of 'history', and nothing would be gained by trying to distinguish between the two. The immediate impact of both within Ruskin's own time was primarily upon the preservation of ancient buildings. The significance of Ruskin's argument was to stress that like poetry, architecture belonged not to anyone in particular, or just to the present, but to all time; the present has only a life interest in it, and its obligation is to protect it for posterity. Ruskin asserts:

it is again no question of expediency or feeling whether we shall preserve the buildings of past time or not. *We have no right whatever to touch them.* They are not ours. They belong partly to those who built them, and partly to all the generations of mankind who are to follow us. (chapter VI, §xx)

The most immediate influence of Ruskin's notion of memory was not so much upon new architecture, but upon the development of a conservation movement in Britain, through William Morris and the Society for the Protection of Ancient Buildings, founded in 1877. (Ruskin's impact upon Morris was not limited to architectural thinking alone though, and Morris was to develop 'memory' also as a substantial element of his political thought.) In Ruskin's later writings on architecture, *St Mark's Rest* and *The Bible of Amiens* (1883), 'memory' continued to be important, but in a different, more generalized sense. In these books, certain buildings provide access to the entire extent of human history, mythology and religion; not so much the embodiment of memory, they are the means of triggering human memory, and of relating it to understanding.

An interesting refinement of Ruskin's ideas about the memorial significance of ancient buildings was to appear a little later in an essay by the Austrian art historian Alois Riegl. Written in 1903 as part of an Austro-Hungarian government proposal for the protection of old buildings, Riegl set out to question what exactly people valued in them. In doing so, he distinguished between 'historic-value', that is to say the evidence the work presented of a particular historical moment, and 'age-value', or a generalized sense of the passage of time, and concluded that as far as the majority were concerned, it was age-value that they sought in ancient buildings.

By the time Riegl was writing his essay, 'memory' was already under attack. Nietzsche's famous assault on memory and celebration of forgetfulness in his essay 'On the Uses and Disadvantages of History' appeared in 1874. Here Nietzsche asserted 'it is possible to live almost without memory ... but it is altogether impossible to *live* at all without forgetting' (62). Whether or not directly acknowledged, Nietzsche's insistence upon the erasure of history, and of memory, was to be one of the most recurrent themes of modernist architecture, and of modernist painting and sculpture.

Within the discourse of modern architecture, 'memory' was rarely mentioned – modernists did not even negate memory, they simply ignored it. For modern

architecture – as for modern art – everything that took away from the immanence of the work, that lay outside the immediate encounter with it, was to be resisted, and foremost among those properties that threatened the work was memory. Characteristic of this thinking is Geoffrey Scott's *The Architecture of Humanism* (1914), a work which drew heavily upon the German tradition of philosophical aesthetics. In his attack upon 'The Romantic Fallacy', Scott writes that 'romanticism is not favourable to plastic form. Romanticism is too much concerned with the vague and the remembered to find its natural expression in the wholly concrete' (39). The emphasis and value of literature, the medium of romanticism, lie

> chiefly in the significance, the meaning and the associations of the sounds which constitute its direct material. Architecture, conversely, is an art which chiefly affects us by direct appeal. Its emphasis and its value lie chiefly in material and in that abstract disposition of material which we call form ... fundamentally, the language of the two arts is distinct and even opposite. (60–61)

But if within the plastic arts of painting, sculpture and architecture memory was rejected, in one form of modernist art – literature – it was paramount. Indeed, for some critics of modernist literature, 'memory' *was* its mode, being the faculty most particularly engaged in the acts of both writing and of reading. Nowhere was this more evident than in Marcel Proust's *A la Recherche du temps perdu* – though what made this book so remarkable was, as Walter Benjamin put it, that it was as much a 'work of forgetting', 'in which remembrance is the woof and forgetting is the warp' (204). Proust's awareness that without forgetting there can be no memory, and that the interest of memory lies in its dialectic with forgetting, is important, and is his point of contact with the other great early twentieth-century student of memory, Sigmund Freud. But Proust is an author partic-ularly interesting in the context of memory and architecture, for he had been an enthusiastic reader of Ruskin, particularly of Ruskin's architectural writing, and indeed had translated *The Bible of Amiens* into French. Proust fully understood Ruskin's notion of a relationship between buildings, literature and memory, and made it his own – he even went so far as to describe the construction

Sant 'Elia, *casa gradinante* for *La Città Nuova*, drawing, 1914. The Futurists, in common with most modernists, rejected 'memory' as a component of aesthetic perception.

Vietnam Memorial, Washington, D.C., Maya Lin, 1982. The popular acclaim for the Vietnam Memorial and other twentieth-century war memorials drew attention to how far modern architecture, by denying memory, had cut itself off from a reservoir of emotive meaning.

of *A la Recherche du temps perdu* as that of a cathedral.[4] However, the notion of memory Proust was to develop was rather different from Ruskin's; whereas for Ruskin architecture was memory, Proust was emphatic that memory had an unstable and elusive relationship to objects, including architecture. As he put it in *Swann's Way*,

> It is a labour in vain to recapture [our own past]: all the efforts of our intellect must prove futile. The past is hidden somewhere outside the realm, beyond the reach of intellect, in some material object (or in the sensation which that material object will give us), of which we have no inkling. And it depends on chance

whether we come upon this object before we ourselves must die. (vol. I, 51)

For Proust, while buildings could trigger involuntary memories, the process was haphazard and unreliable. One can say, then, that while 'memory' was important in modernist aesthetics, its value came from a recognition of the fundamental unlikeness and discontinuity between the physical world of objects, and architecture, and the mental world of memory. This distinction was one that had been absent from the eighteenth- and nineteenth-century conceptions of architectural memory, and, as we shall see, was largely ignored in its late twentieth-century version.

Let us turn now to the third phase of architectural memory, that belonging to the last third of the twentieth century. To grasp the particularities of this phase, some context is necessary. The twentieth century has, in general, been obsessed with memory in a way that no period of history ever was before. Its colossal investment in museums, archives, historical study and heritage programmes are the symptoms of a culture that appears terrified of forgetting. Nowhere has this been more apparent in the astonishing commercial success of that prosthetic memory, the personal computer. Also in the twentieth century there has developed a distinction between 'history' and 'memory', perhaps most persuasively articulated by the German critic Walter Benjamin. For Benjamin, 'history' – a nineteenth-century science – created distorted versions of events that served the interests of dominant power; 'memory', through which fragments of the past entered the present explosively and uncontrollably, was the principal means by which the individual could resist the hegemony of history.

In one particular activity, unprecedented in any previous period of history, Western civilization has shown an extraordinary confidence in the capacity of material objects to resist the decay of memory: that is in the building of war memorials to the dead of its many wars. Memorials commemorating the name of every dead soldier, like those at Thiepval in France, or Monte Grappa in Italy, or more recently the Vietnam memorial in Washington, D.C., have no earlier historical counterparts. Whatever the reasons for these artefacts, whatever purposes they serve, these many memorials rest on the assumptions that forgetting, individually or collectively, these many dead is one of the greatest dangers for modern society; and they demonstrate an unshakeable confidence in the power of physical objects to preserve memory.[5]

In all these various commemorative activities and productions, modern architecture, and modern art, have taken little part, and have been merely onlookers. And when architects, or artists, have tried to involve themselves in these memory-prolonging activities, they have – like Le Corbusier over the Mundaneum project (see ill. p. 166) – quickly attracted hostile criticism.[6] The denial of memory within modernist aesthetics made it virtually impossible for anyone claiming to be a modernist to associate themselves with memorial or commemorative works. And the denigration of memory was reinforced from outside architecture and fine art by philosophy – so for example, the second chapter of Maurice Merleau-Ponty's *Phenomenology of Perception* is an extended attack upon associationism, claiming that memory has no part in perception.

On the other hand, with so much memorial activity going on in Western societies, by the 1960s architects found themselves gazing longingly at this rich reservoir of emotive meaning (and profitable work), from which, so it seemed, they had wilfully cut themselves off. Against the blankness and 'silence' of late modernist architecture, a re-engagement with 'memory' looked particularly appealing, and a strategy that certain literary works of the time seemed to support. The best known was the French philosopher Gaston Bachelard's *The Poetics of Space* (1958), a widely read book, whose true theme might be more accurately described as 'memory' rather than 'space'. Bachelard's aim was to 'show that the house is one of the greatest powers of integration for the thoughts, memories and dreams of mankind' (6). But if this seemed to give *carte blanche* to architects to concern themselves with 'memory', the difficulty was that the memory with which Bachelard was concerned was purely mental, and as he was careful to explain, did not lend itself easily to description, let alone physical construction (13). Again we come up against the fact that while an individual's memories may be triggered by buildings, or even take on a spatial character, built works of architecture are not, as both Freud, and Proust had recognized, a satisfactory analogue for the mental world of memory. The inherent unlikeness of memory and architecture, already established in the early twentieth century, is implicit in Bachelard's book. And more recently, the relation between the two has been pulled even further apart, in the work of the French philosopher Michel de Certeau, for whom 'memory is a sort of anti-museum: it is not localizable' (108). The particular force of memory comes 'from its very capacity to be altered – unmoored, mobile, lacking any fixed position ... Memory is in decay when it is no

longer capable of this alteration'. And he continues, 'Memory comes from somewhere else, it is outside of itself, it moves things about. The tactics of its art are related to what it is, and to its disquieting familiarity' (86–87). Seen in de Certeau's terms, a determinate relationship between buildings and memory looks even less plausible than it did to Proust.

The reintroduction of memory into architectural discourse in the late twentieth century occurred for the relatively straightforward purpose of challenging modernist orthodoxy. As one of those responsible, the German architect O. M. Ungers explained:

> Memory as a bearer of cultural and historical values has been consciously denied and ignored by the Neues Bauen. The anonymity of the functionally correct organization of the environment has asserted itself over collective memory. Historically shaped places and historical peculiarities have been sacrificed on the altar of the functional constraints of *Zweckrationalismus* … Hardly any city remains that corresponds to its historical image. (75–77)

Of those associated with the re-invention of memory, by far the best known, and most discussed (because, amongst other things, of his erratic use of the concept) was the Italian architect Aldo Rossi. In his book *The Architecture of the City* (1966), as part of his critique of orthodox modernism, he suggested that the way to develop new forms of urban architecture was to study those already existing. Not only did the buildings of every existing city reveal a pattern of *permanences* specific to it, but at a deeper level, these characterized its 'collective memory'. As Rossi put it,

> the city itself is the collective memory of its people, and like memory it is associated with objects and places. The city is the *locus* of the collective memory. This relationship between the *locus* and the citizenry then becomes the city's predominant image, both of architecture and of landscape, and as certain artifacts become part of its memory, new ones emerge. In this entirely positive sense great ideas flow through the history of the city and give shape to it. (130)

Summarizing his argument, he wrote 'Memory … is the consciousness of the city' (131).

Housing, Lutzowplatz, Berlin, O. M. Ungers, 1982–84. Ungers's projects from the early 1980s consciously evoked 'memories' of a now lost city.

Rossi's purpose in introducing 'memory' was to find a rationale other than 'functionalism' for modern architecture, a concern common to the circle of architects associated with the Milan journal *Casabella Continuità* in the 1950s and early 1960s.[7] The message of Rossi's argument was that whoever undertook to build in a city would not only change the physical fabric of the city, but more audaciously, alter the collective memory of its inhabitants. Rossi had derived this idea not from any of the precedents that we have so far described, but from, in particular, two pre-war French writers, one a historian, Marcel Poëte, the other a sociologist, Maurice Halbwachs. From Poëte, Rossi derived the idea that the phenomenon of a city cannot adequately be investigated through its functional relations, in the manner attempted by the Chicago sociologists, but only through the record of its past, as manifested in the evidence of the present. It was Poëte who gave to Rossi the idea of 'permanencies', that the very essence of a city's complexity lay in the persistence through time of certain indelible features. The other idea, that the inhabitants of a city shared a collective memory manifested in the buildings of the city, Rossi derived from the sociologist, Maurice Halbwachs. Halbwachs had been a pupil of Emil Durkheim, and it is from Durkheim's theory of society that Halbwachs's 'collective memory', with its shortcomings, originates. Briefly, Durkheim had proposed that society is known to exist through its empirically verifiable institutions – religion, government, culture, etc. – but that what binds it together is the collective consciousness that its members share of being part of that society. The alienation and *anomie* characteristic of modern societies comes about through the decay of the collective consciousness. Maurice Halbwachs's studies of French workers in the 1920s and 1930s claimed that their necessary engagement with matter in the course of their work caused them to lose their sense of connectedness to society, and that this loss presented the greatest danger to France. Its only remedy, he saw, was to strengthen the social *milieu* outside the workplace, so as to compensate for the alienation created within it. Halbwachs was associated with Henri Sellier, and the French Garden City Movement, in the creation of a number of 'garden suburbs' around Paris in the inter-war period with the aim of rehumanizing modern life.[8] *The Collective Memory*, the book from which Rossi took the idea of 'memory', was Halbwachs's last book; in fact, within it, Halbwachs went to some trouble to argue that while social groups may retain their identity as groups through their common memory of certain places, that memory relates not to an actually existing physical space, but to the particular mental image of the space formed by that group.[9] In other words, it is not urban artefacts that are the agents of memory, but their mental images. Rossi's selective, and very literal, reading of Halbwachs hardly took account of the nuances to which Halbwachs attached so much importance. Nor did it pay much regard to the weaknesses inherited from Durkheim's sociology – in particular, the identification of alienation in social, rather than economic causes; and the assumption that individual psychology provides a satisfactory model for the collective behaviour of a society. Not only did Rossi reproduce Halbwachs's assumptions uncritically, but more remarkably, he cast them within a strongly idealist framework that was quite alien to Halbwachs's own thought: so, for example, Rossi wrote, 'the union between the past and the future exists in the very idea of the city that it flows through in the same way that memory flows through the life of a person' (131), and he presented the city as an object with an end of its own, to realize its own idea of itself. But if Rossi's use of Halbwachs bore little relation to Halbwachs's own thinking, we should perhaps accept that Rossi's idea of memory was, as Carlo Olmo says, more poetic than theoretically rigorous; and in any case, while espousing 'memory', Rossi managed also, especially in his subsequent writings and projects, to be thoroughly antihistorical in his attachment to the idea of the autonomy of the urban artefact. Yet for all his inconsistencies, it was Rossi above all who provided European and American architects in the 1970s and 1980s with the idea that the city's fabric constituted its collective memory.

The other, often cited, case of the introduction of 'memory' into the context of modern architecture was the essay 'Collage City' of 1975 by Colin Rowe and Fred Koetter. In this extended reflection on the shortcomings of orthodox modernist architecture and urbanism, the authors questioned modernism's exclusive concentration upon the realization of a future, utopian environment. Explicitly referring to Frances Yates's *The Art of Memory*, they ask whether the ideal city might not 'at one and the same time, behave as both theatre of prophecy *and* theatre of memory' (77); their point was that one should have the liberty to choose between the two, and not be obliged to locate oneself in the future. In general, modernism had been at fault in supposing that novelty was possible without acknowledgment of the memory-laden context from which it necessarily emerged. Within Rowe's *oeuvre*, otherwise devotedly modernist in its

stress upon the immanence of the work, this essay was something of an aberration. However, in its plea for pluralism, it was an important text in the development of architectural postmodernism – and its appeal to memory formed part of this.

From the enthusiastic reception of the ideas of Rossi, Ungers, Rowe, and others, there developed a new orthodoxy, in which as Anthony Vidler has put it, 'Urbanism … might be defined as the instrumental theory and practice of constructing the city as memorial of itself' (1992, 179). One of the difficulties, though, of this proposition was the lack of direct evidence from previous historical periods that anyone had ever actually perceived cities or architecture in this way: it is only as a result of the arguments of Poëte and Halbwachs, as mediated by Rossi and others, that cities had come to be discussed in such terms. Out of the need to legitimate the view of the city as the embodied memory of its inhabitants, there has developed a new kind of historical project, dedicated to proving the presence of this idea in previous ages. The most ambitious and sophisticated of these attempts is Christine Boyer's *The City of Collective Memory* (1994), where the aim is to discover 'how does the city become the locus of collective memory?' (16). Yet while investigating most thoroughly the intellectual origins of this idea, curiously Boyer at no point questions the proposition itself: assuming that cities are the embodiment of memories, she shares the new orthodoxy.

The symptoms of the postmodern orthodoxy of memory as part of the subject of architecture are threefold. First of all, there is a lack of interest in the very extensive investigations into the general phenomenon of memory undertaken in the realms of psychology, philosophy and literature in the twentieth century; in particular, the neglect of the insight of Proust, as of Freud: that 'memory' on its own is not interesting – what matters is the tension between memory and forgetting. Not for nothing did the ancient Greeks place the springs of Lethe (Forgetfulness) and Mnemosyne (Memory) close by, and insist that those who wished to consult the oracle at Trophonios drink from first one, then the other. Secondly, there is a general, and unjustified, assumption that social memory can be explained by reference to individual memory. And thirdly, the supposition that buildings, or indeed any artefacts, provide a satisfactory analogue in the material world for the aleatory world of memory is far from convincing.

In the recent study of social memory, attention has moved away from things and towards activities as the operative agents of memory. Paul Connerton in his book *How Societies Remember* (1989) draws a distinction between 'inscribing' practices and 'incorporating' practices in commemoration, and suggests that 'inscribing' practices – those where memory is recorded in an object – are of less significance than 'incorporating' practices – those involving some kind of bodily action – in the creation of social memory. It is through ceremonies, rituals, codes of behaviour and repetition that collective memories are reproduced among the members of a society, and may become attached to particular places. Seen in these terms, objects like war memorials are less important than the ceremonies and activities that take place around them; and indeed to hope to preserve memories socially through works of architecture would appear futile unless accompanied by some kind of incorporating practice. This is indeed the lesson drawn by Dolores Hayden, who in her book *The Power of Place* (1995) described various projects for the protection of social memories in parts of Los Angeles. None of the projects relied upon buildings or even artefacts except in a secondary way: the principal emphasis was upon public participation through workshops which interpret and re-interpret the historical associations and significance of particular places.

Modernism had good reasons for detaching 'memory' from architecture and urbanism. The attempt to recover 'memory' as a active constituent of them may be understandable in terms of the apparent condition of silence to which modernism seemed to have reduced architecture by the 1960s; but, with the indifference architects and urbanists showed to the investigation of 'memory' that had taken place in other disciplines during the twentieth century, it remains doubtful whether architecture has achieved any distinctive contribution to the 'art of memory'. 'Memory' may well yet prove a short-lived architectural category – and one inherently alien to architecture.

1 See for example Scruton, *Aesthetics*, 1979, 138–43.

2 See for example the various projects of 'Roma Interotta', described in *Architectural Design*, vol. 49, 1979, nos 3–4.

3 See Ballantyne, *Richard Payne Knight*, 1997, chapter 1.

4 See R. Macksey, introduction to Proust, *On Reading Ruskin*, 1987, xxxi. This translation of Proust's prefaces to his translations of *The Bible of Amiens* and *Sesame and Lilies* gives a full account of Proust's absorption in Ruskin.

5 See Gillis (ed.), *Commemorations*, 1994, for some interesting discussions of the range and particularity of twentieth-century war memorials.

6 See Teige, 'Mundaneum', 1929; the project was criticized for its monumentality, and its 'non-modern and archaic character' (88).

7 See Olmo, 'Across the Texts', 1988, *Assemblage*, no. 5, for the circumstances of Rossi's ideas.

8 See Rabinow, *French Modern*, 1989, 321, 336 on Halbwachs.

9 See Halbwachs, *Collective Memory*, especially 140–41.

Nature

Architecture, unlike the other arts, does not find its patterns in nature. G. Semper, 1834 inaugural lecture; quoted in H. Semper, 1880, 7

An architect should live as little in cities as a painter. Send him to our hills, and let him study there what nature understands by a buttress, and what by a dome. J. Ruskin, *The Seven Lamps of Architecture*, 1849, chapter III, §24

What man makes, nature cannot make. Nature does not build a house, nature does not make a locomotive, nature does not make a playground. They grow out of a desire to express. Louis Kahn, 1969, quoted in Wurman, 75

'Any full history of the uses of *nature*', wrote Raymond Williams, 'would be a history of a large part of the history of human thought' (221). The same is true relative to architecture, where for most of the last five hundred years 'nature' has been the main, if not *the* principal category for organizing thought about what architecture is or might be. The only significant break was in the early to mid-twentieth century when, in the era of high modernism, 'nature' was largely put into abeyance; however since the 1960s, with the coming of the environmental movement, a re-invented 'nature' has returned to the vocabulary of architecture.

The distinction between the world created by man – 'culture' – and the world in which man exists – 'nature' – has been perhaps the single most important mental category ever conceived, and there can be few disciplines in whose formation it has not been fundamental. Architecture is no exception. Yet it would seem obvious that within this classification, architecture – a human product – belongs to culture, not to nature, from which it is categorically different. The many attempts to define architecture by relation to nature may indeed seem perverse, yet we must understand these if we are to make any sense of how people have conceived architecture and its products in the

past. It is worth distinguishing in the many accounts of architecture's relationship to nature between those that propose that architecture is *like* nature, in that it follows the same laws or imitates it, and those that say that architecture *is* nature – that in so far as man and woman are objects of nature, architecture's providing them with shelter or symbolic expression makes it a natural product, in the same way that speech is. Architecture in this sense is seen as a condition of mankind's being in the world. The problem faced by those twentieth-century theorists of architecture who rejected both propositions was to establish, if architecture neither is nature nor is like nature, what it then is.

1. *Nature as the source of beauty in architecture.*
The original model for the discussion of beauty in architecture, as of all the arts, was derived by neo-Platonic philosophers from Plato's account of the structure of the natural world in the Dialogue of *Timaeus*. Taking Plato's idea that all things in nature are governed either by numerical relations, or by geometry, neo-Platonists argued that art, in so far as it was satisfying to the human mind, followed the same principles. The outstanding, and most famous application of this argument to architecture was made by Leon Battista Alberti in his *De Re Aedificatoria*, written in the mid-fifteenth century. It is above all where Alberti outlines his theory of *concinnitas* (the principle of harmony that underlies the graceful arrangement of parts in relation to each other and to the whole) that the significance of nature emerges as the model for architecture:

> Neither in the whole body nor in its parts does *concinnitas* flourish as much as it does in Nature herself. ... Everything that Nature produces is regulated by the law of *concinnitas*, and her chief concern is that whatever she produces should be absolutely perfect. ...let us conclude as follows. Beauty is a form of sympathy and consonance of the parts within a body,

according to definite number, outline, and position, as dictated by *concinnitas*, the absolute and fundamental rule in Nature. This is the main object of the art of building, and the source of her dignity, charm, authority and worth. (302–3)

The importance Alberti attached to *concinnitas* might suggest that he believed that nature was the absolute authority for architecture, but elsewhere he was more circumspect. As well as following the Platonic view of the primacy of nature, Alberti also acknowledged Aristotle's notion of art as inherently different from nature. In the *Physics*, Aristotle had written – in a phrase that was to be highly important particularly for seventeenth-century art and architectural theorists – that 'generally art completes what nature cannot bring to a finish, and partly imitates her' (Book II, §8). This view of how art differed from nature appears in the other main section concerned with architectural beauty in Alberti's book (Book VI chapter 2) where he wrote 'rarely is it granted, even to Nature herself, to produce anything that is entirely complete and perfect in every respect', implying that some selection from nature is called for; and this is the task of art, for 'Who would deny that only through art can correct and worthy building be achieved?' (156). Contrary to the received notion of Alberti as an apologist for the identity of architectural with natural beauty, here and elsewhere (see 159), Alberti argued for artifice and skill as the source of beauty, and opened the door to what in the seventeenth century would become a more prevalent view of architecture as an art of the artificial.

The first explicit challenge to the idea that the beauty of architecture was founded in nature came in the seventeenth century from the French theorist and architect Claude Perrault, in his *Ordonnance of the Five Kinds of Columns* (1683). Perrault's denial of the authority of nature for the proportions of architecture was indeed remarkable and radical, and marked the first fundamental reconsideration of architecture's relationship to nature for over two centuries. His remarks in the *Ordonnance* were brief, but unequivocal:

neither imitation of nature, nor reason, nor good sense in any way constitutes the basis for the beauty people claim to see in proportion and in the orderly disposition of the parts of a column; indeed, it is impossible to find any source other than custom for the pleasure they impart. (52)

Categorical though Perrault was, his argument provoked less controversy at the time than has sometimes been supposed. In the long term, however, Perrault's argument marked the beginning of the ultimate demise of the idea that beauty resided in objects, and its replacement by the notion that beauty is a construct of the viewing subject.[1] This theme is discussed below under point 6.

2. *The origin of architecture.* The question of the origin of architecture was a long-running theme amongst architectural theorists.[2] Taking their cue from Vitruvius, who in Book II, chapter 1 of *De Architectura* had described the mythical origins of architecture, Renaissance and post-Renaissance theorists speculated widely, and sometimes wildly, about the form of the first architecture. Whether caves, huts or tents provided the original model of architecture was an issue pursued without the slightest regard for archeological facts – not that any could ever be found – but purely for the purpose of justifying the principles that should be followed in the architecture of the present. The earliest architectural text to develop its argument from the hypothetical buildings of primitive man was Filarete's treatise (1460–64), where it was proposed that the first buildings were huts built of tree trunks, which provided the original form of the column. In the later seventeenth century it became conventional to construct arguments for the present or ideal condition of all human creations (most particularly the State) out of their hypothetical origins in the natural condition in which the first humans found themselves. In architecture, the Vitruvian myth of the first buildings, and of the origins of the orders (*De Architectura* Book IV, chapter 2) provided convenient support for linking architecture to mankind's first, 'natural' state, and was popular amongst Renaissance architectural writers. However, by the eighteenth century, the Vitruvian idea of heroic primitive builders ceased any longer to be taken seriously, and became regarded as mere superstition. Nonetheless, the story of the mythical origins of architecture persisted, but serving a quite different purpose, in order to demonstrate an idea of architecture as a rational system. By far the best known example of the use of the story of architecture's origins in nature to legitimate a contemporary theory was the French writer Marc-Antoine Laugier's *Essai Sur l'Architecture* (1753). The book, an extended critique of rococo, opened as follows:

It is the same for architecture as for all the arts: its principles are founded on simple nature, and in nature's processes its rules are clearly drawn. Let us think of man in his original state, with no means of

Primitive builders, from Filarete's Treatise (1460–64). The Vitruvian myth of the origin of the first buildings linked architecture to mankind's first, 'natural' state.

assistance and no guide other than his natural instinct and needs. He wants a place to rest. Beside a quiet stream, he sees a grassy bank; its fresh greenness pleases his eyes, its tender down invites him; he comes to it, and stretched out idly on this carpet flecked with flowers, he dreams only of enjoying nature's gifts in peace. But soon the heat of the sun burns him, and he is forced to find a shelter.

Having experimented with first the forest and then the cave, and finding neither satisfactory,

he is determined by his own industry to make good nature's unobservant omissions. He wants to make a dwelling which will protect him without burying him. A few fallen branches from the forest are the right material for his purpose. He chooses four of the strongest, and stands them upright on a square. Above he puts four others across; and on these he arranges more inclining towards each other and meet-ing at a point on two sides. This roof is covered with

leaves, tightly enough packed for neither the sun nor the rain to penetrate, and here our man is lodged. ... Such is the course of simple nature; it is to the imitation of its processes that art owes its birth. ... It is by keeping close to the simplicity of this first model that all faults are avoided, and true perfection achieved. The upright pieces of wood give us the idea of columns. The horizontal pieces above them give the idea of the entablature. Finally the inclined pieces which form the roof give us the pediment. This is recognized by all the masters of the art. But take note: never has there been a principle more fertile in its consequences. It is easy henceforth to distinguish the parts fundamental to an architectural order from those introduced only as a result of need, or those added by caprice. (1755, 8–10)

Laugier's originality lay not in his account of the natural origins of architecture, which would have been familiar to his readers, but in the use he then put it to. As Wolfgang Herrmann says, 'His hut is not a curious illustration of a distant past or a factor of an evolutionary theory of architecture, but the great principle from which it now becomes possible to deduce immutable laws' (1962, 48). Laugier does not lose sight of his rustic hut, and proceeds through the book to argue the merits of every aspect of architecture he discusses according to the principles it expressed. Before leaving Laugier, it would be as well to stress the sense he gave to the word 'nature': it is not the source of proportions and their beauty, as Alberti and others had understood it; nor is it something that can be experienced, in the way the Romantics were to consider it; rather it is a principle of construction and decoration for which the closest analogy must be 'reason'.

Laugier was by no means the last architectural thinker to derive his theory of architecture from a hypothetical original building – for both Quatremère de Quincy and Gottfried Semper were to do the same. However, in the early nineteenth century, 'nature' itself underwent such a major philosophic and scientific transformation that to call the hypothetical original building 'natural' was no longer meaningful, and indeed by the time Semper was writing in the 1850s, he was careful to make clear how inappropriate a description this was for what he had in mind.

3. *The valorization of architecture: 'mimesis', or the imitation of nature.* Within the theory of the arts found in classical authors, particularly Cicero and Horace, a fundamental idea was that the essential property of art (in this case primarily poetry) was its capacity to imitate nature.[3] During the fifteenth century, the faithfulness with which a work of art reproduced nature came to be considered the prime criterion of its quality, and this pursuit of the imitation of nature is readily apparent in the work of, say, Leonardo da Vinci. But while poetry, painting and sculpture could all achieve their results by representing nature, architecture was not a representational art: it neither reproduced natural objects, nor, like poetry, human moods and emotions. Architecture's inherent inability to represent nature, and therefore to qualify as a mimetic art, was a serious bar to its acceptance as a liberal art. If architects were to stand on equal social terms with poets and painters, and to differentiate themselves sufficiently from building craftsmen, it was necessary to prove that architecture was an art in which nature was represented. For the best part of three centuries, from the late fifteenth to the late eighteenth, this issue was a major preoccupation within architectural thought.

Broadly speaking, there were two kinds of arguments developed to justify architecture's claim to be a mimetic

Frontispiece, M.-A. Laugier, *Essai sur l'Architecture*, 1753. Architecture points to the natural building, and instructs humanity in its principles.

art. The first claimed that architecture imitated its own natural model – that is to say the hypothetical primitive buildings. In so far as architecture reproduced the forms of the hut or tent, translating the timber or skin into stone, it could be said to be an imitation of nature. This theory, for which some justification could again be found in Vitruvius (Book IV, chapter 2), was developed to the full in the eighteenth century. In that ambitious compilation and classification of all human knowledge, Diderot's *Encyclopédie*, architecture was described, along with painting and sculpture, as an art of imitation. Although no grounds were given for this claim in d'Alembert's *Discours Préliminaire* (1751) to the *Encyclopaedie*, the task of justifying this assertion was to interest architects in the second half of the eighteenth century. William Chambers's pictures in his *Treatise* of the development of architecture from primitive huts derive from this preoccupation.

The second argument, also developed in the eighteenth century, was that while architecture did not represent the superficial appearances of nature, it could and did represent the principles inherent in nature, and in that sense provided a more profound form of mimesis than that found in the other arts whose representation of nature was direct and literal. This approach to representation of nature we have already seen in Laugier, but it was to be elaborated upon extensively in the second half of the eighteenth century. In social and material terms, the purpose of this argument was clear, for it allowed architects to claim, for the first time, that their art was not merely equal to the other arts, but superior to them.

The person responsible for the fullest and most complete development of the justification for the mimetic nature of architecture was the French architectural theorist Quatremère de Quincy, who, in a series of articles written for Pancoucke's *Encyclopédie Méthodique* between 1788 and 1825, evolved an original and intriguing argument. Quatremère's aims were to secure d'Alembert's proposition that architecture was an art of imitation, and to offer a more convincing account than Laugier of how it imitated nature; at the same time, he tried to repair the faults of earlier theories of imitation. Quatremère's starting point (though it does not correspond to the order in which the articles were published) was to confront in a way that no previous writer had done the question of whether the 'nature' that architecture was supposed to imitate referred to the world of physical matter, or to the ideas people held of that

world: his answer was to say that 'nature' was both. He wrote:

> It is necessary to take the word *nature* here in its widest sense, that is, the one which includes the domain of physical beings, and the realm of moral or intellectual things. ... It is not necessary for an art to be called an art of *imitation* that its model be based in an evident and obvious manner on physical and material nature. This sort of model is only accorded to the two arts [painting and sculpture] which address themselves to the eye by the imitation of bodies and colours. ... Therefore when it is understood that nature is the model of all the fine arts, it is necessary to guard against circumscribing the idea of nature within what belongs to her of the evident, the material, in short, within the realm of what falls under the senses. Nature exists as much in what she has of the invisible as in what strikes the eyes. ... To imitate does not necessarily mean to make a resemblance of a thing, for one could, without imitating the work, imitate nature thus, in making not what she makes, but as she makes it, that is, one can imitate nature in her action... ('Imitation')

Quatremère's next issue, likewise avoided by most previous writers, was the question of whether architecture's imitation of nature was literal or metaphorical: his answer, and this was the heart of his remarkable and ingenious theory of architecture, was that it was both. Quatremère argued that architecture was founded upon two principles – the literal imitation of timber buildings in stone, and the imitation by analogy of the principles of order and harmony found in natural objects. To take the theory of the transmutation of timber construction into stone first, Quatremère proposed that primitive building originated in three 'types' (see pp. 304–6), the cave, the tent and the timber hut, each of which provided a natural model for architecture. However, 'of the three models that nature can present to the art, carpentry is without doubt the most perfect and finest of all', and this was the one followed by the Greeks ('Architecture'). Quatremère attached a great deal of importance to the imitation of the timber construction of the hut, indeed it was for him 'one of the principal causes of the pleasure elicited by architecture' (*ibid.*), and constituted a fundamental law of nature. For Quatremère, the representation in stone of other materials, far from being a reprehensible lie, was an agreeable fiction giving

The Third sort of Huts (which gave birth to the Doric Order.)

The Doric Order, in its Improved State.

Primitive huts, from William Chambers, *Treatise on Civil Architecture*. The primary reason for late eighteenth-century architects' interest in the supposedly 'natural' origins of architecture was so as to verify that architecture was indeed an art of imitation.

rise to much of architecture's charm. All the arts, he suggested, achieve their effect by disguising the truth, for man 'wishes to be seduced but not deceived' (*ibid.*). It is through the literal imitation of the natural process of building, represented by the timber hut, that architecture succeeds in producing an impression of imitation as strong as that in the other arts. What is particularly worth noticing about Quatremère's theory is that unlike earlier writers (see 4. below), who saw artifice as the means by which nature was corrected or counteracted and therefore its opposite, he saw no conflict between the two; indeed he regarded the artifice involved in the process of transmutation as itself a quasi-natural process. While he conceded that 'Nature, without doubt, has not made the cabin', he continued, 'but Nature has directed man in his formation, and man, guided by an instinct, coarse if one wishes, but sure, and by a sentiment which in early

times could not mislead, has transmitted to it the true impressions of nature'. At this point though, there was a sleight of hand in the argument, for Quatremère conceded that the hut and the story of the transmutation process had no other basis than myth, and could, he says, even be abandoned altogether without the principles they demonstrated being invalidated. If this is so, then it seems that for Quatremère as for Laugier the principles of which they talk are derived really from reason, and their 'natural' basis was no more than a convention for expounding them. The logical step was to dispense with 'nature' altogether as a step in the argument – which was precisely what Gottfried Semper proceeded to do in the development of his own remarkable theory in the 1850s.

Turning to the second principle, that of imitation by analogy, Quatremère summed up his argument as follows: 'The architect imitates nature when … he has followed

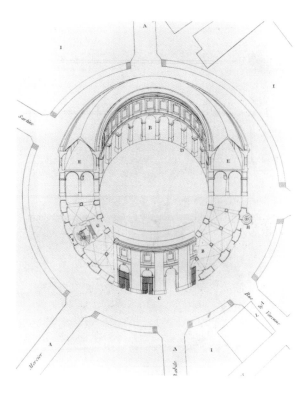

Le Camus de Mézières, Halle au Blé, Paris, 1762–66 (demolished), site plan and cut-away aerial perspective (detail). According to Quatremère de Quincy, architecture – in approved works like the Halle au Blé – was a 'rival of Nature', imitating nature's processes yet without reproducing its visible effects.

and rendered evident the system that nature developed in all her works' ('Imitation'). The absence of verisimilitude to nature makes architecture the most ideal of the arts:

> The general imitation of Nature in her principles of order, of harmony relative to the inclinations of our senses, and to the perceptions of understanding, have given [architecture] a soul, and have made an art no longer copyist, no longer imitator, but a rival of Nature herself... We have seen that Nature offers only analogies [to architecture] on all sides. It imitates its model less than it compares itself to her; ... it does not make what it sees, but as it sees it being made; it is not the effect but the cause that it studies: and from then on it is original even in its imitation. ... Its model being the order of Nature, that exists everywhere, without being visible anywhere. ('Imitation')

Quatremère's theory of natural imitation was, considered historically, a dead end. Its extreme rationalism makes his 'nature' such an artificial construct (particularly when compared to the altogether more vital sense which German writers and philosophers were starting to give to the concept at the time) that it is scarcely credible. Quatremère's arguments about nature belong to mid-eighteenth-century enlightenment debate about the classification of knowledge and had limited application to the practice of architecture, and were not subsequently pursued. On the other hand, his notion of the art of architecture as pure idea was too valuable to be abandoned, and survived stripped of its references to 'nature'.

4. *Nature invoked to justify artistic licence.* It has already been remarked that in some ancient Greek philosophy, the difference between nature and art was that, as Aristotle put it, 'art partly completes what nature cannot bring to a finish'. Increasingly in sixteenth- and seventeenth-century Italy, the notion that nature was always imperfect in its products dominated thinking in the arts and justified the artist's licence in departing from the natural model. The view is associated with Michelangelo and Vasari in the sixteenth century; in the seventeenth, Bernini told the members of the French Academy of Painting on his visit to Paris in 1665 'nature is always feeble and niggardly ... artists who study it should first be skilled in recognizing its faults and correcting them' (Fréart de Chantelou, 166). Such ideas were rapidly absorbed into French artistic circles; André

Félibien, for instance, stated in *L'Idée du Peintre Parfait*, 'Although nature is the source of beauty, art surpasses nature because we find in nature that individual objects are usually imperfect in some way; nature intends that everything should be perfect, but is frustrated by accidents'. This idea had little immediate impact in architecture, where the notion of the natural model had not as yet been developed, but in garden design the results were strikingly clear. The sixteenth-century gardens of Italy, like the Villa Lante, or of seventeenth-century France, like Le Nôtre's at Vaux-le-Vicomte and Versailles, had aimed to make out of organic nature works that demonstrated the superior power of human intellect and artifice over nature's inability to attain beauty when left to itself. In texts on the art of gardening, like J. B. de la Barauderie's *Le Traité du Jardinage* (1638), André Mollet's *Le Jardin du Plaisir* (1651), and Claude Mollet's *Théâtre des Plans et Jardinages* (1652), references to 'Nature' are notable by their absence.

The belief that the imperfections of nature justified the creations of the artist continued to be widely held well into the late eighteenth century. The English architect Sir William Chambers wrote at the beginning of his *Dissertation on Oriental Gardening* (1772), in a statement which closely reproduced the thinking of his friend the painter Sir Joshua Reynolds, 'Nature is incapable of pleasing without the assistance of art'. By this time, however, the argument was also an attack (by Chambers, a prominent Tory) upon the popularity of the 'naturalism' of the landscape gardening of Capability Brown, much favoured by Whig politicians (see 5. below).

5. As a political idea: nature as freedom, lack of constraint. The modern sense of 'natural' as a virtue, as what is free and unaffected, was unknown before the beginning of the eighteenth century. The development of this meaning in the hands of British philosophers took place specifically as a reaction to what was perceived as the denial of the 'natural' rights of liberty, freedom of speech and so on by despotic regimes of Europe, particularly that of Louis XIV, and only too clearly manifested in their approach towards garden design (see ill. p. 228). Although founded in the philosophy of John Locke, its specifically aesthetic dimension was first expounded by Lord Shaftesbury. In *The Moralists* (1709), he wrote as follows:

I shall no longer resist the Passion growing in me for Things of a *natural* kind; where neither *Art*, nor the *Conceit* or *Caprice* of Man has spoil'd their *genuine*

Order by breaking in upon that *primitive state*. Even the rude *Rocks*, the mossy *Caverns*, the irregular unwrought *Grotto's*, and broken *Falls* of Waters, with all the horrid Graces of the *Wilderness* itself, as representing NATURE more, will be the more engaging, and appear with a Magnificence beyond the formal mockery of Princely Gardens. (Hunt and Willis, 124)

Similar sentiments were expressed by Joseph Addison (e.g., *Spectator*, no. 414, 25 June 1712) and Alexander Pope ('Epistle to Lord Burlington', 1731).

These essentially literary ideas about the beauties of nature were applied directly to the design of gardens by the nurseryman and gardener Stephen Switzer in his book *Ichnographia Rustica*, first published in 1718, and reissued in enlarged form in 1742:

the careless and loose Tresses of Nature, that are easily mov'd by the least Breath of Wind, offer more to the Imagination that the most delicate Pyramid, or any of the longest and most elaborately clip'd Espalier, that it is possible to make; for altho' we don't by this absolutely reject, in some few proper Places something of that kind, yet why should that be though such a Beauty, as to exclude things more Natural? (Hunt and Willis, 153)

The setting of country house, should, he suggests combine both sorts of beauty, so that beyond a formal garden immediately by the house,

one would sometimes be passing thro' little Padducks and Corn Fields, sometimes thro' wild Coppices, and Gardens, and sometimes by purling Brooks and Streams, Places that are set off not by nice Art, but by luxury of Nature, a little guided in her Extravagancies by the Artists Hand. (*ibid.*)

Although these ideas were current in the second decade of the century, it was another twenty years before they started to be applied in the practice of landscape gardening. According to Horace Walpole it was William Kent with his Elysian Fields at Stowe in Buckinghamshire in the late 1730s, who first 'leap'd the fence, and saw that all nature was a garden' (1771). Here, at Stowe, the link between political liberty and the freedom offered by nature was made explicit (see ills. pp. 124, 209). While the application of these ideas of nature formed the basis of the English picturesque landscape design and was to

Gardens, Versailles, A. le Nôtre, from 1661. 'The suff'ring Eye inverted Nature sees, Trees cut to Statues, Statues thick as Trees': Alexander Pope's contempt for the artifice of the gardens of European despots encouraged him to see in nature unrestrained a spontaneous beauty.

be a major theme in the later eighteenth-century practice of this art, their extension to architecture came more gradually – and largely in connection with the development of the theory of the aesthetic, which is considered next. Later versions of nature as a basis of liberal politics appear in the nineteenth-century American philosopher Ralph Waldo Emerson, and in the twentieth-century political philosophers Theodor Adorno and Max Horkheimer, in their *Dialectic of the Enlightenment*. The impact of both upon architecture is discussed below.

6. *'Nature' as a construct of the viewer's perception.*
The shift from the notion that the cause of beauty lay in the objective world of matter – or 'nature' – to the view that the source of beauty lay not in the physicality of objects but in the manner in which they were apprehended by the human mind has already been alluded to relative to Claude Perrault (see 1. above). The development of idea that, as David Hume put it, 'Beauty is no quality in things themselves: it exists merely

in the mind which contemplates them; and each mind perceives a different beauty' (1757, 136–37), was undertaken by British philosophers following in the tradition of John Locke. Its application to the arts had been first popularized by Joseph Addison in 1712 in the series of articles on 'The Pleasures of the Imagination' in the *Spectator* (nos 411–21):

we have the power of retaining, altering and compounding those images, which we have once received, into all the varieties of picture and vision that are most agreeable to the imagination; for by this faculty a man in a dungeon is capable of entertaining himself with scenes and landscapes more beautiful than any that can be found in the whole compass of nature. (no. 411)

As a measure of the arts, 'nature' could no longer be simply external objects or phenomena, but had also to include the quality of the human experience by which they were known.

In relation to architecture, the mid-eighteenth-century text that was most widely read and had the most extensive influence was Edmund Burke's *A Philosophical Enquiry into the Origin of our Ideas of the Sublime and the Beautiful* (1757). Like Perrault, Burke dismissed the notion that the proportions of beautiful architecture were derived from natural objects or the human form: 'it appears very clearly to me', Burke wrote, 'that the human body never supplied the architect with any of his ideas'. Amongst other reasons,

> nothing could be more unaccountably whimsical, than for an architect to model his performance by the human figure, since no two things can have less resemblance or analogy, than a man, and an house or temple; do we need to observe that their purposes are entirely different? What I am apt to suspect is this: that these analogies were devised to give a credit to the works of art, by shewing a conformity between them and the noblest works in nature, not that the latter served at all to supply hints for the perfection of the former. (100)

Burke's denial that the effects either of architecture or any of the arts depended upon the imitation of nature's proportions or harmonies allowed him to concentrate upon his main argument, which was that aesthetic sensations, of the sublime and of beauty, are induced by the sight of natural objects, and art succeeds in so far as it can reproduce in the viewer the same sensation of pain or delight. As Burke put it, 'in the imagination, besides the pain or pleasure arising from the properties of the natural object, a pleasure is perceived from the resemblance, which the imitation has to the original' (17). While Burke did not elaborate upon these ideas in relation to architecture, others, in both France and England, did.

The notion that it is the task of the architect to stimulate in the subject the same sensations as he or she might experience from natural objects became a major preoccupation of late eighteenth- and early nineteenth-century architects. The French architect J.-D. Le Roy, in his *Histoire de la Disposition et des formes différentes que les chrétiens ont données à leurs temples depuis le règne de Constantin le Grand à nos jours* (1764), was quick to grasp the potential of Burke's theory:

> All great spectacles impose themselves on men; the immensity of the sky, the vast extent of the earth or

the sea, which we discover at the tops of mountains or in the middle of the ocean, seem to raise our spirit and enlarge our ideas. The greatest of our own works make impressions of the same kind upon us. (50)

The creation of architectural effects to induce particular sensations became a major topic of discussion in French architectural circles, evident in Le Camus de Mézières's book *The Genius of Architecture* (1780), in J.-L. Lequeu's architectural fantasies, and in Boullée's projects.

In his unpublished *Architecture, Essai sur l'Art*, written in the 1790s, Boullée wrote 'If … a man could arouse in us with his art those sensations we experience when we look at nature, such an art would be far superior to anything we possess' (85). It was therefore to the study of natural forms on the one hand, and sensations on the other that Boullée devoted himself with the aim of creating what he called 'the poetry of architecture'. The best and most original example of Boullée's theory of sensations was in his 'architecture of shadows':

> I was in the country, on the edge of a wood in moonlight. My shadow produced by the light caught my eye … Because of my particular mood, the effect of this image seemed to me extremely melancholy. The trees drawn in shadow upon the ground made a deep impression on me. My imagination exaggerated the scene, and thus I had a glimpse of all that is most sombre in nature. What did I see there? The mass of objects stood out in black against the extreme wanness of the light. … Struck by the sensations I was experiencing, I immediately began to wonder how to apply this to architecture. I tried to find a composition made up of the effect of shadows. To achieve this, I supposed the light (as I had seen it in nature) giving back everything that had come alive in my imagination. That was how I proceeded in seeking to discover this new type of architecture. (106)

Apart from the executed works of Boullée (see ills. pp. 50, 230) and Ledoux, and Le Camus de Mézières's Halle au Blé in Paris (see ill. p. 226), perhaps the best built applications of these ideas are to be found in the work of the English architect Sir John Soane, who had indeed studied Le Camus de Mézières's book with close attention, as well as having an intimate familiarity with English picturesque theory. His house at Lincoln's Inn Fields (see ill. p. 127) was, as David Watkin suggests, an attempt to interpret the architecture of sensation

E.-L. Boullée, Project for the King's Library, Paris, drawing, 1788. 'The architecture of shadows', which Boullée claimed as his personal discovery, he learnt from nature, and used to give his schemes appropriate 'character'.

suggested by Le Camus de Mézières.[4] In his lectures, Soane firmly rejected the notion that architecture had any model in nature, and insisted that it was entirely 'an art of invention' (532); his view of the superiority of architecture over the other arts was not far removed from Quatremère de Quincy's description of architecture as 'a rival to Nature herself'.

7. *Art as 'a second nature'*. This description of art, coined by Goethe, marks a fundamental shift in thinking about the entire art–nature relationship in the early nineteenth century, one which rendered obsolete most of the previous uses of nature so far considered. This new formulation of the relationship of art to nature came not – as most previous ideas had – from studying art, but rather from the study of nature. Although Quatremère had implied that architecture was a parallel to nature, by virtue of its non-mimetic, inventive character, Quatremère's idea of nature itself was a stiff, rational construct without the slightest attention to any directly observed natural phenomena. This change in thought, where investigation of nature guides the understanding of art, rather than the

study of art directing the understanding of nature, is most clearly seen in the writings of Goethe, and its diffusion was largely the responsibility of Goethe and his circle.

Goethe's wide-ranging scientific investigations were as important to him as his creative output as a poet and critic – and as far as he was concerned they were not distinct. It was particularly his studies of anatomy and of plant morphology that bear upon the development of his understanding of art's relationship to nature. Goethe's criticism of Linnaeus and the French natural scientists was that they classified species according to their component parts, as if they were constructed in the same way as man-made artefacts; as Goethe put it, in his recollection of a conversation with Schiller in 1794, 'there ought to be another means of representing nature, not in separate pieces, but in living actuality, striving from the whole to the parts' (quoted in Magnus, 69). It is this pursuit of the living whole that characterized Goethe's investigation of nature, and also his recognition that 'in nature nothing stands still'. (See 'Form', pp. 155–57.) Not only did Goethe believe that the artist should proceed in the same way, so that the work becomes the outward expression of the vital force imparted by the artist, but moreover, brought up on Spinoza, he did not consider that there was a sharp distinction to be made between the sensations the mind received and the stimuli arousing them, and that this was as true in the perception of natural objects as it was of artificial ones. As he put it, 'in contemplating nature, at large and in the small, I have always asked myself the question: Is it the object, or is it you that is here expressed? ... The phenomenon is never separate from the observer, but rather interwoven with the latter's individuality' (quoted in Magnus, 236). In other words, the quality of works of art was that they were the outcome of a living spirit, and the seeing of them engaged the active perception of a living subject. In this respect, art was like nature both in its formation, and in its apperception.

Some of these ideas are present in Goethe's youthful essay 'On German Architecture', written in 1772. This was primarily an attack upon Laugier's rationalist conception of 'nature', and proposes that the power of works of architecture (in this case Strasbourg cathedral – see ill. p. 300) lies in their being the outcome of the human instinct for expression. In the key passage, Goethe wrote

> For in man's nature there is a will to create form which becomes active the moment his survival is assured. As soon as he does not need to worry or fear, like a demi-God, busy even in his relaxation, he casts around for a material into which he can breathe his spirit. And so the savage articulates his coconut shell, his feathers, his body with fantastical lines, hideous forms and gaudy colours.

Erwin von Steinbach's cathedral is just such a product of this restless soul.

However, it was during Goethe's stay in Italy in 1786–88, when he encountered for the first time the works of antiquity, that his ideas about architecture and the visual arts really developed. In Rome on 11 August 1787, he wrote: 'now things are unfolding for me, and art is becoming, as it were, a second nature for me, born from the heads of the greatest humans' (*Italian Journey*, 306). After the amphitheatre at Verona and the Temple of Minerva at Assisi, the aqueduct at Spoleto, he recorded, was

> the third ancient structure I have seen ... A second Nature, one that serves civic goals, that is what their architecture is.... Only now do I feel how right I was

to loathe all capricious edifices, like the Winterkasten on the Weissenstein for example, a nothing built for nothing, a huge decorative confection, and it is the same with a thousand other things. They all stand there stillborn, for what has no inner vitality has no life, and can neither be nor become great. (100)

And asking himself how the Greeks achieved perfection in art, he answered 'My supposition is that they proceeded according to the same laws by which nature proceeds, and which I am tracking down' (137). At the same time, part of the 'nature' represented in these works is provided by the active presence of the viewing subject: visiting the ruins of the Ancient Greek temples at Paestum, Goethe writes 'Only by walking around and through them can one really breathe life into them; and one feels it breathe out of them again, which is what the architect intended, indeed built into them' (179).

Despite Goethe's own preference for Greek and Roman architecture, the idea that architecture follows the method of nature and is animated by a living force was to be much more strongly associated with Gothic architecture. Particularly the younger members of Goethe's circle, the Schlegel brothers especially, involved in the German patriotic movement after Napoleon's victory over Prussia in 1805, were far more interested in Gothic, as a German art, and for most of the nineteenth century, Gothic was to be seen as the architecture which corresponded most closely to the natural model.

By far the two most sophisticated developments of the idea of architecture as a 'second nature' are to be found in the writings of the two great nineteenth-century architectural thinkers, the German architect Gottfried Semper, and the English critic John Ruskin. Both writers entirely accepted the distinction made by Goethe and German philosophers of the following generation that architecture, while having some similarities to nature, is itself not nature; as G. W. F. Hegel put it in his *Aesthetics* (1835), architecture 'is manifest as inorganic nature built by human hands', and differs from organic nature which is 'individualized and animated by its indwelling spirit' (vol. II, 653–54).

Semper's intellectual achievement, put bluntly, was by marrying Quatremère de Quincy's theory of imitation and artifice with the German idealist philosophy to produce by far the most sophisticated theory of the artificiality of architecture ever developed. With hindsight, one can say that it was largely Semper's ideas that made it possible for European architects in the early twentieth century to dispense altogether with the natural model of

Amphitheatre, Verona, engraving, F. Masieri, 1744. 'A second Nature.' The first Roman building seen by Goethe, who came to see in ancient architecture exactly the same vital processes as found in organic nature.

architecture. Semper was emphatic that the origins of architecture did not lie in nature. 'Architecture', said Semper in his inaugural lecture at Dresden in 1834, 'unlike the other arts does not find its patterns in nature' (H. Semper, 7; quoted in Ettlinger, 57). Instead, Semper believed that 'the industrial arts … are the key to understanding architectural as well as artistic form and rule in general' ('Attributes of Formal Beauty', 1856–59; Herrmann, *Semper*, 224). Accordingly, the greater part of Semper's writings are taken up not with architecture at all, but with the crafts of weaving, pottery, metalwork, carpentry and masonry. On the other hand, while Semper believed that architecture was not derived from nature, he did acknowledge that there was an analogy with nature in the way architectural forms developed, though he was always careful to stress that it was no more than an analogy. The inspiration for this was Cuvier's zoological

museum at the Jardin des Plantes in Paris, where specimens were arranged in evolutionary order; Semper's training in German idealist thought led him to perceive in these rows of skeletons the presence of pre-existing forms.

> Just as everything there develops and is explained by the simplest prototypical form, just as in nature in her infinite variety is yet simple and sparse in basic ideas, just as she renews continually the same skeletons by modifying them a thousandfold … in the same way, I said to myself, the works of my art are also based on certain standard forms conditioned by primordial ideas, yet which permit an infinite variety of phenomena. ('Prospectus, Comparative Theory of Building', 1852, in Semper, *The Four Elements and Other Writings*, 170)

Semper's notion of artifice is contained in two passages in particular – Part V of *The Four Elements of Architecture* (1851), and §60 of volume 1 of *Der Stil* (1861). In these pages, Semper developed three distinct but related arguments. The first was that historically the technical arts preceded the art of building, which is no more than the application to architectural themes of skills developed originally for other purposes – weaving (see Ill. p. 234), the firing of clay, the laying and cutting of stones for terracing, and carpentry. From these crafts developed the technical symbols, like the woven form of the fence, or the timber joints of carpentry, that give architecture its meaning. The second argument was that historically, man's desire for enclosure preceded his knowledge of the means to achieve it:

the formal creation of the idea of space... undoubtedly preceded the wall, even the most primitive one constructed out of stone or any other material.

The structure that served to support, to secure, to carry this spatial enclosure was a requirement that had nothing directly to do with *space* and the *division of space*. (*Der Stil*, 254)

It was the enclosure of space, not the construction of huts, that was the first architectural act. Accordingly, the art of making enclosures (originally from woven mats and carpets) provided the prime architectural symbol, a symbol which should never be lost sight of though the technical means of making walls may change. Semper writes,

Wickerwork, the original space divider, retained the full importance of its earlier meaning, actually or ideally, when later the light mat walls were transformed into clay tile, brick, or stone walls. Wickerwork was the *essence of the wall*. Hanging carpets remained the true walls, the visible boundaries of space. The often solid walls behind them were necessary for reasons that had nothing to do with the creation of space; they were needed for security, for supporting a load, for their permanence, and so on. Wherever the need for these secondary functions did not arise, the carpets remained the original means of separating space. Even where building solid walls became necessary, the latter were only the inner, invisible structure hidden behind the true and legitimate representatives of the wall, the colourful woven carpets. (*Four Elements*, 103–4)

The transmutation of the idea of the carpet into later walling materials ensured that the original meaning of the wall as a cladding, bounding a space, was not lost.

The third argument, which follows from the previous two, is that it is an inherent characteristic of architecture, once it has passed its most primitive stage, to mask the reality of the materials of which it is made. Semper's concept is similar to Quatremère de Quincy's, though he expresses it differently. Semper proposed that monumental architecture was derived originally from festival structures, timber scaffolds decorated with flowers and plants; when greater permanence was required, these decorative elements were transmuted into other materials, wood or stone. In a footnote, he continues:

I think that the *dressing* and the *mask* are as old as human civilization .... The denial of reality, of the material, is necessary if form is to emerge as a meaningful symbol, as an autonomous creation of man. ... The untainted feeling led primitive man to the denial of reality in all early artistic endeavours; the great, true masters of art in every field returned to it – only these men in times of high artistic development also *masked the material of the mask*. (*Der Stil*, 257)

Thus for Semper, the whole art of architecture rested in the ability to translate ideas or themes from one material to another; whereas for Quatremère, transmutation had been a way to maintain the old proposition that architecture was an art of natural imitation, Semper, with his German background, saw it as the main cause of architecture's meaning, a meaning which derived entirely from it being the work of man, and in no way dependent upon references to nature. It was Semper, therefore, who cut architecture's ties to nature.

If Semper's achievement was to marry Quatremère's Classicism with German Romantic thought, John Ruskin's was to infuse the English picturesque with the theories of the same German philosophical school.[5] Of all the writers in the English-speaking world, none, at any period, devoted as much attention to the relationship of art and of architecture to nature as Ruskin, and his ideas are not easily summarized. Ruskin's strongly religious outlook made him see nature as God's work, and this, together with his admiration for English landscape painting, caused him to believe firmly that nature was the only source of all beauty. His advice to the painter was to 'go to Nature in all singleness of heart, and walk with her laboriously and trustingly, having no other thoughts

The knot – 'the original technical symbol', from *Der Stil*, vol. 1, 1860. Semper was emphatic that architecture, unlike the other arts, derived not from nature, but from the various technical processes developed by mankind, of which weaving was one. Nonetheless, Semper also saw architecture as a 'second nature' in that its development was analogous to that of organic nature.

but how best to penetrate her meaning, and remember her instruction, rejecting nothing, selecting nothing, and scorning nothing' (*Modern Painters*, 1843, part III, section VI, chapter 3, §21). In *The Seven Lamps of Architecture* (1849), Ruskin offered similar advice to the architect: 'An architect should live as little in cities as a painter. Send him to our hills, and let him study there what nature understands by a buttress, and what by a dome' (chapter III, §24). Certainly Ruskin believed that beauty came originally from natural objects, and in 'The Lamp of Power' and of 'The Lamp of Beauty' followed Burke in suggesting that architecture achieved its effects through a 'sympathy' with nature. On the other hand, though, neither in painting, nor even less in architecture, did Ruskin think that the mere imitation of natural forms and objects would achieve anything but a most inferior and derivative beauty: the quality of true art came from the imposition of man's will, and his ability to impress his powers of invention upon the raw material offered by nature. As Ruskin was to put it, all that was noble in architecture came from 'the expression of man's delight in God's work' (*Stones of Venice*, vol. I, 1851, chapter xx, §3). It was this action of the will, first described by Ruskin in 'The Lamp of Life', and closely comparable to Goethe's 'will to create form', that gave architecture its power of mental expression, by which it communicated with and engaged human emotion. In a passage that summarizes his ideas in the early 1850s, Ruskin distinguished between man's

acceptance of the sources of delight from nature, and his development of authoritative or imaginative power in their arrangement: for the two mental elements, not only of Gothic, but of all good architecture … belong to it, and are admirable in it, chiefly as it is, more than any other subject of art, the work of man, and the expression of the average power of man. A picture or poem is often little more than a feeble utterance of man's admiration of something out of himself; but architecture approaches more to a creation of his own, born of his necessities, and expressive of his nature. (*Stones of Venice*, vol. 2, chapter vi, §40, 1853)

The two particular impulses which find their expression in architecture are 'the confession of Imperfection, and the confession of Desire of Change', and it is the presence of these that distinguishes human from natural architecture. 'The building of the bird and the bee needs not express anything like this. It is perfect and unchanging' (*ibid.*). Thus Ruskin was explicit that while architecture may derive its expressive means from the study of nature, there is no sense in which architecture is just the imitation of nature, for what qualifies it as architecture is the evidence it betrays of man's spiritual desire to create beauty himself. These ideas take us far from the sort of contemplation of nature recommended by advocates of the picturesque. Architecture, for Ruskin, is 'a second nature' because it is the outcome of the uniquely human faculty for mental and manual work; while this endows the best works of architecture with a life comparable to that of works of nature, they never attain the perfection of organic nature, against which architecture must always ultimately be judged. The greater part of Ruskin's voluminous writings on architecture are taken up with the question of how this conjunction of the human will with the material of nature is to be realized.

It should be added that in Ruskin's later writings his attitude towards nature changed. In *The Queen of the Air* (1869) and subsequent books, he took the view that the significance of nature was to be appreciated not through the observation of natural phenomena, but through mythology, which, Ruskin believed, expressed the meaning of nature and its essence more completely than mere observation. The significance of these ideas for subsequent architectural thought was limited; W. R. Lethaby's *Architecture, Mysticism and Myth* (1891) was the only attempt to develop these ideas in relation to architecture. In built works of architecture, perhaps the best instance of Ruskin's earlier notion of 'nature' was Deane and

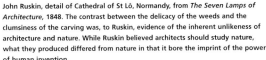

John Ruskin, detail of Cathedral of St Lô, Normandy, from *The Seven Lamps of Architecture*, 1848. The contrast between the delicacy of the weeds and the clumsiness of the carving was, to Ruskin, evidence of the inherent unlikeness of architecture and nature. While Ruskin believed architects should study nature, what they produced differed from nature in that it bore the imprint of the power of human invention.

Interior, Oxford Museum, Deane and Woodward, 1854–60. The inventiveness of the plant and animal carvings, expressive of the museum's purposes, made this one of the best contemporary demonstrations of Ruskin's ideas about the relationship of architecture and nature.

Woodward's Oxford Museum (1854–60); exemplifications of the later, more poetic theory may be found in the works of C. F. A. Voysey and C. H. Townsend.

8. *Nature as the antidote to 'culture'.* The notion that nature was a means of resistance to the artificiality of culture, present in eighteenth-century thought from Lord Shaftesbury's time onwards (see 5. above), was fully exploited by the English Romantic poets, Coleridge and Wordsworth. But it was particularly in the United States

that this idea was to have architectural consequences. The central figure here was the philosopher Ralph Waldo Emerson. Emerson's thoughts about nature were complex. Inspired by Goethe, and by the English Romantic poets, Emerson, writing in the 1830s, saw nature as the quality of things revealed by the power of man's mind: 'Its beauty is the beauty of his own mind' (1837, 87). But in nature, Emerson also saw the revelation of the supernatural: 'Every natural fact is a symbol of some spiritual fact' (1836, 49). Therefore, by means of nature, man realized his own spiritual being: 'every object rightly seen unlocks a new faculty of the soul' (1836, 55). Part of the significance of Emerson's thinking was its American context. Speaking in 1837, he complained 'We have listened too long to the courtly muses of Europe' (104), and he suggested that Americans seek their inspiration from direct experience of the everyday, and of nature:

I ask not for the great, the remote, the romantic; what is doing in Italy or Arabia; what is Greek art, or Provençal minstrelsy; I embrace the common, I explore and sit at the feet of the familiar, the low. Give me insight into today, and you may have the antique and future worlds. (102)

Part of this experience of the everyday was the American's encounter with natural surroundings, unconditioned by history, out of which might come a philosophy of life, and art. Some of the potential of these ideas for architecture were recognized by Emerson's contemporary Horatio Greenough in his essay 'American Architecture' of 1843, but the person upon whom Emerson's ideas had the greatest impact was the architect Louis Sullivan, whose writings not only echo Emerson's style, but whose adulation of nature is entirely in the spirit of Emerson's transcendentalism. Sullivan's essays 'Inspiration' (1886), and particularly 'What is Architecture?' (1906), are pure Emerson, but it was in his architecture, and particularly the ornate decoration (so disturbing to modernists), that Sullivan sought to create work free of cultural convention and tradition, and to realize Emerson's ideal – 'Art [is] a nature passed through the alembic of man' (1836, 47). Louis Sullivan's assistant Frank Lloyd Wright apparently absorbed many of the same Emersonian ideas, but was to realize them architecturally without resorting to naturalistic decoration.

9. *The rejection of nature.* In European thought generally, interest in 'nature' as a putative model for the arts went into sharp decline in the second half of the nineteenth century. This was to some extent due to developments in natural science itself, the theories of Darwin and others, which effectively emphasized the dissimilarity between natural processes and artistic ones. For writers and artists, nature held less and less interest. 'Nature teaches us nothing', wrote Charles Baudelaire in 'The Painter of Modern Life' in 1863, 'Nature can counsel nothing but crime' (31–32); the quality of art for Baudelaire lay in its artificiality. And a similarly categorical distinction between nature and art was a general theme of Friedrich

Nietzsche's: as he wrote in *The Birth of Tragedy* (1872), 'Art is not an imitation of nature, but rather a metaphysical supplement raised up beside it to overcome it' (140 – translated in White, 343). In social and political thought, too, ideas about nature were transformed in this period: Marx and Engels postulated two kinds of nature, the first that from which man takes his materials, the second being the nature *produced* by man as a result of his activities, and which itself becomes a commodity.[6] The distinction between 'nature' and 'culture' – hitherto so important – was now itself called into question.

By the end of nineteenth century, particularly for those architects who espoused the 'modern', nature had nothing to offer. To the Viennese architect Otto Wagner, the first widely acknowledged proponent of a modern architecture in the 1890s, the distinctive quality of architecture was that 'it alone is able to make forms that have no model in nature' (62), and 'is able to present the product as a completely new formation' (81). This point of view, which followed so easily from the arguments of Gottfried Semper, was to be the characteristic attitude of modernist architecture in the early twentieth century, and to dominate architectural thought generally. If 'nature' was no longer any use as an organizing category in thinking about architecture, what were its substitutes? As a general problem, for all the visual arts, this was recognized by the German art historian Wilhelm Worringer in his book *Abstraction and Empathy* (1908). Art as Worringer saw it neither represents nature, nor is a second nature, nor takes its value from references to nature; rather it stands 'beside nature on equal terms and, in its deepest and innermost essence, devoid of any connection with it, in so far as by nature is understood the visible surface of things' (3). Worringer's argument was that art was an independent phenomenon of its own, comprehensible only in terms of its own laws, manifested particularly in the tension in art between tendencies on the one hand to abstraction, and on the other hand to expression. The value Worringer gave to abstraction was to have wide influence on architects as well as artists in the interwar years: for the Dutch De Stijl artist van Doesburg, for example, it was the task of art to negate all aspects of nature, including gravity.

Seen in terms of the subsequent history of twentieth-century architecture, the most significant answer to the question of what would replace 'nature' as the organizing concept for architecture was provided by the Italian Futurists. According to the Futurist architecture Manifesto of 1914, 'Just as the ancients drew the inspiration for their art from the elements of nature, so

Detail, gates of Getty Tomb, Graceland Cemetery, Chicago, L. Sullivan, 1890. Sullivan's florid decoration, which puzzled later modernists, related to a transcendentalist tradition that saw in nature the revelation of the everyday, unpolluted by culture. (See p. 160 for full picture.)

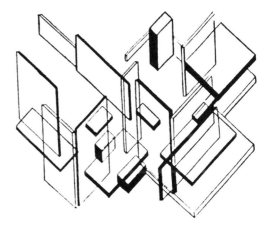

Theo van Doesburg and Cor van Eesteren, isometric drawing of Maison Particulière, 1923. 'A de-naturalized reality': for the neoplasticists, the aim of art was to create a world independent of 'nature'.

we ... must find this inspiration in the elements of the immensely new mechanical world which we have created' (Conrads, 38; see ill. p. 213). This notion that it is in technology that architecture finds its model has without doubt been the single most important idea to replace 'nature' in the twentieth century; and the passion with which the idea has been supported can be at least partly explained by the need to fill the void left by the eviction of 'nature' and the fear of its re-encroachment. But technology has not been the only substitute for nature; the other principal one has been architecture's own tradition. Examples of this argument occur in two English books approximately contemporary with the Futurist architecture Manifesto, Reginald Blomfield's *The Mistress Art* (1908), and Geoffrey Scott's *The Architecture of*

Humanism (1914). Both books were outspoken attacks upon Ruskinian naturalism, and proposed in its stead the study of works of architecture themselves: as Blomfield put it, the science of the architect 'can only be acquired by the study and observation of actual buildings. For these are our "nature" – not trees and caves and rocks. The study of buildings and materials is, to the architect, what the study of anatomy is to the sculptor' (104–5).

However, by no means all twentieth-century modernist architects negated nature. Two outstanding exceptions are the American architect Frank Lloyd Wright, and the Swiss architect Le Corbusier. Wright's emphasis upon nature belongs in the American tradition of Emerson and Sullivan (discussed under 8. above). Of

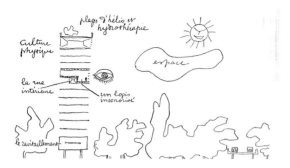

Le Corbusier, man, architecture and nature: diagram of the Unité d'Habitation (see p. 113). 'A man stands on his floor before a wall of glass, facing the sun, space and verdure. His eye sees these things': Le Corbusier saw architecture's purpose as to restore man to nature – and create the conditions for contemplating it in comfort.

Wright's many statements about nature, the following is characteristic: 'Primarily, Nature furnished the materials for architectural motifs out of which the architectural forms as we know them have developed' ('In the Cause of Architecture', 1908, *Collected Writings*, vol. 1, 86). While this sounds like an eighteenth-century writer, its intended meaning was rather different, and concerns the identity of an American architecture. And it is worth adding that when an American architect of the next generation, Louis Kahn, went out of his way to dismiss 'nature' ('What man makes, nature cannot make'), this was partly a sign of an explicit re-engagement by an American with European traditions.

The other exception to the general rejection of 'nature' by modernist architects was Le Corbusier. Le Corbusier's early training had been heavily influenced by his reading of Ruskin, and apart from an interlude in the 1920s when he was more taken up in Futurist, machine-age imagery, the passion for 'nature' inspired by Ruskin was always present. The primary object of Le Corbusier's main town-planning project, the Ville Radieuse, of which the Unité was a built fragment, was to restore to man the relationship with nature that he had lost as a result of urbanization. Le Corbusier's de-urbanization projects of the 1930s and 1940s all belong to a general concern to return man to conditions under which he could contemplate and enjoy 'nature' more perfectly. The Unité was conceived as a complex mechanism to achieve this end: in it, the realization of 'nature' becomes the purpose of architecture.

10. *Environmentalism: nature as ecosystem, and the critique of capitalism.* The previous meanings of 'nature' have been entirely transformed since the late 1960s by the environmental movement, which has taken issue with the old assumption that 'nature' and 'culture' are separate categories, and instead emphasized that they are part of a single system. The effect of this has been to reverse the indifference shown to 'nature' by orthodox modernists (particularly those brought up within the Semper tradition), and to make nature once again a powerful concept within architecture, though imprecise as ever. Recognition that buildings are extravagant users of energy – up to half the world's energy use goes into the production and operation of buildings – and voracious consumers of natural resources – in the USA alone 3000 acres of virgin soil a day are built upon – with major effects on the delicate balance of ecological systems, has led to architecture being seen as a practice with influence over the future of life on the planet. Exemplifying this argument Richard Rogers writes: 'Architecture needs to minimize its confrontation with nature. To do that it must respect nature's laws. ... Working our buildings into the cycle of nature will return architecture to its very roots' (1997, 98). Seen in these terms, architecture is judged by the least disturbance it creates within the ecosystem; Rogers's Bordeaux Law Courts, whose very shape is the result of a 'natural air-conditioning system', exemplifies this approach, and is presented as an antidote to conventional large office buildings, described by Rogers as 'an energy-guzzling environment that isolates people from nature' (88).

The 'nature' to which Rogers and the proponents of 'sustainable' architecture refer is by no means a straightforward concept. The environmental movement, from where these ideas come, is itself characterized by its pluralism, its multiple origins, and widely divergent aims.[7] On the one hand, its intellectual foundation lies in the political philosophy of the Frankfurt School, in particular Theodor Adorno and Max Horkheimer's *The Dialectic of the Enlightenment* (1947), where the primary issue confronting society was presented not as the exploitation of man by man, but the exploitation of nature (in all its senses) by man. Seen in these terms, the critique of capitalism shifted from the social relations of production, to the relations between human beings and 'nature'. This argument provided at least part of the basis of the Green movement, and has sustained its attacks upon international capitalism; it has also stimulated the development of an 'alternative' architecture, employing techniques and processes outside the main system of industrial production, as an intentional critique of the dominant political and economic order. The works of Rogers, nor of most other exponents of green

architecture, would not fall within this category.
On the other hand, the potentially destructive effect
of technology upon the world, a concern first voiced
in Rachel Carson's book *Silent Spring* of 1962 (widely
credited as being one of the main inspirations of the
Green movement), does not itself mean that advanced
technology is inimicable to green buildings. A work
like Foster Associates' Frankfurt Commerzbank uses
non-traditional materials and sophisticated electronic
systems to create a building with low levels of energy
consumption; certainly for Foster, and for many other
architects, respect for nature's laws does not preclude a
high level of artifice in the finished results. Sustainable or
'green' architecture, defined by one writer as 'buildings
which use lightly the earth's resources, and are expressive
also of a way of living which thinks itself in partnership
with nature' (Farmer, 6), is – like the green movement
itself – a very broad church. Environmentalism may have
made 'nature' into a new measure of architectural quality,
but there is far from universal agreement as to what it
means to 'work buildings into the cycle of nature' – a
difference exemplified by the divergence of opinion as to
what are the proper materials for a 'green' architecture.[8]
The persuasiveness of environmentalism, and its many
contradictions, will almost certainly ensure that 'nature'
continues to be an active – and disputed – category
within architecture.

1 See Herrmann, *The Theory of Claude Perrault*, 1973, 42, 140, 168–79;
and introduction by A. Pérez-Gomez to Perrault, *Ordonnance*, 1993, 1–44.

2 See Rykwert, *On Adam's House in Paradise*, 1972, for the history of
this theme.

3 See Lee, *Ut Pictura Poesis*, 1967, for a full account of the post-Renaissance
development of the theory of mimesis. On the relationship of this theory to the
relative social value of the different arts, see P. O. Kristeller, 'The Modern System
of the Arts', 1951.

4 Watkin, *Sir John Soane*, 1996, 213–15.

5 See Swenarton, *Artisans and Architects*, 1989, chapter 1, for Ruskin's debt
to German philosophy.

6 See Neil Smith, *Uneven Development*, 1984, especially 16–28.

7 For a discussion of the contradictoriness of 'nature' within environmentalism,
see Soper, *What is Nature?*, 1995, especially chapter 8.

8 See Hagan, 'The Good, the Bad and the Juggled', 1998.

Law Courts, Bordeaux, Richard Rogers and Partners, 1993–98.
'Nature' as eco-system. The aim of architecture becomes to cause the least
interference with nature: here the shape of the timber oval domes above the
court rooms was designed to optimize natural ventilation and do away with
the need for energy-consuming mechanical ventilation.

To create architecture *is to put in order*. Put what in order? Functions and objects. Le Corbusier, *Precisions*, 68

Now architecture consists of Order, which in Greek is called *taxis*. ... Order is the balanced adjustment of the details of the work separately, and, as to the whole, the arrangement of the proportion with a view to a symmetrical result. Vitruvius, *De Architectura*, Book I, chapter 2

The English word 'order' has a superabundance of meanings – the Oxford English Dictionary gives thirty-one for the noun and nine for the verb. Only a couple of these are specific to architecture, but it would be too much to expect that in its architectural currency, 'order' should have resisted promiscuous relations with at least some of the thirty-eight other meanings. The clearest way to understanding 'order' in architecture is to look at the ends to which it has been directed. Until the early 1970s (when the entire significance of order shifted) these were four: 1. the attainment of beauty, through a relationship of parts to the whole; 2. the representation of the ranks (orders) of society; 3. the avoidance of chaos, through architecture's use as model, or instrument, of social and civil order; 4. in an urbanistic sense, to resist the inherent tendency of cities to disorder. These senses are not necessarily always distinct – indeed from their overlapping comes much of the interest of the concept. 'Order' was a property highly valued by the first generation of modernist architects (as the quotation from Le Corbusier suggests), but of all the modernist concepts, it was one of the most susceptible to attack; it was variously criticized from within architecture during the 1960s, and then from without, in a way that altered its entire significance, as will be described.

1. *The attainment of beauty, through the relationship of parts to the whole*. The passage from Vitruvius quoted above gives the original sense of 'order' as it was understood in architecture in antiquity, a sense which has continued into the present. However, even in antiquity, there was already an ambiguity between this general sense, and the various particular systems of order, the 'Orders', Doric, Ionic, Corinthian etc. Throughout the history of the classical tradition, the overlapping of these two senses, the general and the particular, has been to their mutual advantage, as one may see in a remark by the architect Charles Moore in 1977: 'we'll have to do more than clothe our buildings in the semantically appropriate Orders. We will have to bring comprehensible Order to them'.

Vitruvius, in his choice of the term 'order' to describe the harmonious arrangement of parts, borrowed it – as presumably had Greek architects before him – from Aristotle's notion of *taxis*. In his *Metaphysics*, discussing mathematics, Aristotle had stated 'The chief forms of beauty are order and symmetry and definiteness, which the mathematical sciences demonstrate in a special degree' (1078b). Aristotle made use of the same idea, but this time as a biological analogy, in his discussion of plot structure in chapter 7 of the *Poetics*: 'to be beautiful, a living creature, and every whole made up of parts, must not only present a certain order in its arrangement of parts, but also be of a certain definite magnitude. Beauty is a matter of size and order...'. The meaning of 'order' as the beauty of a mathematical, or biological, relationship of parts to the whole, adopted by Vitruvius, has been used successively from antiquity to the Renaissance, and into our own times, though not, as Rykwert (1996) shows, in a direct continuity. From Alberti to the present there have been repeated attempts to find mathematical, or geometric principles that could supply architecture with a system of 'order'. Le Corbusier's proportional system, the Modulor, and Christopher Alexander's

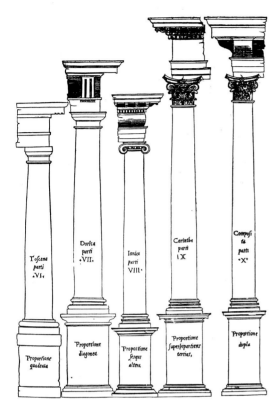

The Orders, from S. Serlio, *Dell'Architettura*, Book IV, 1537. The sixteenth-century architect Sebastiano Serlio was the first to systematize the 'orders' as 'five styles of building'; but since antiquity 'order' had been used to signify both the general arrangement of parts in relation to the whole, and a species of column.

mathematical sets are among the more recent examples.

All these various attempts to define the order within architecture present some fairly major epistemological problems. First of all, what exactly is it that architecture orders? Matter? Space? Flows? Perception? Social relations? Until one can say in what the order consists, no scheme of order can be created – but by defining what is to be ordered (always a mental abstraction from reality of the object), the order created is already circumscribed and predetermined after the model of the abstraction. Or, to put this slightly differently, 'order' is invariably about abstractions, rather than things, so that if we find 'order' in architecture, it is, tautologically, the reconstitution as an object of what we first knew as an abstraction. The second problem is where does the order come from? Out of the mind, evidently, but in what form? Mathematics, as we have seen, has been a

popular source for order in architecture, but there have been other models too, principally nature, also suggested by Aristotle, and pursued by Renaissance theorists. When the eighteenth-century French theorist Quatremère de Quincy wrote that architecture's model lay 'in the order of nature', and went on to add that such an order 'exists everywhere without being visible anywhere' ('Architecture', 33), he was in a sense reiterating what was a very old idea. But even during Quatremère's lifetime, developments in scientific thought were to change 'nature' itself from a generalized abstraction into a phenomenon whose inner workings were susceptible to analysis, and so to diversify the possible invisible 'orders' of nature, thereby creating a highly fertile source of new models for architecture. John Ruskin's studies in the nineteenth century of crystal and mineral formations (see ill. p. 129), and the interest among twentieth-century architects in the biologist D'Arcy Thompson's study of the growth patterns of plants and animals in his *On Growth and Form* (1917), are but two instances of the employment of other notions of 'order' than those deriving from mathematics. In the post-1945 era, interest in 'order' has shifted to the psychology of perception, to the study of human perception as the key to order in the world of artefacts: Christopher Alexander's research on mathematical sets was predicated on the principle that these were the patterns most easily grasped by human perception; and the basis of Kevin Lynch's analysis of the order of cities was not the cities themselves, but the perceptual apparatus through which people knew them.

2. *As a representation of the ranks (orders) of society.*
That architecture both designated, and protected, social rank was understood in antiquity. Vitruvius outlined the variations between the houses of different occupations in Book VI, chapter V of *De Architectura*, remarking that 'if buildings are planned with a view to the status of the client … we shall escape censure'. With the craze for domestic building that affected Europe after about 1450, the architectural expression of social distinctions became an important business: a major feature of the post-Renaissance classical tradition was attention to 'decorum' and 'propriety', the signification of social rank. These matters that were just as fundamental a part of the classical system as an understanding of the Orders themselves – and indeed the correct use of the Orders demanded a knowledge of the principles of decorum. The importance of the relationship between social rank and domestic architecture was made clear by Sir Henry Wotton in his *Elements of Architecture* (1624), where

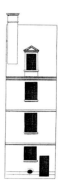

Houses of different sizes maintained differences of social rank by the *decorum* of their appearance. From Le Muet, *Manière de Bien Bastir*, 1647.

he says 'Every Mans proper Mansion House and Home' deserves 'according to the degree of the Master, to be decently and delightfully adorned' (82). What made 'decorum' such an inflammatory issue was the social discourse that had developed in the sixteenth century around the extravagance of domestic building: on the one hand, those who had the means were considered under an obligation to build lavishly, particularly if they held political office; but on the other hand, magnificent building excited the envy of social inferiors, whose tendency to emulate their superiors' extravagance caused the initial distinction of rank to vanish, and so threatened the existence of social hierarchy, and thereby civil order.[1] This tension was everywhere felt in sixteenth- and seventeenth-century Europe – a French example of 1515 indicates the kind of argument:

> those gentlemen who have no stipend or benefice from the king, or only a little one, want to imitate completely or in part the style of the court. It could not happen otherwise, for never have the remainder of the subjects yearned to do anything other than live according to the example of princes and their courts. By this means the nobility is destroyed for lack of proper ordering... (Seyssel)

It was to regulate these pretensions, and so protect social hierarchy, that the notion of 'decorum', of forms of architectural decoration appropriate to the station of the patron, was developed. After the French Revolution interest in decorum declined, presumably because it had proved worthless in protecting social rank. Whatever sense of it persisted into the twentieth century was subverted finally by architects like Lutyens, whose small houses for bourgeois clients were built with the mannerisms of aristocratic mansions (see ill. p. 54).

3. *The avoidance of chaos, through the use of architecture as a model, or instrument, of social order.* From the late eighteenth century, there was a perceived connection between architectural 'order' and social 'order' – whether taken in the sense of keeping 'good order', or in a more specific sense of a naturally existing, pre-ordained arrangement of society. The connection was presented both as a loose association, and also as an exact correspondence, capable of regulation. As an example of the loose association, we may take the English architect C. R. Cockerell's Royal Academy lectures in 1841. Cockerell's main interest in 'order' came from his criticisms of the picturesque, whose practitioners had, he felt, gone too far in cultivating variety and irregularity, 'forgetting that the building is to derive its chief effect from the contrast of its regularity and order with the surrounding irregular objects and scenery' (159). However, Cockerell also drew a connection between architectural and social order: 'If we call to mind the fact, that the greatest architectural efforts have usually followed periods of political and moral disorder, we may recognize in such works that natural love of order, which revolutions and tumults have denied' (159).

If Cockerell thought that ordered architecture was the natural response to political disorder, the prospect of a precise regulation of the body politic through architectural means was brought to a high degree of perfection in the institutional buildings developed in the late eighteenth and early nineteenth centuries.

Undoubtedly the most famous exponent of this theme was the English philosopher Jeremy Bentham, with his Panopticon scheme for a model prison (see ill. p. 191), whose architecture he believed would create within all who entered it 'a sense of clockwork regularity' to the degree that 'action scarcely follows thought'.[2] While the Panopticon, developed in the late 1780s, was undoubtedly the clearest instance of a building conceived to restore ordered relationships within a world otherwise chaotic and lacking in order, it is by no means the only example. Indeed, Bentham thought that one of the great merits of the Panopticon was that it was a model capable of being applied to any institution. There had already in the 1780s been built in Britain a series of prisons designed by William Blackburn, under the influence of the prison reformer John Howard, that contrived to restore the inmates to an understanding of a desired model of social relations. Interest in these experiments was stimulated by the events of the French Revolution, an event which seemed to confirm what many had previously suspected, that society was inherently disordered and unstable, and in need of corrective measures if it was to continue. In the first part of the nineteenth century, much attention was given in all European countries to the means of regulating society by, amongst other things, architecture; the considerable interest in not just prisons, but all institutional buildings, hospitals, schools, workhouses, asylums and factories, all derived from a concern to regulate social relations, and curb the entropic tendencies of those at the margins of society, the sick, poor, the insane, and the young.

When Bernard Tschumi, discussing architectural modernism, wrote in 1977 'De Stijl's insistence on elementary form was not only a return to some anachronistic purity but also a deliberate regression to a secure order' (82), the 'order' to which he refers is clearly moral, just as Cockerell's was, but directed not at society at large, but at the psychology of the individual.

4. *Counteracting the disorder of cities*. There have been complaints about the disorder of cities for as long as there have been cities: indeed, it has been generally supposed that cities are inherently chaotic and need to have imposed upon them some sort of order to make them fit to live in. In the thinking about this subject since the early Renaissance, it has been assumed that a city with clearly defined parts (see ill. p. 244) will be orderly, and moreover that a city whose buildings, streets and squares are arranged to look regular will have order. The seeds of this idea are present in Alberti, who to achieve order advised attention to the layout and composition of roads and squares, and recommended the segregation of foreigners into zones of their own (191). The supposition that what looks ordered will be orderly, has, it must be said, been one of the great fallacies of the modern era, but it has neverthless been taken for granted by exponents of urban design, from Alberti, to Baron Haussmann, to Daniel Burnham and to the master-planners of the 1950s and 1960s. The history of, say, St Petersburg, or Paris, in the twentieth century, will rapidly confirm that there is no reason to assume that a place with physical order will be politically stable.

What can be seen over the last two hundred and fifty years is a series of attempts to escape from this fallacy, to recognize that the visual appearance of order is a mere phantasm intended to make what is inherently chaotic appear well regulated, and to acknowledge that discord is what makes a city a city. It has not been an easy argument to make, for if one is not to have visual order in a city, is one then to have disorder? And since disorder is what cities produce of their own accord, what need would there then be left for an architect or planner, whose principal skill, as they have frequently reminded us, is in the creation of *order*? One of the earliest instances of an attempt to break with the baroque illusion occurs in Laugier's *Essay on Architecture* of 1753, where, after the usual complaints about the disorder of Paris, Laugier made the surprising plea that a city should contain a multitudinous variety in its details, 'so that there is yet order and a sort of confusion' (224). This plea for variety he took up again, reversing the argument, in his *Observations sur l'Architecture* of 1765: 'Whoever knows how to design a park will have no difficulty in tracing the plan for a city.... It must have regularity and fantasy, relationships and oppositions, accidents which vary the picture, great order in the details, confusion, uproar, tumult in the whole' (312–13). Laugier's successors did not follow his advice – Haussmann's Paris is, if anything, the opposite, ordered in the whole, chaotic in the details. In recent times, there has been a return to an interest in the disorder of cities. Kevin Lynch, in *The Image of the City* (1960), while concerned that cities should be seen as a coherent pattern, recognized that in many American cities 'areas of formal order have little character' (22). Lynch insisted that 'complete chaos … is never pleasurable', but at the same time wanted to avoid an environment so ordered as to inhibit future patterns of activity: 'what we seek is not a final but an open-ended order, capable of continuous further development' (6). A growing fascination with urban disorder appears in

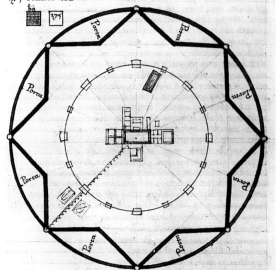

Senentrione: Questi quadretti sono ciascuno uno stadio ilquale stadio e 375 braccia .00.

I nella testa doriente Io fo lachiesa maggiore & inquella occidente fo ilpalazzo reale lequali grandezze alpresente non tocho pche quando la faremo allora intenderete tutto dalla parte della piazza inuer settentrione Io fo lapiazza demercatim laqual fo larga uno quarto di stadio cioe nouanta tre braccia & tre quarti & lungha mezzo stadio & dalla parte meredana della piazza fo unaltra piazza oue sora come due uno mercato & iui suiendera cose damangare & come e labeccheria & frume & herbe & altre simili cose plobisogno della uita delhuomo & questa sora largha interzo distadio & lungha due terzi cioe braccia dugento cinquanta a ppresso diquesta intesta glifo ilpalazzo delcapitano dacento appresso lacorte che solo lastrada lasparte & inquella demercatim dauna testa fo ilpalazzo delpodesta & dallaltra parte opposita quello doue siiene laragione del comune Dalla parte settentrionale fo laprigione comune laquale uiene nesse direto alpalazzo della ragione Dalla parte orientale dacento della piazza fo lerario cioe doue sifa & conserua lomoneta & appresso ladoghana nella piazza delmercato sora come o detto ilpalazzo delcapitano & dauna

Filarete, plan of the ideal city of Sforzinda, c. 1460–64. Perfect form as the image of perfect society – but history does not show that orderly plans necessarily produce social stability.

Venturi and Scott Brown's *Learning from Las Vegas* of 1972: quoting Henri Bergson's definition of disorder as 'an order we cannot see', they present the environment of Las Vegas's main street, the Strip, as one not readily apparent, but only emergent:

> the order of the Strip *includes*; it includes at all levels, from the mixture of seemingly incongruous land uses to the mixture of seemingly incongruous advertising media plus a system of neo-Organic or neo-Wrightian restaurant motifs in Walnut Formica. It is not an order dominated by the expert and made easy for the eye. (52–53)

Quoting August Heckscher, they say 'Chaos is very near; its nearness, but its avoidance, gives … force'. But without question, the work which most completely broke apart the old connection between visual order and urban order was Richard Sennett's *The Uses of Disorder* (1970). Sennett was critical of the purified, seemingly secure world of the white middle-class suburbs of America, and the withdrawal of most aspects of social interaction into the domain of the family. He argued that the problem of American cities lay in urban planning's misguided goal of aiming to reduce or avoid social conflict altogether in the city; instead, argued Sennett,

> What should emerge in city life is the occurrence of social relations, and especially relations involving social conflict, through face-to-face encounters. For experiencing the friction of differences and conflicts makes men personally aware of the milieu around their own lives … To make the experience of conflict a maturing one requires the destruction of an assumption regnant since the work of Baron Haussmann in Paris, an assumption that the planning of cities should be directed to bring order and clarity to the city as a whole. Instead of this idea … the city must be conceived as a social order of parts without a coherent, controllable whole form. … Encouraging unzoned urban places, no longer centrally controlled, would thus promote visual and functional disorder in the city. My belief is that this disorder is *better* than dead, predetermined planning, which restricts effective social exploration. (138–42)

Sennett's call for disorder meant dispensing with city planning as it was known; would the same be true of architecture?

Within modernist architectural circles, from the 1920s

Paris, junction of Boulevard Voltaire and Boulevard Richard-Lenoir, nineteenth-century postcard. 'An assumption that the planning of cities should be directed to bring order and clarity to the city as a whole': Haussmann's Paris was the principal example of an orderliness against which radical urbanists rebelled in the 1960s.

to the 1960s, 'order' was a strong concept – indeed for many practitioners it was the concept that legitimated their activity and gave them the right to intervene in the social domain. As Le Corbusier's remarks in *Precisions* (quoted at the beginning of this entry) made clear, 'order' was a term that subsumed both compositional and functional considerations – and this was its appeal to the English architects Alison and Peter Smithson, who in the 1950s routinely described what they did as 'ordering', rather than 'designing'. The range of meaning incorporated by 'order' could be bafflingly large, as shown in Mies van der Rohe's inaugural address on his appointment to the Armour Institute (later Illinois Institute of Technology) in 1938. It is worth quoting part of this:

> The idealistic principle of order, however, with its over-emphasis on the ideal and the formal, satisfies

neither our interest in truth and simplicity nor our practical sense.

> So we shall emphasize the organic principle of order that makes the parts meaningful and measurable while determining their relationship to the whole.

> And on this we shall have to make a decision.

> The long path from material through purpose to creative work has only a single goal: to create order out of the godforsaken confusion of our time.

> But we want an order that gives to each thing its proper place, and we want to give each thing what is suitable to its nature. (Neumeyer, 317)

Mies saw order as a key concept in architecture: what he meant by it includes the first of the senses described above (the relationship of parts to the whole), the third (a remedy for chaos and confusion), and even a hint of

860–880 Lakeshore Drive, Chicago, Mies van der Rohe, 1948–51. 'Uniform and orderly pattern': modern architecture's love of 'order' became a soft target in the 1960s.

the second, in his claim that each thing (rather than person) have its proper place.

In the 1950s, Mies van der Rohe's work was valued by American critics for amongst other things, its order; for example, Peter Blake commented that 860 Lakeshore Drive 'presents a uniform and orderly pattern to the outside world' (194). Architects in the 1960s reacting against orthodox modernism picked on this category in particular as a soft target – soft partly because of the flabbiness it had acquired from overuse in the previous decades, partly because of the paradoxes inherent to it. The first extensive critique of what he called the modernist architects' 'prim dreams of pure order' (104) came from Robert Venturi, in his *Complexity and Contradiction in Architecture* of 1966. Venturi's book was not an argument against order – on the contrary, it was strongly in favour of it – but suggested that it was to be understood in a different way, and found in different places, to the assumptions made by orthodox modernism. There were two not connected arguments. The first, the book's most explicit theme, proposed that it was possible to have an orderly whole in works of architecture while the relationship of the parts themselves was complex and contradictory; they should be able to accommodate inconsistencies and irregularities demanded by the needs of programme and use without losing their overall coherence. Indeed, for Venturi, what gives architecture its interest is when order is broken by such anomalies. 'A building with no "imperfect" part can have no perfect part, because contrast supports meaning. An artful discord gives vitality to architecture' (41). But, he insists, 'Order must exist before it can be broken', and 'Indeed a propensity to break the order can justify exaggerating it' (41). Venturi's wish was to see buildings whose overall order was sufficiently strong to accommodate unanticipated alterations and additions: 'Our buildings must survive the cigarette machine' (42). The first of Venturi's arguments concerning order was essentially one to do with composition, and while original, still belonged within the original, Vitruvian sense. The second of Venturi's arguments was entirely different, and took issue with the conventional view amongst American architects, critics and urbanists that the landscape of American cities was disordered. Taking his cue from Pop artists, Venturi, discussing photographs of American streets, argued that

in some of these compositions there is an inherent sense of unity not far from the surface. It is not the obvious or easy unity derived from the dominant binder or the motival order of simpler, less

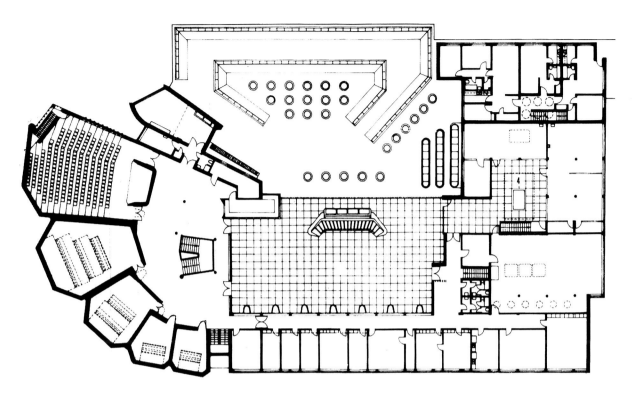

Plan, Cultural Centre, Wolfsburg, A. Aalto, 1958–63. 'He does not disperse the parts nor make them similar as Mies does…': Venturi admired Aalto for refusing to succumb to modernism's compulsion for orderliness.

contradictory compositions, but that derived from a complex and illusive order of the difficult whole. (104)

In other words, Venturi argued that urban scenes which most people had dismissed as chaos, if one chose to look carefully, in fact manifested an order. 'It is perhaps from the everyday landscape, vulgar and disdained, that we can draw the complex and contradictory order that is valid and vital for our architecture as an urbanistic whole' (104). This was the theme pursued in *Learning from Las Vegas*.

Other architects and critics in the late 1960s also started to take an interest in disorder – Robert Maxwell, quoting Robert Herrick's poem 'A sweet disorder in the dresse', saw the architect's or city planner's problem as 'how to generate a satisfying complexity from a simple and essentially controllable system' (26). While it was one thing to talk of 'disorder', it was another to build it: one work in particular, Alvar Aalto's Wolfsburg

Cultural Centre, had aroused interest as a building which accommodated a number of distinct parts, each with their own separate geometrical system. Venturi had commented on this building, and it was written about at length by Dimitri Porphyrios – though however disparate the various spaces within, the overall form is strongly unified.

The entire re-orientation of the significance of 'order' occurred in the late 1960s through the work of two French philosophers, Michel Foucault and Henri Lefebvre. Neither were concerned directly with 'order' in architecture as such, but rather with 'order' in general, though both were aware of architecture's peculiar concern with 'order'. For both Foucault and Lefebvre, the creation of systems of order had been one of the main features of modern capitalism, and those systems of order pervaded thought, social life, economic relations, time, space, indeed everything. For both thinkers, the propensity to reduce the totality of experience to systems of abstract order was the single most distinctive feature of the modern world. Space is no exception, and according to

Foucault, 'In our era, space presents itself to us in the form of patterns of ordering' (351), that is to say not as direct experience, but in the various abstract schemes of series, trees and networks developed to comprehend it. In so far as architecture manifests 'order', it is merely reproducing more of what is already everywhere present. Within this scheme, the interest shown by architects in 'order' might be seen as a trivial game entirely internal to their own practice, and of no wider concern; but both Foucault, and more particularly Lefebvre, saw architects as carrying a general partial responsibility for the widespread prevalence of abstract models of thought. Lefebvre was critical of the *reductivism* of all forms of thought as they present themselves in the modern world, the tendency to privilege a single concept, and make everything else fit that concept. The reduced models developed by specialists are particularly dangerous because applied within a particular practice they impose an order, with its own self-fulfilling justification and finality. 'Urbanism and architecture provide good examples of this. The working class, in particular, suffers the effects of such "reduced models", including models of space, of consumption, and of so-called culture' (107).

The effect of Foucault's and Lefebvre's writing was that it was no longer possible to talk about 'order' innocently in architecture: in works of architecture, one was looking at a particular manifestation of the same formations, the same ordering processes that were encountered in all other aspects of life. Probably the first architect to appreciate this, and to try to turn it to advantage, was Bernard Tschumi. For Tschumi, the alliance of modern science and capitalism had resulted in the reduction of the world to models and concepts; his often repeated concern was to resist the dematerialization of architecture into the realm of concepts, making him suspicious of all categories of thought created around architecture, and particularly those which proclaimed architecture as having a 'unity'. The 'unity' of works of architecture was a product of the myth of 'the unified, centered, and self-generative subject, whose own autonomy is reflected in the formal autonomy of the work' ('Disjunctions', 208). Tschumi's aim was to conceive, and present, his work as free of the conceptual models which had allowed modern architecture to become enmeshed with capitalism and modern science. In particular, this meant questioning notions of unity and order. Of two works, one theoretical (*Manhattan Transcripts*, 1978 – see ill. p. 194), the other built (Parc de la Villette, Paris – see ill. p. 285), Tschumi wrote 'As they are conceived, both works have no beginnings, no

ends. They are operations composed of repetitions, distortions, superpositions, and so forth. Although they have their own internal logic … The idea of order is constantly questioned, challenged, pushed to the edge' (209). In other words, for Tschumi, to question 'order' was to be concerned neither with the pursuit of beauty, nor with the avoidance of chaos, but rather with defining what an architect could still do in the post-structuralist era without becoming an accomplice in the general reduction of all things to abstract models.

It will be noticed though, that Tschumi did not suggest that 'order' could be dispensed with altogether, simply that it could be questioned. And other architects whose works appear entirely lacking in 'order', Coop Himmelblau, or Morphosis, however chaotic and all-inclusive they try to make the process of designing or constructing their buildings, remain surprisingly strongly attached to 'order', albeit open-ended: Thom Mayne of Morphosis, while committed to the ideas that architecture should reflect the flux of modern culture through its incompleteness, nonetheless insists 'Our concern is to establish and work within coherences, or orders, that are general and multivalent' (8). One recent commentator, Paul-Alan Johnson, remarks that 'Order in architecture is undoubtedly considered by many architects to be too well-known to excite interest now' (240). While it may be true that 'order' is less talked about now than it was thirty years ago, this is hardly to do with its becoming 'too well-known'; rather the reason is that it has become *too difficult* to talk about, for the issues it raises are too large, and too threatening. If architecture does not create 'order', there would be no need to have architecture at all and the processes of environmental change can be left to get on with it on their own; but if architecture is in the business of producing 'order', it is involved in something far bigger than it can possibly handle, the process by which experience is filtered, transformed and fed back to us in reduced form, all in the name of 'culture'. In these circumstances, one can well understand why an architect might choose to remain silent on the question of 'order'.

1 See Lubbock, *The Tyranny of Taste*, 1995, and Thomson, *Renaissance Architecture*, 1993, for rewarding discussions of these issues.
2 Bentham, 1791, quoted in Evans, *Fabrication of Virtue*, 215. See chapter 5 of Evans's book for discussion of the Panopticon.

Simple

If the work being created is to be a true reflection of our time, the simple, the practical, the – one might almost say – military approach must be fully and completely expressed. Otto Wagner, 1902, 85

My perception of building is so very simple. Mies van der Rohe, 1925, quoted in Neumeyer, 23

I would like to think that our work is not simple. James Stirling, 1984, in Stirling 1998, 151

'Simple' must be one of the most overworked words in the architectural vocabulary. Although not a modernist term, in so far as it had already accumulated a superabundance of meaning before the twentieth century, it was nonetheless used ubiquitously by modernist architects to characterize the distinctiveness of their works, and for that reason has been treated widely as a defining property of modernist aesthetics. This impression has been heavily reinforced by its having been singled out by late modernist architects – notably Robert Venturi – as the feature of modernism most particularly to be resisted. As a result since the late 1970s, almost every architect has been at pains to reject, or at least, like James Stirling, to distance themselves from 'simplicity'.

Most of the principal precursors of modernism – Otto Wagner, Adolf Loos, Hendrik Berlage, Hermann Muthesius, Louis Sullivan, Frank Lloyd Wright – went out of their way to stress that the style they were inaugurating would be marked by its 'simple' quality. And almost all modern architects of the following generation routinely described their own work, or buildings they admired, in terms of simplicity. A few examples will suffice to show how general this was: Le Corbusier in 1930 writes, 'Great art is made of simple means, let us repeat this tirelessly. History shows us the tendency of the mind towards simplicity. Simplicity is the result of judgment, of choice, it is the sign of mastery'

Interior, German Pavilion, World Exhibition, Barcelona, Mies van der Rohe, 1929. 'Simultaneously simple and complex.'

(1930, 80). Philip Johnson in his 1947 book *Mies van der Rohe* wrote of the Barcelona pavilion, 'the design is simultaneously simple and complex' (58); of 'the simple beauty' of the Tugendhat house interior (60); and of 'the simplicity characteristic of every campus building' at IIT (140); and it was Johnson who, in the same book, first publicized Mies's aphorism 'less is more'. And Eero Saarinen's description of his own CBS building (1965): 'Its beauty will be, I believe, that it will be the simplest skyscraper statement in New York'; 'When you look at this building you will know exactly what is going on. It will be a very direct and simple structure. It does just what it has to do' (16). Or Kevin Lynch's remarks that urban design should aim at 'formal simplicity: clarity and simplicity of form in the geometric sense, limitations of parts … Forms of this nature are much more easily incorporated in the image, and there is evidence that observers will distort complex facts to simple forms' (1960, 105).

As these examples make abundantly clear, the

'simplicity' of modernism applied to no single aspect of architecture, but covered anything from the method of design, to structural expression, to perceived effect. When we turn to the reaction against modernism's 'simplicities', these are just as diverse. They range from Jane Jacobs's attack upon modernist urban theory's mistaken assumption 'that cities were properly problems of simplicity' (1961, 449), to Robert Venturi's appeal for an architecture of complexity and contradiction. Venturi's argument is set out in chapter 2 of *Complexity and Contradiction in Architecture* (1966), where he characterized the simplification of modernism as a tendency to suppress the complications and contradictions. This was essentially an argument against the kind of compositional simplification which excluded awkward or irreconcilable elements: 'Blatant simplification means bland architecture. Less is a bore' (17). Venturi did not reject simplicity outright as an aim, only when it is forced: 'The recognition of complexity in architecture does not negate what Louis Kahn has called "the desire for simplicity". But aesthetic simplicity which is a satisfaction to the mind derives, when valid and profound, from inner complexity' (17). Venturi's purpose was to show how the complexity of the programme could be acknowledged and reconciled with the need to produce a coherent building. This theme formed the greater part of the last chapter, 'The Obligation Towards the Difficult Whole'.

Since the late 1960s, when Venturi's book appeared, 'simple' has been acceptable as a positive critical category only when qualified by some manifest complexity. For example, this is how William Curtis describes the work of the British architect Denys Lasdun: 'Forced simplicity and false simplicity are both anathema in this framework. By examining the design process of several buildings, it has been possible to show how the apparent "simplicity" of Lasdun's designs in fact masks a tense unification of opposites' (1994, 198).

What, if anything, did 'simple' mean in the modernist vocabulary? As a critical category much of its value clearly comes from what it opposes, rather than any inherent meaning it has in itself. Throughout the eighteenth and nineteenth centuries, the term's appeal came from the force of its opposition to one critical value or another. The question relative to modernism is whether in the twentieth century it acquired any new senses beyond those already attaching to it from its previous usage.

Ballroom, Palazzo Gangi, Palermo, 1750s. For eighteenth-century architects, 'simplicity' was primarily a term of opposition to the excesses and licence of rococo.

1. *Eighteenth-century attack upon the rococo.* Although Serlio in the sixteenth century had adopted 'simple' as one of the positive terms in his critical vocabulary (see p. 43), and it was a commonplace description for the architecture of antiquity thereafter, it first became a *polemical* word in the attack upon the rococo in mid-eighteenth-century France and Italy. By the 1750s, the virtues of 'simplicity' were being regularly asserted by opponents of the rococo. For example, Pierre Patte in 1754: 'out of the wish to give architecture an air of ingeniousness, that quality of grandeur and noble simplicity which was always its principal attribute is removed' (15); or the Italian architectural writer Francesco Milizia in 1768, 'The ills of architecture arise out of over-abundance. Therefore in order to perfect architecture, one must rid it of those superfluities, and tear off those trimmings with which stupidity and caprice have disfigured it. The simpler architecture is, the more beautiful it is' (1768, 66). But the most celebrated propagandist of 'simplicity' was the Abbé Laugier in his *Essay on Architecture*, the originality of which was to present 'simplicity' as not simply an attribute of ancient architecture, but to argue that it was a fundamental property of architecture, founded in its natural origins. Following his well known account of primitive man's building the first hut (see p. 222), he

explained 'It is by approaching the simplicity of this first model that fundamental mistakes are avoided and true perfection is achieved' (10). For Laugier, the perfection of Greek architecture lay in its approximation to the simplicity of nature, by employing only such elements as could be accounted for by relation to their structural purpose. In fact, the only ancient building Laugier cited for conforming to 'the true principles of architecture' was the Maison Carré at Nîmes, whose 'simplicity and nobility strikes everyone' (11).

Where Laugier's criticism of rococo differed from that of his contemporaries was that rather than merely complain about its lack of simplicity, Laugier made the 'simple' into a positive quality, rooted in nature, that a skilful architect could manipulate to effect.

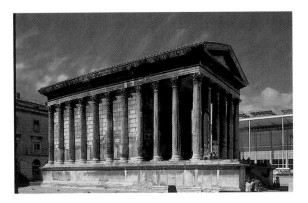

Maison Carré, Nîmes, late first century BC. 'Its simplicity and nobility strike everyone': Laugier saw the 'simplicity' of antiquity as a corrective to the architecture of his own time.

> It is true that I remove from architecture much that is superfluous; that I strip it of the mass of trinkets and baubles with which it is ordinarily adorned; and that I leave it only its natural state and its simplicity. But do not be mistaken: I take nothing away from the architect, from his work or from his means. I require him always to proceed simply and naturally, and never to present anything that savours of art and constraint. Those engaged in the occupation will agree that far from shortening their labours, I sentence them to much study, and to extraordinary precision. … An architect is drawn to superfluities only because he lacks genius; he only overloads his work because he lacks the wit to make it simple. (56–57)

Laugier's idea that 'simplicity' was a positive quality that a skilful architect might handle to great effect was taken up and reiterated by other eighteenth-century writers. This, for example, is J.-F. Blondel in his *Cours*:

> A simple architecture should be the most esteemed of all; simplicity is the property of the works of great masters; it bears a character that art cannot define, and that the most able professor cannot teach; it alone can enchant the spirit and the eyes; it leads to the sublime, and it is always preferable, whatever may be said, to those forced compositions that betray the art and to that multitude of ornaments with which unprincipled men overload their productions, because it is easier to please the crowd by the confusion of elements and the prodigality of sculpture than by the simplicity of which we speak. There is only a very small number of connoisseurs who know how to feel it and to appreciate it. (vol. 1, 396–97)

This sense of simplicity as the antidote to ornamental excess became routine in neo-classicism; it is for example, one of the several ways in which the English architect Sir John Soane (for whom it was a favourite critical epithet) used it in his Royal Academy Lectures. In decoration, Soane warned, 'the young architect is too often led astray, thinking that a profusion of ornaments always increases the beauty of a building. This is a mistake; it is in simplicity that all real decoration is to be found' (637). 'Simplicity' for Soane was the opposite of 'wildness'; as he recorded in a footnote, 'Simple figures, in a word, simplicity, is always preferable to too much wildness. Simplicity may be reproduced without too much monotony, and pleasing movement without excess of variety' (603).

Soane, like others before him and since, was aware though of the risk that too much simplicity could produce banality or monotony (590) – he may have had in mind Sir Joshua Reynolds's warning in his *Discourses on Art* that simplicity pursued as an end in itself becomes 'disagreeable and nauseous' (151), and that it should be treated merely as a 'negative virtue', a 'corrector of excess' (149).

2. *The maximization of sensation.* The mid-eighteenth-century philosophical innovation that the aesthetic lay not in objects, but in the mind's perception of them brought about a new and particularly important validation of the simple. According to Lord Kames in his *Elements of Criticism* of 1762, one of the earliest and most influential works advancing these ideas in relation to architecture, 'simplicity ought to be the ruling principle. Profuse

ornament hath no better effect than to confound the eye, and to prevent the object from making an impression as one entire whole' (vol. 2, 387). Rather, the aesthetic aim of works of art should be 'to touch the mind like one entire impression made as it were at one stroke' (vol. 1, 181). A more long-winded but similar argument appeared in the German writer J. J. Winckelmann's *The History of Ancient Art* (second ed. 1776):

> All beauty is heightened by unity and simplicity, as is everything which we do and say; for whatever is great in itself is elevated, when executed and uttered with simplicity. It is not more strictly circumscribed, nor does it lose any of its greatness, because the mind can survey and measure it with a glance, and comprehend and embrace it in a single idea; but the very readiness with which it may be embraced places it before us in its true greatness, and the mind is enlarged, and likewise elevated by the comprehension of it. Everything which we must consider in separate pieces, or which we cannot survey at once, from the number of its constituent parts, loses thereby some portion of its greatness, just as a long road is shortened by many objects presenting themselves on it, or by many inns at which a stop can be made. The harmony which ravishes the soul does not consist in arpeggios, and tied and slurred notes, but in simple, long drawn tones. This is the reason why a large palace appears small, when it is overloaded with ornament, and a house large, when elegant and simple in style. (43–44)

Amongst late eighteenth- and early nineteenth-century architects, this particular sense of the simple was widespread. Another quotation from Soane, this time on the required qualities of classical architecture, shows him including simplicity among the properties necessary to that effect on the senses that he considered the ultimate aim of the art of architecture: 'There must be order and just proportion; there must be intricacy and simplicity in the component parts, variety in the mass, light and shadow, so as to produce the varied sensations of gaiety and melancholy, of wildness, and even of surprise and wonder' (587). Nor were the merits of simplicity restricted to exponents of neo-classical architecture – witness Ruskin in *The Seven Lamps of Architecture*: 'get but gloom and simplicity, and all good things will follow in their place and time' (chapter 3, §xxiii).

There is little doubt that even if this was not often articulated, 'simple' as what enabled the immediate and maximum effect of the work upon the senses was an

important meaning of the word throughout its use into the modernist era.

3. *Economy of means.* The desirability of the 'simple' because it might cost less only appears as a feature of architectural discourse in the early nineteenth century, and is primarily associated with the French architect J. N. L. Durand. In his *Précis*, intended to instruct engineers at the Ecole Polytechnique in the basics of architecture, 'simplicity' was a key term, reiterated throughout. The particular, innovative sense in which Durand used it is illustrated in the following passage: 'it will be concluded that a building will be less costly the more symmetrical it is, the more regular, and the more simple. There is no need to add that if economy prescribes the greatest simplicity in all the necessary parts, it proscribes absolutely anything useless' (vol. 1, 8).

Although Durand's simplicity was not restricted to the sense of economy – he also referred to it in terms of effect: 'the projects most suited to producing the grandest effects in their execution are those disposed in the simplest manner' (vol. 1, 34) – it was for making economy into a principle of design that Durand was famous. It should be stressed that the 'simplicity' to which Durand referred related solely to the organization of the plan, to the distribution and to arrangements of masses – all matters of design, not of construction. Durand's principles became standard within French engineering circles, and are repeated in, for example, his successor Léonce Reynaud's *Traité d'Architecture* (1850).

4. *As a stage in the history of art and architecture.* It was the intellectual achievement of Winckelmann in the eighteenth century to have shown that art was subject to progressive development. Winckelmann's research concentrated on the arts of ancient Greece, and their classification into three historical phases of rise, classic excellence, and then decadent decline. The arts of the first phase were marked by 'froth and bombast', an excess of passion, but in the classic period this gave way to 'noble simplicity and sedate grandeur' (13). Winckelmann emphasized that the simplicity of the great art of the classic period was not achieved without difficulty – and it was the loss of this control and restraint that precipitated art into decadence. Most subsequent philosophers and historians of art accepted this notion that 'the simple style' represented the highest phase of achievement within any given culture. For example, G. W. F. Hegel in his *Aesthetics* insisted that the simple style should not be

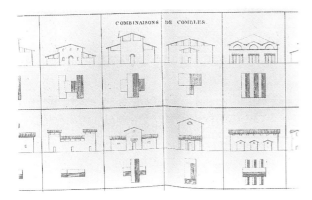

J. N. L. Durand, various arrangements of roofs, from *Précis*, 1817. 'Economy prescribes the greatest simplicity in all the necessary parts': Durand favoured 'simplicity' – as in the composition of roofs – because it saved money.

associated with the crude and savage features of the original stage.

> Those beginnings which are simple and natural in the sense of being crude have nothing to do with art and beauty ... the simple, as the simplicity of beauty, as ideal proportion, is rather a result which only after manifold intermediate steps has reached the point where multiplicity, variety, confusion, extravagance and laboriousness have been overcome ... This is like the manners of a cultured man. (vol. 2, 615)

Within nineteenth-century German art history, the notion that the 'simple' marked the mature phase of historical development of a style was accepted axiomatically – and there can be no doubt that when modernist architects described their work as simple they sought by this association to affirm its maturity and historical legitimacy. It might be added that the Viennese architect Adolf Loos's assertions about the primitive and degenerate nature of ornament in his essays of 1900–10 were an ironic formulation within the same general theory.

5. *The simple life, matter-of-factness.* At the end of the nineteenth century, critics seized hold of the idea that the renewal of architecture was to be achieved by pursuing the practical and matter-of-fact, taking as the principal model the domestic comfort of the middle-class dwelling. The main exponent of this idea was the German architect and critic Hermann Muthesius; in his book *Style-Architecture and Building-Art*, he explained as follows,

> Just as today we all work, just as everyone's clothing is middle class, just as our new tectonic forms (in so far as they are not the work of architects) move in the track of complete simplicity and straightforwardness, so also we want to live in middle class rooms whose essence and goal is simplicity and straightforwardness. (94)

The key to this lay in the word *sachlich* that Muthesius adopted. Untranslatable in English, it means variously 'practical', 'material', 'factual', 'matter-of-fact', 'artless', 'straightforward' and 'functional' (see pp. 180–81).[1] Muthesius's model for a *sachlich* architecture was the domestic work of the English Queen Anne movement, in particular that of Richard Norman Shaw. Alongside monumental architecture, Muthesius saw having existed in previous times

> a simple middle-class building art ... which satisfied one's everyday needs in dwellings and in other ordinary artifacts. In this production ... One remained simple and natural, limited oneself to the necessary and familiar, and generally followed a timeless local guild tradition on which the changes in monumental architecture had only a limited effect. (75)

The achievement of the British late nineteenth-century architects was to have revived this tradition, 'a simple and natural, reasonable way of building' (96), and made it into the expressive means of their domestic work; the results stood in sharp contrast to the decorative excesses of German and Austrian Jugendstil architecture.

Muthesius's idea that 'simplicity' lay in the comfort of the ordinary and everyday he derived from William Morris, whose writings are full of the merits of simplicity. It is to Morris that must be attributed the notion that in the simple life and surroundings of the ordinary man or woman there exists the essential material for artistic work. To take one of many examples, Morris writes 'simplicity of life, even the barest, is not a misery, but the very foundation of refinement. ... From simplicity of life would rise up the longing for beauty' (1881, 149–50). Thanks to Muthesius and the Deutsche Werkbund, this sense of 'simplicity' as the expression of ordinary life was to carry considerable weight in modernist circles, particularly in Weimar Germany.

6. *Rationalization of production.* The final, and only sense of 'simple' particular to modernism, derived from Henry Ford's methods of manufacturing cheap cars.

Living room, house for Stanley Parker, Letchworth, Hertfordshire, Barry Parker and Raymond Unwin, c. 1907. The 'simple life': inspired by William Morris, sparse interiors became the sign of a way of life.

Model T Ford. Introduced in 1909, Ford's mass-produced car became the primary exemplar of 'simplicity' for architects in the early twentieth century.

The impact of these ideas in Europe in the 1920s, and the widespread, if misplaced, expectation that they could revolutionize not only building production and architectural practice but the entire quality of life, make this one of the strongest connotations of 'simple' in the modern era. In his autobiography *My Life and Work* (1922) Henry Ford set out the doctrine:

> My effort is in the direction of simplicity. People in general have so little and it costs so much to buy even the barest necessities (let alone that share of the luxuries to which I think everyone is entitled) because nearly everything that we make is much more complex than it needs to be. Our clothing, our food, our household furnishings – all could be much simpler than they are now and at the same time be better looking. ... Start with an article that suits and then study to find some way of eliminating the entirely useless parts. This applies to everything – a shoe, a dress, a house, a piece of machinery, a railroad, a steamship, an airplane. As we cut out useless parts and simplify necessary ones we also cut down the cost of making. (13–14)

Ford went on to describe how the principle of simplification was applied in the development and improvement of his own product, the Model T.

Ford's idea of simplification was deliberately and knowingly employed by architects in the 1920s – as Mies van der Rohe acknowledged in 1924, 'What Ford wants is simple and illuminating' (250). The expectation that the methods of mass-production would lead to the standardization of building, and in turn to the simplification of the form of buildings and entire cities, had certainly been present at least since Gropius's 1910 'Programme for the Provision of Housing on Aesthetically Consistent Principles'; and when for example, the Russian architect Moisei Ginzburg referred to 'the rational utilization of space by logical simplicity' (79) in the workers' housing of the future, what he had in mind was the potential benefits of modern mass-production methods upon design.

The 'simplicity' offered by Henry Ford was not, it should be stressed, the same as the 'simplicity' of Durand. Whereas for Durand, simplicity was economy in the design of the building, and its organization, Ford's simplicity lay in the reorganization of the means of production, of labour, materials, and plant: any simplification of the design of the resulting product, whether car or house, was not conceived as an end in itself, but merely as the means towards realizing the various economies of production.

Faced with the overinvestment of meaning in 'simple', one might wonder why modernist architects and critics carried

Chapel, Illinois Institute of Technology, Chicago, Mies van der Rohe, 1949–52.
'It was meant to be simple; and, in fact, it is simple': to Mies, 'simplicity' had
transcendental connotations.

on using it at all. So hedged about with qualifications and
contradictions was Mies van der Rohe's 1953 description
of his chapel at Illinois Institute of Technology that it
seems almost impervious to meaning: 'There is nothing
spectacular about this chapel: it was not meant to be
spectacular. It was meant to be simple; and, in fact, it is
simple. But in its simplicity it is not primitive, but noble,
and in its smallness it is great – in fact monumental'
(328). Yet, Fritz Neumeyer has suggested, what Mies
was trying to convey was his sense of architecture as the
means to the revelation of transcendental knowledge.[2]
Beyond the eighteenth-century writers, for whom the
simple was the means to gain the maximum mental effect,
the aim might be, as Nietzsche required of the historian in
On the Uses and Disadvantages of History, to 'remint the
universally known into something never heard of before,
and to express the universal so simply and profoundly
that the simplicity is lost in the profundity and the
profundity in the simplicity' (94). For Mies van der Rohe
it was perhaps this sense that redeemed the term from
the other, *sachlich* and productivist, meanings for which
he had no time.

1 See S. Anderson, Introduction to Muthesius, *Style-Architecture and
Building-Art*, 1902, especially 14–19, 34–35, and 38 n.10.
2 See Neumeyer, *The Artless Word*, 1991, chapter VI.

Space

What I am really interested in is designing
architectural space. Neil Denari, 1993, 95

Space is the most luxurious thing anybody can give anybody in the name of architecture. Sir Denys Lasdun, 1997

Any definition of architecture itself requires a prior
analysis and exposition of the concept of space.
Henri Lefebvre, 1974, 15

These remarks, two by contemporary architects and
one by a philosopher, might lead us to suppose that in
'space' we have found the purest, irreducible substance of
architecture – the property unique to it, that sets it apart
from all other artistic practices. But if this might seem
reassuringly consensual and certain, our confidence will
go as soon as we discover how little agreement there is as
to what is meant by 'space'. And any remaining faith that
space might be the fundamental category of architecture
becomes even more precarious when we realize that any
of the above remarks, had they been uttered before 1890,
would have been entirely meaningless outside a small
circle of German aesthetic philosophers: as a term, 'space'
simply did not exist in the architectural vocabulary until
the 1890s. Its adoption is intimately connected with the
development of modernism, and whatever it means,
therefore, belongs to the specific historical circumstances
of modernism, just as is the case with 'space's' partners,
'form' and 'design'.

Since the eighteenth century, architects had talked
about 'volumes' and 'voids' – and they occasionally used
'space' as a synonym: Soane, for example, referred to
'void spaces' (602), and to the need in devising the plan
to avoid 'loss of space' (603).[1] Although 'space' is often
still used in this sense, it was to convey something more
that 'space' was adopted by modernist architects, and it
is with these superposed meanings that we shall entirely
concern ourselves here.

Much of the ambiguity of the term 'space' in modern
architectural use comes from a willingness to confuse it
with a general philosophical category of 'space'. To put
this issue slightly differently, as well as being a physical
property of dimension or extent, 'space' is also a property
of the mind, part of the apparatus through which we
perceive the world. It is thus simultaneously a thing
within the world, that architects can manipulate, and
a mental construct through which the mind knows the
world, and thus entirely outside the realm of architectural
practice (although it may affect the way in which the
results are perceived). A willingness to connive in a
confusion between these two unrelated properties seems
to be an essential qualification for talking about architectural space. This confusion is present in most of what
is said about architectural space; it finds its expression in
the commonly held belief that architects 'produce' space –
a belief implicit in the statements of Denari and Lasdun
quoted at the opening of this entry. It was part of the
purpose of Henri Lefebvre's *The Production of Space*
(1974) to expose the problem created by this distinction
between space conceived by the mind and the 'lived' space
encountered by the body; Lefebvre's book, the most
comprehensive and radical critique of 'space', calls
into question almost everything about space within
architecture described in what follows – but despite its
force, it has had, as yet, little impact upon the way space
is still customarily talked about within architecture.

The development of space as an architectural category
took place in Germany, and it is to German writers that
one must turn for its origins, and purposes. This
immediately presents a problem for an English-language
discussion of the subject, for the German word for space,
Raum, at once signifies both a material enclosure, a
'room', and a philosophical concept. As Peter Collins
pointed out, 'it required no great power of the
imagination for a German to think of room as simply
a small portion of limitless space, for it was virtually

impossible for him to do otherwise' (1965, 286). In neither English nor French can a material enclosure so easily be linked to a philosophical construct, and consequently 'space', as a translation for the German *Raum*, lacks the suggestiveness of the original. An example of the possibilities present in German, but lacking in English, can be seen in the translation of Rudolf Schindler's 1913 'Manifesto', discussed below.

As well as an awareness of the effects of translation upon the meaning of the term, we should also take into account the effects of time. 'Space's' meanings in architecture are not fixed; they change according to circumstances and the tasks entrusted to it. When Denari and Lasdun enthuse about space, we should not assume that they mean by it what, say, Mies van der Rohe meant by it in 1930. We must, as always, proceed by asking to what the category spoken of – in this case 'space' – is being opposed: the reasons for valuing 'space' in the 1990s are not the same as those in 1930. Despite the tendency of speakers to imply that they are talking about an immutable absolute, 'space' is no less transient a term than any other in architecture.

The preconditions of modernist architectural space
How far the terms used in architecture are borrowed from previously developed philosophical discourses, and how far they arise from experiences and perceptions articulated within the practice of architecture, is sometimes hard to say: in the case of 'space', though, there seems to be clear evidence that the development of a discourse about space within philosophical aesthetics preceded its coming into use within architecture. While we should not conclude from this that philosophy supplied the entire framework for the architectural concept, there is no doubt that it partly provided it. In so far as architectural 'space' originated out of philosophical concerns in nineteenth-century Germany, there are two distinct traditions of thought to be taken into account. One, the attempt to create a theory of architecture out of philosophy rather than out of architectural traditions, centres on Gottfried Semper; the other, concerned with a psychological approach to aesthetics, though it has some links to Kant's philosophy, only emerged in the 1890s. While in practice, the distinction between the two schools of thought was not so great, it will be helpful to consider them separately.

More than anyone else, it was German architect and theorist Gottfried Semper who was responsible for the introduction of 'space' as the principal theme of modern architecture. In advancing his wholly original theoretical account of the origins of architecture, the first to do so

without reference to the orders, Semper proposed that the first impulse for architecture was the enclosing of space. The material components are only secondary to spatial enclosure, so 'the wall is that architectural element that formally represents and makes visible the *enclosed space as such*' (*Der Stil*, 254). In this and other remarks about the primacy of enclosure over material, Semper suggested that in space creation lay the future of architecture. Just how he arrived at this insight is uncertain: in so far as his ideas about architecture were developed from philosophical origins, as distinct from architectural ones, it is probable that they owed something to his reading of Hegel's *Aesthetics*. For Hegel, 'enclosure' was a feature of architecture's purposiveness, and as such, therefore, entirely distinct from, and inadequate to its aesthetic, idea-bearing property. However, the whole thrust of Hegel's account of architecture was to address the question of how what arose originally out of the satisfaction of human material needs might at the same time be purely symbolic and purposeless, the independent embodiment of the Idea (see vol. II, 631–32). In his exploration of this question, Hegel did briefly discuss enclosed space, and although his remarks were undeveloped they are nonetheless highly suggestive, particularly in relation to Gothic religious architecture, which he saw as transcending its purposiveness, and in which, by means of its spatial enclosure – 'differentiated in length, breadth, height and the character of these dimensions' (vol. II, 688) – an independent religious idea was realized. According to Harry Mallgrave, 'enclosure' was being talked about amongst architects as a theme of architecture in Germany in the 1840s – he cites Carl Bötticher's essay 'Principles of Hellenic and Germanic Ways of Building' (1846) – but no one went so far as Semper in suggesting that spatial enclosure was *the* fundamental property of architecture.[2] Although Semper's remarks about space were brief, his influence, both on those who agreed with his arguments and those who did not, was great. For those German-speaking proto-modern architects who first articulated 'space' as the subject of architecture in the first decade of the century, there is no question but that he was the source of their conception of space. We find Adolf Loos in his article 'The Principle of Cladding' of 1898 claiming in Semperian terms that 'The architect's general task is to provide a warm and liveable space'; he went on to say that 'effects are produced by both the material and the form of the space' (66). The Dutch architect H. P. Berlage, in a 1905 lecture ('Thoughts on Style') published in German, stated 'Since architecture is the art of spatial enclosure, we must emphasize the architectonic nature of space, in both a constructive and a decorative sense. For this reason a building should not be considered primarily from the outside' (152). In a subsequent article in 1908, he declared even more categorically, 'the purpose of architecture is to create space, and it should thus proceed from space' (209). Or in 1910, the German architect Peter Behrens said, again in a lecture, subsequently published as 'Art and Technology', 'For architecture is the creation of volumes, and its task is not to clad but essentially to enclose space' (217). What is significant about the formulation of space by all these architects, all of whom had a profound influence on the generation of 1920s modernists, was that, following Semper's model, they saw it entirely as a matter of *enclosure*. It is without doubt this sense of space as enclosure that architects found easiest to apply in practical terms, and however else people might describe architectural space, this was for a long time the most widely used sense of the term, even after other meanings were introduced.

A further architectural thinker whom we might mention here, also German-speaking, also a disciple of Semper, and also to be of great influence on the post-1918 generation of architects, was the Viennese architect Camillo Sitte, whose book *City Planning According to Artistic Principles* was published in 1889. Sitte saw urban design as 'an art of space' (*Raumkunst*), and his prescriptions for the modelling of cities are all based upon the principle of creating enclosed spaces. Where other architects saw spatial enclosure purely in terms of the interior, Sitte cleverly translated this theme of architecture to exterior space. This insight, that 'space' belonged not only inside buildings but also outside them, was to be crucial during the 1920s.

Turning now to the other tradition that contributed to the new understanding of space in the 1920s, we shall look at the late nineteenth-century developments in the theory of aesthetic perception. According to Kant, effectively the founder of this philosophical tradition, space is a property of the mind, part of the apparatus by which the mind makes the world intelligible. In *The Critique of Pure Reason* (1781) Kant had outlined what he meant by space: 'Space', he wrote, 'is not an empirical concept which has been derived from outer experiences' (68). 'Space does not represent any property of things in themselves, nor does it represent them in their relation to one another' (71). Instead, space exists 'in the mind *a priori*... as a pure intuition, in which all objects must be determined' and contains 'prior to all experience, principles which determine the relations of these objects. It is, therefore, solely from the human standpoint that we can speak

Lina Loos's bedroom in Loos's flat, Vienna, Adolf Loos 1903. 'The architect's first task is to provide a warm and liveable space'.

of space, of extended things, etc.' (71). The possibilities that space, as a faculty of mind, might have for aesthetic judgments were not developed by Kant. Schopenhauer, though, in his interesting essay on architecture in *The World as Will and Idea* (1818), recognized this possibility, remarking that 'architecture has its existence primarily in our spatial perception, and accordingly appeals to our *a priori* faculty for this' (vol. 3, 187). But this was no more than a one-line observation, and it was not until the development of the theory of empathy, in the 1870s, that anything was made of this. The philosopher Robert Vischer, who first saw the possibilities of empathy for architecture, wrote principally about the projection of bodily sensation as a means of interpreting the meaning of form, but in the preface to his essay explained that his understanding of empathy was gained from the study of dreams, and the way in which 'the body, in responding to certain stimuli in dreams, objectifies itself in spatial forms' (92). However, despite this suggestion of bodily projection into spaces, rather than forms, he did not go on to develop this aspect of the argument.

At the same time as Vischer was evolving the notion of empathy, the philosopher Friedrich Nietzsche was engaged in writing the works which were so profoundly to affect art practice. It is hard to calculate Nietzsche's influence – it seems that in German-speaking countries, if there was one philosopher read by every young artist and architect in the late nineteenth and early twentieth century, it was Nietzsche. And even though he wrote virtually nothing about architecture, and not much directly about the visual arts, there is no doubt that his writings were widely absorbed by Jugendstil and early modernist architects alike, for whom they were quite as important as anything in architectural theory. What concerns us here is Nietzsche's contribution to the theories of space, about which he wrote little directly, although the implications of his theory of art probably had just as much, if not more, effect upon modernist thinking than any of the specifically architectural theories of space we shall look at. In *The Birth of Tragedy* (1872), Nietzsche's first book, he famously declared 'that existence and the world seem justified only as an aesthetic phenomenon' (141). If art and life were one, then the distinctions between subject and object on which most theories of aesthetics had rested could be forgotten about, and art, as well as life, could be approached from the point of view of pure subjectivity. Nietzsche argued that culture in general derived from two instincts, the Apollonian – the realization of the images presented to the mind in dreams; and the Dionysian – the intoxication experienced in song and dance. The Apollonian provided a pleasure in appearance, in vision, but the Dionysian, Nietzsche's great discovery, involved the body's whole being; it is the implications of the Dionysian for the understanding of space that we shall consider. Nietzsche expressed the Dionysian instinct as follows:

> In song and in dance man expresses himself as a member of a higher community; he has forgotten how to walk and speak and is on the way toward flying into the air, dancing. His very gestures express enchantment. ... he feels himself a god, he himself now walks about enchanted, in ecstasy, like the gods he saw walking in his dreams. He is no longer an artist, he has become a work of art. (37)

And he continues, 'the entire symbolism of the body is called into play, not the mere symbolism of the lips, face, and speech but the whole pantomime of dancing, forcing every member into rhythmic movement' (40). What drives the Dionysian spirit is the excess of energy, 'the overflow of primordial delight' (142). This superfluity of force, expressed in rhythmic dance, was enacted within a space, which was in its turn animated by that activity. Nietzsche recognized the importance of space as the field within which the Dionysian instinct made its presence felt; as he put it in his notebooks (published as *The Will to Power*), 'I believe in absolute space as the substratum of force: the latter limits and forms' (293). And later, answering his own rhetorical question, 'What is "the world" to me?', he replies,

> This world: ... not something blurry or wasted, not something endlessly extended, but set in a definite space as a definite force, and not a space that might be 'empty' here or there, but rather as force throughout, as a play of forces and waves of forces, at the same time one and many, increasing here and at the same time decreasing there. (550)

If Nietzsche's notion of space as a force field, generated by the dynamism of bodily movement, is one that he only alluded to and never developed, the allusion was not lost on the generation of German and Italian architects who read him.

Returning to the theory of empathy, the possibilities suggested by Schopenhauer's remark remained undeveloped until three remarkable essays appeared almost simultaneously – and apparently independently of each other – in the year 1893. The first of these, *The Problem of Form in the Fine Arts* by the German sculptor Adolf Hildebrand, argued that attention to the process of perception of things in the world might itself lead to grasping the inherent themes not only of sculpture but also of painting and of architecture. In his understanding of architecture, Hildebrand was influenced by his friend Conrad Fiedler, whose reading of Semper had already suggested to him that enclosed space, identified by Semper as the original impulse of architecture, might itself become the principal object to consider in thinking about architecture.[3] For Hildebrand, the business of the artist was to distinguish between those aspects of things presented simply through their appearance, and the 'idea of form', 'a sum total that we have extracted by comparing appearances' and therefore known only in the imagination. In arriving at the clear idea of form, Hildebrand emphasized movement, both of the eye, and of the body in space, in order to supply the mind with the requisite range of images from which the imaginatively constituted perception might occur. The task of visual art was to reconstitute within a single image the natural space within which objects existed, and the viewing subject's movement through which their forms were revealed. His stress upon space as the prerequisite for understanding form was certainly original, as was his manner of describing it:

> By a spatial continuum we mean space as three-dimensional extension and as a three-dimensional mobility or kinesthetic activity of our imagination. Its most essential attribute is continuity. Let us therefore imagine the spatial continuum as a body of water in which we can submerge containers and thus define

individual volumes as specifically formed individual
bodies without losing the conception of the whole
as one continuous body of water. (238)

Artistic representation is concerned precisely with evoking
this idea of space, and he continues:

If we now set for ourselves the task of making visible
the appearance of this natural space as a whole, then
we first have to imagine it three-dimensionally as
a void filled in part by the individual volumes of
objects and in part by the air. The void exists not as
something externally limited but rather as something
internally animated. Just as the boundary or form
of an object indicates its volume, it is also possible
to compose objects in such a way that they evoke
the idea of a volume of air bounded by them.
The boundary of an object is, strictly speaking, also
the boundary of the body of air surrounding it. (239)

In these few sentences, Hildebrand suggested no fewer
than three of the ideas about space that were to be of so
much significance in the 1920s: that space itself was the
subject matter of art, that it was a continuum, and that it
was animated from within. After this astonishing passage,
Semper's idea of space as enclosure is left far behind,
looking decidedly leaden.

Hildebrand formulated the problem for painting as
to how a single image on a flat surface was to convey
this space that he had described so vividly; for sculpture
the task was more difficult, for a detached figure had
somehow to convey the surrounding spatial continuum
from which it had, of necessity, become detached. But for
architecture, the problem was slightly different, for 'Our
relation to space finds its direct expression in architecture,
which evokes a definite spatial feeling instead of the mere
idea of the possibility of movement in space'. The work
itself already orientates us in space, so no effort of
imaginative perception is involved. This led Hildebrand to
his remarkable conclusion that 'Space itself, in the sense
of inherent form, becomes effective form for the eye'
(269). In other words, whereas in the other arts, the artist
had to represent space by means of the human figure, or
inanimate objects, in architecture this was unnecessary:
since space can be directly apprehended, there is no need
to reconstitute it through other objects, and space itself
is the form with which the eye is concerned (see also
'Form', pp. 159–60). And where all previous architectural
commentators, Semper included, had seen either walls
or load-bearing members as the elements upon which

architecture relied to convey its theme, Hildebrand was
able to argue that these 'assume specific relative values
only within the effect of the total spatial image' (269). In
other words, unless the mind had first grasped the space
as a form, it would be unable to see the physical elements
as anything other than just matter. 'It is only within the
spatial context of a specific perceptual whole that the
functional idea [of load, or support] can develop into a
specific form' (269). Though Hildebrand's remarks about
architecture are brief, they opened up the possibility of a
whole new discourse of architecture, one which was to
occupy a great many people in the twentieth century.

No less remarkable than Hildebrand's remarks about
space is the more specifically architectural argument of
August Schmarsow's essay 'The Essence of Architectural
Creation', given as a lecture in 1893 and published the
following year. The essay is a speculative enquiry as to
what constitutes the aesthetic of architecture. Like
Hildebrand, Schmarsow denied that the aesthetic
of architecture lay in its material components. He
asks rhetorically

Do the massive pile of purposely hewn stone, the
well-jointed beams, and the securely arched vaults
constitute the architectural work of art, or does the
work of art come into being only in that instant when
human aesthetic reflection begins to transpose itself
into the whole and to understand and appreciate all
the parts with a pure and free vision? (285)

That vision, he goes on to argue, is constituted through
the sense of space; and if one contemplates the entirety
of the history of architecture, the property common to all
works is that they are realizations of spatial constructs.
Like Hildebrand, Schmarsow equates space in architecture
with form. But at this point, any similarity between
the two writers' conception of space dissolves, and
Schmarsow embarks on his wholly original 'aesthetics
from within', derived from the theory of empathy – that
in perceiving things the mind projects into them its
knowledge of bodily sensations. But whereas the theory of
empathy had hitherto been entirely reserved for the perception of solid objects, Schmarsow cleverly transposed it
to the encounter with space. From our bodily experience
of the world, through the various optical and muscular
sensations, we acquire an intuited sense of space.

As soon as we have learned to experience ourselves
and ourselves alone as the centre of this space, whose
co-ordinates intersect in us, we have found the

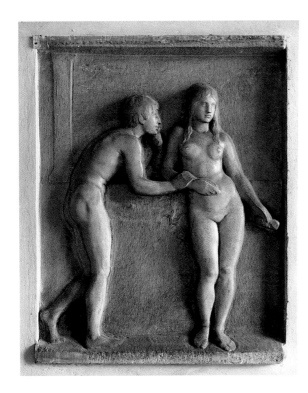

A. Hildebrand, *Courting*, marble relief, 1880. Hildebrand saw the task of sculpture as to represent the spatial continuum within which objects existed; but architecture had no need to *represent* such a space, and instead it was the presence of space in works of architecture that gave aesthetic significance to their material elements.

precious kernel, the initial capital investment so to speak, on which architectural creation is based. ... Our sense of space [*Raumgefühl*] and spatial imagination press towards spatial creation; they seek their satisfaction in art. We call this art architecture; in plain words, it is the *creatress of space*. (286–87)

For Schmarsow, space exists because we have a body – 'The spatial construct is, so to speak, an emanation of the human being present, a projection from within the subject, irrespective of whether we physically place ourselves inside the space or mentally project ourselves into it' (289). In other words, constructed space is a kind of three-dimensional negative of the subject body's own sense of space; or, as he put it later, 'we perceive the spatial construct as a body outside ourselves with its own organization' (293).

These highly suggestive ideas in fact far exceeded in their possibilities the limits of understanding of

architectural space current amongst architects even in the 1920s. In particular, Schmarsow stressed that the 'spatial construct' is a property of the mind, and not to be confused with the actual geometrical space present in buildings; this point, later developed by the philosopher Martin Heidegger, largely passed architects by. If, in their full extent, Schmarsow's ideas had a limited impact upon architectural practice, this was not to be the case with architectural history. It followed logically from Schmarsow's scheme that the study of past architecture should deal with it as the realization of the intuitive sense of space at different stages in history – as he put it, '*The history of architecture is the history of the sense of space*' (296). This lesson was to be taken up and pursued vigorously by successive historians, notably Alois Riegl and Paul Frankl – and we should perhaps acknowledge that 'spatiality', through the work of these and other historians, acquired another life as an object of art-historical enquiry, and that this sense should be distinguished from its currency amongst architects, even if the two sometimes met, as in the well known writings of Sigfried Giedion.

The third of three accounts of space to appear in 1893 was that of the aesthetic philosopher Theodor Lipps in his essay 'Raumästhetik und Geometrisch-Optische Tauschungen'. Lipps is best known for his development of the theory of empathy; in this essay he argued that there were two kinds of seeing, optical, which was concerned with matter, and aesthetic, which was concerned with what was left after matter was removed. For Lipps, space was this dematerialized object: as he put it, 'Since forceful or vital space is the single object of the arts of abstract space creation, nothing can prevent us from eliminating the material carrier. So it is possible that in the art of abstract representation of space, the spatial form can exist purely, unmaterialized'.[4] The aesthetic of this space he explained in a later essay: 'The beauty of spatial forms is my ability to live out an ideal sense of free movement in it. Opposed to this is the ugly form, where I am not able to do this, where my underlying compulsion to freely move within and observe the form is hindered and not possible'.[5] Lipps's theory is quite distinct from Schmarsow's, in that he has no conception of space as enclosure – rather his interest in space is as a way of visualizing the inner life of matter. Although Lipps's ideas are less specific to architecture than those of either Hildebrand or Schmarsow, of the three he probably had the most influence in the short term upon architects, particularly upon the practitioners of Jugendstil;[6] it is also worth remarking that he is the only one of the various German theorists of space to be mentioned by the English writer Geoffrey Scott, who in *The Architecture of Humanism* of 1914 presented the first English-language account of the new sense of spatiality as the theme of architecture (see 226–30 especially).

Up to this point we have been looking at the intellectual, philosophical preconditions for a discourse about architectural space before it had yet become a theme talked about by architects. The variety of conceptions of 'space' in existence by 1900 can in part be explained by the variety of intellectual problems to which it had been developed as a solution. We can summarize these briefly as follows:

1. To describe the original *motive* of architecture: for Hegel, and particularly for Semper, the significance of spatial enclosure was as the purpose from which architecture, as an art, had developed.

2. To describe the cause of aesthetic perception in architecture: as developed by Schmarsow and Lipps particularly, 'space' provided an answer to the question of what in works of architecture stimulated aesthetic perception.

3. To satisfy the expectation, fundamental to all nineteenth-century art theory, that works of art should reveal *movement*. How works of architecture, inherently static, might express motion was a longstanding concern. A suggestive passage written by Goethe in 1795 has been linked to the solutions developed a century later:

> It might well be thought that, as a fine art, architecture works for the eye alone, but it ought primarily – and very little attention is paid to this – to work for the sense of movement in the human body. When, in dancing, we move according to certain rules, we feel a pleasant sensation, and we ought to be able to arouse similar sensations in a person whom we lead blindfold through a well-built house. (Gage, 196–97)

The significance of Hildebrand's essay in particular was to suggest 'space' as the means of talking about *movement*, in terms of the kinetic bodily experience of the subject.

From 'space' to 'spatiality'

The incorporation of some of these ideas about space into the everyday language of architecture began to occur after 1900. We will take two early examples of architects talking about their work as the 'art of space'. The first is the Munich architect August Endell, who had attended

some of Lipps's lectures. In his 1908 book *Die Schönheit der Grosser Stadt*, Endell was concerned with what he called 'the life of space'. He explained:

> The human being creates, with his body, what the architect and painter call space. This space is entirely different from the mathematical and epistemological space. The painterly and architectural space is music and rhythm, because it meets our extensions as certain proportions because, in turn, it releases and encloses us ... Most people think of architecture as the corporeal members, the facades, the columns, the ornaments. But all that is secondary. Essential is not the form, but its reversal, space; the void that expands rhythmically between the walls, and is defined by walls. (71–76; quoted in van de Ven, 150)

In his notion of space as the negative of form, it is not too hard to see the imprint of Lipps's ideas. However, the remarks about space being created by the body indicate a rather different understanding of space, which in some respects corresponds to Schmarsow's 'spatial construct', particularly in his emphasis upon its categorical difference from mathematical space; at the same time, though, the description of the rhythmic, musical quality of space is not Schmarsow's, and suggests an origin in Nietzsche's notion of the Dionysian spirit.[7]

The second early account of 'space' by an architect comes from the Viennese architect Rudolf Schindler, who subsequently emigrated to the USA. His 1913 Manifesto starts by arguing that in the past 'The aim of all architectural effort was the formal conquest of material-mass', but in the present this attention to structure no longer applies.

> We no longer have plastically shaped material-mass. The modern architect conceives the room [*Raum*] and forms it with wall – and ceiling – slabs. The only idea is space [*Raum*] and its organization. Lacking material-mass, the negative interior space [*Raum*] appears positively on the exterior of the house. Thus the 'box-shaped' house has appeared as the primitive form of this new line of development. (10)

This account of space belongs primarily to the tradition of space as enclosure articulated by Semper, Loos and Berlage; but Schindler's stress on elimination of the structural mass, of matter, is reminiscent of all, or any, of the three 1893 essays by Hildebrand, Schmarsow and Lipps.[8] Schindler wrote in 1934 an article describing the

Staircase, Atelier Elvira, Munich, A. Endell, 1898. 'The human being creates, with his body, what the architect and painter call space': Endell's work was influenced by his knowledge of Theodor Lipps's theory of aesthetic space.

revelation of space that had inspired this manifesto; in the article he made it clear that he had been looking for a way to think about architecture free from its materiality. On the evidence of Endell and Schindler at least, we might conclude that of the various new conceptions of space developed in the 1890s, the most sophisticated – Schmarsow's 'spatial construct' – was the least interesting to practising architects.

In the field of historical thinking, though, it was Schmarsow's ideas that were to be the most productive. Between 1900 and 1914, there was a particularly active period within the history of architecture, when ideas about the subject were rethought in the light of the discourse about space begun in the previous decade; in the process, several refinements were introduced into that discourse, particularly in terms of defining what might be described as 'spatiality', the space-perceiving faculty of the human mind. Two authors in particular contributed to this, Alois Riegl and Paul Frankl. Riegl, whose first book *Stilfragen* (Problems of Style) had appeared in 1893, was above all concerned with showing that the development of art was not to be understood in relation to contingent external factors, purpose, material or technique, but relative to its own internal development, which could only be accounted for in terms of the different aesthetic perceptions of people at successive stages of history. In a subsequent book, *Spätrömische Kunstindustrie* (Late Roman Art and Industry, 1901), Riegl argued that differing ways of seeing manifest in the works of antiquity were to be understood primarily in terms of changes in their sense of spatiality. Riegl introduced his discussion of architecture as follows:

> The particular characteristic of late Roman architecture is its relation to the problem of space. It recognized space as a cubic material quantity – it differs in that from near Eastern and classical architecture; but it does not recognize it as an unlimited shapeless quantity – which makes it different from modern architecture. (43)

Riegl went on to elaborate the various distinguishing features of spatial perception manifested in late Roman architecture, but what is significant about this whole enterprise is the supposition that if the human mind's ability to interpret the material world has indeed followed a historical progression, then the evidence of this progression is to be found in an evolution of architectural space as built. The implications of this for modern architecture were obvious, for if modernity had any

meaning as a new phase of historical development, it must be accompanied by a new spatial perception, which must in turn be manifested in a new sort of architecture. Leaving aside the confusion as to what is cause and which effect, the impact of this upon the historians who took up the cause of modern architecture in the 1920s, Sigfried Giedion in particular, are plain to see.

The second major historical study of spatiality in architecture was Paul Frankl's *Principles of Architectural History* (1914), in which, following the suggestions of Schmarsow and Riegl that space was the essential subject of the history of architecture, he developed a scheme for the analysis of space in Renaissance and post-Renaissance architecture. Frankl's main contribution was to distinguish between the 'additive space' of early Renaissance buildings, and the 'spatial division' of post-Renaissance buildings. By additive space, Frankl meant that the spatiality of buildings was built up by a series of distinct compartments; in baroque churches, this distinctness started to be broken:

> Every lunette has the effect of an interpenetration, a fusing together of two spaces, so that their bounding surfaces cannot be determined with certainty ...
> To the average observer, space seems to penetrate the large barrel vault and overflow that geometrical boundary. This causes an uncertainty that cannot be tolerated. (30)

The opposite of additive space, developed after 1550, was spatial division; here, rather than space being constituted as a series of compartments, 'there is a smooth flow of space' (46) through the whole, which is conceived as a part of a larger, endless space. As the contours of the interior become less interesting, the more one is aware of the 'infinite, formless, universal space' without (47). In buildings of this period, one sees 'the desire to represent the *entire interior space* as a fragment, as something incomplete' (47). This tendency becomes even more pronounced in eighteenth-century baroque, where the interior 'takes on the appearance of a fortuitous, undefined fragment of universal space' (61), like the pilgrimage church at Banz in Germany, where 'the interior has the effect of a continuous, cohesive unit to which the side chapels and the galleries belong, and which, as an undulating structure, seems to be in contact with the infinite exterior space' (65). While Frankl's scheme offers a more precise account of spatiality in specific buildings than anything we have so far encountered, it has to be acknowledged that this was at the cost of the concept of spatiality itself: Schmarsow's spatial construct was unequivocally an effect of the mind, and was not be confused with the actual geometric space found within buildings. This distinction was lost by Frankl, for whom spatiality had become a property of buildings: while this might seem to have made it of more practical use to those involved with architecture, at the same time it undermined the value of the concept, and brings us back to the physical senses of space as enclosure or continuum.

'Built' space

By 1920, space was well established as a category in the architectural vocabulary, but in terms of built work there was little to be seen that could be said to justify the claim that architecture was an art not of materials, but of space. The pre-war work of Berlage and of Behrens is not notable for its spatial qualities, nor is that of Adolf Loos, whose work, though later expressive of his term *Raumplan*, before 1914 was distinctive primarily for its materials and surfaces. The only architect whose buildings could be identified as 'spatial' (as they were by Berlage) was Frank Lloyd Wright – though Wright himself did not describe his work in terms of 'space' until 1928.[9] In terms of architectural production, one of the outstanding features of the 1920s was without question the many and various efforts to realize architecture as an 'art of space'. The history of this built work is well known, and this is not the place to describe it again. We should emphasize though that the *vocabulary* and the concepts through which this work was discussed were already in place by 1920, and were not an outcome of the work.

Yet we should not assume that 'space' was adopted by modernist architects simply because there already existed a discourse about it. As we have seen, the motives for the development of this discourse had been as an answer to three distinct problems, historical, philosophical, and aesthetic, none of which, though they might have interested architects, were ultimately architectural. The specific problem facing architects in the first decades of the century was rather different: it was to identify and legitimate the modern, and to establish a way of talking about it. In this, 'space' served their purposes. In the first place the concept of 'spatiality', in its definition of the distinctive and historically specific features of modern perception, offered as good a case as there could be for a new sort of architecture. Secondly, 'space' offered a non-metaphorical, non-referential category for talking about architecture, and one which at the same time allowed architects to rub shoulders with the socially superior discourses of physics and philosophy. In so far as

Interior, Pilgrimage Church at Banz, 1710. 'An undefined fragment of universal space': in Frankl's interpretation 'space' turned from a property of mental perception into a property of buildings.

architecture had always suffered the slur of being no more than a trade, or a business, the claim to deal with the most immaterial of properties – 'space' – allowed architects decisively to present their labour as mental rather than manual. Ultimately the motives for the architectural interest in space differ from the philosophical and scientific motives for interest in it: that they shared the same terminology should not mislead us into thinking that they were talking about the same thing.

At the risk of drastic oversimplification, we can attempt a summary of what happened with the recently emerged category of 'space' in the period between 1920 and 1930. As Van de Ven's book makes clear there was almost no limit to the production of meanings of 'space' in this period, every architect and writer inventing new inflections: Moholy-Nagy in *The New Vision*, to illustrate the problem, listed forty-four adjectives describing different kinds of space. But without going into too much subtlety, we can say that there were broadly three different senses in which 'space' was used by architects and critics during the 1920s: space as enclosure; space as continuum; and space as extension of the body.

1. *Space as enclosure.* This will be familiar from the tradition established by Semper, and developed by Berlage and Behrens. For most architects in the early 1920s, this was the most commonly understood sense of space. It was just such a meaning that was incorporated in Adolf Loos's term *Raumplan*, a word that he first started to use in the 1920s to describe his volumetric house interiors.

2. *Space as continuum.* The notion that inside and outside space were continuous and infinite was important to the Dutch De Stijl group, and to the Bauhaus group around El Lissitsky and Moholy-Nagy. The idea had been suggested in a pre-war book by the historian Albrecht Brinckmann, *Platz und Monument* (1908), but the development of the theme was one of the most original aspects of spatial thinking in the 1920s. One of the first and most explicit demonstrations of this idea was the Viennese architect Frederick Kiesler's *Cité dans l'Espace* (City in Space), an installation at the Austrian pavilion of the 1925 Paris exhibition; Kiesler described it as follows in *De Stijl* no. VII,

> A system of tension in free space
> A change of space into urbanism
> No foundation, no walls
> Detachment from the earth, suppression of the static axis
> In creating new possibilities for living, it creates a new society
> (Quoted in Banham, *Theory and Design*, 1960, 198)

The idea was developed most clearly in Moholy-Nagy's *The New Vision* (discussed below).

3. *Space as extension of the body.* The notion that space was perceived in terms of the body's imagined extension within a volume was known from Schmarsow. However, an original variant of this appeared in a book by the Bauhaus teacher Siegfried Ebeling, *Der Raum als Membran* (Space as membrane, 1926), whose influence upon Mies van der Rohe has recently been stressed by Fritz Neumeyer.[10] Ebeling saw space as a membrane, a protective covering, like the bark of a tree, between man and the outer world. It was thus directly formed by man's activity, and equalized his relationship with the external world. Space, formed by the biological sensibility of man,

F. Kiesler, *La Cité dans l'Espace*, Austrian Pavilion, Paris Exhibition of Decorative Arts, 1925. Space as a continuum. Kiesler's installation was one of the first modernist expressions of space as a gravity-free, non-material element of urbanism.

became 'a continuous force field', activated by man's movement and desire for life. This unusually existential view of space was referred to in Moholy-Nagy's *The New Vision*.

Of the many versions of architectural space described in the 1920s, by far the most interesting is Moholy-Nagy's *The New Vision*, originally published in 1928. Moholy-Nagy, in charge of the curriculum at the Bauhaus, was faced with the problem of how, if 'space' was the true subject of architecture, it was to be taught. While the sources of most of the ideas in Moholy's book can be recognized in the discourse about space that had developed in the previous thirty years, he managed a remarkably sophisticated synthesis of them, and above all, he turned what had previously been a matter of speculative aesthetics concerned with the perception of architecture into a scheme that could be applied practically to the creation of new work. (In doing this, Moholy was obliged to ignore Schmarsow's warning and to allow 'space', as a thing, to become confused with 'spatiality', its mental perception.) 'The root of architecture', wrote

Moholy, 'lies in the problem of the mastery of space' (60): which, given that aesthetics had declared architecture to be an art of space, but left it to architects to make it happen, was indeed true. Following Schmarsow and the psychologists, Moholy accepted that space was a biological faculty, but, following Riegl and Frankl, recognized that 'spatiality' was historically conditioned, and specific to each period of history. The task of architecture was therefore to bring to mankind awareness of the present consciousness of space. It is hardly possible to summarize Moholy's rich and diverse account of how this was to be made to happen, but some of the main points can be drawn out. In describing how space was to be understood, he explicitly rejected the notion of it as enclosure:

> It will not be long before ... architecture will
> be understood, not as a complex of inner spaces,
> not merely as a shelter from the cold and from
> danger, nor as a fixed enclosure, as an unalterable
> arrangement of rooms, but as an organic component
> in living, as a creation in the mastery of space
> experience. (60)

In this and other remarks, he makes plain his rejection of the Semper tradition of space, and equally of Adolf Loos's *Raumplan* compositions. He was also explicit in rejecting the equation of 'space' with 'volume'. A single sentence and accompanying diagram explain as well as anything what he meant: 'If the side walls of a volume (i.e., a clearly circumscribed body) are scattered in different directions, spatial patterns or spatial relations originate' (60–61). We might note in this example both the already established idea that space is not concerned with materials (which he also discusses elsewhere), but also that space is achieved by detaching the structural members, so that in the voids between them is created a continuum of space that runs through the building and connects inside with outside. Part of what he means by this is conveyed in a caption to an illustration of Le Corbusier's Maison La Roche, where he writes 'a "section of space" is cut out of "cosmic" space by means of a network of strips, wires, and glass, just as if space were a divisible, compact object' (58). But he also means more than this, for in the continuum of space, 'Boundaries become fluid, space is conceived as flowing... Openings and boundaries, perforations and moving surfaces, carry the periphery to the center, and push the center outward. A constant fluctuation, sideways and upward, radiating, all-sided, announces that man has taken possession... of... omnipresent space' (63–64). So in addition to the notion

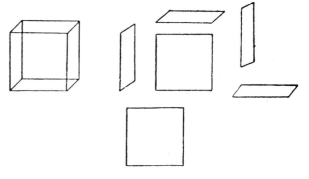

'Volume and Space relationships. If the side walls of a volume (i.e. a clearly circumscribed body) are scattered in different directions, spatial patterns or spatial relations originate'. One of Moholy-Nagy's various explanations of architectural space, from L. Moholy-Nagy, *The New Vision* (1928).

that space is a simple cosmic continuum, made visible by the buildings, he also has the idea that space is a product of motion, and that it changes as man himself moves in space – this idea, reminiscent of his colleague Ebeling's *Raum als Membran*, is certainly an important one to Moholy, so the building becomes 'a plan of creative expression in space'. But even this does not exhaust his concepts of space, for he also suggests that space has its own 'dynamic fields of force' (62), independent of man's occupation of it – an idea which Banham suggests he derived from Boccioni and the Italian Futurists. Both in his text, and in his highly original choice of illustrations, Moholy suggested how architecture as the art of space creation might be approached.

We might at this point take a characteristic remark about space by an architect in the early 1930s, and consider in some detail what purposes it served. Mies van der Rohe, for a 1933 pamphlet on the possibilities of mirrorglass, wrote of the opportunities provided by this material, 'Only now can we articulate space, open it

up and connect it to the landscape' (Neumeyer, 314).[11]
Why should Mies have considered this desirable? Why
should he have presented the aim of architecture in terms
of space? We must consider to what 'space' was being
opposed here. For an architect like Mies, the problem in
the 1920s was to be 'modern'. Among the means then
available to realize this aim there were two that Mies
was particularly concerned with. The first was, following
Nietzsche, to live in the present, free from the constraints
of history, of culture; translated into building, this
meant affirming the free movement of the subject, the
opportunity for the unfolding of life, as against the
previous idea that building was a solid physical mass
that contained and constrained the life of the subject.
It also meant the rejection of everything 'historical'
about building, its massiveness, its materiality. Mies's own
approach to this was to realize it through an insubstantial
architecture of 'skin and bones'. The second approach
was the eradication of 'symbolism'; the line of thinking
developed in pre-war German circles was that
architecture, to be modern, should be *sachlich* (that
is 'matter-of-fact', or 'real') and should not achieve its
end through symbolic means. The criticism of the work
of Mies's Berlin contemporaries Mendelsohn and Häring
was that it was heavily symbolic, as well as being
massive, both properties inconsistent with the 'modern'
as understood by Mies. Around 1930, Mies realized
two works, the German Pavilion at Barcelona, and the
Tugendhat house at Brno, Czechoslovakia, which are
generally regarded as having broken free from both these
properties. Mies's aim seems to have been to make an
architecture that would, through the subject's encounter
with it, bring to consciousness the 'modern spirit'; in
particular, this was to be achieved by the freedom of
movement, and the opportunity, as Mies put it 'to seize
life', unrestricted by mass and matter. As Mies's friend
Ludwig Hilbersheimer commented perceptively of the
Tugendhat house, 'one must move in this space, its
rhythm is like music' (Neumeyer, 186). When, therefore
Mies talks about space, it is a way of signifying his
engagement with an aesthetic property which is
'modern', and the antithesis of everything represented
by 'traditional' architecture, but in terms which privilege
subjectivity. For Mies, 'space' was without question the
pure essence of architecture – but not of the architecture
of all times, only that representative of the 'modern'.

The adoption in English of 'space' as a term happened
relatively slowly. Apart from the unique case of Geoffrey
Scott's *Architecture of Humanism* of 1914, nothing
written in English before 1940 communicated the richness

of the German discourse about space. As has been noted,
Wright (who might have been expected to have had some
notion of 'space' after Schindler went to work in his
office in 1918), did not use the word until 1928; and
remarkably, when Hitchcock and Johnson wrote *The
International Style* for the Museum of Modern Art
exhibition in New York, they described the new
architecture purely in terms of the old word 'volume',
venturing only one reference to 'space': 'Volume is felt
as immaterial and weightless, a geometrically bounded
space' (44). In general, it appears that 'space' as an
English term only became widespread following the
emigration to Britain and the United States of German
architects, for whom the word was by then a natural part
of their vocabulary. The translation of Moholy-Nagy's
The New Vision into English in 1930 provided the main
source for the understanding of 'space' in the English-
speaking world, while the Swiss historian Sigfried
Giedion's Norton lectures at Harvard in 1938–39,
published as *Space, Time and Architecture* in 1940,
provided the first substantial English language account
of the history of architecture as an art of space, and
probably marks the point at which the term became
accepted in English. Although in terms of ideas of 'space'
and 'spatiality' it contained nothing not found in previous
writers, Giedion's book was significant, because with its
enormously wide readership by architects in the English-
speaking world, it diffused and normalized the discourse
of architectural space. Moreover, through his persuasive
combination of text and illustrations, Giedion successfully
presented architectural space not as a concept, but as
actually existing and recognizable in a corpus of modern
built work. And no one had shown so well as Giedion
how modern architecture, of all the arts, had best
succeeded in giving expression 'to this new space
sense' (428), the spatiality distinctive to modern vision
and consciousness.

Through Giedion's influence, and the authority carried
by the first generation of modernist architects, 'space' had
by the 1950s and 1960s become a normal category in
architectural discourse throughout the world, leading
Robert Venturi and Denise Scott Brown to remark in
1972, in *Learning from Las Vegas*, 'Perhaps the most
tyrannical element in our architecture now is space …
If articulation has taken over from ornament … space is
what displaced symbolism' (148). As this remark implies,
the attempt to lessen the importance attached to 'space'
was one characteristic of postmodern architecture in the
late 1970s and 1980s. As summarized by Charles Jencks,
the postmodernist approach to space was deliberately

Interior, Tugendhat House, Brno, Czechoslovakia, Mies van der Rohe, 1929. 'One must move in this space, its rhythm is like music': Ludwig Hilbersheimer's perception of the interior of the Tugendhat House.

unambitious, and ambiguous, compared to modernist practice: 'The boundaries are often left unclear, the space extended infinitely without apparent edge' (50). More striking though was the widely observed tendency of postmodern architecture towards flatness and towards exaggeration of the work's image, an effort which led people to complain about its neglect of 'space'. The remarks of Denari and Lasdun, quoted at the beginning of this entry, may be seen as reactions to the perceived denigration of space by postmodernism.

What has above all kept interest in 'space' alive in architectural circles during the 1980s and 1990s, however, has been resistance to the linguistic models of architecture, prevalent from the late 1950s to the 1970s. This opposition is evident in the otherwise very different work both of the architect Bernard Tschumi and the theorist Bill Hillier. Tschumi, in his very first published

Chiat Day offices, Ocean Park, Los Angeles, Frank Gehry and Claes Oldenburg, 1989–91. More symbolism than 'space' in postmodern architecture.

essay in 1975, attacked 'claims that the architectural object is pure language and that architecture is an endless manipulation of the grammar and syntax of the architectural sign' (1975, 36). Tschumi's repulsion for the tendency always to refer architecture back to a concept, to render it a thing of the mind, precipitated his interest in space. As he wrote, 'My voyage into the abstract realm of language, into the dematerialized world of concepts, meant the removal of architecture from its intricate and convoluted element: space. ... Space is real, for it seems to affect my senses long before my reason' (1975, 39). However, in so far as architectural discourse acknowledged space, it did so by rendering it into a concept. In a subsequent essay, Tschumi recognized – apparently the first time that anyone from within architecture had done so – that the peculiarity of 'space' lay in its both being a concept ('spatiality') and something experienced:

> By definition architectural concepts were absent from the experience of space. Again *it was impossible to question the nature of space* and at the same time make or experience a real space. The complex opposition between ideal and real space was certainly not ideologically neutral, and the paradox it implied was fundamental. (1976, 69)

The exploration of this paradox became a major theme of Tschumi's thinking in the succeeding years. As he put it, 'it is my contention that *the moment of architecture* is that moment when architecture is life and death at the same time, when the experience of space becomes its own concept' (1976, 74); or later, 'the architecture of pleasure lies where concept and experience of space abruptly coincide ' (1977, 92). This rare insight – at least from within the world of architecture – into the peculiar difficulty of 'space' owed a good deal to Tschumi's familiarity with the work of Henri Lefebvre.

In the case of the architectural morphologist Bill Hillier, his work in developing a syntax of space likewise derives from a resistance to the tendency of architectural discourse to borrow its concepts from other disciplines (particularly linguistics), and a determination to find a way of describing and analysing architecture based upon the phenomenon of architecture itself. In the question of the relationships between buildings and the life that takes place within and around them, Hillier argued that it is as spatial configurations, rather than as physical matter that buildings are to be approached. Avoiding analogues with other disciplines, Hillier proposes 'the paradigm of architecture is a configuration paradigm' (391);

'Buildings are... probabilistic space machines, able to absorb as well as generate social information through their configuration' (395). Hillier's interest in finding a means to describe and analyse buildings and environments in terms of spatial configuration alone derives from the view that the only valid theories of architecture are those taken from what is unique to architecture.

Heidegger and Lefebvre

We have so far considered the discourse about space in terms largely internal to architecture. If we turn our attention to the two major philosophical investigations undertaken in the twentieth century, the first by the German philosopher Martin Heidegger, the second by the French philosopher Henri Lefebvre, some of the limitations of specifically architectural notions about space will be made apparent.

Heidegger's understanding of space was that space is neither, as Kant had proposed, a property of mind by means of which the world is perceived, nor does it exist previous to one's being in the world; in short, there is no space independently of one's being in it. 'Space is not something that faces man. It is neither an external object nor an inner experience. It is not that there are men, and over and above them *space*' ('Building, Dwelling, Thinking', 358). This argument first appeared in *Being and Time* (1927), with the following fundamental proposition: '*Space is not in the subject, nor is the world in space*. ... Space is not to be found in the subject, nor does the subject observe the world "as if" that world were in a space; but the "subject" [*Dasein*], if well understood ontologically, is spatial' (*Being and Time*, 146). While spatiality is a major aspect of our encounters with things in the world, space as such is not something that can be known apart from things, but only by their relation to other things. As he puts it, 'anything constantly ready-to-hand of which circumspective Being-in-the-world takes account beforehand, has its place. The "where" of its readiness-to-hand is ... orientated towards the rest of what is ready-to-hand' (*Being and Time*, 137), and he gives the example of the way the rooms of a house are orientated in relation to another object, the sun. And often the regions where things are, he suggests, do not 'become accessible explicitly as such a region until one fails to find something in *its* place' (*Being and Time*, 138).

In the essay 'Building, Dwelling Thinking' of 1952, Heidegger presented these ideas with a more concrete relationship to building. Heidegger is emphatic that – contrary to the conventional architectural thinking about this subject – 'Building never shapes "pure" space' (360). Rather, he argues, we should see a 'locale' (the term he uses instead of a 'where' in *Being and Time*), as being created by the presence of an object within it: the example he gives is of the bridge – the 'locale' of a particular stretch of river bank 'comes into existence only by virtue of the bridge' (356). What he understands as space, which he describes as 'that for which room has been made, that which is let into its bounds', can only occur in an already existing locale: '*Accordingly, spaces receive their essential being from locales and not from "space"* ' (356). In considering the relationship between locale and space, he explains that a particular locale may have places that are near or far from it, and that these distances, which can be measured, constitute a particular sort of space, an interval. Also, by substituting markers for the actual objects, it is possible to abstract the interval and consider it as an extension, which can be presented purely mathematically, as 'space' – but this impoverished sort of space (which he always distinguished by putting it in inverted commas, and which corresponds fairly closely to what is commonly understood as the space of architects), being a mere abstraction that can be translated anywhere, lacks the essential relationship to locale wherein lay the original quality of space. This distinction between on the one hand space which is contingent upon specific objects and oneself being in it, and which lacks boundaries, and on the other hand space as a mathematical abstraction that can be plotted by co-ordinates and which has boundaries defined externally, is fundamental to Heidegger's account of space. It will be apparent by now that Heidegger's notion of space contradicts almost all the notions about space developed by architects between 1890 and 1930; not only did he aim to abolish distance and all quantifiable aspects from its description, but he also denied any recognition to its bodily interpretation or resonance that had been so important to Schmarsow and his successors. It was in particular Heidegger's absence of any account of the subject's own body in the account of space that provoked Maurice Merleau-Ponty's alternative account of space, developed in chapter 3 of *Phenomenology of Perception*, where he argued the need to recognize the body's own spatiality: as he puts it, 'far from my body's being for me no more than a fragment of space, there would be no space at all for me if I had no body' (102). And he concludes, 'The body is our general medium for having a world' (146).

Heidegger's influence upon architecture, not noticeable until the early 1960s, was twofold: firstly, in certain circles, 'place' superseded 'space' as the buzzword. For example, the Dutch architect Aldo van Eyck wrote in 1961 about his Amsterdam orphanage (see ill. pp. 272–73):

> I arrived at the conclusion that whatever space and time mean, place and occasion mean more, for space in the image of man is place, and time in the image of man is occasion. Split apart by the schizophrenic mechanism of determinist thinking, time and space remain frozen abstractions .... A house should therefore be a bunch of places – a city a bunch of places no less. (237)

Secondly, Heidegger's insistence that 'space' is unmeasurable and non-quantifiable may be seen as relevant to attempts in some recent architecture to draw attention to these aspects. Given that Heidegger's arguments were addressed to philosophy, rather than architecture, it is not easy to see the immediate relevance of his ideas to architectural practice; it is probably true to say that more influential for architecture have been the interpretations of his ideas offered through the books of Christian Norberg-Schulz, and Gaston Bachelard's widely read *The Poetics of Space*, first published in French in 1958.

Turning now to Henri Lefebvre's *The Production of Space*, first published in French in 1974, we come to consider the first and only comprehensive critique of 'space' which at the same time attempts a general theory of space. *The Production of Space* calls into question virtually everything that has been said so far in this entry about 'space' as it applies to architecture. It is impossible to summarize adequately the argument of this exceptionally clever and complex book, and the remarks that follow do no more than bring out the aspects of Lefebvre's discussion that most directly touch on architecture.

Lefebvre's starting point is the neglect, not only by philosophy but by all the human sciences, of what 'space' is: the mind thinks of space, but it does so within a space, a space that is at once both conceptual, but also physical, a space that is the embodiment of social relations, and of ideology. One of the aims of the work is to expose the nature of the relationship between the space produced by thought, and the space within which thought happens. Yet this schism, Lefebvre stresses, has not been a feature of all societies, and one of his main purposes is to confront this as a feature of modern culture.

At the heart of *The Production of Space* is the category of 'social space'. One must attempt to understand this elusive concept before approaching any aspect of Lefebvre's theory. Social space is what

(above and opposite) Interiors, orphanage, Amsterdam (now Berlage Institute), A. van Eyck, 1958–60. 'Whatever space and time mean, place and occasion mean more.' Partly under Heidegger's influence, 'place' replaced 'space' as architectural buzzword in the 1960s.

the cultural life of societies takes place within, what 'incorporates' the social actions of individuals (33); yet it is not to be understood as a 'mere "frame" … nor a form or container of a virtually neutral kind, designed simply to receive whatever is poured into it' (93–94). Nor is social space a 'thing', to be treated 'in itself' (90); and although it is a product, it 'is never produced in the sense that a kilogram of sugar or a yard of cloth is produced' (85), but rather is to be understood as 'at once both *work* and *product* – a materialization of "social being"' (101–2). As Lefebvre puts it, in a particularly expressive metaphor, societies 'secrete' space, producing and appropriating it as they go along (38). The particular, and most reprehensible, feature of modern societies is that they reduce this complex space, which is at once perceived (through the social relations of everyday life), conceived (by thought), and lived (as bodily experience), to an abstraction. The whole tendency of Western history has been to render the entirety of social space into an abstraction, which he designates by the shorthand description of 'mental space'. Lefebvre's project is to regain consciousness of social space. 'Social space will be revealed in its particularity to the extent that it ceases to be indistinguishable from mental space (as defined by the philosophers and mathematicians) on the one hand, and physical space (as defined by practico-sensory activity and the perception of "nature") on the other' (27).

Let us turn now to the implications of this for architecture. It is worth appreciating that Lefebvre drew a distinction between 'architectural space' and the 'space of architects' (300). 'Architectural space', by virtue of

the experience that people have of it, is one of the means through which social space is produced:

> Architecture produces living bodies, each with its own distinctive traits. The animating principle of such a body, its presence, is neither visible nor legible as such, nor is it the object of any discourse, for it reproduces itself within those who *use* the space in question, within their lived experience. (137)

The 'space of architects', on the other hand, is what the whole of this entry has been about: it is the manipulation of space effected by architects in their professional practice, and the discourse in which that activity takes place. While 'architectural space', which simply reproduces within individual subjects the features of the society in which it is found and is therefore no better or no worse than the society in which it belongs, 'the space of architects' is anathema to Lefebvre. When Lefebvre writes 'any definition of architecture itself requires a prior analysis and exposition of the concept of space' (15), it might be supposed, taken out of context, that he shared the view that space is the exclusive quality of architecture. Nothing could be further from the truth. As far as Lefebvre was concerned, all disciplines are involved with space (107), and there is no sense in which architecture, by virtue of its relation to building, has any more right to space than any other discipline. At the same time, no individual discipline is capable of giving a satisfactory account of social space, because

of the tendency of each discipline to render it into an abstraction appropriate to its own purposes. In this respect, architecture is worse than most: 'Surely it is the supreme illusion to defer to architects, urbanists or planners as being experts or ultimate authorities in matters relating to space' (95). Although architects, by virtue of traditional involvement with space, claim authority in its practice, they are as responsible as any for the schism of mental and physical space, a schism which they have reinforced and perpetuated in their service to the rulers and manipulators of consciousness. Lefebvre returns to this later in the book, when he writes 'It is easy to imagine that the architect has before him a slice or piece of space cut from larger wholes, that takes this portion of space as a 'given' and works on it according to his tastes, technical skills, ideas and preferences' (360). But, Lefebvre continues, this is a misapprehension. First of all, the space given to the architect is not the neutral, transparent stuff of Euclidean geometry: it has already been produced. 'This space has nothing innocent about it: it answers to particular tactics and strategies; it is, quite simply, the space of the dominant mode of production, and hence the space of capitalism' (360). This fundamental point, which derives from Lefebvre's whole analysis of 'social space', is his single most telling criticism of the entire tradition of architectural space as developed in the first half of the twentieth century, and challenges its implicit assumption that space is a pre-existing, neutral given. The second reason why it is a misapprehension is that architects are deluded if they think that they create in a condition of 'pure freedom' – for the eye of the architect is not altogether his or her own, but is constituted through the space in which they live. Thirdly, the apparatus employed by architects – such as their techniques of drawing – are not transparent, neutral mediators, but are themselves part of the discourse of power; and moreover, the practice of drawing is itself one of the prime means through which social space is turned into an abstraction, homogenized for the purposes of exchange, and drained of lived experience. Fourthly, the techniques of drawing practised by architects, indeed the whole practice of architecture, privilege the eye above all other senses and sustain the tendency for image, and spectacle, to take the place of reality, a tendency manifested throughout modern capitalism.

> The eye … tends to relegate objects to the distance, to render them passive. That which is merely *seen* is reduced to an image – and to an icy coldness. The mirror effect thus tends to become general. Inasmuch as the act of seeing and what is seen are confused, both become impotent. By the time this process is complete, space has no social existence independently of an intense, aggressive and repressive visualization. (286)

Architecture, for Lefebvre, is complicit in the reduction of space to its visual image. Fifthly, architecture, and this is particularly so of modernism, was partly responsible for making space appear homogeneous, 'the reduction of the "real"… to a "plan" existing in a void and endowed with no other qualities' (287). In short, architecture carries much of the responsibility for perpetuating the deceptions perpetrated by space, for 'spaces sometimes lie just as things lie' (92).

Underlying Lefebvre's criticisms of the 'space of architects' is his critique of 'abstract space'. 'Abstract space' is the form into which social space has been rendered by capitalism; its fundamental feature is the separation of mental space, from 'lived' space, with the result that human subjects are alienated not just, as Marx saw it, from the results of their labour, but from the entire experience of everyday life. This abstract space, the creation of philosophy and of the sciences, 'is formulated in the head of a thinker before being projected onto social and even physical "reality"' (398); the result is that consciousness of space occurs not through its being lived, but via the representations of it, always thin and reductive, that are provided through the intellectual disciplines and other ideological practices of capitalism. Among the effects of this process of reduction are the rendering of space to appear uniform, so it can be treated as interchangeable, and the suppression of evidence of contradictions within it.

> Abstract space, which is the tool of domination, asphyxiates whatever is conceived within it. … This space is a lethal one which destroys the historical conditions which gave rise to it, its own (internal) differences, and any such differences that show signs of developing, in order to impose an abstract homogeneity. (370)

Within abstract space, its occupants find that they themselves become abstractions, as 'users', and are unable to see space other than in the mutilated, sliced-up form in which is presented to them (313); and while the space they find themselves within *appears* to be coherent, and seems transparent, this too is part of the flattening and reduction achieved by abstract, mental space.

Of all the occupations responsible for perpetuating the schism between mental and lived space that is characteristic of modern abstract space, few according to Lefebvre have been quite so guilty as architects. As he puts it, 'architects and city-planners offered – as an *ideology in action* – an empty space, a space that is primordial, a container ready to receive fragmentary contents, a *neutral* medium into which disjointed things, people and habitats might be introduced' (308). It is this indictment, which Lefebvre returns to again and again in the book, which makes clear how much the whole discourse of 'space' in architecture, far from being an assertion of architecture's independence, has linked it to the exercize of power and domination in the modern era.

Lefebvre's analysis sets him apart from almost everything said or written previously about architectural space. Although there is a strong phenomenological element in *The Production of Space*, Lefebvre also distanced himself from Heidegger, primarily because of Heidegger's neglect of history, his omission of the body as a dimension of space, and his failure to account for how 'being' is produced in anything other than mythical terms (121–22). Of the writers on space discussed here, those with whom Lefebvre had most in common were Nietzsche and Merleau-Ponty. Lefebvre's aim, as he puts it at one point, 'is to treat social practice as an extension of the body', an attitude which is fundamentally Nietzschean; but in the same sentence he continues, '[this] extension… comes about as part of space's development in time, and thus too as part of a historicity itself conceived of as *produced*' (249). In that respect, in his concern to develop a *historical* analysis of space, he departs from Nietzsche.

The question raised earlier, and to which we will now return, was the reason for 'space's' supremacy within architectural discourse in this century. On page 265, various suggestions were put forward, considering the problem from the point of view of the occupational and artistic status of architects. We might now return to this question with the benefit of the thinking of Heidegger and Lefebvre. What both these writers make clear is that the space of which architects talk is not space in general, but an understanding of it quite specific to their own *métier* – it is a category invented for purposes of their own. At the same time, though, as Lefebvre makes clear, this 'space' does not simply serve their own purposes, but is part of the dominant discourse of power and domination of modern capitalist societies. The particular value of Lefebvre's book is to resist the tendency to see architecture as a self-determining practice, setting its own objectives and inventing its own principles; on the contrary, as Lefebvre makes clear, architecture is just one social practice among many, and in its space-regulating operations it serves not its own ends, but those of power in general.

One question that remains unexplained within Lefebvre's argument is why the articulation of a discourse about space did not occur earlier, since according to his thesis, the development of 'abstract' space, of which the space of architects is one of the servants, began long before the twentieth century. Lefebvre leads us to suppose, though he does not actually say this, that there existed a discourse about space in architecture before the term itself entered the vocabulary; if this was so, are we then to suppose that the enthusiastic adoption by architects of the term 'space', from the restricted and exclusive corner of aesthetic philosophy where it was first developed, arose out of the wish to give a name to what they had long been engaged in, but had lacked the means to speak about? Or are we to assume that the adoption of the language of space was a naive wish on the part of architects to identify themselves with the sources of power and authority from whom came their likely sources of employment? By realizing both physical space, and a discourse about space, architects might be said to be fulfilling their traditional role of finding the means to represent what otherwise existed only as ideology. This indeed is a view which Lefebvre does partly suggest. If either of these arguments are correct, then we must regard the success of the discourse about space within architecture as less to do with architecture, and more with the needs of ruling power to present an acceptable and seemingly uncontradictory account of its dominion in the realm of space.

1 Robin Middleton, 'Soane's Spaces' (1999), points out that the philosopher Lord Kames in his *Elements of Criticism* (1762) had stressed the importance of the subjective experience of space in the perception of architecture – 'space as well as place enter into the perception of every visible object' (1817 ed., vol. 2, 476) – and that Soane had read and noted Kames's book carefully.

2 Mallgrave, *Semper*, 1996, 288.

3 See C. Fiedler, 'Observations on the Nature and History of Architecture' (1873), in Mallgrave and Ikonomou, 130, 135, 142; see also their introduction, 29–35.

4 Quoted van de Ven, 81.

5 T. Lipps, *Aesthetik*, 1923, 247; quoted M.Schwarzer, 53.

6 See Mallgrave and Ikonomou, 47.

7 See Neumeyer, *The Artless Word*, 181–83, for discussion of Endell's book and its influence.

8 See Mallgrave, 1992, for a discussion of Schindler's text.

9 Berlage in 1912 commented on the interiors of Wright's houses that they were 'plastic – in contrast to European interiors which are flat and two-dimensional'. See Allen Brooks, *Writings on Wright*, 131. Wright's first use of the term 'space' is in 'In the Cause of Architecture IX, The Terms', published in 1928; see Wright, *Collected Writings*, vol. 1, 315.

10 See Neumeyer, *The Artless Word*, 171–77.

11 See Neumeyer, *The Artless Word*, 177*ff.* for discussion of the significance of this statement.

Structure

In fact, all architecture proceeds from structure, and
the first condition at which it should aim is to make
the outward form accord with that structure.
E.-E. Viollet-le-Duc, *Lectures*, vol. 2, 1872, 3

In the English language you call everything structure.
In Europe we don't. We call a shack a shack and not a
structure. By structure we have a philosophical idea.
The structure is the whole, from top to bottom, to the
last detail – with the same ideas. That is what we call
structure. Mies van der Rohe, quoted in Carter, 1961, 97

One cannot speak about structures in terms of forms,
and vice versa. Roland Barthes, 'Myth Today', 1956, 76

The architect is not meant to question structure. The
structure *must* stand firm. After all, what would happen
to insurance premiums (and to reputations) if the
building collapsed? Bernard Tschumi, 'Six Concepts',
1991, 249

'Structure' in relation to architecture has had three uses:

1. Any building, in its entirety. For example, Sir William
Chambers, 1790: 'Civil architecture is that branch of the
builder's art which has for its object all structures, either
sacred or profane ...' (83); or Sir John Soane, 1815:
'Inigo Jones, Sir Christopher Wren, and Kent have
been justly blamed, their taste arraigned, their judgment
doubted, because they sometimes blended Roman and
Gothic architecture in the same structure' (600). Until
well after the middle of the nineteenth century, in
the English language, this was the only recognized
architectural sense of 'structure'.

2. The system of support of a building, distinguished
from its other elements, such as its decoration, cladding,
or services. This is the sense implied by Viollet-le-Duc, in

the quotation above. It entered general currency in the
second half of the nineteenth century.

3. A schema through which a drawn project, building,
group of buildings, or entire city or region become
intelligible. The schema may be identified through any
one of a variety of elements: the most usual are the
arrangement of tectonic parts; the masses – or their
negative, volumes or 'spaces'; systems of interconnection
or of communication. None of these are themselves a
'structure', only signs that give cause for the perception
of 'structure'. The main feature of the twentieth century
has been the increase in the number of elements
perceived as bearing 'structure'.

The first meaning is straightforward, and little more
need be said about it. The other two are where all the
complications lie. The second and third meanings
cannot be dissociated, for 2. is really no more than
a particular case of 3., even though in practice they
are often spoken about as if they were distinct. The
confusion between 2. and 3., inherent to the modernist
use of 'structure', is compounded further (particularly
in English, where it is stronger than in other languages)
by the existence of 1., giving rise to the impression that
a structure is a *thing*, and moreover a thing over which
architects have a peculiar claim to expertise. The
resulting muddle is only too apparent in a sentence like
the following, by the architect Nicholas Hare, writing in
1993 about the work of Peter Foggo for Arup Associates
at Broadgate: 'on both the exterior and interior the parts
are articulated with the greatest precision, yet ordered
into a coherent whole through a hierarchical logic of
structure and construction'. It is impossible to tell
whether 'structure' here means the physical supports of
the building, or a different, invisible schema manifested
through some other element.
    The key to untangling the muddle is to recognize

that 'structure' is a *metaphor*, which, while it may have started in building, only returned to architecture after much foreign travel. Furthermore, 'structure' is not one, but *two* metaphors, each borrowed from a different field: first from natural history, which gave it its nineteenth-century meaning; and second, from linguistics, which provided its twentieth-century meanings. Whereas in other fields – ethnography for example – when the new linguistic sense of structure was introduced, there was a vigorous campaign to cleanse the older biological metaphor from the discipline, in architecture this never happened; what has been remarkable in architecture has been the prolonged coexistence within a single word of two essentially hostile metaphors. No doubt this has much to do with the original, first sense of 'structure', which has permitted architects to claim a privilege in matters of 'structure'. Were the third, linguistic sense of 'structure' to be upheld to the exclusion of the others, this right would vanish, for an architect could no more claim to 'make' structure than might an individual by speaking a language.

Structure as that distinct element of the whole concerned with its means of support

This sense is principally associated with the French mid-nineteenth century architect and theorist Viollet-le-Duc, who, while he did not invent it, certainly popularized it, and through the wide readership that his works enjoyed not only in France, but also in translation in Britain and the United States, is responsible for its present familiarity. Viollet's view that structure was the basis of all architecture he expressed repeatedly, and was his justification for the superiority of Gothic architecture. Characteristic of his point of view is the following:

> it is impossible to separate the form of the architecture of the thirteenth century from its structure [*structure*]; every member of this architecture is the result of a necessity of that structure, as in the vegetable and animal kingdom there is not a form or a process that is not produced by the necessity of the organism ... I cannot give you the rules by which the form is governed, inasmuch as it is of the very nature of that form to adapt itself to all the requirements of the structure; give me a structure, and I will find you the forms that naturally result from it, but if you change that structure, I must change the forms. (*Lectures*, vol. 1, 283–84)

No. 1, Finsbury Avenue, Broadgate, City of London, Arup Associates, 1982–84. 'A hierarchical logic of structure and construction'. But can 'structure' be visible?

The analytical drawings with which Viollet illustrated his writings to show the 'structure' of ancient buildings make it clear how far 'structure' was an abstraction: under the eyes of onlookers, substantial masses of masonry dissolve into nothing, leaving only a pure system of thrusts and restraints, invisible in life. Viollet's conception of 'structure' was quite rapidly taken up in the United States, and made use of by the Vienna-educated architect and theorist Leopold Eidlitz, and his friend the influential critic Montgomery Schuyler, best known for his reviews of Adler and Sullivan's office buildings. Eidlitz, in his book *The Nature and Function of Art* (1881), took from Viollet the notion that 'structure' was basic to architecture, but employed it within a framework of German philosophical idealism. Instead of perceiving the perfection of 'structure' as the subject of architecture, Eidlitz saw 'structure' as the means by which the underlying Idea was represented; as he put it, 'It is the problem of the architect to depict the emotions of the structure he deals with; to depict as it were, the soul of that structure' (287). Much of what Eidlitz was concerned with was the relationship between Idea and 'structure'. Montgomery Schuyler, preoccupied with the search for a 'modern' architecture, had a conception of 'structure' rather closer to Viollet's; and we also see plainly in what Schuyler writes the blurring of tectonic abstraction with physical component that is so characteristic of the English use of the word: for example, in his 1894 essay 'Modern Architecture',

> The real structure of these towering buildings, the 'Chicago construction', is a structure of steel and baked clay, and when we look for an architectural expression of it, or an attempt at an architectural expression of it, we look in vain. No matter what the merits or demerits may be of the architectural envelope of masonry, it is still an envelope, and not the thing itself, which is nowhere, inside or out, permitted to appear. The structure cannot be expressed in terms of historical architecture, and for that reason the attempt to express it has been foregone. (113–14)

Like Viollet, Schuyler conceived 'structure' in terms of biology: 'In art as in nature an organism is an assemblage of interdependent parts of which the structure is determined by the function and of which the form is an expression of the structure' (115), and he proceeded to quote from the biologist Cuvier. Viollet's best-known English disciple was W. R. Lethaby, who characterized the

Sanctuary, Saint-Leu d'Esserent (Oise). In Viollet-le-Duc's analytical drawings, substantial masses of masonry dissolve to the point of instability before the spectator's eyes, so as to reveal the 'structure'.

history of architecture as 'the delight in experimental structure' (70). In France, Viollet's influence was extensive: of the proto-modernists who absorbed his ideas, Auguste Perret is perhaps the best-known – and in describing his approach, Perret habitually used the category 'structure' as he had learnt it from Viollet. For example, 'The great buildings of our day permit the use of a body-structure, a framework in steel or in reinforced concrete, which is to the building what the skeleton is to the animal'.

The distinction between the 'structure' and the outward appearance of the work of architecture, the essential issue with which all these post-Viollet architects and writers were concerned, is not as natural as it might now seem. Accustomed as we are to the professional separation of structural engineers from architects, it is easy for us to talk of the 'structure', the system of support, as a property apart from the rest of the building. While it was Viollet who introduced this way of thinking into general currency, and who popularized 'structure' as the name for this abstraction, he was only able to do so because of developments within French architecture and engineering in the latter part of the eighteenth century. As Antoine Picon has shown, a capacity to describe and analyse the system of support independently of the conventions of building, and of assumed notions of 'stability' – in other words to think about the system of support independently of any actual building – was an achievement of the late eighteenth-century French engineers.[1] While there exist earlier precedents for this approach, in the work of Sir Christopher Wren, and of Claude Perrault, it only developed as an effective way of perceiving architectural issues in the debates around the the work of the architects Soufflot, Patte, and of the engineer Peronnet in the late eighteenth century. Within these debates, there was a marked hesitancy to depart from the accepted conventions of what *looked* stable, and only Soufflot and particularly Perronet were prepared to take this risk. What is significant is the way in which Perronet presented his arguments: in a letter of 1770 supporting Soufflot's slender piers at Sainte Geneviève, Perronet praised the qualities of Gothic buildings:

> The magic of these latter buildings consists largely in the fact that they were built, in some degree, to imitate the structure [*structure*] of animals; the high, delicate columns, the tracery with transverse ribs, diagonal ribs and tiercerons, could be compared to the bones, and the small stones and voussoirs, only four to five inches thick, to the flesh of these animals. These buildings could take on a life of their own, like a skeleton, or the hulls of ships, which seem to be constructed on similar models. (Picon, 1988, 159–60)

While this sounds like the well known passage where Alberti compared the construction of buildings to the skin and bones of animals (Book III, chapter 12), the underlying purpose was entirely different.[2] Whereas Alberti was concerned with the connectedness of the parts of the construction, Perronet was more concerned with their lightness, relative to conventional norms of building. Two things in particular about Perronet's remark are worth noting in the present context. The first is that it was natural history, not the simple, load-bearing systems of building construction, that provided Perronet with his model for 'structure'. And as we have seen from the previous quotations, a great many architects who

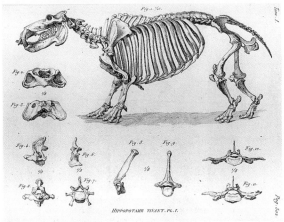

(top) Interior, Sainte Geneviève (Panthéon), Paris, J.-G. Soufflot, begun 1757. The slenderness of Soufflot's columns gave rise to concerns about their stability, and led to comparisons with the 'structure' of animals.
(bottom) Skeleton of Hippopotamus, from Cuvier, *Ossemens Fossiles*, 1821, vol. 1. The hippopotamus's great weight was borne on the tiniest bones.

subsequently adopted the 'structural' thesis went out of their way to draw attention to the fact that it was a biological, not a building metaphor.[3] It would appear, then, that 'structure' as term for the support system in architecture was originally a metaphor drawn from biology, and not from building – even if the biological usage may itself have been borrowed from building.

This brings us to the second point raised by Perronet's quotation, one that explains why he, and others, were so keen on the biological sense of 'structure'. According to Antoine Picon, what Perronet wanted was a theory of construction – or 'structure' – distinct from the practice of construction, or building. *Construction*, a term long familiar to architects, comprised the whole generic practice of building, combining not just principles, but also conventions, and labour practices; thus, in mid-eighteenth-century France, Blondel divided architecture into 'distribution', 'decoration' and 'construction', a division which roughly corresponded to the Vitruvian triad of commodity, firmness and delight. But for Perronet and subsequent rationalists, the categorization of everything to do with stability under the heading of 'construction' was not satisfactory, because 'construction' was encumbered with all the know-how, and prejudices, of building; for 'construction' as J. N. L. Durand put it at the beginning of the nineteenth century 'expresses the meeting of the different mechanical arts employed in architecture, such as masonry, carpentry, joinery, ironwork etc.' (vol. 1, 31). The significance of 'structure' was that it allowed them to think about the system of support without the interference of two thousand years' worth of accumulated customary wisdom derived from the knowledge of existing objects. Although implied by Perronet in the 1770s as a means to think about architecture free from traditions of the various mechanical arts, he did not in fact use the term 'structure' relative to building – later in the same letter to Soufflot, he retained the term 'construction' – 'In imitating nature in our constructions [*constructions*], we could make very durable works with a lot less material'. When exactly 'structure' started to be used to describe the abstraction of the system of support is not clear: Rondelet's *Traité Théorique et Pratique de l'Art de Bâtir* (1802–17), for example, did not use the word, and called the subject we would now recognize as 'structure' *'théorie des constructions'*. One of the first people to make use of the modern concept of 'structure' was an English author, Robert Willis, whose analysis of Gothic architecture was clearly influenced by French rationalist ideas – but he still hardly used the word itself. Writing in 1835, he used the

phrase 'Mechanical Construction' to signify what would later be called 'structure'. Willis explained his category as follows:

> there are two things to be observed in the construction of a building; how the weights are really supported, and how they seem to be supported. The first I shall call the *Mechanical*, or actual construction, and the second the *Decorative*, or apparent construction, and it is necessary to make a strong distinction between them. (15)

Willis did occasionally use the term 'structure' instead of 'construction', but always qualified it with the adjective 'mechanical' when he meant by it the 'real' system of support: evidently Willis did not expect his readers to understand 'structure' on its own in the modern sense. Pugin, whose famous formulation at the beginning of *The True Principles of Christian Architecture* (see p. 298) was likewise derived from French and Italian rationalism, used the word 'construction', not 'structure', which would, on its own, have been meaningless in Britain in 1841 in the sense he intended. Even into the 1870s, English authors continued to use the phrase 'mechanical structure' when they wanted to signify the system of support independent of material substance. There is no doubt that it was Viollet-le-Duc both in France, and in English translation, who was responsible for popularizing 'structure' as a free-standing metaphor.

Once it became possible, and later customary, to conceive the mechanical system of the structure apart from the material facts of construction, most controversy about 'structure' became concerned with how far it should, or should not be visible in the resulting work. This has been a familiar modernist debate: consider for example Mies van der Rohe's 1922 article 'Skyscrapers', which presented the issue in terms that Viollet-le-Duc (and even more Leopold Eidlitz) would have approved:

> Only skyscrapers under construction reveal the bold constructive thoughts, and then the impression of the high-reaching steel skeletons is overpowering. With the raising of the walls, this impression is completely destroyed; the constructive thought, the necessary basis for artistic form-giving, is annihilated and frequently smothered by a meaningless and trivial jumble of forms. (Neumeyer, 240)

While Mies clearly conceived of the structure as idea, 'the bold constructive thoughts', which he saw as quite distinct from their actual physical manifestation in the building, this distinction, particularly in English, is always collapsing, however often it is reconstituted: what Willis and others had been so keen to establish, that 'structure' was an abstraction, a relationship between parts, not visible in reality, always ends up regarded by modern architects as a physical object, a thing. Mies's remark about huts and structures, quoted at the beginning of the entry, draws attention to this paradox.

The primacy of mechanical, or tectonic 'structure' put forward by Viollet-le-Duc, and subscribed to by Mies van der Rohe and a great many other modernist architects, was by no means universally accepted. In the nineteenth century, the entirely different theory of architecture of Viollet's German contemporary, Gottfried Semper, attached minimal importance to structure, and treated it as entirely secondary to the primary purpose of creating enclosed space. Thus in *Der Stil* he wrote, 'The structure that served to support, to secure, to carry this spatial enclosure was a requirement that had nothing directly to do with *space* and the *division of space*. It was foreign to primitive architectural thinking and was in the beginning not a form-determining element' (vol. 1 §60, 1989, 254). Semper's Viennese disciple Adolf Loos showed a similar indifference to structure: 'The architect's general task is to provide a warm and liveable space', to which carpets and tapestries contribute. 'Both the carpet on the floor and the tapestry on the wall require a structural frame to hold them in the correct place. To invent this frame is the architect's second task' (1898, 66). More recently, the relegation of tectonic structure to an obviously subordinate place has been the most literal sense of architectural 'Deconstruction'. For example, the Viennese partnership Coop Himmelblau (whose approach has an uncanny similarity to that of their compatriot, Adolf Loos) declares that 'In the initial stages structural planning is never an immediate priority, but it does become very important when the project is being realized' (Noever, 23). It is ironic that the work of Coop Himmelblau (see ill. p. 282), and of other deconstructive architects, often turns out to demand far more structural ingenuity than works developed with a 'rational' approach to structure. As Robin Evans remarks, 'What follows from the architect's emancipation from structure is the architect's release from it, not the building's' (1996, 92).

None of this grapples with the more fundamental problem of why a separate category called 'structure' should be there at all. For, as we have seen, 'structure', far from being a divinely ordained category, is an abstraction,

860–880 Lakeshore Drive, Chicago, under construction, Mies van der Rohe, 1950. 'Only skyscrapers under construction reveal the bold constructive thoughts…'

invented in the late eighteenth century out of a metaphor from natural history, so as to free architects from the normalizing constraints of the word 'construction', the everyday practice of building. The remarkable feature of this term is that what began as an abstraction, whose very significance lay in its invisibility, has been turned in modern parlance into a *thing*.

'Structure' in fields other than architecture

At the same time as 'structure' became part of the architectural vocabulary, it was also undergoing development in other fields. It is worth considering briefly what it was about the notion of 'structure' within natural history that offered such a potent image both for architects and others.

The main work of eighteenth-century natural history was in the classification of species. The initial method, established by Linnaeus, was to classify a specimen through the visual evidence of its parts, each assessed according to four values: number, form, proportion and situation. These four values comprised the *structure*: 'By the structure of a plant's parts we mean the composition and arrangement of the pieces that make up its body' (Tournefort, 1719; quoted in Foucault, 1970, 134). Michel Foucault has argued that what this method entirely failed to do was to distinguish the property of *life* in the plants or animals so classified; indeed, as described by these natural historians, they might as well not have been living things at all.[4] It was the attempt to overcome this fault, and to describe the quality of life in plants and animals, that distinguished the work of the later eighteenth-century naturalists, Lamarck, Vicq d'Azyr and Cuvier; the parts, previously classified on visual evidence alone, were now classified within a hierarchy of their relative importance to the organism as a whole, a scheme which necessarily involved defining them according to their functions. Within this method, 'structure' now became the feature that conveyed the relative functions of the parts, and it ceased to be a property based upon visible criteria alone. The result, as Foucault puts it, was that 'To classify ... will mean ... to relate the visible to the invisible, to its deeper cause, as it were' (229). 'Structure' is what makes possible this relationship of the visible to the invisible, and it becomes the way to define 'life', the organic property of living things.

In its appeal to Perronet and the engineers, and later to Viollet-le-Duc, the significance of the naturalists' notion of 'structure' was first of all that it allowed them to conceive buildings as hierarchically arranged relationships of functional parts, and to disregard the evidence their appearance presented to the eye; and secondly, that it allowed them to think of buildings as like living things, whose forms were not fixed according to some predetermined ideal, but might vary according to the relative functions of the parts. The attraction of this notion of 'structure', as the property of life in organic things, is obvious to anyone who, like the late-eighteenth-century architects and engineers, wanted to question the formulae prescribed by the conventions of the classical tradition. It was from the naturalists that architects, by an analogy, developed their notion of 'structure' as a relationship of the mechanical functions of parts, a relationship that is perceived independently of the visual evidence of the building.

The other main field where 'structure' was to be important (apart from linguistics, which will be discussed in the next section) was sociology. Here again, it was the naturalists' notion of 'structure' that provided the model for the study of sociology. The key figure in this development was Herbert Spencer, for whom the study of

Funder-Werk 3, St Veit/Glan, Austria, Coop Himmelblau, 1988–89. The architect's emancipation from 'structure' is not necessarily the building's.

society was not distinct from the study of natural history: as he put it, 'just as Biology discovers certain general traits of development, structure and function, holding throughout all organisms ... so Sociology has to recognize truths of social development, structure, and function' (1873, 59). 'Structures' for Spencer were the functional units of society, and he distinguished between those that were 'operative' (i.e. productive), and those that were 'regulative', institutions like the church, the law, the army. As societies grew in size, and became more complex, so too did their structures: 'It is also a characteristic of social bodies, as of living bodies, that while they increase in size they increase in structure' (1876, §215, 467). The 'structure' was always the outcome of a particular function: 'distinct duties entail distinct structures' (§254, 558); and 'Changes of structures cannot occur without changes of functions' (§234, 504). In Spencer's theory of 'structures' we see what we have already seen in the biological, and the architectural theory, the notion of a direct and determinate relation between 'function' of the organ or building component, and the structure. Spencer's mechanistic notion of 'structure' is worth drawing attention to if only because it underlines the extent to which the concept of 'structure' developing out of biology was linked to 'function'; however, as he was very widely read in the late nineteenth century (both Louis Sullivan and Frank Lloyd Wright mention him), if one is looking for metaphors for 'structure' outside architecture, Spencer may be as influential as the earlier biologists in giving 'structure' its modern significance. Spencer's theory of society also happens to be the underlying object of attack in the notion of structure to be discussed next.

'Structure' as the means by which things become intelligible

Whereas previously biology had provided the model for 'structure', in the early twentieth century its place was to be taken by linguistics, which henceforth provided 'the true science of structure' (Barthes, 1963, 213). Saussure's proposition, that 'Language is a system of interdependent terms in which the value of each term results solely from the simultaneous presence of the others' (114) suggested that the study of language could be approached by asking not *what* words meant, only *how* they carried meaning. What made language intelligible was not meanings attached to particular words, but the system within which they were used. The 'structure' of language ceased to be a matter of a functional relationship between words and what they signified, but became the study of the system of differences within language. This uncoupling of 'structure' from 'function' has been fundamental to the remarkable development of linguistics in the twentieth century, a field distinguished by the creativeness of its practitioners in the invention of alternative models for the structure of language. Of all the other disciplines where there has been developed the understanding of 'structure' as an intellectual schema through which things are made intelligible, none has attracted more notice than structural anthropology. Whereas traditionally anthropologists and sociologists had, like Herbert Spencer, approached the study of societies by asking what their institutions and practices were *for*, what function they served in the organization of society, structural anthropology ignored this, for it led to a purely empirical, anecdotal description of societies. Instead, structural anthropology treated all products of social activity as inherently transferable, and interchangeable; it is the system within which these products, be they rituals, institutions, or artefacts, are transferred and substituted that reveals the structure, indeed the 'life' of the society, rather than any particular meanings or functions that might be attached to them. 'Structure', considered in these terms, ceases to be a property of objects, though it may be perceived through them.

The most promising material for the application of the linguistic sense of 'structure' lay not in architecture, but in space. While interior space has routinely been discussed in terms of a biological/mechanical metaphor of structure – for example, Rowe and Slutsky's remarks about 'the spatial structure' of Le Corbusier's Villa Stein at Garches (1963, 168–69) – the linguistic sense of

structure offered the possibility of a wholly different order of analysis. Space, like language, is not a substance, and, when considered as 'social' space rather than as enclosed 'architectural' space, is one of the properties through which societies constitute themselves. The anthropologist Claude Lévi-Strauss remarked on this, writing that

> It has been Durkheim and Mauss's great merit to call attention for the first time to the variable properties of space which should be considered the structure of several primitive societies … There have been practically no attempts to correlate the spatial configurations with the formal properties of the other aspects of social life. This is much to be regretted, since in many parts of the world there is an obvious relationship between the social structure and the spatial structure of settlements, villages or camps. (1963, 290–91)

As he went on to say, though, the absence of any obvious relationship between social space and social structure in other parts of the world, and the complications it presented elsewhere, made it very difficult to devise any sort of structural model for it. Nonetheless, his own analysis of the South American Bororo villages, described in *Tristes Tropiques* (284–320), was an elegant and persuasive example of the potential for the structural analysis of social space, and was an inspiration to the development of research into the morphology and structure of space.

A slightly different, more obviously poetic, account of the relationship of 'structure' in its new linguistic sense to objects was put forward by Roland Barthes:

> The goal of all structuralist activity … is to reconstruct an 'object' in such a way as to manifest thereby the rules of functioning (the 'functions') of this object. Structure is therefore actually a *simulacrum* of the object, but a directed, *interested* simulacrum, since the imitated object makes something appear which remained invisible or, if one prefers, unintelligible in the natural object. Structural man takes the real, decomposes it, then recomposes it.

Structural activity, says Barthes, is 'a veritable fabrication of a world which resembles the primary one, not in order to copy it but to render it intelligible' (1963, 214–15). Barthes's own example of this is presented in his essay on 'The Eiffel Tower' (1964), in which the literary bird's-eye view of Paris and of France presented by Hugo and Michelet respectively permits us to transcend sensation and see things *in their structure*. ... Paris and France become under Hugo's pen and Michelet's ... intelligible objects, yet without – and this is what is new – losing anything of their materiality; a new category appears, that of concrete abstraction; this, moreover, is the meaning which we can give today to the word *structure*: a corpus of intelligent forms. (1964, 242–43)

The possibility that architects might themselves make 'structure', in the sense that Barthes suggested that writers and other artists could, is one that intrigued and fascinated from the late 1950s, when structuralism and semiology became widely studied. The interest in this linguistic metaphor is discussed at length in chapter 5. An example of the way this perceived analogy between architecture and linguistic structure was developed is illustrated by the group of Dutch architects whose work was published in *Forum* magazine, and in particular Herman Hertzberger. Hertzberger's view was that the forms produced by architects were cold and lifeless, repressive rather than liberating; his aim was to develop forms that would be interpreted and completed by the occupants of buildings in their own way. To describe what he meant, he suggested the relationship of available architectural forms and their capacity for individual interpretations might be understood as like that between language and speech; and within this framework 'we assume an underlying "objective" structure of forms – which we call arch-forms – a derivative of which is what we see in a given situation' (144). The architect, as he saw it, was committed to working within this existing structure of socially established 'arch-forms', and could never create anything totally afresh, but might nonetheless realize objects that could be reconstituted by the users of buildings to mean new and unexpected things. While amongst these Dutch architects, the presentation of this relationship between social perception and architecture as one of 'structure' in a linguistic sense was never more than the loosest of analogies, it should be stressed that this 'structural' impulse, this desire to discover a system that would render the world intelligible and to reconstitute it in architectural form, was a major preoccupation of architecture in the late 1960s and 1970s.

The turning against structuralism, on account of its own self-confessed contradictions, and of its tendency to render the world as an abstraction, was also a major feature of the late 1960s and 1970s, particularly evident in the writings of Henri Lefebvre and Jacques Derrida.

Whereas Lefebvre questioned the turning of life into an abstract concept, Derrida disputed the notion of 'intelligibility' on which structuralism was predicated (see particularly Derrida's essay 'Structure, Sign and Play in the Discourse on the Human Sciences'). Both arguments attracted some interest in architecture, where linguistic models and structuralist thinking had been so attractive in the 1960s.

Bernard Tschumi's work and writing in the 1970s were motivated by his objections to the structuralists' tendency 'to dematerialize architecture into the realm of concepts', to make a 'split between discourse and the domain of daily experience' (1976, 68, 69). From early on, Tschumi made 'structure' a particular object of contempt: '*language* or *structure* are words specific to a mode of reading architecture that does not fully apply in the context of pleasure' (1977, 95). Of his various strategies, the questioning of 'structure' was a major theme, as in the Parc de la Villette scheme:

> We know that architectural systems are always noted for the coherence they represent. From the Classical era to the Modern Movement ... the notion of an incoherent structure is simply without consideration. The very function of architecture, as it is still understood, precludes the idea of a dis-structured structure. However, the process of superimposition, permutation and substitution which governed the Parc de la Villette plan could only lead to a radical questioning of the concept of structure... (1986, 66)

However, it is far from clear in what way Parc de la Villette 'questioned structure': the fact that the scheme has three superimposed systems (a grid, movement patterns, surfaces) if anything confirms, rather than casts doubt upon, the necessity of 'structure'. But more than this, the scheme ignores the problem of how far a percept, a mental 'structure', is necessary for this scheme, or any other piece of a city, to become intelligible to its occupants, and of whether that 'structure' is in any way within the architect's competence. Jacques Derrida was, according to Tschumi, surprised when Tschumi expressed interest in 'deconstruction', and asked him 'But how could an architect be interested in deconstruction? After all, deconstruction is anti-form, anti-hierarchy, anti-structure, the opposite of all that architecture stands for' (1991, 250). Derrida's initial surprise remains. Would the practice of architecture survive the elimination of 'structure'? What would the result be? The answer is as ambiguous as 'structure' itself, and depends entirely to which metaphor, biological or linguistic, the question is addressed. If to the biological, it would lead to the collapse of buildings, formlessness, chaos; or if to the linguistic, the result would be blindness, incomprehension and ultimately the annihilation of the subject. As neither prospect will be tolerated, 'structure', in all its ambiguity, seems unlikely to be displaced as an architectural concept.

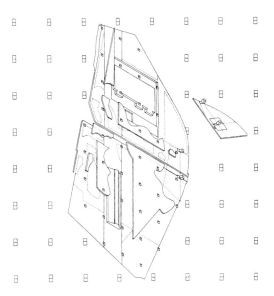

1 See Picon, *French Architects and Engineers*, 1992, especially chapter 7.
2 The various translations of Alberti's *De Re Aedificatoria* indicate the difficulties caused by the historical shifts in the meaning of 'structure'. Book III chapter 4 opens with the sentence '*Reliquum est, ut structuram aggrediamur*'. Bartoli, in 1565, translated this as '*Restaci a dare principio alla muraglia*', which Leoni in 1726 translated into English as 'We now come to begin our wall'; Rykwert, Tavernor and Leach in 1989 translate the original Latin as 'It now remains for us to deal with the structure'. While this would have been acceptable in the eighteenth century, it runs the risk of being misunderstood by a modern reader, who might be led to think, wrongly, that Alberti had a conception of 'structure' in the modern sense of an abstraction of the system of support. In another place, Alberti wrote '*structurae genera sunt haec*' (Book III, chapter 6), which was translated into Italian as '*Le maniere degli edifici sono queste*'; Leoni translated this as 'The different sorts of structures are these'; and Rykwert et.al. more accurately translated the original Latin as 'These are the kinds of construction' – which, since the passage refers to methods of building walls, is undoubtedly what '*structura*' means here in modern terminology.
3 Steadman, *The Evolution of Designs*, 1979, chapter 4, elaborates on this point.
4 See Foucault, *The Order of Things*, 1966, 160–61; see also 132–38 and 226–32 for the argument on which this discussion is based.

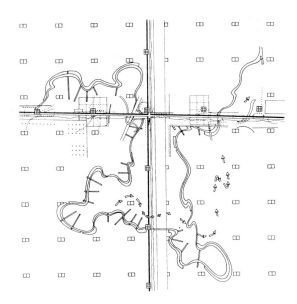

B. Tschumi, 'La Case Vide', drawings for Parc de la Villette, Paris, 1985. Tschumi's scheme for Parc de la Villette questioned received notions of both 'order' and 'structure'.
(top) 'The points, a grid of *folies* superimposed on the surfaces.'
(bottom) 'The lines and points combine – the Gallery and the Cinematic Promenade collide with the *folies*'.

Ideas concerning transparency are one of the most relevant features of our time. T. Mayne, 1991, 79

'Transparency' is a wholly modernist term, unknown in architecture before the twentieth century. This is not merely to do with the developments in the architectural use of glass, for to think of 'transparency' as limited to a description for the properties of glass would be to miss much of its significance. There are three senses in which the word exists in architecture: the distinction between the first two, 'literal' and 'phenomenal', was first made explicit in two articles by Colin Rowe and Robert Slutsky. The third sense, 'transparency of meaning', is more diffused and has never been codified so precisely.

1. *Literal transparency*, meaning pervious to light, allowing one to see into or through a building, was made possible by the development of frame construction and techniques for fixing large areas of glass. These developments, undeniably important to architectural modernism, were seized upon by modernist architects for their aesthetic significance – in dissolving the wall as an architectural element, and in reversing the traditional relation between exterior and interior. This, for example, was how the German architect Arthur Korn saw the matter in 1929:

> The contribution of the present age is that it is now possible to have an independent wall of glass, a skin of glass around a building: no longer a solid wall with windows. Even though the window might be the dominant part – this window is the wall itself, or in other words, this wall is itself the window. And with this we have come to a turning point. It is something quite new compared to the achievements through the centuries … it is the disappearance of the outside wall – the wall, which for thousands of years had to be made of solid materials such as stone or timber or clay products. But in the situation now, the outside wall is

no longer the first impression one gets of a building. It is the interior, the spaces in depth and the structural frame which delineates them, that one begins to notice through the glass wall. This wall is barely visible, and can only be seen when there are reflected light distortions or mirror effects. (170)

The aesthetic possibilities Korn outlined were described by László Moholy-Nagy in the same year in *The New Vision* (*Von Material zu Architektur*) as 'transparency' – and this is the term that has stuck. Literal transparency has continued throughout the period of architectural modernism, and was only temporarily abandoned with the postmodernists' taste for fake solid walls; the purging of postmodernism was marked by a return to glass skins of unprecedented expanse and invisibility. In France especially, where the tradition of technocratic rationalism was strong, the word has been used with specific political connotations: as Colquhoun wrote of the literal 'transparency' of the Centre Pompidou: 'the building is seen as an object which is accessible to everyone and can be appropriated by the public' (1977, 114). The same could be said of some of the works of Jean Nouvel, and Foster's Carré d'Art at Nîmes.

2. *Phenomenal transparency* – the apparent space between solid objects – was the subject of two articles written by Colin Rowe and Robert Slutsky in 1955–56.[1] Their discussion of it was introduced by a quotation from Gyorgy Kepes's *Language of Vision* (1944):

> If one sees two or more figures overlapping one another, and each of them claims for itself the common overlapped part, then one is confronted with a contradiction of spatial dimensions. To resolve this contradiction one must assume the presence of a new optical quality. The figures are endowed with transparency: that is, they are able to interpenetrate without an optical destruction of each other.

Transparency however implies more than an optical characteristic, it implies a broader spatial order. Transparency means a simultaneous perception of different spatial locations. Space not only recedes but fluctuates in a continuous activity. The position of the transparent figures has equivocal meaning as one sees each figure now as the closer, now as the further one. (160–61)

Kepes's sense of transparency obviously related to the spatial devices of Cubist painting, and the first part of Rowe and Slutsky's discussion was devoted to this. Yet to apply the same idea to architecture gave rise, as they noted, to 'inevitable confusions':

> For, while painting can only imply the third dimension, architecture cannot suppress it. Provided with the reality rather than the counterfeit of three dimensions, in architecture, literal transparency can become a physical fact; but phenomenal transparency will be more difficult to achieve – and is, indeed, so difficult to discuss that generally critics have been entirely willing to associate transparency in architecture exclusively with a transparency of materials (166).

They proceeded then to show how certain works of Le Corbusier – the Villa Stein at Garches, the League of Nations competition design, and the office block project for Algiers – created by implied layers of planes an illusion of spatial depth that was at variance with the spatial reality of the buildings, and so created in the viewer's mind the 'equivocal meaning' noted by Kepes. In the second of the two articles, they went on to show that such illusions were not exclusive to modern architecture, but could, for example, be found in the facades of Renaissance *palazzi*, and in Michelangelo's proposed facade for San Lorenzo in Florence.

Although Kepes, in 1944, was apparently the first to give this type of transparency the name 'phenomenal', the property had certainly been remarked upon previously in architecture. Rowe and Slutsky themselves noted that in Moholy-Nagy's references to 'transparency' in *The New Vision*, there were implications of this sort of transparency. And in another book published the year before Moholy-Nagy's, and equally important in the dissemination of architectural modernism, the Swiss historian and critic Sigfried Giedion's *Building in France* (*Bauen in Frankreich*, 1928), there was reference to 'transparency' in terms suggestive of the 'phenomenal'. Following comparison of the purist paintings of Le Corbusier and Ozenfant with

Institut du Monde Arabe, Paris, J. Nouvel, G. Lezens, P. Soria and Architecture Studio, 1987. Literal transparency.

Housing scheme at Pessac, near Bordeaux, Le Corbusier, 1925–28 © FLC L2(6)1-46. Sigfried Giedion drew attention to the similar illusions of 'transparency' created by the interpenetration of objects in Le Corbusier's cubist paintings, and by overlapping solids in photographs of his architecture.

Le Corbusier's villas (see also ill. p. 25), Giedion wrote 'Not only in photos but also in reality do the edges of the houses blur. There arises – as with certain lighting conditions in snowy landscapes – that dematerialization of solid demarcation that distinguishes neither rise nor fall and that gradually produces the feeling of walking in clouds' (169). Like his successors, Giedion attributed the discovery of this effect to painters: 'We owe it to the Dutch, to Mondrian and Doesburg, that they first opened our eyes to the oscillating relations that may arise from surfaces, lines, air' (176).

3. *Transparency of meaning*. This sense, and its significance within modernist aesthetics, is best explained by the American critic Susan Sontag in 'Against Interpretation' (1964). '*Transparence* is the highest, most liberating value in art – and in criticism – today. Transparence means experiencing the luminousness of the thing in itself, of things being what they are' (13). This idea, that there should be no distinction between form and content, between object and meaning, lies at the very heart of modernist aesthetics, in all the arts, and not just architecture. The ideal of modernist art was that it should need no interpretation, because whatever meaning it had was immanent in the sensory experience of the work; it was, to quote Sontag again, 'by making works of art whose surface is so unified and clean, whose momentum is so rapid, whose address is so direct that the work can be … just what it is' (11). Others have called this property by different names: the American sculptor Robert Morris called it 'presentness' (1978), and Donald Judd 'directness'.

Within architecture, there has been a strong predisposition to assume that diaphonous materials are the natural means of achieving this property which Sontag called 'transparence' – 'the luminousness of the thing in itself'. An early instance of this occurred when Mies van der Rohe, writing in 1933 in answer to the question 'What Would Concrete, what Would Steel be without Mirror Glass?', responded

> The glass skin, the glass walls alone permit the skeleton structure its unambiguous constructive appearance and secure its architectonic possibilities. … Now it becomes clear again what a wall is, what an opening, what is floor and what ceiling. Simplicity of construction, clarity of tectonic means, and purity of material reflect the luminosity of original beauty. (Neumeyer, 314)

Alternative models – as transparent, and as a solid – of competition entry for French National Library, Paris, OMA, 1989. Uncertainty whether the building would appear clear or opaque, depending on time of day and weather conditions, could be anxiety-inducing: not at all the intention of modernist 'transparency'.

Similar assumptions underlie recent and more remarkable feats with glass than Mies van der Rohe was able to achieve.

Transparency of meaning is more commonly expressed in relation to its converse, 'opacity' – the condition to which, as Anthony Vidler has pointed out, many buildings with literal transparency revert for much of the time.[2] After postmodernism, which rejected transparency (in all senses), Vidler saw signs of the emergence of a new approach to modernism that accepted its technological and ideological heritage, but sought to problematize its premises. As an instance of this, he suggested that OMA's 1989 competition entry for the French National Library – a glass cube with various amorphous solids suspended within it – might be seen as 'at once a confirmation of transparency and its complex critique' (221). The impossibility of making out exactly what the various amoebic shapes within are, through the sometimes translucent exterior (depending on weather or light conditions), is such as to throw the subject into a state of anxiety and estrangement that Vidler saw as presaging the 'uncanny'. In Vidler's essay, there is, therefore, the suggestion that 'transparency' might lead to aesthetic results not envisaged by the modernist pioneers.

1 'Transparency: Literal and Phenomenal', Part 1, (first published 1963) in Rowe, *Mathematics of the Ideal Villa*, 1982, 159–83; Part 2 (first published 1971), in Ockman (ed.), *Architecture Culture*, 1993, 206–25.
2 See Vidler, *The Architectural Uncanny*, 1992, 'Transparency', 216–25.

...the striving toward truth must be the guiding star of the architect. Otto Wagner, 1896, 83

A modern building should derive its architectural significance solely from the vigour and consequence of its own organic proportions. It must be true to itself, logically transparent, and virginal of lies or trivialities. Walter Gropius, 1935, 82

Architecture is the reaching out for the truth. Louis Kahn, 1968 – Wurman, 28

1. *Truth in modernism and after*

As these remarks from various moments in the history of modernism suggest, 'truth' was undeniably an important concept within architectural modernism. Yet 'truth' was not itself a modernist concept, for neither was it invented by the modernists, nor did they bring to it any significant new meanings; as a critical category within architecture, 'truth' was a creation of the late eighteenth and nineteenth centuries, and the modernists did no more than reproduce the various meanings that it had acquired in its nineteenth-century heyday. Although, in the most oversimplified terms, the principal distinction between a modernist and a postmodernist sensibility is generally taken as the attachment to, or rejection of 'truth', we should not therefore regard 'truth' as a defining concept of modernism. The recent assault upon 'truth' in critical theory has not just been an assault upon modernism, but upon the whole tradition of Western thought; and within architecture the 'truth' attacked is not a concept particular to twentieth-century modernism, but one inherited from earlier centuries. While we shall start by outlining the various senses in which 'truth' was used by twentieth-century modernists, and describing the main features of the subsequent attack upon 'truth', the most interesting debates about 'truth' relative to architecture all belong to the eighteenth and nineteenth centuries, and it is these therefore that occupy the bulk of this entry.

As used by modernist architects and critics, 'truth' occurs in three senses, though they are not always distinct: Louis Kahn's remark could refer to any one – or all three. First, there is 'expressive truth', the sense of a work being true to its inner essence, or to the spirit of its makers: this is the meaning intended by Gropius. Secondly, there is 'structural truth', the expectation that the outward appearance of a work should conform to its structural system, and to the properties of the materials of which it is made. For example, speculating in 1955 as to what might constitute a universal architectural language of the present, the engineer Ove Arup said, 'The nearest approach I can find to a common ideology is the frequently expressed conviction that a regeneration of architecture in our new technical age must come through the truthful expression of structure' (19). And thirdly, there is 'historical truth', the requirement that a work should be of its time, and be true to the stage of historical development reached within the art. This is, for example, the sense conveyed by Mies van der Rohe in his 1924 article '*Baukunst und Zeitwille*' ('Building Art and the Will of the Epoch'), where he wrote

> Greek temples, Roman basilicas and mediaeval cathedrals are significant to us as creations of a whole epoch rather than as works of individual architects ... They are pure expressions of their time. Their true meaning is that they are symbols of their epoch. ... Our utilitarian buildings can become worthy of the name of architecture only if they truly interpret their time. (Johnson, *Mies*, 186)

Historical truth, as might be expected, was particularly apparent in the work of modernist historians, whose project was to prove that modern architecture was indeed historically destined. Thus Sigfried Giedion, at the beginning of his 1928 book *Building in France, Building* in Iron, Building in Ferro-Concrete, asserted 'We see ... that the architecture we now describe as "new" is a legitimate part of an entire century of development' (86). Similar concerns underlie the work of the historian Nikolaus Pevsner, and are evident in his 1936 book *Pioneers of the Modern Movement*. And in his remarkable forty-six volume publication *The Buildings of England*, the buildings selected are by and large those which manifested historical truthfulness; those lacking this quality he either ignored or, if their size or prominence made inclusion unavoidable, condemned – like the neo-baroque Council House at Nottingham of 1927–29, which he compared unfavourably to the contemporary Stockholm Town Hall, remarking 'the Ionic columnation is no more inspiring or truthful than the interiors' (1951, 130). All these three senses of truth, expressive, structural and historical, were developed in the nineteenth century, and the process of their development will be discussed more fully later.

The assault upon 'truth' that has been such a major feature of criticism since the 1960s has come primarily from literary criticism. Although resistance to 'truth' has certainly been evident in architecture, the economic realities of building have not made it easy to give up, and rejection of truth has in large part been a matter of applying to architecture theories developed in the reading of literature. There are though a few significant exceptions, which can be dealt with briefly. The first is in the writings of Robert Venturi. In his 1966 book *Complexity and Contradiction in Architecture*, Venturi wrote 'I like elements which are ... inconsistent and equivocal rather than direct and clear' (16). His enthusiasm was for the ambiguity of baroque architecture, which he contrasted with the singularity of modern architecture; not so much an attack on 'truth', *Complexity and Contradiction* was more of a return to an older, baroque idea, that truth could coexist with deception. In *Learning From Las Vegas* (1972), Venturi and Scott Brown were more outspoken against 'truthfulness', but here the attack was on the inappropriateness of moral criteria in relation to architectural values. As they put it in relation to an apartment block designed by Paul Rudolph, 'Our criticism of Crawford Manor and the buildings it stands for is not moralistic, nor is it concerned with so-called honesty in architecture or a lack of correspondence between substance and image *per se*; ... We criticize Crawford Manor not for "dishonesty", but for irrelevance today' (101). At about the same time, the notion of 'historical truth' was put under scrutiny. Two texts in particular stand out. Charles Jencks's 'History

as Myth', in which he took issue with the claims of Giedion, Pevsner and others for the historical legitimacy of modernism, argued instead that the history of modern architecture was open to a plurality of interpretations, all of them equally mythical, and so devoid of truth. David Watkin's *Morality in Architecture* (1977) was a more extended attack upon the attempt by modernist historians to give modernism a moral authority; the argument drew heavily upon Karl Popper's anti-Hegelian *The Poverty of Historicism* (1957).

However, it has been from outside architecture that the major attacks upon 'truth' have derived. These attacks, a product of literary theory in France in the late 1960s, were part of the reaction against structuralist theory. Structuralist literary criticism, based upon Saussure's theory of semiotics, had accepted the arbitrariness of separation between the signifier and the signified, and so challenged traditional literary criticism's claims that works of literature carried definitive meanings. The lessons of this theory, evident in the collection of Roland Barthes's early essays entitled *Mythologies*, disputed literary criticism's ability to produce 'truths'. A good example of this argument directed at modernist design appeared in Jean Baudrillard's *For a Critique of the Political Economy of the Sign* (1972):

> In summary, the formula of the Bauhaus is: for every form and every object there is an objective, determinable *signified* – its function. This is what is called in linguistics the level of *denotation*. The Bauhaus claims to strictly isolate this nucleus, this level of denotation – all the rest is coating, the hell of *connotation*: residue, superfluity, excrescence, eccentricity, ornamentation, uselessness. Kitsch. The thing denoted (functional) is beautiful, the connoted (parasitical) is ugly. Better yet: the thing denoted (objective) is true, the connoted is false (ideological). In effect, behind the concept of objectivity, the whole metaphysical and moral argument of truth is at stake.
>
> Now today this postulate of denotation is in the process of breaking up. It is finally beginning to be seen ... that it is arbitrary, not merely an artifact of a method, but a metaphysical fable. *There is no truth of the object, and denotation is never more than the most beautiful of connotations.* (1981, 196)

Yet for Baudrillard, Barthes and others, there was an unsatisfactoriness in Saussure's assumption that for every sign, there was always a determinate signified. The circle of French structuralist critics became increasingly uncomfortable about this obligation towards an ultimate, transcendental signified; inspired partly by the irrationalism of Georges Bataille, and by the attacks upon 'truth' mounted by Friedrich Nietzsche a century earlier (see particularly Part 1 of *Beyond Good and Evil*), they started exploring other ways of describing the relationship between readers and texts. In Barthes's case, his criticism underwent a marked shift away from interest in the structure of the work itself as responsible for the generation of meaning, and towards an interest in the subject's own experience and possession of language, the language through which they read the work, and in the act of reading as a process of acquiring an identity. Barthes described this new conception of the relationship between reader and text as follows:

> To be with the one I love and to think of something else: this is how I have my best ideas, how I best invent what is necessary to my work. Likewise for the text: it produces, in me, the best pleasure if it manages to make itself heard indirectly; if, reading it, I am led to look up often, to listen to something else. (1973, 24)

This shift towards the subject put an end to any idea that a work could itself produce a 'truth'. As Barthes put it, 'Criticism is not a translation but a periphrase. It cannot claim to rediscover the "essence" of the work, for this essence is the subject itself, that is to say an absence' (1966, 87).

The person who first, and perhaps still most successfully, tried to bring to architectural thinking this new theory of criticism, driven by irrationality and desire, was Bernard Tschumi.[1] In a series of essays written in the 1970s, he addressed the split between the objective nature of architectural works, and the subject's presence within them. In 'The Architectural Paradox' (1975), he ascribed the dissatisfaction felt by many people with architecture to the difference between 'conceived space' – that which is known intellectually – and 'perceived space' – that which derives from bodily experience – and the difficulty of relating one to the other. The problem, as Tschumi put it, is that

> architecture is made of two terms that are interdependent but mutually exclusive. Indeed, *architecture constitutes the reality of experience while this reality gets in the way of overall vision. Architecture constitutes the abstraction of absolute truth, while this very truth gets in the way of feeling.*

Crawford Manor, New Haven, Paul Rudolph, 1962–66. Criticized by Venturi and Scott Brown for the irrelevance of its pretensions to moral values of 'honesty'.

We cannot both experience and think that we experience (48).

Tschumi's solution to the paradox was suggested by Bataille and Barthes, to surrender rationality and truth in favour of an erotic, sensual, 'experienced space' that bridged sensory pleasure and reason.

Another attempt to incorporate the post-structuralist rejection of 'truth' into architecture occurred in Peter Eisenman's collaboration with Jacques Derrida for a project for La Villette, called *Choral Works*. Here Derrida's view of language as an endless play of meanings was to be translated into the physical work.

> Its structure of stone and metal, the superposition of layers … plunges into the abyss of the 'platonic' *chora*. … the truth of *Choral Work*, the truth which *lyre* or *layer* says and does and gives is not a truth: it is not presentable, representable, totalizable; it never shows itself. … For all these layers of meanings and forms, of visibility and invisibility extend (lie, as in layers) *into* each other, *on* or *under* each other, *in front of* or *behind* each other, but the truth of the relationship is never established, never stabilized in any judgment. It always causes something else to be said – allegorically – than that which is said. *In a word*, it causes one to lie. The truth of this work lies in this lying strength. (344)

In this calculated irrationality, we see, as Eisenman had earlier described it, evidence 'of the effort to dissociate architecture from its metaphysic of center' (1987, 181).

The other main attempt to weaken the hold of truth upon Western thought comes from the theory of simulation developed by Jean Baudrillard. In a neo-Marxist version of post-structuralism, Baudrillard argued that part of the reason for the alienation of advanced capitalist societies was the tendency to replace the commodity as the unit of exchange, by its simulacrum. The characteristic of modern societies is less their attachment to commodities than to commodity signs, such as the advertised image; in these circumstances, it becomes impossible to distinguish the commodity from its simulacrum. As Baudrillard puts it, 'The simulacrum is never that which conceals the truth – it is the truth which conceals that there is none. The simulacrum is true' (1983, 1). The simulacrum is neither true nor false: 'it is always a false problem to want to restore the truth beneath the similacrum' (1983, 48). There has been little direct application of these ideas to architecture,

despite their obvious relevance to the circumstances of architecture, a practice concerned simultaneously with both image production and with building production.

Against the abrasion of 'truth' by structuralism and post-structuralism, against the notion that people's engagement with the world occurs not in relation to things, but to signs and images, there has been resistance. Because of the physical materiality of works of architecture, and their considerable unlikeness to 'text', architecture has provided a particular focus for this counter-attack. The recent arguments for the existence of an inherent and essential truth of works of art are various, but are all derived from phenomenology. One attacks the convention of Western thought which sees a division between the visible and the invisible world, one known to the senses, the other to the mind. As the French philosopher Maurice Merleau-Ponty put it, 'The senses translate each other without any need of an interpreter, and are mutually comprehensible without the intervention of any idea' (235). Thus the world is not known independently of being in it, and the meaning of objects in the world cannot be separated from the experience they offer to the senses. Some of the architectural implications of this argument have been suggested by, amongst others, Alberto Pérez-Gomez and Louise Pelletier.

A rather different, historical, line of argument proposes that the collapse of 'truth' in architecture is the result of the rise of the aesthetic, and of its separation from science, relative to their previous unity in antiquity and the Middle Ages. Here, it is perceived that the central problem of architecture is its inability any longer to bear a transcendental truth. The result of the separation of artistic from scientific practices is, as the philosopher Hans Gadamer put it, that 'Instead of art and nature complementing each other, as had always seemed to be the case, they were contrasted as appearance and reality' (74). As a consequence of this 'aesthetic differentiation', the work of art, failing to attain the level of scientific 'truth', has no other purpose than merely to please the senses. Some of the implications of this problem were explored by Pérez-Gomez in his book *Architecture and the Crisis of Modern Science*, and more particularly in a 1985 article by the architectural theorist Dalibor Vesely, whose attachment to the possibility of architectural 'truth' is clear – despite his doubts as to its present attainability. As far as Vesely is concerned, all the 'truths' of architecture aspired to by the modernists (and described later in this entry) are false, being the partial truths produced by either modern science or by modern aesthetics. While once it had been possible for art, when undifferentiated from science, to embody an absolute, transcendental truth, the development of positivist scientific method since the seventeenth century brought this to an end. Summarizing his own argument, Vesely wrote that his purpose was to show 'how art, a revelation of the truth of reality preserved in the symbolic representation, differs from aesthetic representation, created and experienced as a source of pleasant sensation' (32). Against the false truths of the post-Renaissance world, Vesely explained 'By "truth in a positive sense", I understand the capacity of the work of art (architecture) to reveal the truth of existing reality – the human situation – but also the capacity to preserve it in the work as symbolic representation' (38, n.65). Critical both of modern science's mistaken assumption that it can give an exhaustive account of nature, and of art's failure to do more than produce forms that are judged beautiful, Vesely was disturbed by the prospect of 'replacing architectural reality as a whole by aesthetic or scientific fiction and, by manipulating the fiction, believing that we are manipulating or even creating reality itself' (32). The best prospect for the reclamation of truth Vesely saw to be through an understanding of continuous principles manifested through architecture's history – though pessimistically he acknowledged that attempts at this in the previous two decades had led to nothing more than a nostalgia for the pre-industrial city, and various other misguided borrowings from history. All these attempts foundered upon the mistaken belief that the renewal of architecture could be brought about by the mere manipulation of 'form'.

Although the post-structuralist assault on 'truth' has made the term less talked about than it was forty years ago – and when it is talked about, has caused it to be treated more circumspectly – it is clear that it has not been displaced, and that there is a real possibility that through these phenomenological readings it may yet return, but to hold a different position within the verbal apparatus of architecture.

2. 'Truth' in Renaissance art theory: the imitation of nature

Renaissance neo-Platonism valorized 'truth' as a quality of art, making in particular the degree to which an art offered faithful representation of a natural ideal a measure of its standing. Poetry and drama, regarded by Aristotle and Horace as the most faithful in this respect, became regarded as the superior arts, and a major theme of Renaissance art theory was taken up with demonstrating the equivalence of the visual arts of painting and sculpture in their ability to represent the natural ideal.[2] Architecture, not being a representational art, stood at a disadvantage in this respect relative to the other arts, and a recurrent concern of its practitioners was to demonstrate that it too could aspire to the level of representational truth. This was not merely idle philosophical speculation, but affected their livelihood and social standing; for the relatively recent social differentiation of architecture from building relied in part upon architects being able to prove that theirs was a 'liberal' rather than a 'mechanical' art.[3] However, it was not at once obvious that architecture was an art of representation in the way that poetry and painting were, for what, if anything, did it represent? Here Vitruvius came to their rescue, for in one brief passage, he described the ornaments of the Doric and Ionic orders as made in the image of the earliest timber buildings, and claimed that this dictated their arrangement. Thus for the Greeks, Vitruvius wrote, 'what cannot happen in reality cannot (they thought) be correctly treated in the imitation. For by an exact fitness deduced from the real laws of nature, they adapted everything to the perfection of their work, and approved what they could show by argument, to follow the method of reality' (Book IV, chapter II, §§5–6). Whatever Vitruvius had meant, for architectural thinkers from the sixteenth to the eighteenth centuries, this was sufficient to make architecture an art concerned with the truthful representation of nature, and so on a par with poetry and painting. From the sixteenth to the mid-eighteenth century, whenever architectural writers mention 'truth' they invariably do so in the sense of the truthful representation of architecture's natural model. Thus Palladio in 1570, listing the abuses of architecture, condemned everything which deviated from nature, which provided 'the true, good and beautiful method of building' (Book I, chapter xx).

What is particularly noticeable is that throughout the sixteenth and seventeenth centuries, architectural commentators had no difficulty in reconciling the deceptiveness of architecture with its claims to truthfulness. Fully aware that architecture creates an artificial reality, and that it is largely concerned with making things seem other than they are, Renaissance and Baroque architects saw no contradiction between this and architecture's supposed truthfulness. It was only in the second half of the eighteenth century that the notion broke down that architecture could be both an art of deception and at the same time an art of truth, and that this seeming paradox became intolerable. The reasons for this, as we shall see, were to do with the redefinition of 'truth'. In the seventeenth, and well into the eighteenth centuries, it was taken for granted that the pleasure of art in general, and of architecture in particular, derived from its capacity to deceive. Thus the architect Guarino Guarini wrote in 1686 that 'architecture, although it depends on mathematics, is nonetheless an art of flattery, in which the senses do not want to be disgusted by reason' (10–11). If the primary purpose of art was to please the senses, as was generally held in late seventeenth- and early eighteenth-century theory, then it was the duty of art to adjust reality to suit. So, for example, Bernini held that one of the most important things for an architect 'was to have a good eye in assessing the *contrapposti*, so that things should not appear to be simply what they were, but should be drawn in relation to objects in their vicinity that change their appearance' (Fréart de Chantelou, 139). And to take an example from the eighteenth century, and one with a considerable subsequent influence, we may quote Edmund Burke's *A Philosophical Enquiry into the Origin of our Ideas of the Sublime and Beautiful* of 1757, where Burke argued that to achieve the effect of the sublime, apparent size was always more important than actual size: 'A true artist should put a generous deceit on the spectators .... No work of art can be great, but as it deceives' (76).

However, around the middle of the eighteenth century, acceptance of architecture as both an art of truth and an art of deception began to break down, with the eventual result that to value one invariably compromised the other. Although some architectural theorists, notably Quatremère de Quincy, tried to preserve the unity of the two against the development of the new and more exclusive conceptions of truth, theirs was to be a losing battle. The reasons for the demise of the baroque coexistence of truth and deception were entirely external to architecture.

The first is to do with developments in other branches of thought in the seventeenth and eighteenth century. The 'scientific revolution' of the seventeenth century – the discoveries of Galileo, Newton, William Harvey and others – came about from a willingness to renounce what the ancients said about the natural world, and to look for explanations based on direct observation and the application of reason. If this led to advances in the natural sciences, should not the same attitude be applied to architecture – rather than being bound by deference to antiquity, should not architecture rest on principles arrived at by reason? This was exactly the analogy used by Carlo Lodolí, who, as we shall see shortly, was the first person to develop a new notion of architectural truth. We do not, Lodolí said, insist on sticking to Hippocrates

and Galen but we follow the new medical discoveries of William Harvey and others, so likewise in architecture we should follow our reason rather than ancient traditions and the doubtful authority of Vitruvius.[4] Specious though this argument was for architecture – not a natural science – it was nonetheless compelling.

The second reason for dissatisfaction with the truthfulness to nature came from developments in philosophy. Until the latter part of the eighteenth century, aesthetics and morals were not regarded as separate kinds of knowledge. In Plato and Aristotle, and in all subsequent Western philosophy, beauty and truth had been compatible, even interchangeable concepts, a view repeated in the early eighteenth century by Lord Shaftesbury, who is generally regarded as the founder of modern aesthetic philosophy: 'the most natural beauty in the world is honesty and moral truth. For all beauty is truth' (241). Similar statements abound in eighteenth-century writing on the arts. Only with Kant's *Critique of Judgment* (1790) was aesthetics decisively established as an independent branch of knowledge, separate from morals and ethics. From Kant onwards, to speak of beauty in terms of truth became a philosophical transgression, and even if most writers on the arts remained ignorant of the details of Kant's philosophy, the effect was to make truth into an altogether more rigorous concept. Although there have been many lapses in the policing of the border between morals and aesthetics,[5] there is no doubt that 'truth' became a more exclusive category than it had been before, and one that could no longer coexist peacefully with the deceptions of art.

3. Structural truth

The first serious challenge to the notion of architecture as an art of deception came simultaneously in the 1750s from two different sources, in Italy from Carlo Lodolí, and in France from the Abbé Laugier.

Carlo Lodolí (1690–1761) was a Franciscan friar who lived most of his life in Venice. His reputation as 'the Socrates of architecture' came from his evidently provocative teaching; but as he published nothing, and all his papers perished after his death, his ideas are known to us only at secondhand, through Francesco Algarotti's 'Saggio Sopra l'Architettura' (1753) and Andrea Memmo's *Elementi d'Architettura Lodoliana*. These two present significantly different accounts of Lodolí's ideas: Memmo's account is generally thought more reliable than Algarotti's, whose essay was not only very short, but prejudiced against Lodolí. Both however agree on the importance of 'truth' to Lodolí: 'Having no other end

Interior of Dome of Capella della S. Sindone, G. Guarini, Turin, 1667–90.
'The senses do not want to be disgusted by reason': baroque architects saw no
contradiction between architecture's truthfulness and its capacity to deceive.

than the truth, which he would expound and show in all its various facets and guises, he intended to purge architecture, as so to speak Socrates did philosophy, of empty words and the fallacies of the Sophists' (Algarotti, 34); and Memmo lists as one of Lodolí's maxims 'no architectural beauty can be found which does not proceed from truth' (Memmo, vol. 2, 59). Truth, for Lodolí, was the antidote to the two main abuses that he saw in architecture, on the one hand the capriciousness of those (like Borromini) who disregarded all rules and followed only their own, and on the other, uncritical obedience to the authority of the ancients. Lodolí based his own rational principle on a two part division of architecture into 'function' (see pp. 174–75) and 'representation', or in other words, a distinction between the structural, static properties of the building and its materials, and what is seen by the eye.⁶ Memmo implies that 'truth' is the unity of function with representation; but there was also a more specific sense in which Lodolí used truth, concerning materials. Lodolí argued that the form taken by the ornaments of a building should follow the essential properties of the materials of which they were made: this was a direct attack on the Vitruvian doctrine of the transmutation of timber details into stone architecture, and on baroque artifice in general. Lodolí (who was fond of metaphors) argued

> that without truth essential beauty could not be conceded. Sometimes he would say that crystal, however many facets were worked on it, when placed beside a genuine cut diamond could never be considered as anything but a fine imitation; that a woman's cheeks could never be thought rosy if the colour on them were vermilion powder: that one could never call beautiful false hair known to be the work of artifice: as reasonably could a wig imitating a lovely head of hair be judged beautiful, etc. Applying such images to architecture, he reflected that giving marble the appearance of wood was the same as putting money to deplorable use ... Why do we never enquire whether it would be as or more pleasing to give marble true and scientific forms of its own, so that what to an intelligent eye must appear deformed would not be discerned. (Memmo, vol. 2, 81–82)

From Lodolí comes the notion that for architecture to be truthful, its ornaments must be consistent with the materials in which they are made.

The other mid-eighteenth-century contribution to the theory of architectural truth came from Laugier's *Essai*

sur l'Architecture, first published in 1753. Laugier, like Lodolí, wanted to purge architecture of baroque excesses, and establish general principles arrived at by reason. In fact, Laugier's principles rest upon what is 'natural' (see pp. 221–23), that is to say what accords with the structural logic of the primitive hut, and only once does he use the word 'true' of architecture (his proposal for church architecture 'is entirely natural and true' [1756, 104]). However, Laugier's 'natural' is not very far from Lodolí's 'truth', sufficiently close for the two to become, as we shall see, mixed up by the Italian writer Francesco Milizia. Milizia (1725–98), a prolific author of architectural books, drew material from a variety of sources; his books enjoyed a wide readership, went into several editions, and were translated variously into French, Spanish and English. It was really Milizia, rather than Algarotti or Memmo, who was the main publicist of the obscure Lodolí, and it is thanks to Milizia that Lodolí's notions of truth gained the currency that they later did. However, Milizia was not an original, nor a systematic writer, and he had no hesitation in combining ideas from different authors. Thus we find in the following an amalgam of Laugier and Lodolí:

> Never do anything unnecessary, or for which a good reason cannot be given. The reasons must be deduced from the origins and from the analysis of the primitive natural architecture of the cabin, which has produced that fine art of imitation, civil architecture. That is the directing norm for artists in their work, and for critics in examination of it. *Everything must be founded on truth, or on verisimilitude. What cannot be sustained truthfully and in reality cannot be approved* ... (1785, xxvii)

It is in another of Milizia's books, *L'Arte di Vedere*, which was translated into both French and Spanish, that we find the most lucid of all eighteenth-century statements of the concept of structural truth (though without using the word itself). This translation is from the French edition, not the original Italian (from which it differs in some details) for reasons that will become apparent later.

> Architecture being founded on necessity, it follows: 1st that its beauty must borrow its character from this same necessity; 2nd that the ornaments must derive from the very nature of the edifice, and result from the need it may have for them. Nothing should be seen in a building which has not its use there, and which is not an integral part of it; 3rd that everything

visible must be for something; 4th that nothing be admitted whose existence cannot be justified by good reasons; 5th that these reasons must be evident, because evidence is the principal ingredient of beauty; architecture can have no other beauty than that which is derived from necessity; that necessity is straightforward and self-evident, it never shows itself in elaborate work, and is revolted by all contrived ornament.

Those who wish to learn to look at buildings must always go back to these unquestionable, constant, general and unbending principles, which are all drawn from reason and from the very essence of architecture. You must ask of every part, who are you? what are you doing there? how do you do your job? do you contribute in some way to usefulness, or to solidity? do you fulfil your functions better than another could if he were in your place? (1797–98, 75)

Against the persuasive arguments for constructional truth put forward by Lodolí and Milizia there was one last ditch stand to preserve the old baroque idea that architecture could be both true and false. The brilliant argument put forward by the French architectural theorist Quatremère de Quincy in the 1780s is worth repeating for its ingenuity, even though it failed to preserve the old notion of 'truth' against the incursion of new meanings. Briefly, Quatremère set out to do what no one before had attempted, to give a rational account of the paradox of architecture's simultaneous truth and falsity. Quatremère argued that all his predecessors had made the mistake of supposing that the 'natural' model of architecture was the primitive timber hut itself; instead, Quatremère said, 'nature' (see pp. 224–26) was an ideal concept of which physical objects, the timber hut included, were simply representations. The imitation of nature performed by architecture was not in the copying of timber details into stone, but in the translation into stone of the ideal of nature, which those timber details happened to represent.[7] Thus Greek architecture was at once both truthful (because it showed truthfully the translation of the ideal), and at the same time fictive, because of the act of imagination necessary to the imitation and its appreciation. This enabled Quatremère to refute Lodolí's demand that stone should copy nothing but stone, and to propose instead that the imitation of the timber hut was at once real and illusory. He continues:

Let us have no doubt about it, it is through this happy deception that man enjoys the pleasure of imitation in architecture. Without such a deception, there would be no place for that pleasure which accompanies all the arts and is their charm. This pleasure of being half-deceived, which endears man to the fictitious and the poetic, makes him prefer truth disguised to truth naked. We like to find in art a lie, though it should not impose too much; it is a deception to which we submit willingly, because it lasts only as long as we wish, and because we can always undeceive ourselves of it. Man fears the truth as much as the lie: he likes to be seduced but not led astray. It is on this knowledge of man's soul that the arts, those friendly and truthful liars, have founded all their empire. Skilful flatterers of the sovereign they delight, they know that they risk as much by speaking the truth as by lying. Their craft is to keep always close to both the truth and the lie. ('Architecture', 1788, 115)

But for all its cleverness, Quatremère's argument led nowhere. Among early nineteenth-century European architects, the principles of structural truth put forward by Lodolí, and propagated by Milizia, became increasingly widespread. Thus the Prussian architect Karl Friedrich Schinkel, in a passage written around 1825 in his unpublished *Lehrbuch*, regarded structure as providing a truth for the architect: 'architecture is construction. In architecture everything must be true, any disguise or concealment of structure is an error. The proper task is to create every part of construction beautifully and in accordance with its character' (1979, 115). Similarly, on materials, Schinkel wrote in terms that closely follow Lodolí, 'any fully perfected construction in a particular material has its own definite character and could not rationally be executed in the same way in another material' (1979, 114–15). And revealing is Schinkel's dismissive response on visiting Sir John Soane's house in London in 1826 – 'Everywhere little deceptions' (1993, 114). The person who imported the new terminology of structural truth into the English language was A. W. N. Pugin, whose *The True Principles of Pointed or Christian Architecture* (1841) set out in its very title the ground to which it laid claim. The double significance of Pugin's book was not only that he introduced to the English-speaking world the notion of structural truth that had been developed in France and Italy at the end of the eighteenth century, but also that it was he who first linked Gothic architecture with structural truth. At the very beginning of *The True Principles* Pugin set out two rules: '*1st, that there should be no features about a building which are not necessary for convenience, construction, or propriety; 2nd, that all ornament should consist of enrichment of the essential construction of the building*'. He then went on to add two supplementary principles: 'In pure architecture the smallest detail *should have a meaning or serve a purpose*; and even the construction itself *should vary with the material employed*, and the designs should be adapted to the material in which they are executed'. These principles, it will be noticed, bear an extraordinarily close similarity to those put forward by Milizia in the passage from *L'Arte di Vedere* quoted earlier, and it is likely that it was from the French edition of Milizia's book that Pugin acquired the notion of structural truth. Armed with these principles, Pugin had little difficulty in setting about distinguishing true architecture from false. The architecture of the Middle Ages satisfied Pugin's principles best on all grounds, though what most of all appealed to him was what he saw as its religious truthfulness:

> the severity of Christian architecture is opposed to all deception. We should never make a building erected to God appear better than it really is by artificial means. These are showy worldly expedients, adapted only for those who live by splendid deception, such as theatricals, mountebanks, quacks and the like. Nothing can be more execrable than making a church appear rich and beautiful in the eyes of men, but full of trick and falsehood, which cannot escape the all-searching eye of God. (1853 ed., reprinted 1969, 38)

As telling as Pugin's demonstration of the truth of Gothic architecture was what he had to say about the false architecture of his own time. In the castellated country house, for example,

> we find guard-rooms without either weapons or guards; sally-ports, out of which nobody passes but the servants, and where a military man never did go out; donjon keeps which are nothing but drawing-rooms, boudoirs, and elegant apartments; watch-towers, where the house-maids sleep, and a bastion in which the butler cleans his plate: all is a mere mask, and the whole building an ill-conceived lie. (49)

Pugin's fulminations against the deceptions of picturesque Gothic perpetrated by Nash, Repton and Soane was, however, not just an argument grounded in their structural untruths: it was also a moral argument, which linked the decay of society with its adoption of false architecture. In making a moral argument through an aesthetic one, Pugin was committing the error that Kant

A. W. N. Pugin, 'The Scales of Truth', endpiece, from *Contrasts*, 1836. Pugin's vivid image – in which the nineteenth century is weighed in the balance of truth against the fourteenth century, and found wanting – contributed to 'truth' becoming current in the English architectural vocabulary.

had ruled against – but it was an error to be repeated to great effect by Pugin's successors, amongst them John Ruskin and William Morris. Morris was outspoken in his exploitation of this philosophical confusion: for him, art was not separate from politics, morals or religion – 'Truth in these great matters of principle is one, and it is only in formal treatises that it can be split up decisively' (*Works*, vol. XXII, 47).

If there is one name with which the principle of structural truth will remain forever linked, it is the French architect Eugène-Emmanuel Viollet-le-Duc (1814–79). In Viollet-le-Duc's voluminous writings we find by far the most compelling theory of structural truth, reinforced by notions of historical truth. Viollet-le-Duc's understanding of structural method came in part from the English archeologist Robert Willis, whose *Remarks on the Architecture of Middle Ages* (1835) and article 'On the Construction of Vaults' (1841) offered a much better-observed analysis of structural systems than that provided by Pugin. (Willis never described the construction in terms of truth, and was critical of Pugin's nomenclature, which he believed to be unjustified and misleading.)[8] Viollet-le-Duc's argument appears most explicitly in his *Entretiens*

A. W. N. Pugin, caricature of Gothic revival villa, from *True Principles*, 1843. 'On one side of the house machiolated parapets, embrasures bastions, and all the show of a strong defence, and round the corner of the building a conservatory leading to the principal rooms, through which a whole company of horsemen might penetrate at one smash into the very heart of the mansion!' Pugin invoked 'truth' to make the picturesque seem absurd.

sur l'Architecture (1863), translated into English as *Lectures on Architecture* (1877). The whole project was, as he explained in the Preface, not to promote one system or style above another, but rather to attain 'the knowledge of the True' (vol. 1, 7). The failure of the architecture of the nineteenth century was its neglect of the principle of truth, 'the alliance of the form with the requirements and the means of construction' (vol. 1, 447). As far as Viollet was concerned,

> There are in architecture … two indispensable modes in which truth must be adhered to. We must be true in respect of the programme, and true in respect of the constructive processes. To be true in respect of the programme is to fulfil exactly, scrupulously, the conditions imposed by the requirements of the case. To be true in respect of the constructive processes is to employ the materials according to their qualities and properties. What are regarded as questions purely belonging to art, symmetry and external form, are only secondary conditions as compared with those dominant principles. (vol. 1, 448)

In Lecture X, Viollet elaborated at length on the truths of architecture, but it can be said that his real purpose was to displace the traditional 'principles' of architecture, like symmetry and proportion, which were really regulated by taste, and to put in their place 'truth'. Rather than the arbitrary aesthetic criteria of the so-called laws of

architecture, he proposed instead that 'Laws based on geometry and calculation, and resulting from a nice observation of the principles of statics, naturally give rise to true expression, – sincerity' (vol. 1, 480). That Viollet's ideas were so influential was partly due to his comprehensiveness – although Viollet believed Gothic to be the purest development of constructional truth, the *Lectures* and the *Dictionnaire Raisonné* dealt fully with Greek, Roman and other architectures too. The assurance and clarity with which Viollet pressed his arguments gave him a popularity that his predecessor, Willis, had never enjoyed, while the translation of the *Lectures* into English ensured him a wide readership in the English-speaking world; and two of the leading nineteenth-century architectural journals, *The Builder*, under the editorship of George Godwin, and the *Encyclopédie d'Architecture*, edited by Adolphe Lance, were both supporters. But what made Viollet's arguments particularly appealing was their relevance to the developing technologies of iron and reinforced concrete; and it was their application in France to reinforced concrete by Auguste Perret, Freyssinet and others, that carried their influence through to the modernist architects of the 1920s in France and Italy.[9] Auguste Perret himself continued throughout his life to use Viollet's term 'truth' to designate the alliance of form with the means of construction: speaking in 1948, he says, 'It is only by the splendour of truth that a building attains beauty. That which is true is everything that has the honour and the burden to carry or to protect'.

4. *Expressive truth*

The sense of 'truth' as the expression of a building's essence, or as of the spirit of its maker, was a creation of the Romantic movement in late eighteenth-century Germany. The first, outstanding exposition of it was in the passionate essay 'On German Architecture' (1772) by the young J. W. von Goethe. Goethe's experience of Strasbourg cathedral led him to dismiss the account Laugier – 'the frivolous Frenchman' – gave of the origins of architecture: 'not one of thy conclusions can soar into the region of truth: all float in thy system's atmosphere'. In Strasbourg cathedral, Goethe saw expressed the genius of its mason, Erwin von Steinbach, and it was this that gave it its truth. The origin of architecture, Goethe proposed, lay not so much in any idealized primitive hut, but in man's instinctive will to create symbolic forms: as he puts it, as soon as man's existence is secure, 'he gropes around for matter to breathe his spirit into'. It was this spirit, the expression of Erwin von Steinbach's instinct to create symbolic form, that Goethe saw in Strasbourg

Strasbourg Cathedral, early nineteenth-century engraving. 'Step hither, and discern the deepest sense of truth': for Goethe, the directness of expression of the spirit of its builder was the 'truthfulness' of Strasbourg.

cathedral – 'Here stands his work: step hither, and discern the deepest sense of truth and beauty of proportions, quickening out of strong, rough, German soul, out of the strait, gloomy, pope-ridden stage of the *medium aevum*'.

Goethe's essay ranges over all sorts of ideas, without being particularly logical about any of them. In his desire to find a better account of architecture's truthfulness to nature, he started by accepting the post-Vitruvian idea that architecture was the imitation of natural or primitive construction – though rather than vertical tree trunks with a roof above, he proposed that the original building was 'two poles crossed at the top at the one end, two at the other, and one pole across as a ridge'. From this he writes of Gothic architecture as comparable to the forms of nature, and it is only towards the end that he arrives at the wholly original suggestion that what truthfulness in architecture really means is truthful expression of the spirit of its maker.

The appearance of Kant's *Critique of Judgment* in 1790, by calling into doubt 'truth' as an aesthetic category, put some pressure upon the interpretation of art being developed by Goethe and the other German Romantics. It was to overcome this problem that Goethe's friend Friedrich Schiller, in his *On the Aesthetic Education of Man*, distinguished between two kinds of untruth, 'aesthetic semblance' and 'logical semblance'. Schiller argued that 'To attach value to semblance of the first kind can never be prejudicial to truth, because one is never in danger of substituting it for truth' (193). And he went on to explain that it was not necessary that 'an object in which we discover aesthetic semblance must be devoid of reality; all that is required is that our judgment of it should take no account of that reality; for inasmuch as it does take account of it, it is not an aesthetic judgment' (199). By separating the aesthetic from the moral, Schiller preserved a notion of truth within art.

Schiller's distinction was to be important for the person who, without doubt, was the greatest exponent of 'expressive truth' in the field of architecture, the English critic John Ruskin. First in 'The Lamp of Life', chapter V of *The Seven Lamps of Architecture* (1849), and then in 'The Nature of Gothic' in volume two of *The Stones of Venice*, Ruskin developed his argument as to the manner in which works of architecture demonstrated the spirit and character of their makers, how their quality lay 'in the vivid expression of the intellectual life which has been concerned in their production' (1849, chapter V, §I); yet Ruskin never used the word 'truth' to describe this property, always preferring 'life' or 'living architecture'. While the principle Ruskin advanced in 'The Lamp of

Life', and later developed in 'The Nature of Gothic', has often been referred to by commentators as 'expressive truth', Ruskin avoided the term 'truth' in this context, possibly because of the strong overtones of structural rationalism it already carried in England by 1850. In 'The Lamp of Truth', however, Ruskin did put forward an argument that superficially ressembled Pugin's doctrine of truth – the deceptions Ruskin identified were 'The suggestion of a mode of structure or support other than the true one'; 'The painting of surfaces to represent some other material than that of which they actually consist'; and thirdly 'The use of cast or machine-made ornaments of any kind' (§VI) – but what is interesting is that he immediately qualified both the first two cases with the conditions under which fictions were permissible. This was where Schiller's 'aesthetic semblance' came in, for Ruskin's point was 'that, when the mind is informed beyond the possibility of mistake as to the true nature of things, the affecting it with a contrary impression, however distinct, is no dishonesty, but on the contrary a legitimate appeal to the imagination' (§VII). Many of Ruskin's readers, their minds no doubt deadened by too much structural rationalism, assumed that Ruskin was recommending a theory of structural truth, and misunderstood that in fact, on the contrary, he was arguing for the legitimacy of structural deception when it created an aesthetic response in the beholder's mind.[10] The misapprehension that Ruskin's notion of 'truth' was the same as Pugin's was widespread: for example, the architect T. G. Jackson referred in his *Recollections* to 'the passion for truth, as inculcated by Ruskin, which made me at Mr Tate's vicarage expose the brick corbel course … in all its nakedness as a cornice round the rooms' (89); and the same misreading is evident in the attacks upon Ruskin mounted in the early twentieth century by writers like Geoffrey Scott and Trystan Edwards. Possibly because of the potential confusion in Ruskin's theory of aesthetic truth through the pleasure in deception, when in 1854 he came to summarize his architectural thought in the Addenda to the first two of the *Lectures on Architecture and Painting*, he made no mention of 'truth' at all, and stressed instead the quality of Gothic architecture as the expression of 'the liberty of the workman'.

Of all nineteenth-century architects, perhaps the most explicit in his use of 'expressive truth' was the American Louis Sullivan. Familiar with German Romantic thought through Emerson, and his Chicago education, the notion that architecture is the outward expression of the individual and of society is a recurring theme of Sullivan's

National Farmers' Bank, Owatonna, Minnesota, L. Sullivan, 1906–8. 'Every building you see is the image of a man whom you do not see': Louis Sullivan was an enthusiast for expressive truth.

writings. Take, for example, Lecture 3 of *Kindergarten Chats* (1901–2): '*every building you see is the image of a man whom you do not see*. That the man is the reality, the building its offspring'. And he continues 'if we would know why certain things are as they are in our disheartening architecture, we must look to the people; for our buildings, as a whole, are but a huge screen behind which are our people as a whole' (24). The absence in American architecture of 'truthful' buildings, about which he constantly berated his audiences, were for Sullivan the result of a lack of 'a genuine feeling existing in you' (1906, 188). But as well as Sullivan's belief that 'truthful' architecture meant truthful in expression, he certainly also understood 'truthful' in the constructive sense – and a passage in his *Autobiography of an Idea* describes his awakening to this other notion of 'truth' (249–50). A tendency to interpret the word in terms both of expressive and constructional truth is quite marked amongst late nineteenth-century American architects. Particularly interesting are the remarks by Leopold Eidlitz, whose Austrian origins gave him a familiarity with German idealist thought, but who in his American architectural practice was an enthusiastic follower of Viollet-le-Duc. But Eidlitz made it clear that he regarded constructional truth as only partially valid, for 'Architecture deals with ideas, and with ideas only. In the forming of a structure, it attempts to depict the soul of the structure, not merely to minister to the physical wants of its occupants' (226). Louis Sullivan, and the young Frank Lloyd Wright, too, like Eidlitz and Sullivan before him, habitually compressed expressive and structural truth.

5. Historical truth
The third of three senses of 'truth' to become current in

the nineteenth century also comes from late eighteenth-century Germany. The idea originates from two sources – the study of ancient art by Winckelmann; and the development, in particular by Herder and Hegel, of the notion that history as a whole is not a random series of events, but follows a plan that can be uncovered by reason. Winckelmann argued that the style of Greek art progressed from the simple, to the noble, and finally to the decadent stage; this idea that art followed a characteristic pattern of development was taken up and applied by Hegel in particular to the entire history of art. As Hegel put it,

> Each art has its time of efflorescence, of its perfect development as an art, and a history preceding and following this moment of perfection. For the products of all the arts are works of the spirit and therefore are not, like natural productions, complete all at once within their specific sphere; on the contrary, they have a beginning, a progress, a perfection, and an end, a growth, blossoming and decay.
> (*Aesthetics*, 614)

Architecture, like all other arts, underwent a progress from what Hegel termed the symbolic, to the classical, and then the romantic stage. Without going into Hegel's use of this scheme, it is clear that any work not conforming to the characteristics of the historical stage to which it belonged might be judged not only unhistorical, but also, since Hegel attributed to art a special capacity to reveal the truth underlying the processes of history, as untruthful (*Aesthetics*, 7–8). Versions of historical truth occur in many nineteenth-century architectural writers – among them Pugin and Viollet-le-Duc, both of whom argued for certain principles on the grounds that they were historically sanctioned. But the architectural writer who made fullest use of historical truth was James Fergusson, author of the first comprehensive history of architecture in the English language. In his first book, *An Historical Inquiry into the True Principles of Beauty in Art* (1849), Fergusson attacked copying: 'the only path by which any nation, at any age or in any country, ever accomplished any thing that was great or good either in science or in art, was by steady progressive aggregation of experience, without ever looking back or attempting to copy' (1849, 162). Fergusson argued that until the sixteenth century these principles had held true, but had since been lost and copying had become general. Seen historically, nineteenth-century architecture was a failure:

No rule of true art will apply to ours. … it is the history of a nation that neglected all the true forms of the beautiful, and were earnest only in the pursuit of the most literal utilitarian utterances, and who were in consequence content to imitate, like monkeys, without understanding what they were doing, or why they did it, what men, using their intellect as such, had elaborated with half our means out of the rudest materials. (1849, 182)

Subsequently Fergusson developed his concept of 'true architecture' further, ultimately classifying all architecture as either true or false. In a letter to *The Builder* in 1850, Fergusson distanced himself from the Gothic revivalists: 'Mr Pugin strongly insists on the truthfulness of his architecture. That he is the most truthful of copyists I fully admit; but according to my definition, truth in art consists in representing the wants and feelings of the people who use it' (vol. VIII, 148). Here, Fergusson made use of expressive truth – which is never far from historical truth. But in the third volume of his history of world architecture, the *History of the Modern Styles of Architecture* (1862), which dealt solely with post-Renaissance architecture, is Fergusson's most explicit application of historical truth. The introduction, which must be among the most remarkable of all the disquisitions on truth in this period, opens with the statement, 'It is, perhaps, not too much to say that no perfectly truthful architecture has been erected in Europe since the Reformation' (2). Truthful architecture was, as he had defined it before, that 'arranged solely for the purpose of meeting, in the most direct manner, the wants of those for whom they were designed' (1). Of the world's architectures, only Egyptian, Greek, Roman and Gothic had been true, and so, astonishingly, Fergusson proceeded to devote virtually the entire 500-odd pages of the volume to false architecture – in the hope, as Fergusson put it, that people

> may be led to perceive how false and mistaken the principles are on which modern Architecture is based, and how easy, on the contrary it would be to succeed if we were only content to follow in the same path which has led to perfection in all countries of the world and in all ages. (x)

A few rare examples of truthful post-Reformation buildings stand out: the Bibliothèque Sainte Geneviève in Paris 'gives a promise of common sense being once more thought compatible with Architectural Art' (229); and of King's Cross station in London, 'Externally the design has

Interior, Bibliothèque Sainte Geneviève, Paris, H. Labrouste, 1838–50. The Bibliothèque Sainte Geneviève was one of the few nineteenth-century buildings regarded by James Fergusson as satisfying the demands of 'truth'.

the merit of being entirely truthful' (479).

The pressing question of historical truth posed by Viollet-le-Duc at the beginning of Lecture X – 'Is the nineteenth century destined to close without possessing an architecture of its own?' (vol. 1, 446) – was one that troubled a great many nineteenth-century architects; and it was just as important to early modernist architects, for many of whom it became the legitimation of their whole practice.

1 See Martin, 'Interdisciplinary Transpositions: Bernard Tschumi's Architectural Theory', 1998.

2 See Lee, *Ut Pictura Poesis*, 1967.

3 See Kristeller for a full account of the contoversy over classification of the arts.

4 Memmo, *Elementi d'Architettura Lodoliana*, vol. 2, 1834, 86–87.

5 For a recent attempt to tighten border security, see Scruton, *The Aesthetics of Architecture*, 1979, 164–65, 238–39.

6 See Rykwert, *The First Moderns*, 1980, 324, for elucidation of Lodoli's use of these two terms.

7 See Lavin, *Quatremère de Quincy and the Invention of a Modern Language of Architecture*, 1992, 102–13.

8 See Buchanan, 'Robert Willis', PhD thesis, 1995.

9 See Banham, *Theory and Design in the First Machine Age*, 1960, chapters 1–3.

10 For example, Pevsner, *Ruskin and Viollet-le-Duc*, 1970, described Ruskin's qualifications of the principles of truth as a 'sleight of hand' (16).

Architectural history shows that the development of types is essential to the architectural system.
C. Norberg-Schulz, 1963, 207

Ultimately, we can say that type is the very idea of architecture, that which is closest to its essence.
A. Rossi, 1966; 1982, 41

There are few disciplines that have not benefitted from the concept of the 'type', and architecture is no exception. Within architecture, the two most common schemes of typological classification have been by use – churches, prisons, banks, airports, etc.; and by morphology – buildings with long hall-shaped interiors, centrally planned buildings, buildings with courtyards, buildings with interconnecting compartments, or with separated compartments, and so on. Although, as we shall see, these are not the only classificatory systems to have been devised, much of the debate around 'types' has been concerned with how far functional types correspond to morphological types.

A basic classification by use of religious buildings, secular buildings, theatres, private houses, and fortifications was inherent to the classical system of architecture since antiquity. In the mid-eighteenth century, the French architectural writer and teacher J.-F. Blondel in his *Cours d'Architecture* compiled a very much longer list of varieties of building (sixty-four altogether), and this formed the basis for his architectural system (see 'Character', p. 122–23). It has sometimes been said that Blondel's typological classification was the origin of the modern system of functional types, but this is slightly misleading. First of all, Blondel did not call them 'types' but 'genres', which indicates the literary basis to his scheme; and secondly, his main purpose in listing all these varieties of building was to identify for each the appropriate 'character'. Nonetheless, a typological classification of buildings by purpose has been in constant use since the late eighteenth century; a recent example is Nikolaus Pevsner's *A History of Building Types* (1976) in which the 'types' are all descriptions of uses.

The beginning of morphological classification is usually located in the French teacher and writer J. N. L. Durand's scheme of architectural education set out in his *Précis* (1802–5). There, Durand provided techniques for the composition of different architectural forms without regard to their use – though in the second volume, Durand showed his students how to adapt these forms to the programmes for buildings of different purposes, which, following Blondel, he called not 'types', but 'genres'.

The literature of architectural types and typology is large, particularly as a result of developments in the last three decades.[1] Rather than attempt inadequately, as would inevitably be the case, to summarize all the meanings architects have attributed to 'type', what is offered here is a short enquiry into the various *purposes* for which the concept has been used in architecture.

1. *Protection of the idea of architecture as the imitation of nature*

In the eighteenth century, the view that architecture was an art imitative of 'nature' (see pp. 223–26) was central to architectural thought and to claims that architecture was a 'liberal', as opposed to 'mechanical' art. From the middle of the century, pressure started to be put upon the mimetic theory of architecture by, in particular, the rationalist arguments of Carlo Lodoli (see pp. 174–75 and 295–96), and it was in order to protect the mimetic theory that the French architectural thinker Quatremère de Quincy developed his remarkably ingenious theory of imitation (see pp. 224–26, 297). According to Quatremère, architecture does not imitate nature literally, but only metaphorically, so that everyone knows that the imitation is fictitious, while being nonetheless being aware

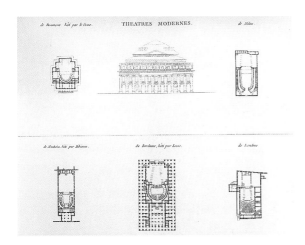

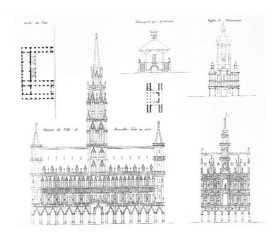

J. N. L. Durand, Theatres and Market Halls, from *Recueil et parallèle des édifices*, 1801. Durand produced the first systematic comparison of buildings by use; following Blondel, he described these as '*genres*'.

of its supposedly real reference to 'nature'. It was so as to explain what it was in 'nature' that architecture referred to, that Quatremère introduced the 'type'. In his now often-quoted entry on 'Type' in the *Encyclopédie Méthodique*, Quatremère drew a distinction between 'type' and 'model' as follows:

> The word 'type' presents less the image of a thing to copy or imitate completely than the idea of an element which ought itself to serve as a rule for the model. … The model, as understood in the practical execution of the art, is an object that should be repeated as it is; the type, on the contrary, is an object after which one may conceive works of art with no resemblance one to another at all. All is precise and given in the model; all is more or less vague in the type. (148)

Quatremère then went on to explain why the 'type' was so necessary to architecture: 'Everything must have an antecedent. Nothing, in any genre, comes from nothing, and this must apply to all the inventions of man'. But Quatremère was careful to stress that the 'type' was not the primitive cabin, the tent or the cave, which previous writers had posited as the original architecture – these were 'models'; but the 'type' was (in the case of timber building) 'that kind of combination to which the use of wood is susceptible, once adopted in each country' (149), or, in other words, the process modified by circumstance. The distinction between the 'type' – 'the original reason

of the thing, which can neither command nor furnish the motif or the means of an exact likeness', and 'model' – 'the complete thing, which is bound to a formal resemblance', was critical, because it was what enabled Quatremère to argue that while not copying nature, architecture nonetheless imitated nature.

Quatremère formulated his theory of 'types' in the 1780s, and it belongs to the architectural debate of that time; however, the encyclopedia entry on 'Type' was not published until 1825, and only after that date were the implications of Quatremère's ideas taken up, principally by the German architect and theorist Gottfried Semper. The problem that had so exercized Quatremère – to prove that architecture, while not copying nature, still imitated nature – was of no concern at all to Semper who, familiar with Goethe's theory of art as a 'second nature', could accept that architecture might be like nature in its formative processes yet be quite independent of nature. But Semper was interested in architecture's origins, seeing, like Quatremère, that 'nothing can come from nothing'. Although attracted by Quatremère's analysis of the problem, Semper was critical of the strongly idealist character of Quatremère's thought, and wanted, without losing the force of Quatremère's 'type' as a generic idea, to give it greater identity and substance so that it might be of more practical use to the architect. Semper also had the advantage that by the time, in the 1830s, that he became interested in these questions, developments in natural science had produced a more sophisticated account of both 'nature' and of 'types' than had been

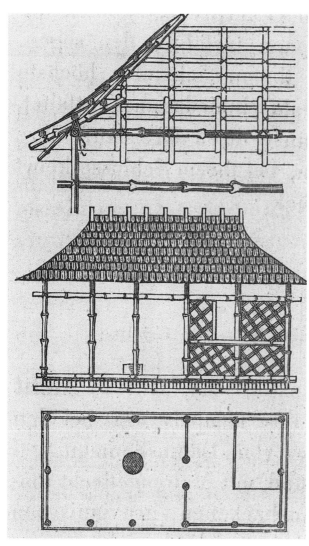

G. Semper, Caraib Hut, from *Der Stil* vol. 2, 1863. Semper's idea that the 'types' of architecture were to be understood through the potential of each of the four main processes involved in building – terracing, roofing, walling, and the hearth – he illustrated by reference to the West Indian bamboo hut he had seen at the Great Exhibition of 1851.

available to Quatremère; it was by direct analogy from his knowledge of animal and plant morphology that Semper formulated his theory of architectural types. As Semper wrote in a letter in 1843 to his prospective publisher, 'Just as everything there [in nature] develops and is explained by the simplest prototypical form, just as nature in her infinite variety is yet simple and sparse in basic ideas … in the same way, I said to myself, the works of my art are also based on certain standard forms conditioned by primordial ideas, yet which permit an infinite variety of phenomena'. Semper's project was 'to trace these prototypical forms of architecture' (*The Four Elements etc.*, 170). His terminology for the 'prototypical forms' varied, between *Urformen*, *Normalformen*, *Urkeim*, and *Urmotiven* – all of them words drawn from Goethe's theory of plant and animal morphology – but when he lectured in English in London in 1853, the word he used was 'type': works of industrial art, he said, 'are like those of nature, connected together by some few fundamental ideas, which have their simplest expression in *types*' (1853, 8).[2] Following Quatremère's suggestion in his encyclopedia article on 'Type', that the 'type' of timber construction was 'that kind of combination to which the use of wood is susceptible', Semper proposed that architecture's 'types' were to be understood through the potentiality of four main processes involved in building: terracing (masonry), roofing (carpentry), the hearth (ceramics), and walling (textiles). 'This plan', Semper explained, 'should make apparent the derivation of objects and forms from their primordial motives [*Urmotiven*] and style changes conditioned by circumstances' (*The Four Elements etc.*, 132–33). (It may be no coincidence that Semper identified in architecture the same number of 'types' – four – as the biologist Cuvier, whose system he referred to frequently, had in the animal kingdom.) The example referred to by Semper as objective proof of the existence of the four primordial motives was the 'Caraib hut' he had seen at the Great Exhibition of 1851; although Semper stressed that this hut had nothing in common with architecture, because each of the four motives was treated distinctly without any attempt to merge them into an expressive whole, it nonetheless made each motive, or 'type', demonstrably clear. The merit of Semper's classificatory scheme was to preserve the 'type' as a generic idea, and to give it determinacy and practical application, but without letting it become confused with a 'model'.

2. As a means of resistance to mass culture

In the Deutsche Werkbund from 1911, a major topic of debate was *Typisierung* – a word that has in the past been translated as 'standardization', but which according to present consensus would be best translated as 'type'.[3] The Werkbund debate was initiated by Muthesius's 1911 lecture, 'Where Do We Stand?', in which he attacked the tendency towards stylistic individualism in the arts of the time as 'simply horrifying'. Against this, 'Of all the arts, architecture is the one which tends most readily towards a type [*typisch*] and only thus can it really fulfill its aims' (50). Muthesius returned to the theme at the 1914 Werkbund Congress in Cologne, when, listing a ten-point policy for the Werkbund, he described the first two as follows:

> 1. Architecture, and with it the whole area of the Werkbund's activities, is pressing towards types [*Typisierung*], and only through types [*Typisierung*] can it recover that universal significance which was characteristic of it in times of harmonious culture.
> 2. Types [*Typisierung*], to be understood as the result of a beneficial concentration, will alone make possible the development of a universally valid, unfailing good taste. (1914, 28)

Although there was an argument that the standardization of products could, in the manner of Henry Ford (see ill. p. 254), lead to economies of production, and so improve German economic competitiveness, and this was certainly an interpretation taken up by economists and management experts, that was not, it seems, what Muthesius and the other members of the Werkbund were most concerned with. Rather, the type was a means of bringing order to the chaotic world of mass consumption, ruled by fashion, individualism and *anomie*. In this respect, the 'type' occupied a position very close to that of 'form' (see pp. 161–65) in the same debates. As one member of the Werkbund, the entrepreneur Karl Schmidt, wrote after the 1914 Werkbund debate, 'for me the matter of types means nothing other than replacing disorder and lack of discipline with order' (quoted in Schwartz, 127); or as the critic Robert Breuer put it, 'the concept of the type becomes a force which impedes every form of arbitrariness … with inescapable severity' (quoted in Schwartz, 127). It was not without significance that the products designed by Peter Behrens for the AEG were referred to as 'types'.

Although before 1914, the immediate concern in these debates about 'types' had been the design of commodities,

Peter Behrens, kettles, from AEG catalogue 1912. 'The concept of the type becomes a force which impedes every form of arbitrariness': Behrens's designs for AEG were referred to as 'types'.

increasingly after 1920 they extended to architecture too. Outside Germany, the best-known exposition of this theme was in Le Corbusier's *Decorative Art of Today* (1925), where the illustrations of steel office desks, filing cabinets, and travel luggage, described as '*objets-type*', or 'type-objects', were offered as the rational alternatives to the 'hysterical rush of recent years towards quasi-orgiastic decoration' (96) manifested by furnishings manufacturers. 'We have', wrote Le Corbusier, 'only to introduce this method [of developing type-obects] into our apartments and decorative art will meet its destiny: type-furniture and architecture' (77). The architectural 'types' developed by Le Corbusier, the Maison Citrohan, and the Pavillon de l'Esprit Nouveau, served the same purpose, distilling the chaotic disorder of bourgeois individualism into a rational, ordered existence. The 'type', in this context, was a means of protecting civilization against the the disintegration of cultural values brought about by capitalism, and its agent, fashion.

3. To achieve '*continuità*'

The reintroduction of 'type' into the discourse of architecture around 1960 – the phase described by Anthony Vidler as 'the third typology' – started in Italy.[4] With hindsight, it is possible to see that there were in this 'third typology' two quite distinct motives, one linked to the specifically Italian debates about *continuità*, the other to Anglo-American preoccupations with 'meaning'. Although many of those who talked about 'type' often talked with a view to both motives, for the purposes of historical analysis it is helpful to consider them separately.

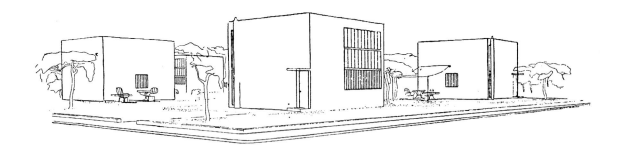

Le Corbusier, mass-production houses for artisans, drawing, 1924, from *L'Oeuvre complète*, vol. 1. 'Type architecture' – the solution to the disintegration of culture threatened by capitalism and the hysteria of fashion.

Continuità, the theme developed in the second half of the 1950s by Ernesto Rogers, the editor of *Casabella*, was in part a critique of orthodox modernism, and partly a solution to specifically Italian difficulties (see pp. 200–1). The three related concepts that came out of the debates about *continuità*, 'History' (see p. 196), 'Context' (see p. 132) and 'Type', all became key terms in the architectural discourse of the 1970s and 1980s. The distinctive feature of 'type' in these discussions, and which set it apart from earlier notions of 'type', was the emphasis, as Vidler put it, on 'the *city* as the site for urban typology' (1977, 3). Typology was a means of describing the relationship between buildings and the city of which they formed part, and thereby of showing how individual buildings were manifestations of the collective, and historical processes of urban development; it was a way of showing that an 'architectural event' was not just four walls and a roof, but something that existed only as part of the general urban phenomenon, considered both spatially, socially, and historically.

It was in a book by an architecture teacher at the University of Venice, Saverio Muratori, that this conception of 'type' made its first appearance in print. Muratori's *Studi per una Operante Storia Urbana di Venezia* (1960), based on research begun in 1950, was a study of the morphology of building plots and open spaces in Venice; the significance that Muratori attached to the 'types' he identified was that it enabled one to demonstrate in concrete terms all those aspects of the process of the city – growth, *milieu*, class – which historical geographers had previously treated only as abstractions. By the time Muratori's book appeared, it seems that others, among them the architects Carlo Aymonino, Vittorio Gregotti and Aldo Rossi, were already talking about 'types' in similar terms. Although there were disagreements, particularly between those who saw typology essentially as simply a method of urban analysis, and those, like Rossi, who saw it as providing a general theory for architecture, they all agreed upon the value of typology as a means of describing the relationship of architecture to cities, and of founding *continuità* in the objective reality of the built world. Of the various expositions of 'typology', that put forward by Rossi in

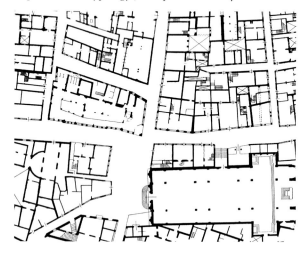

S. Muratori, Map of Quartiere S. Bartolomeo, Venice (detail), from *Studi per una operante storia urbana di Venezia*, vol. 1, 1959.

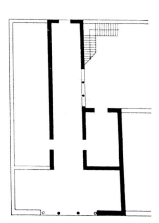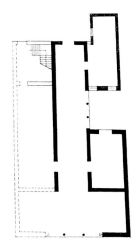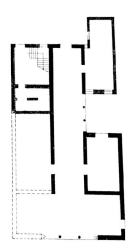

S. Muratori, plan of Casa Barizza on the Grand Canal in the twelfth, fifteenth and eighteenth centuries. In post-war Italy, the 'type' became a way of describing the relation between individual buildings and the city. Muratori's pioneering study showed in great detail the progressive development of many individual buildings in Venice, and how the city as a whole consisted of a limited number of historically evolved 'types'.

The Architecture of the City is probably the best known and, at least outside Italy, has been the most influential.

For Rossi 'type' served two explicit purposes: firstly, it offered a means of thinking about urban architecture independently of the functions to which it was put – and thus provided a critique of orthodox modern architecture; and secondly, the evidence that certain building forms and street patterns persisted throughout the history of cities regardless of the various uses to which they were put, could be taken as manifestations of 'type', that irreducible element in which the historical 'permanencies' of the city were encoded (1982, 35–41). It was from the concept of the 'type' that Rossi subsequently developed his idea of 'analogies', of an 'analogical architecture', whereby a whole city might be represented through a single building; thus, describing his experiences of the United States, Rossi remarked 'in the villages of New England ... a single building seems to constitute the city or village, independent of its size' (1981, 76). It was this idea in particular, from Muratori's research onwards, that fascinated Italian architects.

4. *In the pursuit of meaning*

By the 1960s it was becoming a commonly voiced complaint against architectural modernism that it had drained architecture of meaning. While the first generation of modern architects had done this with the best of intentions – so as to remove from architecture the insignia of social class which it had traditionally borne – the results had been to produce what, in the 1960s, was to become known as 'the crisis of meaning'. This issue certainly formed a subtext to Rossi's *The Architecture of the City*, but as Rossi throughout his career maintained a calculatedly equivocal stance towards this whole question, he never addressed it directly. However, in a book written by another member of the Milan circle, Vittorio Gregotti, *Il Territorio dell'Architettura*, and published in the same year, 1966, there was far more direct attention to the problem of signification and meaning. Gregotti suggested that the 'semantic crisis' of modern architecture was in part related to typology. Referring back to late eighteenth-century architects, specifically Ledoux, these architects, with their projects for public buildings in urban settings had, Gregotti claimed, 'intended to bring the problem of the semantics of the type under control', establishing 'the possibility of an urban semantics' (100). Architectural modernism had rejected all schemes of signification, and precipitated 'the semantic crisis of the type' – 'the crisis of the power of architecture to transmit messages as effectively as other channels of communication' (101). The two remedies to this lay in the revalorization of the 'type', and in the configuration of 'context' [*ambiente*] as

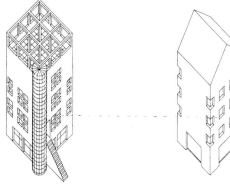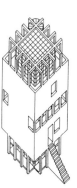

part of architecture. This view that in the 'type' – whether the discovery of new types, or the recovery of existing ones – lay the solution to the modern architecture's lack of meaning formed an important part of Italian architectural debate in the 1960s. When the English-speaking world started to take notice of the Italian discourse about 'types' in the late 1960s and early 1970s, it was this aspect in particular, more than the theory of *continuità*, that attracted architects and critics. Writing in 1977, the historian and critic Anthony Vidler, who was particularly responsible for disseminating the new theory of 'types', laid most stress upon the way 'types' were productive of meaning, such as to create 'one comprehensible experience of the city' (1977, 4). And the critic Alan Colquhoun, writing in 1989, suggested that 'type' provided the means through which structuralism, as a theory of meaning, could be translated to architecture:

> Just as language always pre-exists a group or individual speaker, the system of architecture pre-exists a particular period or architect. It is precisely through the persistence of earlier forms that the system can convey meaning. These forms, or *types*, interact with the tasks presented to architecture, in any moment in history, to form the entire system. (1989, 247–48)

Or, to give another example, when Demetri Porphyrios (a Greek who had studied at Princeton) discussed the works of Alvar Aalto in terms of typology, it was so as to press the case for their having semantic meaning: 'By utilizing the associational richness of already operative and socially legitimate iconographic types ... Aalto achieves the ultimate poetic aspect of language: that of polysemy (the

manifold levels of signification; the profusion of secondary and tertiary meanings)' (1979, 144).

Christian Norberg-Schultz suggested, in the sentence quoted at the beginning of this entry, that 'type', in its various manifestations, has on successive occasions provided architects with a means of renewing their discipline. While this is certainly true, the lesson of this particular enquiry has been that its force has always been felt through its opposition to some other concept. Despite 'type' having the appearance of the purest of ideal categories, an absolute if ever there was one, in architectural usage at least, its appeal has in practice been less from an inherent strength of content of its own than from its value as a means of resistance to a variety of other ideas. The only 'pure' theory of types, that developed by Gottfried Semper, architects have found remarkably difficult to put to any practical use; on the other hand, set against structural rationalism, mass consumption, functionalism, or loss of meaning, 'type' and 'typology' become, as Micha Bandini says, 'almost magical words which by their mere utterance yield hidden meanings' (1984, 73).

1 Useful general discussions of 'type': Vidler, 'The Idea of Type', 1977; Moneo, 'On Typology', 1978; Bandini, 'Typology as a Form of Convention', 1984.
2 On Semper's terminology, see Semper, *The Four Elements etc.* 1989, introduction by Mallgrave and Herrmann, 23, 30; also Rykwert, 'Semper and the Conception of Style', 1976. Semper's familiarity with Goethe's theory of types he gained from the naturalist Alexander Humboldt's *Cosmos*, 1843 (see Mallgrave, 1985, 75).
3 See Schwartz, *The Werkbund*, 1996, 238 n.213, and Anderson's introduction to Muthesius, *Style-Architecture and Building-Art*, 1902, 30. This discussion of 'type' as a means of resisting the effects of capitalism on culture is derived from Schwartz, 121–46.
4 Vidler, 'The Third Typology', 1977, pp.1–4

(above) Aldo Rossi, *Citta Analogica*, drawing, 1976. 'The type is a constant, it can be found in all the areas of architecture': Rossi was fascinated by the poetic possibility of representing a whole city by means of a single building.

(below) O. M. Ungers, 'Typology of Detached Houses based on a Constant Grid', 1982. 'Types' seemed to offer a way of putting meaning back into architecture.

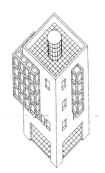   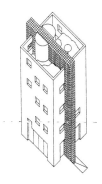

'User' was one of the last terms to appear in the canon of modernist discourse. Unknown before about 1950, the term became widespread in the late 1950s and 1960s; on the wane in the 1980s, it has returned to currency in the 1990s serving a different purpose to that it maintained in the modernist era. The term's origins coincide with the introduction of welfare state programmes in Western European countries after 1945, and it is in relation to these that its first phase of currency should be interpreted.

What the 'user' is meant to convey in architecture is clear enough: the person or persons expected to occupy the work. But the choice of 'user' in place of 'occupants', 'inhabitants' or 'clients' has held strong connotations of the disadvantaged or disenfranchised – it particularly implied those who could not normally be expected to contribute to formulating the architect's brief. Furthermore, the 'user' was always a person unknown – and so in this respect a fiction, an abstraction without phenomenal identity. The 'user' does not tolerate attempts to be given particularity: as soon as the 'user' starts to take on the identity of a person, of specific occupation, class or gender, inhabiting a particular piece of historical time, it begins to collapse as a category. Deprived of its abstract generality, its value disintegrates; for its merit is to allow discussion of peoples' inhabitation of a building while suppressing all the differences that actually exist between them. Describing them simply as 'the users' strips them, or any sub-group of them, of their discordant, non-conformist particularities, and gives them a homogeneous – and fictional – unity. It was just this tendency to abstraction that made the French philosopher Henri Lefebvre suspicious of the term. In *The Production of Space* (1974), he writes: 'The word "user" [*usager*] ... has something vague – and vaguely suspect – about it. "User of what?" one tends to wonder. ... The user's space is *lived* – not represented (or conceived)' (362). As far as Lefebvre was concerned, the category of the 'user' was a particular device by which modern societies, having

deprived their members of the lived experience of space (by turning it into a mental abstraction) achieved the further irony of making the inhabitants of that space unable even to recognize themselves within it, by turning them into abstractions too (93). Lefebvre's remarks are among the earliest attacks upon the 'user'. Yet for Lefebvre 'use' and 'user' were by no means wholly negative concepts – indeed his ultimate desire was to see users regain the means to appropriate space and make it their own. He was, as he put it, '*For* appropriation and for use, ... and *against* exchange and domination' (368). Use is what would unify spatial practice against all the forces that dispersed it: '*use* corresponds to a unity and collaboration between the very factors that such dogmatisms insist on dissociating' (369).

A similar view of the emancipatory power of 'use' against functional determinism is to be found in the writings since the early 1960s of the Dutch architect Herman Hertzberger. 'User' is a recurrent term in Hertzberger's articles, and it is clear that he sees the whole purpose of architecture as to enable 'users [to] become inhabitants' (1991, 28), to create for 'the users ... the freedom to decide for themselves how they want to use each part, each space' (1967; in 1991, 171). The measure of an architect's success for Hertzberger is the way spaces are used, the diversity of activities which they attract, the opportunities they provide for creative reinterpretation (see ills. pp. 116, 313). Hertzberger's analogy for describing this process is language: 'The relation between a collective given and individual interpretation as it exists between form and usage as well as the experience thereof may be compared to the relation between language and speech' (1991, 92).

However, this very particular, positive sense of the user did not enter general currency until the 1990s. Until then, the most common reason for interest in the 'user' was as a source of information from which design could proceed. It is hard now to appreciate the excitement and

Interior, De Drie Hoven, Home for the Elderly, Amsterdam, H. Hertzberger, 1964–74. To create for 'the users... the freedom to decide for themselves how they want to use each part, each space': to Hertzberger, 'users' are the ultimate measure of an architect's work.

anticipation surrounding studies of the 'user' in the early 1960s. An English schools architect, Henry Swain, speaking in 1961, announced that 'To evolve techniques to help us to analyse the needs of the users of buildings is the most urgent task of our profession' (508). Swain's choice of the word 'user' in place of the more conventional 'client' or 'occupant' can be seen as serving at least three purposes. Firstly Swain, like many other architects, believed that analysis of user needs would lead to new architectural solutions – to a truly 'modern' architecture liberated from dependence on conventional architectural programmes or formulae. The 'user' would provide the material through which architecture might finally realize its potential. Characteristic of the confidence in the results that would follow from the study of 'user needs' (although the term 'user' was not employed in it) was the British Ministry of Housing and Local Government Report *Homes for Today and*

Tomorrow of 1961 (usually known as the Parker Morris Report) that recommended a new basis for defining the standards of state-subsidized housing. In it, the authors took issue with the previous policy of statutory minimum room sizes, to which they objected because it tended to produce a conventional arrangement for the dwelling, with little scope for flexibility either in the design or the subsequent use of the dwelling. Instead of minimum room sizes, they recommended a minimum size for the entire dwelling, arrived at 'by looking at the needs as a whole of the intended occupants of a dwelling'. As they set out their rationale,

> This approach to the problem of design starts with a clear recognition of these various activities and their relative importance in social, family and individual lives, and goes on to assess the conditions necessary for their pursuit in terms of space, atmosphere,

efficiency, comfort, furniture and equipment.... The approach is flexible, questioning such widespread assumptions as that equal floor areas should be devoted to sleeping, dressing and sanitary needs as to all other needs put together, or that houses should generally have two storeys rather than one, one and half, two and a half or three. The approach is also indirect. Arrangement and rooms are the results, and not the starting point; arrangement flows from the inter-relation of the ways in which the needs can be satisfied within the limitations and opportunities provided by the site, the structural possibilities and the cost; rooms grow from the needs and provide for the needs – they evolve as a consequence of thought and not in the copying of what has gone before. (4)

Striking in this passage – and wholly characteristic of the widespread interest in the study of the 'user' – were the confidence that attention to people's activities and needs would lead to non-traditional architecture; and a vagueness – characterized by the words 'flows from' and 'grows from' – as to exactly how this information about the user would inform architectural practice.

Secondly, the choice of the term 'user' may be understood in terms of the expansion of the functionalist paradigm – if a relationship was said to exist between buildings and social behaviour, then it was necessary to have a word to represent those upon whom buildings were perceived to act. The 'user' satisfied this need, providing, as it were, the required second variable in the functionalist equation. The 'user' therefore may be seen as a result of the functionalist model – and some of its unsatisfactoriness flows from the shortcomings of this model.

The third purpose of the 'user' was to sustain architects' belief-systems during a period of astonishing favour and good fortune for the profession. The two decades after the end of the Second World War saw the growth of the welfare state in Western European countries, and of welfarist policies in the USA. Within this political system, designed to stabilize relations between capital and labour but without effecting any major redistribution of the ownership of wealth, architecture was widely adopted by Western governments as an important part of their strategy. Not only was it a matter of providing new schools, housing and hospitals, but of doing so in such a way that those who occupied these buildings would be convinced of their 'equal social worth'[1] with all other members of society. The task given to architects, and in the execution of which they were

entrusted extraordinary freedom, was to create buildings that would induce – in the face of persisting social differences – a sense of belonging to a society of equals. For the many architects employed on public-sector projects, it was necessary to convince themselves – and the public at large – that the 'client' was not the bureaucracies or elected committees that actually commissioned the buildings, but those who would actually inhabit them. Although these people were almost invariably unknown to the architects, the professional claims of architects to serve the greater good of society depended upon being able to show that the true beneficiaries of the new schools or social housing were indeed those destined to occupy them. The 'user', and the extensive analysis of 'user needs', allowed architects to believe that notwithstanding their employment by ministries and government, the people whom they truly served were the occupants of the buildings.[2] By privileging 'the user', it could be claimed the expectations within a welfare state democracy for the disempowered to be treated as citizens of 'equal social worth' was being realized. It might, therefore, be said that the purpose of the 'user' in the 1950s and 1960s was partly to satisfy architects' own belief-systems, to legitimate their claim to be working for the underprivileged class, while in reality working for the state; and partly to allow architecture to hold its particular, and peculiar place within the welfare state democracy as the service which provided the appearance of a society moving rapidly towards social and economic equality, when in reality such differences persisted.

The decline of interest in the 'user' and 'user needs' corresponded to the decline in public-sector commissions in the 1980s. Not only was the 'user' no longer of value to architects, but moreover, as their social authority declined, the 'user' became a positive threat, the personification of uncontrollable disorder that frustrated the architect's intentions.

Perhaps another reason for dissatisfaction with the 'user' has been that it is such an unsatisfactory way of characterizing the relationship people have with works of architecture: one would not talk about 'using' a work of sculpture. Yet with architecture, there is still no better alternative, and a recent book has reinstated the word 'as a more appropriate term ... than either the occupant, occupier or inhabitant because it also implies both positive action and the potential for misuse' (Hill, 1998, 3). By the late 1990s, it appears that 'user' has lost its earlier connotation of the disadvantaged and disenfranchised and become a means for architects to

Washroom, Little Green Lane School, Croxley Green, Hertfordshire. 1949.
'Users' wash their hands in the small size washbasins specially designed by
David Medd for primary schools. Introduced in the post-war era, the word's
purpose was primarily to describe those whose interests the building programme
of the welfare state was intended to serve.

criticize their own practice. It was a peculiarity of
Lefebvre's book *The Production of Space* that 'use' and
'user' appeared in two contrary senses; Lefebvre's second,
emancipatory sense, also used by Herzberger from the late
1960s, now seems to have displaced the previous sense
produced out of the circumstances of the welfare state.

1 This was the phrase coined by the political theorist T. H. Marshall in 1950.
See Forty, 1995, 28.
2 See Lipman, 'The Architectural Belief System', 1968, for an interesting
discussion of this dilemma.

Bibliography

Dates in brackets are of original publication; where a second date is given after a semi-colon, it refers to the date of the edition quoted here, or of the edition from which the translation quoted here was made.

Titles of foreign works are given in English when a published translation exists, and in their original language when no translation exists.

Aalto, A., 'The Humanising of Architecture', *Architectural Forum*, vol. 73, Dec. 1940, pp. 505–6

Addison, J., *The Spectator*, in *The Works of Joseph Addison*, six vols, ed. R. Hurd, G. Bell and Sons, London, 1902

Adler, D., 'Influence of Steel Construction and of Plate Glass upon the Development of the Modern Style', *Inland Architect*, vol. 28, November 1896, pp. 34–37 (quoted in Johnson, *Theory of Architecture*, p. 304)

Adorno, T., and Horkheimer, M., *Dialectic of the Enlightenment* (1947), trans. J. Cumming, Herder and Herder, New York, 1972

Alberti, L.-B., *De Re Aedificatoria* (c. 1450), trans. J. Leoni, as *Ten Books on Architecture* (1726), London, 1775; and trans. J. Rykwert, N. Leach and R. Tavernor, *On the Art of Building in Ten Books*, MIT Press, Cambridge, MA and London, 1988 (citations from this edition unless indicated otherwise)

Alexander, C., *Notes on the Synthesis of Form*, Harvard University Press, Cambridge, MA, 1964

——, Ishikawa, S., and Silverstein, M., *A Pattern Language: Towns, Buildings, Construction*, Oxford University Press, New York, 1977

Algarotti, F., 'Saggio Sopra l'Architettura' (1756), in Algarotti, *Saggi*, Laterza e Figli, Bari, 1963, pp. 31–52

Alison, A., *Essays on the Nature and Principles of Taste* (1790), A. Constable and Co., Edinburgh, 1825

Allen Brooks, H., *Writings on Wright*, MIT Press, Cambridge MA , 1981

Alsop, W., 'Speculations on Cedric Price Architects' Inter-Action Centre', *Architectural Design*, vol. 47, nos 7–8, 1977, pp. 483–86

Ambasz, E. (ed.), *Italy: The New Domestic Landscape, Achievement and Problems of Italian Design*, Museum of Modern Art, New York, 1972

Anderson, S., '*Sachlickeit* and Modernity, or Realist Architecture', in Mallgrave (ed.), *Otto Wagner*, 1993, pp. 323–60

Andrew, D. S., *Louis Sullivan and the Polemics of Modern Architecture*, University of Illinois Press, Urbana and Chicago, 1985

Antoni, C., *From History to Sociology* (1940), trans. H. White, Merlin Press, London, 1962

Arendt, H., *The Human Condition* (1958), Doubleday, New York, 1959

Argan, G.C., 'Roma Interotta', *Architectural Design*, vol. 49, nos 3–4, 1979, p. 37

Aristotle, *The Basic Works of Aristotle*, ed. R. McKeon, Random House, New York, 1941

Arup, O., 'Modern architecture: the structural fallacy', *The Listener*, 7 July 1955; reprinted *Arup Journal*, vol. 20, no. 1, Spring 1985, pp. 19–21

Ashton, D., *Picasso on Art*, Thames and Hudson, London, 1972

Bachelard, G., *The Poetics of Space* (1958), trans. M. Jolas, Beacon Press, Boston, 1969

Bacon, E., *Design of Cities* (1967), revised edition, Thames and Hudson, London, 1978

Baltard, L. P., *Architectonographie des Prisons*, Paris, 1829 (quoted Evans, 1982, p. 208)

Bandini, M., 'Typology as a Form of Convention', *AA Files*, no. 6, 1984, pp. 73–82

Banham, R., 'The New Brutalism', *Architectural Review*, vol. 118, December 1955, pp. 354–59 (reprinted *A Critic Writes*, pp. 7–15)

——, *Theory and Design in the First Machine Age*, Architectural Press, London, 1960

——, *The Architecture of the Well-Tempered Environment*, Architectural Press, London, 1969

——, *A Critic Writes. Essays by Reyner Banham*, selected by M. Banham, P. Barker, S. Lyall, C. Price, University of California Press, Berkeley, Los Angeles and London, 1996

Barbaro, D.: Vitruvius, *I Dieci Libri dell'Archittetura*, tradotti e commentati da Daniele Barbaro (1556; 1567), facsimile edition, ed. M. Tafuri, Edizioni Il Polifilo, Milan, 1987

Barthes, R.: *A Roland Barthes Reader*, ed. S. Sontag, Vintage, London, 1993

——, 'Myth Today' (1956), in *A Roland Barthes Reader*, pp. 93–149

——, *Mythologies* (1957), trans. A. Lavers, Vintage Books, London, 1993

——, 'The Structuralist Activity' (1963), in *Critical Essays*, trans. R. Howard, Northwestern University Press, Evanston, 1972, pp. 213–20

——, 'The Eiffel Tower' (1964), in *A Roland Barthes Reader*, pp. 236–50

——, *Criticism and Truth* (1966), trans. K. P. Keuneman, University of Minnesota Press, Minneapolis, 1987

——, *The Fashion System* (1967), trans. M. Ward and R. Howard, University of California Press, Berkeley and Los Angeles, 1990

——, 'Semiology and the Urban' (1967b), in Leach (ed.), *Rethinking Architecture*, pp. 166–72

——, *The Pleasure of the Text* (1973), trans. R. Miller, Blackwell, Oxford, 1990

Bataille, G., 'Formless' (1929), in *Visions of Excess, Selected Writings 1927–1939*, trans. A. Stoekl, University of Minnesota Press, Minneapolis, 1985, p. 31

Baudelaire, C., *The Painter of Modern Life and Other Essays*, trans. J. Mayne, Phaidon Press, London, 1964

Baudrillard, J., *For a Critique of the Political Economy of the Sign* (1972), trans. C. Levin, Telos Press, St Louis, MO, 1981.

——, *Simulations*, trans. P. Foss, P. Patton, P. Beitchman, Semiotext(e), New York, 1983

Baxendall, M., *Patterns of Intention. On the Historical Explanation of Pictures*, Yale University Press, New Haven and London, 1985

Behne, A., 'Art, Craft, Technology' (1922), trans. C. C. Collins, in F. Dal Co, *Figures of Architecture and Thought*, pp. 324–38

——, *The Modern Functional Building* (1926), trans. M. Robinson, Getty Research Institute, Santa Monica, CA, 1996

Behrendt, W. C., *Modern Building*, Martin Hopkinson, London, 1938

Behrens, P., 'Art and Technology' (1910), in T. Buddensieg (ed.) *Industriekultur. Peter Behrens and the AEG*, trans. I. Boyd Whyte, MIT Press, Cambridge, MA, 1984, pp. 212–19

Benjamin, W., *Illuminations*, trans. H. Zohn, Collins/Fontana, London, 1973

Benton, T., 'The Myth of Function', in P. Greenhalgh (ed.), *Modernism in Design*, Reaktion Books, London, 1990, pp. 41–52

——, Benton, C. and Sharp, D., *Form and Function. A Source Book for the History of Architecture and Design 1890–1939*, Crosby Lockwood Staples, London, 1975

Beresford Hope, A. J., *The Common Sense of Art*, London, 1858

Bergren, A., 'Dear Jennifer', *ANY*, vol. 1, no. 4, January/February 1994, pp. 12–15

Berkeley, G., *The Querist* (1735), in *The Works of George Berkeley Bishop of Cloyne*, ed. A. A. Luce and T. E. Jessop, vol. VI, 1953

Berlage, H. P., 'Thoughts on Style' (1905) and 'The Foundations and Development of Architecture' (1908), trans. I. Boyd Whyte and W. de Wit, *Hendrik Petrus Berlage: Thoughts on Style 1886–1908*, Santa Monica, CA, 1996, pp. 122–56, pp. 185–257

Blake, P., *The Master Builders*, Victor Gollancz, London, 1960

Bletter, R. H., 'Introduction' to A. Behne, *The Modern Functional Building*, 1996, pp. 1–83

Blomfield, R., *The Mistress Art*, Edward Arnold, London, 1908

Blondel, J.-F., *Architecture françoise ou receuil des plans, élévations, coupes et profiles*, vol. 1, Paris, 1752

———, *Cours d'architecture*, 4 vols, Paris, 1771–77

Blundell Jones, P., *Hugo Häring: the organic versus the geometric*, Axel Menges, Stuttgart and London, 1999

Boffrand, G., *Livre d'architecture*, Paris, 1745

Bonta, J. P., 'Reading and Writing about Architecture', *Design Book Review*, no. 18, 1990, pp. 13–16

Bötticher, C. G. W., 'The Principles of the Hellenic and Germanic Ways of Building with Regard to Their Present Application to Our Present Way of Building' (1846), in W. Herrmann, *In What Style Should We Build? The German Debate on Architectural Style*, Getty Center, Santa Monica CA, 1992, pp. 147–67

Boullée, E.-L., 'Architecture, Essay on Art' (c. 1790), in H. Rosenau, *Boullée and Visionary Architecture*, Academy Editions, London, and Harmony Books, New York, 1976

Boyer, M. C., *The City of Collective Memory. Its Historical Imagery and Architectural Entertainments*, MIT Press, Cambridge, MA and London, 1994

Brett, L., 'Detail on the South Bank', *Design*, no. 32, Aug. 1951, pp. 3–7

Broadbent, G., *Design in Architecture*, John Wiley and Sons, London, 1973

Buchanan, A. C., *Robert Willis and the Rise of Architectural History*, unpublished Ph.D thesis, University of London, 1995

Burckhardt, J., *Reflections on History* (1868–1871), trans. M. D. H., G. Allen and Unwin, London, 1943

Burgess, W., *The Builder*, vol. 19, 1861, p. 403

Burke, E., *A Philosophical Enquiry into the Origin of our Ideas of the Sublime and Beautiful* (1757; 1759), ed. J. T. Boulton, Basil Blackwell, Oxford, 1987

Burns, H., with L. Fairbairn and B. Boucher, *Andrea Palladio 1505–1580, The Portico and the Farmyard*, catalogue of exhibition at the Hayward Gallery, London, Arts Council of Great Britain, 1975

Carroll, L., *Alice's Adventures in Wonderland* (1865) and *Through the Looking Glass* (1872), Penguin Books, Harmondsworth, Middlesex, 1962

Carter, P., 'Mies van der Rohe', *Architectural Design*, vol. 31, March 1961, pp. 95–121

Chambers, Sir W., *A Treatise on the Decorative Part of Civil Architecture* (1759; 1791), Priestley and Weale, London, 1825

———, *A Dissertation on Oriental Gardening*, London, 1772

Chermayeff, S., and Alexander, C., *Community and Privacy* (1963), Penguin Books, Harmondsworth, Middlesex, 1966

Ching, F. D. K., *Architecture Form, Space and Order*, van Nostrand Reinhold, New York, 1979

Choisy, A., *Le Histoire d'Architecture*, 2 vols., Gauthier-Villars, Paris, 1899

Chomsky, N., *Cartesian Linguistics*, Harper and Row, New York and London, 1966

CIAM (Congrès International d'Architecture Moderne), 'La Sarraz Declaration' (1928), in Conrads, *Programmes and Manifestoes*, pp. 109–13

Cockerell, C. R.: Royal Academy Lectures on Architecture, reported in *The Athenaeum*, vol. VI, 1843

Coleridge, S. T., *Biographia Literaria* (1817), 2 vols, ed. J. Shawcross, Oxford, 1907

———, *Lectures and Notes on Shakspere*, ed. T. Ashe, G. Bell, London, 1908

Collins, G. R. and C. C., 'Monumentality: a Critical Matter in Modern Architecture', *Harvard Architectural Review*, no. IV, Spring 1984, pp. 14–35

Collins, P., *Concrete*, Faber and Faber, London, 1959

———, *Changing Ideals in Modern Architecture 1750–1950*, Faber and Faber, London, 1965

———, 'The Linguistic Analogy', in *Language in Architecture*, ed. J. Meunier, Proceedings of the 68th Annual General Meeting of the Association of Collegiate Schools of Architecture, Washington, D.C., 1980, pp. 3–7

Colquhoun, A., 'Plateau Beaubourg' (1977), in *Essays in Architectural Criticism*, MIT Press, Cambridge, MA and London, 1981, pp. 110–19

———, *Modernity and the Classical Tradition*, MIT Press, Cambridge MA and London, 1989

Connerton, P., *How Societies Remember*, Cambridge University Press, Cambridge, 1989

Conrads, U. (ed.), *Programmes and Manifestoes on Twentieth Century Architecture*, Lund Humphries, London, 1970

Constant, 'The Great Game to Come' (1959), in I. Andreotti and X. Costa (eds), *Theory of the Dérive and other situationist writings on the city*, Museu d'Art Contemporani, Barcelona, 1996, pp. 62–63 (also in Ockman, ed., *Architecture Culture*, pp. 314–15)

Cook, P. and Parry, E., 'Architecture and Drawing: Editing and Refinement', *Architects' Journal*, vol. 186, 16/23 December 1987, pp. 40–45

Cox, A., 'Highpoint II', *Focus*, no. 2, 1938, pp. 76–79

Crinson. M. and Lubbock, J., *Architecture: Art or Profession?*, Manchester University Press, Manchester and London, 1994

Curtis, W., *Denys Lasdun: architecture, city, landscape*, Phaidon, London, 1994

Cuvier, G., *Recherches sur les Ossemens Fossiles*, 4 vols, 'Discours préliminaire', vol. 1, Paris, 1812 (trans. by R. Kerr as *Essay on the Theory of the Earth*, Edinburgh and London, 1813)

Dal Co, F., *Figures of Architecture and Thought, German Architecture Culture 1880–1920*, trans. S. Sartarelli, Rizzoli, New York, 1990

Daly, C., 'Reform Club', *Révue Générale d'Architecture et des Travaux Publics*, vol. XV, 1857, pp. 342–48

de Certeau, M., *The Practice of Everyday Life*, trans. S. Rendall, University of California Press, Berkeley, Los Angeles, London, 1984

Denari, N.: Peter Zellner, 'Interview with Neil Denari', *Transition*, no. 41, 1993

Derrida, J., *Writing and Difference*, trans. A. Bass, Routledge, London, 1978

———, 'Structure, Sign and Play in the Discourse of the Human Sciences', 1966, in *Writing and Difference*, pp. 278–93

———, 'Why Peter Eisenman Writes Such Good Books', *Threshold*, vol. 4, Spring 1988, pp. 99–105; reprinted Leach (ed.), *Rethinking Architecture*, pp. 336–47 (source quoted here)

Descartes, R.: *The Philosophical Writings of Descartes*, vol. 1, trans. J. Cottingham, R. Stoothoff and J. Murdoch, Cambridge University Press, 1985

Doordan, D. P., *Building Modern Italy, Italian Architecture 1914–1936*, Princeton Architectural Press, New York, 1988

Dorfles, G., *Simbolo, Communicazione, Consumo* (1959), excerpt trans. as 'Structuralism and Semiology in Architecture', in C. Jencks and G. Baird (eds) *Meaning in Architecture*, Barrie and Rockliff: The Cresset Press, London, 1969, pp. 39–49

Durand, J. N. L., *Précis des leçons d'Architecture données à l'École polytechnique*, 2 vols (1802–5), Paris, 1819

Eco, U., 'Function and Sign: the Semiotics of Architecture' (1986), in Leach (ed.), *Rethinking Architecture*, pp. 182–202

Edwards, T., *Good and Bad Manners in Architecture* (1924), Tiranti, London, 1946

Egbert, D. D., *The Beaux Arts Tradition in French Architecture*, Princeton University Press, Princeton, NJ, 1980

Eidlitz, L., *The Nature and Function of Art, More Especially of Architecture*, Sampson Low, London, 1881

Eisenman, P., 'From Object to Relationship II: Giuseppe Terragni Casa Giuliani Frigerio', *Perspecta* 13/14, 1971, pp. 36–61

———, 'House I 1967', in *Five Architects: Eisenman Graves, Gwathmey, Hejduk, Meier*, Oxford University Press, New York, 1975, pp. 15–17

———, *House X*, Rizzoli, New York, 1982

Eliot, T. S., 'Tradition and the Individual Talent' (1917), in T. S. Eliot, *Points of View*, Faber and Faber, London, 1941, pp. 23–34

Ellis, C., 'Prouvé's People's Palace', *Architectural Review*, vol. 177, May 1985, pp. 40–48

Elmes, J., 'On the Analogy Between Language and Architecture', *Annals of the Fine Arts*, vol. 5, 1820, pp. 242–83

Emerson, R. W., 'Nature' (1836), 'The American Scholar' (1837), in *Selected Essays*, Penguin Books, New York and London, 1985

———, *Journals*, 10 vols, Houghton Mifflin Co., Boston and New York, 1909–14

Endell, A., 'Möglichkeit und Ziele einer neuen Architektur', *Deutsche Kunst und Dekoration*, vol. 1, 1897–98, quoted in Mallgrave, Introduction to O. Wagner, *Modern Architecture*, p. 44

———, *Die Schönheit der grossen Stadt*, Stuttgart, 1908

Ettlinger, L. D., 'On Science, Industry and Art, Some Theories of Gottfried Semper', *Architectural Review*, vol. 136, July 1964, pp. 57–60

Evans, R., *The Fabrication of Virtue. English Prison Architecture 1750–1840*, Cambridge University Press, 1982

———, 'In front of lines that leave nothing behind', *AA Files*, no. 6, 1984, pp. 89–96

———, 'Postcards from Reality', *AA Files*, no. 6, 1984, pp. 109–11

———, 'Translations from Drawing to Building', *AA Files*, no. 12, 1986, pp. 3–18

———, *The Projective Cast. Architecture and its Three Geometries*, MIT Press, Cambridge, MA, and London, 1995

Evelyn, J.: *The Diary of John Evelyn*, ed. E. S. de Beer, Oxford University Press, London, 1959

Farmer, J., *Green Shift, Towards a Green Sensibility in Architecture*, Butterworth-Heinemann, Oxford, 1996

Fergusson, J., *An Historical Inquiry into the True Principles of Beauty in Art, more especially with reference to Architecture*, London, 1849

———, *A History of the Modern Styles*, London, 1862

Fiedler, C., 'Observations on the Nature and History of Architecture' (1878), in Mallgrave and Ikonomou, *Empathy, Form and Space*, pp. 126–46

Filarete (Antonio di Piero Averlino), *Treatise on Architecture* (before 1465), trans. J. R. Spencer, 2 vols, Yale University Press, New Haven and London, 1965

Fink, K. J., *Goethe's History of Science*, Cambridge University Press, 1991

Ford, H., *My Life and Work*, Heinemann, London, 1922

Forty, A., 'Being or Nothingness: Private Experience and Public Architecture in Post-War Britain', *Architectural History*, vol. 38, 1995, pp. 25–35

——, 'Masculine, Feminine or Neuter?', in K. Rüedi, S. Wigglesworth and D. McCorquodale (eds), *Desiring Practices. Architecture Gender and the Interdisciplinary*, Black Dog Publishing Ltd., London, 1996, pp. 140–55

——, '"Spatial Mechanics": Scientific Metaphors in Architecture', in P. Galison and E. Thompson (eds), *The Architecture of Science*, MIT Press, Cambridge, MA, and London, 1999, pp. 213–31

Foucault, M., *The Order of Things* (1966), Routledge, London, 1992

——, 'Of Other Spaces: Utopias and Heterotopias' (1967), in Leach, *Rethinking Architecture*, pp. 350–56; and in Ockman, *Architecture Culture*, pp. 420–26

Frampton, K., 'Stirling in Context', *RIBA Journal*, vol. 83, March 1976, pp. 102–4

Frankl, P., *Principles of Architectural History* (1914), trans. J. F. O'Gorman, MIT Press, Cambridge, MA, and London, 1968

Fréart de Chambray, R., *A Parallel of the Antient Architecture with the Modern ... To which is added An Account of Architects and Architecture by John Evelyn Esq.* (1650), trans. J. Evelyn, London, 1664

Fréart de Chantelou, P., *Diary of the Cavaliere Bernini's Visit to France* (1665), ed. A. Blunt, trans. M. Corbett, Princeton University Press, 1985

Freud, S., *Civilization and its Discontents*, trans. J. Riviere, ed. J. Strachey, Hogarth Press, London, 1969

Gadamer, H., *Truth and Method*, New York, 1975

Gage, J., *Goethe on Art*, Scolar Press, London, 1980

Garnier, C., *Le Théâtre*, Paris, 1871

Ghirardo, D., *Architecture after Modernism*, Thames and Hudson, London, 1996

Giedion, S., *Building in France Building in Iron Building in Ferro-Concrete* (1928), trans. J. Duncan Berry, Getty Center, Santa Monica, CA, 1995

——, *Space, Time and Architecture* (1941), 9th printing, Oxford University Press, London, 1952

Gillis, J. R. (ed.), *Commemorations, The Politics of National Identity*, Princeton University Press, Princeton, NJ, 1994

Ginzburg, M., *Style and Epoch* (1924), trans. A. Senkevitch, MIT Press, Cambridge MA and London, 1982

——, 'Constructivism as a Method of Laboratory and Teaching Work', *SA* 1927, no. 6: in C. Cooke ed., *Russian Avant Garde Art and Architecture*, Academy Editions and Architectural Design, London, 1983, p. 43

Girouard, M., *Life in the English Country House*, Yale University Press, New Haven and London, 1978

Goethe, J. W. von, 'On German Architecture' (1772), trans. N. Pevsner and G.Grigson, *Architectural Review*, vol. 98, Dec. 1945, pp. 155–59. There are less poetic translations by J. Gage, *Goethe on Art*,

pp. 103–12; and in *Goethe The Collected Works*, vol. 3, trans. E. and E. H. von Nardroff, Princeton University Press, Princeton, NJ, 1986, pp. 3–14.

——, *Italian Journey* (1816–17), trans. R. R. Heitner (vol. 6 in *Goethe: The Collected Works*), Princeton University Press, Princeton, NJ, 1989

Göller, A., *Zur Aesthetik der Architektur*, 1887

——, 'What is the Cause of Perpetual Style Change in Architecture?' (1887), trans. Mallgrave and Ikonomou, *Empathy, Form and Space*, pp. 193–225

Goodman, N., *Languages of Art*, Harvester Press, Brighton (UK), 1981

Great Britain: Ministry of Housing and Local Government, *Homes for Today and Tomorrow* (Parker Morris Report), HMSO, London, 1961

Greenberg, C., 'Modernist Painting' (1960), in Harrison and Wood (eds), *Art in Theory*, pp. 754–60

Greenough, H., *Form and Function. Remarks on Art, Design, and Architecture*, selected and edited by H. A. Small, University of California Press, Berkeley and Los Angeles, 1958

Gregotti, V., *Le territoire de l'architecture* (1966), French trans. from Italian by V. Hugo, L'Équerre, Paris, 1982

Groák, S., *The Idea of Building*, E. and F. N. Spon, London, 1992

Gropius, W., 'Programme for the Establishment of a Company for the Provision of Housing on Aesthetically Consistent Principles' (1910), in Benton, Benton and Sharp, *Form and Function*, pp. 188–90

——, 'The Theory and Organisation of the Bauhaus' (1923) in Benton, Benton and Sharp, *Form and Function*, pp. 119–27

——, 'Principles of Bauhaus Production' (1926), in Conrads, *Programmes and Manifestoes*, pp. 95–97

——, *The New Architecture and the Bauhaus* (1935), Faber and Faber, London, 1965

——, 'Blueprint of an Architect's Education' (1939), in *The Scope of Total Architecture*, George Allen and Unwin, London, 1956

——, 'Eight Steps toward a Solid Architecture' (1954), reprinted in Ockman (ed.), *Architecture Culture*, pp. 177–80

Guadet, J., *Éléments et Théories d'Architecture*, Paris, 1902

Guarini, G., *Architettura Civile* (written 1686, published 1737), Gregg, London, 1964

Guillerme, J., 'The Idea of Architectural Language: a Critical Enquiry', *Oppositions*, no. 10, 1977, pp. 21–26

Hagan, S., 'The Good, the Bad and the Juggled: the New Ethics of Building Materials', *The Journal of Architecture*, vol. 3, no. 2, 1998, pp. 107–15

Halbwachs, M., *The Collective Memory* (1950), trans. F. J. and V. Y. Ditter, Harper and Row, New York, 1980

Hare, N., 'Peter Foggo' (obituary), *The Guardian*, 17 July 1993, p. 30

Häring, H., 'Approaches to Form' (1925), in Benton, Benton and Sharp, *Form and Function*, pp. 103–5

Harris, E. and Savage, N., *British Architectural Books and Writers 1556–1785*, Cambridge University Press, 1990

Harris, J. and Higgott, G., *Inigo Jones Complete Architectural Drawings*, The Drawing Center, New York, 1989

Harrison, C. and Wood, P. (eds), *Art in Theory 1900–1990*, Blackwell, Oxford, 1992

Harvey, Sir W., 'The Movement of the Heart and Blood in Animals' (1635), in Sir William Harvey, *The Circulation of the Blood and Other Writings*, translated by Kenneth J. Franklin, Dent, London, 1963

Hawksmoor, N., letter to Lord Carlisle, 5 October 1732, *Walpole Society*, vol. XIX, 1930–31, p. 132

Hayden, D., *The Power of Place. Urban Landscapes as Public History*, MIT Press, Cambridge, MA, and London, 1995

Hegel, G. W. F., *Aesthetics*, trans. T. M. Knox, 2 vols, Oxford University Press, 1975

Heidegger, M., *Being and Time* (1927), trans. J. Macquarrie and E. Robinson, Blackwell, Oxford, 1962

——, 'Building Dwelling Thinking' (1951), in *Martin Heidegger: Basic Writings*, ed. D. F. Krell, Routledge, London, 1993, pp. 347–63. Also reprinted in Leach, *Rethinking Architecture*, pp. 100–9

Herder, J. G. von, *Treatise on the Origin of Language* (1772), trans., London, 1827

Herrmann, W., *Laugier and Eighteenth Century French Theory*, Zwemmer, London, 1962

——, *The Theory of Claude Perrault*, A. Zwemmer, London, 1973

——, *Gottfried Semper: in search of architecture*, MIT Press, Cambridge, MA, and London, 1984

Hertzberger, H., 'Flexibility and Polyvalency', *Forum*, vol. 16, no. 2, February–March 1962, pp. 115–18; abstracted in *Ekistics*, April 1963, pp. 238–39; and partly reprinted in Hertzberger, *Lessons for Students in Architecture*, pp. 146–47

——, 'Identity' (1967), partly reprinted in Hertzberger, *Lessons for Students in Architecture*, pp. 170–71

——, 'Architecture for People', *A+U*, March 1977, pp. 124–46

——, *Lessons for Students in Architecture*, Uitgeverij 010 Publishers, Rotterdam, 1991

——, interview in L. Hallows, MSc Report, University College London, 1995

Higgott, G., '"Varying with reason": Inigo Jones's theory of design', *Architectural History*, vol. 35, 1992, pp. 51–77

Hildebrand, A., 'The Problem of Form in the Fine Arts' (1893), in Mallgrave and Ikonomou, *Empathy, Form and Space*, pp. 227–79

Hill, J. (ed.), *Occupying Architecture*, Routledge, London, 1998

Hill, R., *Designs and their Consequences*, Yale University Press, New Haven and London, 1999

Hillier, B., *Space is the Machine*, Cambridge University Press, Cambridge, 1996

——, and Hanson, J., *The Social Logic of Space*, Cambridge University Press, Cambridge, 1984

Hitchcock, H.-R. and Johnson, P., *The International Style* (1932), Norton, New York, 1966

Hofstadter, A. and Kuhns, R., *Philosophies of Art and Beauty. Selected Readings in Aesthetics from Plato to Heidegger* (1964), University of Chicago Press, Chicago and London, 1976

Horace, 'On the Art of Poetry', in Aristotle/Horace/Longinus, *Classical Literary Criticism*, trans. T. S. Dorsch, Penguin Books, London, 1965

Huet, B., 'Formalisme–Réalisme', *Architecture d'Aujourdhui*, vol. 190, April 1977, pp. 35–36

Hugo, V., *Notre Dame de Paris* (1831; 1832), trans. J. Sturrock, Penguin Books, London, 1978

Humboldt, W. von, *On Language, The Diversity of Human Language-Structure and its Influence on* the *Mental Development of Mankind* (1836), trans. P. Heath, Cambridge University Press, 1988

Hume, D., 'Of the Standard of Taste' (1757), in D. Hume, *Selected Essays*, Oxford University Press, 1993, pp. 133–54

Hunt, J. D. and Willis, P., *The Genius of the Place, The English Landscape Garden 1620–1820*, MIT Press, Cambridge, MA, and London, 1988

Iversen, M., 'Saussure versus Peirce: Models for a Semiotics of Visual Arts', in A. L. Rees and F. Borzello (eds), *The New Art History*, Camden Press, London, 1986, pp. 82–94

Jackson, T. G., *Recollections of Sir Thomas Graham Jackson*, ed. B. H. Jackson, Oxford University Press, 1950

Jacobs, J., *The Death and Life of Great American Cities* (1961), Penguin Books, Harmondsworth, 1974

Jakobson, R., 'Two Aspects of Language and Two Types of Aphasic Disturbances' (1956), in *Selected Writings*, vol. 3, 'Word and Language', Mouton, The Hague and Paris, 1971, pp. 239–59

Jencks, C., 'History as Myth', in C. Jencks and G. Baird (eds), *Meaning in Architecture*, Barrie and Rockliff, The Cresset Press, London, 1969, pp. 245–66

Jencks, C., *The Language of Post-Modern Architecture*, 1978

Johnson, P., *Mies van der Rohe*, Museum of Modern Art, New York, 1947

——, 'The Seven Crutches of Modern Architecture', *Perspecta*, no. 3, 1955, pp. 40–44; reprinted in Ockman (ed.), *Architecture Culture*, pp. 190–92

Johnson, P.-A., *The Theory of Architecture. Concepts, Themes, and Practices*, Van Nostrand Reinhold, New York, 1994

Kahn, A., 'Overlooking: A Look at How we Look at Site or... site as "discrete object" of desire', in K. Rüedi, S. Wigglesworth and D. McCorquodale (eds), *Desiring Practices. Architecture Gender and the Interdisciplinary*, Black Dog Publishing Ltd, London, 1996, pp. 174–85

Kahn, L., 'Order is', *Zodiac* no. 8, Milan, June 1961, p. 20; reprinted in Conrads, *Programmes and Manifestoes*, pp. 169–70

——: A. Latour (ed.), *Louis I. Kahn: Writings, Lectures, Interviews*, Rizzoli, New York, 1991

Kames, Lord, *Elements of Criticism* (1762), 9th ed., 2 vols, Edinburgh, 1817

Kant, I., *Critique of Pure Reason* (1781), trans. N. Kemp Smith, Macmillan, London, 1929

——, *The Critique of Judgment* (1790), trans. J. C. Meredith, Clarendon Press, Oxford, 1952

Kerr, R., 'English Architecture Thirty Years Hence' (1884), in Pevsner, *Some Architectural Writers*, pp. 291–314

Kiesler, F., 'Manifesto' (1925), in Benton, Benton and Sharp, *Form and Function*, pp. 105–6

——, 'Magical Architecture' (1947), in Conrads, *Programmes and Manifestoes*, pp. 150–51

Koolhaas, R., *Delirious New York* (1978), 010 Publishers, Rotterdam, 1994

——, and Mau, B., *S,M,L,XL*, 010 Publishers, Rotterdam, 1995

Korn, A., 'Analytical and Utopian Architecture' (1923), in Conrads, *Programmes and Manifestoes*, pp. 76–77

——, *Glass in Modern Architecture* (1929), excerpts in Benton, Benton and Sharp, *Form and Function*,

pp. 170–71

Kristeller, P. O., 'The Modern System of the Arts', *Journal of the History of Ideas*, vol. 12, 1951, pp. 496–527, and vol. 13, 1952, pp. 17–46; reprinted in P. O. Kristeller, *Renaissance Thought and the Arts*, Princeton University Press, Princeton, NJ, 1990, pp. 163–227

Lane, B. M., *Architecture and Politics in Germany 1918–1945*, Harvard University Press, Cambridge, MA, 1968

Lasdun, D., 'An Architect's Approach to Architecture', *RIBA Journal*, vol. 72, April 1965, pp. 184–95

——, interview on video shown at Royal Academy, London, 1997

Laugier, M.-A., *An Essay on Architecture* (1753; 1755), trans. W. and A. Herrmann, Hennessey and Ingalls, Los Angeles, 1977. (Citations are not from this translation, but from the French edition, Paris, 1755, reprinted P. Mardaga, Brussels and Liège, 1979)

——, *Observations sur l'Architecture* (1765), P. Mardaga, Brussels and Liège, 1979

Lavin, S., *Quatremère de Quincy and the Invention of a Modern Language of Architecture*, MIT Press, Cambridge, MA, 1992

Leach, N. (ed.), *Rethinking Architecture. A Reader in Cultural Theory*, Routledge, London, 1997

Le Camus de Mézières, N., *The Genius of Architecture; or the Analogy of that Art with Our Sensations* (1780), trans. D. Britt, Getty Center, Santa Monica, CA, 1992

Le Corbusier, *Towards a New Architecture* (1923), trans. F. Etchells, Architectural Press, London, 1970

——, *The Decorative Art of Today* (1925), trans. J. Dunnett, Architectural Press, London, 1987

——, 'Standardisation cannot resolve an architectural difficulty' (1925a), *L'Almanach d'Architecture Moderne*, Crés, Paris, 1925, pp. 172–74; trans. in Benton, Benton and Sharp, *Form and Function*, p. 138

——, *Precisions on the Present State of Architecture and City Planning* (1930), trans. E. S. Aujame, MIT Press, Cambridge, MA, and London, 1991

Ledoux, C.-N., *L'Architecture considerée sous le rapport de l'art, des moeurs et de la législation*, Paris, 1804

Lee, R. W., *Ut Pictura Poesis the humanistic theory of painting*, Norton, New York, 1967

Lefebvre, H., *The Production of Space* (1974), trans. D. Nicholson-Smith, Blackwell, Oxford, 1991

Le Muet, P., *Manière de Bien Bastir* (1647), reprinted Gregg, London, 1972

Le Roy, J.-D., *Histoire de la disposition et des formes différents que les chrétiens ont données à leurs temples depuis le règne de Constantin le Grand à nos jours*, Paris, 1764

Lethaby, W. R., 'The Builder's Art and the Craftsman', in R. N. Shaw and T. G. Jackson, *Architecture, a Profession or an Art*, London, 1892

——, 'The Architecture of Adventure' (1910), in *Form in Civilization*, pp. 66–95

——, *Architecture, an Introduction to the History and Theory of the Art of Building* (1911; 1929), revised edition, Thornton Butterworth, London, 1935

——, *Form in Civilization* (1922), Oxford University Press, London, 1936

——, *Philip Webb and His Work* (1935), Raven Oak Press, London, 1979

Levine, N., 'The book and the building: Hugo's theory

of architecture and Labrouste's Bibliothèque Ste-Geneviève', in R. Middleton (ed.), *The Beaux Arts and Nineteenth Century French Architecture*, Thames and Hudson, London, 1982, pp. 138–73

——, *The Architecture of Frank Lloyd Wright*, Princeton University Press, 1996

Lévi-Strauss, *Introduction to the Works of Marcel Mauss* (1950), trans. F. Baker, Routledge and Kegan Paul, London, 1987

——, *Tristes Tropiques* (1955), trans. J. and D. Weightman, Penguin Books, Harmondsworth, 1976

——, *Structural Anthropology*, trans. C. Jacobson and B. G. Schoepf, Basic Books, New York, 1963

Libeskind, D., *Countersign*, Academy editions, London, 1991

——, 'Libeskind on Berlin', *Building Design*, 8 April 1994, pp. 17–18

Lipman, A., 'The Architectural Belief System and Social Behaviour', *British Journal of Sociology*, vol. 20, no. 2, June 1969, pp. 190–204

Llewelyn Davies, R., 'The Education of an Architect', Inaugural lecture delivered at University College London, 1960, H. K. Lewis and Co., London, 1961

Loos, A., 'The Principle of Cladding' (1898) in *Spoken Into the Void. Collected Essays 1897–1900*, trans. J. O. Newman and J. H. Smith, MIT Press, Cambridge, MA, 1982, pp. 66–69

——, 'Ornament and Crime' (1908), in Conrads, *Programmes and Manifestoes*, pp. 19–24

——, 'Regarding Economy' (1924), trans. F. R. Jones, in M. Risselada (ed.), *Raumplan versus Plan Libre*, Rizzoli, New York, 1988, pp. 137–41

Lotze, H., *Microcosmos: An Essay Concerning Man and his Relation to the World* (1856–64), trans. E. Hamilton and E. E. Constance Jones, Scribner and Welford, New York, 1886

Loudon, J. C., *Encyclopaedia of Cottage, Farm and Villa Architecture*, Longman, London, 1833

Lubbock, J., *The Tyranny of Taste*, Yale University Press, New Haven and London, 1995

Lukács, G., 'Realism in the Balance' (1938), trans. R. Livingstone, in E. Bloch, G. Lukács, B. Brecht, W. Benjamin, T. Adorno, *Aesthetics and Politics*, New Left Books, London, 1979, pp. 28–59

Lynch, K., *The Image of the City*, MIT Press, Cambridge MA and London, 1960

Magnus, R., *Goethe as a Scientist* (1906), trans. H. Norden, Henry Schuman, New York, 1949

Mallgrave, H. F., 'Gustav Klemm and Gottfried Semper: the Meeting of Ethnological and Architectural Theory, *RES: Journal of Anthropology and Aesthetics*, no. 9, Spring 1985, pp. 68–79

——, 'Schindler's Program of 1913', in L. March and J. Sheine (eds), *R. M. Schindler. Composition and Construction*, Academy, London, 1992, pp. 15–19

——, 'From Realism to *Sachlichkeit*: the Polemics of Architectural Modernity in the 1890s', in Mallgrave (ed.), *Otto Wagner*, 1993, pp. 281–321

——(ed.), *Otto Wagner, Reflections on the Raiment of Modernity*, Getty Center, Santa Monica, CA, 1993

——, *Gottfried Semper. Architect of the Nineteenth Century*, Yale University Press, New Haven and London, 1996

——, and Ikonomou, E., *Empathy, Form and Space. Problems in German Aesthetics 1873–1893*, Getty Center, Santa Monica, CA, 1994

Mandeville, B., *The Fable of the Bees* (1714), 2 vols,

Clarendon Press, Oxford, 1966

Markus, T., *Buildings and Power*, Routledge, London, 1993

Martin, Leslie, 'An Architect's Approach to Architecture', *RIBA Journal*, vol. 74, May 1967, pp. 191–200

Martin, Louis, 'Interdisciplinary Transpositions: Bernard Tschumi's Architectural Theory', in A. Coles and A. Defert (eds), *The Anxiety of Interdisciplinarity*, BACKless Books, London, 1998, pp. 59–88

Maxwell, R., *Sweet Disorder and the Carefully Careless*, Princeton Architectural Press, New York, 1993

——, 'Sweet Disorder and the Carefully Careless' (1971), reprinted in *Sweet Disorder and the Carefully Careless*, pp. 21–30

Mayne, T., 'Connected Isolation', in Noever (ed.), *Architecture in Transition*, 1991, pp. 72–89

——: *Morphosis Buildings and Projects 1989–1992*, Rizzoli, New York, 1994

McDonough, T. F., 'Situationist Space', *October*, no. 67, 1994, pp. 59–77

McKean, J., *Learning from Segal*, Birkhauser Verlag, Basel, Boston and Berlin, 1989

Medd, D., 'Colour in Buildings', *The Builder*, vol. 176, 25 February 1949, pp. 251–52

Memmo, A., *Elementi d'Architettura Lodoliana* (vol. 1, 1780), 2 vols., Zara, 1834

Merleau-Ponty, M., *Phenomenology of Perception* (1945), trans. C. Smith, Routledge and Kegan Paul, London, 1962

Meyer, H., 'Building' (1928), in C. Schnaidt, *Hannes Meyer*, A. Niggli, Teufen, Switzerland, 1965, pp. 94–97; and in Conrads, *Programmes and Manifestoes*, pp. 117–20

Middleton, R., 'Soane's Spaces and the Matter of Fragmentation', in M. Richardson and M.-A. Stevens (eds), *John Soane Architect*, Royal Academy of Arts, London, 1999, pp. 26–37

Mies van der Rohe, L. All writings are reproduced and translated in Neumeyer, *The Artless Word*: this is the source quoted, unless otherwise stated.

Milizia, F., *Vite degli Architetti*, 1768

——, *Memorie delle Architetti Antichi e Moderni*, Parma, 1781

——, *Memorie degli Architetti* (4th ed.), Bassano, 1785

——, *L'Art de Voir dans les Beaux Arts*, Paris, Year VI (1797–98)

Mitchell, W. J., *Logic of Architecture: Design, Computation and Cognition*, MIT Press, Cambridge, MA, and London, 1990

——, *Iconology: Image, Text, Ideology*, University of Chicago Press, Chicago and London, 1986

——, *Picture Theory*, University of Chicago Press, Chicago and London, 1994

Moholy-Nagy, L., *The New Vision* (1929), 4th revised edition, trans. D. M. Hoffman, Geo. Wittenborn, New York, 1947

——, *Vision in Motion*, Paul Theobold, Chicago, 1947

Moneo, R., 'On Typology', *Oppositions*, no. 13, 1978, pp. 22–45

Moore, C., 'Charles Moore on Postmodernism', *Architectural Design*, vol. 47, no. 4, 1977, p. 255

Mordaunt Crook, J., *The Dilemma of Style, Architectural Ideas from the Picturesque to the Post-Modern*, John Murray, London, 1989

Morris, R., 'The Present Tense of Space' (1978), in R. Morris, *Continuous Project Altered Daily. The Writings of Robert Morris*, MIT Press, Cambridge,

MA, and London, 1993, pp. 175–209

Morris, W., 'Architecture and History' (1884), in *Collected Works of William Morris*, vol. XXII, 1914, pp. 296–314

——, 'Gothic Architecture' (1889), in *William Morris Stories in Prose, Stories in Verse, Shorter Poem, Lectures and Essays*, ed. G. D. H. Cole, Nonesuch Press, London, 1948, pp. 475–93

——, 'Antiscrape' (1889b), in May Morris (ed.), *William Morris Artist Writer Socialist*, vol. 1, Blackwell, Oxford, 1936, pp. 146–57

——, 'News from Nowhere' (1890), in *William Morris Stories in Prose, Stories in Verse, Shorter Poem, Lectures and Essays*, ed. G. D. H. Cole, Nonesuch Press, London, 1948, pp. 3–197

——, 'The Woodcuts of Gothic Books' (1892), in May Morris (ed.), *William Morris Artist Writer Socialist*, vol. 1, Blackwell, Oxford, 1936, pp. 318–38

Mumford, L., 'Monumentalism, Symbolism and Style', *Architectural Review*, vol. 105, April 1949, pp. 173–80

——, 'East End Urbanity' (1953), in Mumford, *The Highway and the City*, pp. 26–34

——, 'Old Forms for New Towns' (1953), in Mumford, *The Highway and the City*, pp. 35–44

——, 'The Marseille "Folly"' (1957), in Mumford, *The Highway and the City*, pp. 68–81

——, *The Highway and the City*, Secker and Warburg, London, 1964

Munro, C. F., 'Semiotics, Aesthetics and Architecture', *British Journal of Aesthetics*, vol. 27, no. 2, 1987, pp. 115–28

Muratori, S., *Studi per una Operante Storia Urbana di Venezia*, 2 vols, Istituto Poligrafico dello Stato, Rome, 1960

Muthesius, H., *Style-Architecture and Building-Art: Transformations of Architecture in the Nineteenth Century and its Present Condition* (1902; 1903), trans. and Introduction by S. Anderson, Getty Center, Santa Monica, CA, 1994

——, *The English House* (1904, 2 vols) trans. J. Seligman, Crosby Lockwood Staples, London, 1979

——, 'Where do we Stand?' (1911); excerpts translated in Benton, Benton and Sharp, *Form and Function*, pp. 48–51; and Conrads, *Programmes*, pp. 26–27

——, 'Werkbund Theses' (1914), in Conrads, *Programmes and Manifestoes*, pp. 28–29

Nerdinger, W., 'From Bauhaus to Harvard: Walter Gropius and the Use of History', in G. Wright and J. Parks (eds), *The History of History in American Schools of Architecture 1865–1975*, Princeton Architectural Press, New York, 1990, pp. 89–98

Neumeyer, F., *The Artless Word. Mies van der Rohe on the Art of Building*, trans. M. Jarzombeck, MIT Press, Cambridge, MA, 1991

Nietzsche, F., *The Birth of Tragedy* (1872), trans. W. Kaufmann, Vintage Books, New York, 1967

——, 'On the Uses and Disadvantage of History for Life' (1874), trans. R. J. Hollingdale, in F. Nietzsche, *Untimely Meditations*, Cambridge University Press, Cambridge, 1983, pp. 57–123

——, *Beyond Good and Evil* (1886), trans. R. J. Hollingdale, Penguin Books, London, 1990

——, *The Will to Power* (1901), trans. W. Kaufmann and R. J. Hollingdale, Vintage Books, New York, 1968

Noever, P. (ed.), *Architecture in Transition*, Prestel-Verlag, Munich, 1991

Norberg-Schulz, C., *Intentions in Architecture*, Scandinavian University Books, Oslo, and Allen and Unwin, London, 1963

——, 'The Phenomenon of Place', *Architectural Association Quarterly*, vol. 8, no. 4, 1976, pp. 3–10. (Reprinted in C. Norberg-Schulz, *Genius Loci Towards a Phenomenology of Architecture*, Academy, London, 1980)

Nuffield Provincial Hospitals Trust, *Studies in the Functions and Design of Hospitals*, Oxford University Press, London, New York, Toronto, 1955

Ockman, J. (ed.), *Architecture Culture 1943–1968. A Documentary Anthology*, Rizzoli, New York, 1993

Olmo, C., 'Across the Texts: the Writings of Aldo Rossi', *Assemblage*, vol. 5, 1988, pp. 90–120

Onians, J., *Bearers of Meaning. The Classical Orders in Antiquity, the Middle Ages, and the Renaissance*, Cambridge University Press, Cambridge, 1988

Palladio, A., *The Four Books on Architecture* (1570), trans. I. Ware, London, 1738, facsimile edition Dover Publications, New York, 1965; and trans. R. Tavernor and R. Schofield, MIT Press, Cambridge, MA, and London, 1997

Panofsky, E., *Idea, a Concept in Art Theory* (1924), trans. J. J. S. Peake, University of South Carolina Press, Columbia, SC, 1968

Parker, B., *Modern Country Homes in England* (1912), ed. D. Hawkes, Cambridge University Press, 1986

Patetta, L., *L'Architettura in Italia 1919–1943. Le Polemiche*, clup, Milan, 1972

Patte, P., *Discours sur l'architecture*, Paris, 1754

——, *Mémoires sur les objets les plus importans de l'architecture*, Paris, 1769

Payne Knight, R., *An Analytical Enquiry into the Principles of Taste* (1805), 3rd ed., London, 1806

Pérez-Gomez, A., *Architecture and the Crisis of Modern Science*, MIT Press, Cambridge, MA, and London, 1983

—— and Pelletier, L., *Architectural Representation and the Perspective Hinge*, MIT Press, Cambridge, MA, and London, 1997

Perrault, C., *Ordonnance for the Five Kinds of Columns after the Method of the Ancients* (1683), trans. I. K. McEwen, Getty Center, Santa Monica, CA, 1983

Perret, A., 'M. Auguste Perret Visits the AA', *Architectural Association Journal*, vol. 63, May 1948, pp. 217–25; reprinted in *Architectural Association 125th Anniversary Special Commemorative Publication*, London, 1973, pp. 163–65

Pevsner, N., *Pioneers of the Modern Movement*, Faber, London, 1936

——, *An Enquiry into Industrial Art in England*, Cambridge University Press, 1937

——, *The Buildings of England: Nottinghamshire*, Penguin Books, Harmondsworth, Middlesex, 1951

——, 'Modern Architecture and the Historian or the Return of Historicism', *RIBA Journal*, vol. 68, no. 6, April 1961, pp. 230–40

——, *Some Architectural Writers of the Nineteenth Century*, Clarendon Press, Oxford, 1972

—— and Nairn, I., *The Buildings of England: Surrey* (1962), Penguin Books, Harmondsworth, Middlesex, 1971

Picon, A., *French Architects and Engineers in the Age of Enlightenment* (1988), trans. M. Thom, Cambridge University Press, 1992

Piranesi, G. B., *Prima parte di architetture* (1743), text

and trans. in *Giovanni Battista Piranesi Drawings and Etchings at Columbia University*, Columbia University, New York, 1972

Plato: *The Dialogues of Plato*, 3 vols, trans. B. Jowett, Clarendon Press, Oxford, 1953

——, *The Republic*, trans. H. D. F. Lee, Penguin Books, Harmondsworth, Middlesex, 1967

——, *Timaeus and Critias*, trans. H. D. F. Lee, Penguin Books, London, 1977

Podro, M., *The Critical Historians of Art*, Yale University Press, New Haven and London, 1982

Popper, K. R., *Conjectures and Refutations. The Growth of Scientific Knowledge* (1963), Routledge and Kegan Paul, London, 1969

Porphyrios, D., '"The Burst of Memory": An Essay on Alvar Aalto's Typological Conception of Design', *Architectural Design*, vol. 49, 1979, nos 5/6, pp. 143–48

Potts, A., *Flesh and the Ideal, Winckelmann and the Origins of Art History*, Yale University Press, New Haven and London, 1994

Pratt, Sir R.: R. T. Gunther (ed.), *The Architecture of Sir Roger Pratt*, Oxford University Press, 1928

Price, C., 'Fun Palace', *New Scientist*, vol. 22, 14 May 1964, p. 433

Price, U., *Essays on the Picturesque*, 3 vols, London, 1810, reprinted Gregg, Farnborough, Hampshire, 1971

Proust, M., *On Reading Ruskin*, trans. and ed. J. Autet, W. Burford and P. J. Wolfe, Yale University Press, New Haven and London, 1987

——, *In Search of Lost Time* (1922), vol. 1, *Swann's Way*, trans. C. K. Scott Moncrieff and T. Kilmartin, revised D. J. Enright, Vintage, London, 1996

Pugin, A. W., *The True Principles of Pointed or Christian Architecture*, Henry Bohn, London, 1841

Quatremère de Quincy, A.-C., 'Architecture' (1788), 'Character' (1788), 'Idea' (1801), 'Imitation' (1801), 'Type' (1825), *Encyclopédie Méthodique: Architecture*, 3 vols, Paris and Liège, 1788, 1801, 1825. Translations of excerpts of 'Architecture' and 'Character', and of 'Idea' and 'Imitation' in full by T. Hinchcliffe, *9H*, no. 7, 1985, pp. 27–39; of 'Type' by A. Vidler, *Oppositions*, no. 8, 1977, pp. 148–50

——, *De l'Architecture Égyptienne considerée dans son origine, ses principes et son goût, et comparée sous les mêmes rapports à l'architecture Grecque* (written 1785), Paris, 1803

Rabinow, P., *French Modern. Norms and Forms of the Social Environment*, University of Chicago Press, Chicago and London, 1989

Repton, H., *Sketches and Hints on Landscape Gardening* (1795), reprinted in J. C. Loudon, *The Landscape Gardening and Landscape Architecture of the late Humphry Repton Esq.*, London, 1840

Reynolds, Sir J., *Discourses on Art* (1778; 1797), ed. R. R. Wark, Yale University Press, New Haven and London, 1975

Richards, J. M., *An Introduction to Modern Architecture* (1940), Penguin Books, Harmondsworth, 1956

Richardson, M., *Sketches by Edwin Lutyens*, Academy Editions, London, 1994

Riegl, A. *Problems of Style* (1893), trans. E. Kain, Princeton University Press, 1992

——, *Late Roman Art and Industry* (1901), trans. R. Winkes, Giorgio Bretschneider Editore, Rome, 1985

Robbins, E., *Why Architects Draw*, MIT Press, Cambridge, MA, and London, 1994

Robertson, H., *Modern Architectural Design*, London, 1932

Rogers, E. N., 'Continuità', *Casabella Continuità*, no. 199, January 1954, pp. 2–3

——, 'Preexisting Conditions and Issues of Contemporary Building Practice' (1955), in Ockman (ed.), *Architecture Culture*, pp. 201–4

——, 'L'Architettura Moderna dopo la generazione dei Maestri', *Casabella Continuità*, no. 211, June–July 1956, pp. 1–5

——, *Gli Elementi del Fenomeno Architettonico* (1961), Guida editori, Naples, 1981

Rogers, R., *Cities for a Small Planet*, Faber and Faber, London, 1997

Rossi, A., *The Architecture of the City* (1966), trans. D. Ghirardo and J. Ockman, MIT Press, Cambridge, MA, and London, 1982

——, 'Une Education Réaliste', *Architecture d'Aujourdhui*, Avril 1977, p. 39

——, *A Scientific Autobiography*, trans. L. Venuti, MIT Press, Cambridge, MA, and London, 1981

——, 'Interview by Antonio de Bonis', *Architectural Design*, vol. 52, nos 3/4, 1982, pp. 13–17

Rowe, C., 'The Mathematics of the Ideal Villa' (1947), in *The Mathematics of the Ideal Villa and Other Essays*, 1982, pp. 1–27

——, 'Character and Composition; Some Vicissitudes of Architectural Vocabulary in the Nineteenth Century' (written 1953–54, first published 1974), in *The Mathematics of the Ideal Villa and Other Essays*, 1982, pp. 59–87

——, 'La Tourette' (1961), in *The Mathematics of the Ideal Villa and Other Essays*, 1982, pp. 185–203

——, *The Mathematics of the Ideal Villa and Other Essays*, MIT Press, Cambridge, MA, and London, 1982

——, 'James Stirling: a Highly Personal and Very Disjointed Memoir', in *James Stirling Buildings and Projects*, ed. P. Arwell and T. Bickford, 1984

——, *As I was Saying. Recollections and Miscellaneous Essays*, 3 vols, ed. A. Carragone, MIT Press, Cambridge, MA, and London, 1996

——, and Koetter, F., 'Collage City', *Architectural Review*, vol. 158, August 1975, pp. 66–91; revised and expanded as *Collage City*, MIT Press, Cambridge, MA, and London, 1978

——, and Slutsky, R., 'Transparency: Literal and Phenomenal': Part 1 (1963) in Rowe, *Mathematics of the Ideal Villa and Other Essays*, 1982, pp. 159–83; Part 2 (1971), in Ockman (ed.), *Architecture Culture*, 1993, pp. 206–25

Rowe, P. G., *Civic Realism*, MIT Press, Cambridge, MA, and London, 1997

Ruskin, J., *The Seven Lamps of Architecture*, London, 1849

——, 'The Nature of Gothic', in *The Stones of Venice*, vol. 2, chap. 2, London, 1853

——, *The Two Paths*, Smith Elder and Co., London, 1859

Rykwert, J., 'The Necessity of Artifice' (1971), reprinted in *The Necessity of Artifice*, Academy Editions, London, 1982, pp. 58–59

——, *On Adam's House in Paradise*, Museum of Modern Art, New York, 1972

——, 'Lodolí on Function and Representation', *Architectural Review*, vol. 161, July 1976; reprinted in *The Necessity of Artifice*, pp. 115–21

——, 'Semper and the Conception of Style' (1976), in *The Necessity of Artifice*, pp. 122–130

——, *The First Moderns*, MIT Press, Cambridge,

MA, and London, 1980.

——, *The Necessity of Artifice*, Academy Editions, London, 1982

——, *The Dancing Column On Order in Architecture*, MIT Press, Cambridge, MA, and London, 1996

Saarinen, E., *Eero Saarinen on His Work*, ed. A. B. Saarinen, Yale University Press, New Haven and London, 1968

Sant'Elia, A., and Marinetti, F. T., 'Manifesto of Futurist Architecture' (1914), in Conrads, *Programmes and Manifestoes*, pp. 34–38

Saussure, F. de, *Course in General Linguistics* (1915), trans. W. Baskin, Fontana, London, 1978

Scammozzi, V., *L'Idea della Architettura Universale*, Venice, 1615

Schelling, F. W. J., *The Philosophy of Art* (1859), trans. D. W. Scott, University of Minnesota Press, Minneapolis and London, 1989

Schiller, F., *On the Aesthetic Education of Man* (1795), trans. and ed. E. M. Wilkinson and L. A. Willoughby, Clarendon Press, Oxford, 1967

Schindler, R. M., 'Modern Architecture A Program' (1913), trans. H. F. Mallgrave, in L. March and J. Sheine (eds), *R. M. Schindler. Composition and Construction*, Academy, London, 1992, pp. 10–13. (A slightly different version of the text is translated in Benton, Benton and Sharp, *Form and Function*, pp. 113–15; for the German original of this version, see A. Sarnitz, *R. M. Schindler Architekt 1887–1953*, Academie der Bildenden Kunst, Wien, 1986)

——, 'Space Architecture' (1934), in Benton, Benton and Sharp, *Form and Function*, pp. 183–85

Schinkel, K. F., *Das architektonische Lehrbuch*, ed. G. Peschken, Deutscher Kunstverlag, Berlin, 1979

——, *The English Journey*, ed. D. Bindman and G. Riemann, trans. F. Gayna Walls, Yale University Press, New Haven and London, 1993

Schlegel, A. W., *A Course of Lectures on Dramatic Art and Literature* (1809–11), trans. J. Black, Henry Bohn, London, 1846

Schmarsow, A., 'The Essence of Achitectural Creation' (1893), in Mallgrave and Ikonomou, *Empathy, Form and Space*, pp. 281–97

Schopenhauer, A., *The World as Will and Idea* (1818), trans. R. B. Haldane and J. Kemp, 3 vols, 8th ed., n.d

Schumacher, T., 'Contextualism: Urban Ideals and Deformations', *Casabella*, no. 359/60, 1971, pp. 79–86

Schuyler, M., *American Architecture and Other Writings* (2 vols), ed. W. H. Jordy and R. Coe, The Belknap Press of Harvard University Press, Cambridge, MA, 1961

——, 'Modern Architecture' (1894), in *American Architecture and Other Writings*, vol. 1, pp. 99–118

——, 'A Great American Architect: Leopold Eidlitz' (1908), in *American Architecture and Other Writings*, vol. 1, pp. 136–87

Schwartz, F. J., *The Werkbund. Design Theory and Mass Culture before the First World War*, Yale University Press, New Haven and London, 1996

Schwarzer, M. W., 'The Emergence of Architectural Space: August Schmarsow's Theory of *Raumgestaltung*', *Assemblage* no. 15, 1991, pp. 50–61

Scott, G., *The Architecture of Humanism* (1914), Architectural Press, London, 1980

Scott, Sir G. G., *Remarks on Secular and Domestic*

Architecture, Present and Future, London, 1857

Scruton, R., *The Aesthetics of Architecture*, Methuen, London, 1979

Scully, V., *Modern Architecture* (1961), Studio Vista, London, 1968

Segal, W.: *Architects' Journal*, vol. 187, 4 May 1988 (special issue on Walter Segal)

Semper, G., *Der Stil in den technischen und tektonischen Künsten oder praktische Aesthetik*, 2 vols, Frankfurt, 1860, 1863

——, *The Four Elements of Architecture and Other Writings*, trans. and introduction by H. F. Mallgrave and W. Herrmann, Cambridge University Press, 1989 (includes translation of part of *Der Stil*)

——, 'London Lecture of November 11, 1853', *RES: Journal of Anthropology and Aesthetics*, no. 6, Autumn 1983, pp. 5–31

——, '"On Architectural Symbols", London Lecture of autumn 1854', *RES: Journal of Anthropology and Aesthetics*, no. 9, 1985, pp. 61–67

Semper, H., *Gottfried Semper: Ein Bild seines Lebens und Wirkens*, Berlin, 1880

Sennett, R., *The Uses of Disorder. Personal Identity and City Life* (1970), Allen Lane The Penguin Press, London, 1971

Serlio: *Sebastiano Serlio on Architecture*, vol. 1, Books I–V of *Tutte l'opere d'architettura e prospectiva* (1537–1551), trans. V. Hart and P. Hicks, Yale University Press, New Haven and London, 1996

Seyssel, C. de, *Monarchie de France*, 1515 (quoted Thomson, *Renaissance Architecture*, p. 32)

Shaftesbury, 3rd Earl of (A. Ashley Cooper), *The Moralists*, 1709, excerpt reprinted in J. Dixon Hunt and P. Willis, *The Genius of the Place*, 1988, pp. 122–24

——, *Characteristics of Men, Manners, Opinions, Times* (1711), excerpt in Hofstadter and Kuhns, *Philosophies of Art and Beauty*, pp. 241–66

Shane, G., 'Contextualism', *Architectural Design*, vol. 46, Nov. 1976, pp. 676–79

Shepheard, P., *What is Architecture? An Essay on Landscapes, Buildings and Machines*, MIT Press, Cambridge, MA, and London, 1994

Shute, J., *The First and Chief Groundes of Architecture*, London, 1563

Simmel, G., *On Individuality and Social Forms*, Selected Writings ed. D. N. Levine, University of Chicago Press, Chicago and London, 1971

Sitte, C., *City Planning According to Artistic Principles* (1889), in G. R. and C. C. Collins, *Camillo Sitte: The Birth of Modern City Planning*, Rizzoli, New York, 1986

Smith, L. P., 'The Schlesinger and Mayer Building', *Architectural Record*, vol. 16, no. 1, July 1904, pp. 53–60

Smith, N., *Uneven Development*, Blackwell, Oxford, 1984

Smithson, A. (ed.), *Team X out of CIAM*, 1982

——, and P., 'The Built World – Urban Reidentification', *Architectural Design*, vol. 25, June 1955, pp. 185–88

——, 'Cluster City', *Architectural Review*, vol. 122, November 1957, pp. 333–36

——, 'The "As Found" and the "Found"', in D. Robbins (ed.), *The Independent Group: Postwar Britain and the Aesthetics of Plenty*, MIT Press, Cambridge, MA, and London, 1990, pp. 201–2

Soane, Sir J., 'Royal Academy Lectures' (1810–19), in D. Watkin, *Sir John Soane. Enlightenment Thought and the Royal Academy Lectures*, Cambridge University Press, 1996

Sontag, S., 'Against Interpretation' (1964) in S. Sontag, *Against Interpretation* (1966), Vintage, London, 1994, pp. 3–14

Soper, K., *What is Nature? Culture, Politics and the Non-Human*, Blackwell, Oxford, 1995

Sorkin, M., *Exquisite Corpse. Writings on Buildings*, Verso, London and New York, 1991

Souligné, M. de, *A Comparison Between Rome in Its Glory as to the Extent and Populousness of it and London as at Present*, 2nd ed., London, 1709

Spencer, H., *The Study of Sociology*, Henry S. King, London, 1873

——, *The Principles of Sociology*, vol. 1, Williams and Norgate, London and Edinburgh, 1876

Steadman, P., *The Evolution of Designs. Biological analogy in architecture and the applied arts*, Cambridge University Press, 1979

Stern, R., *New Directions in American Architecture*, Studio Vista, London, 1969

——, 'At the Edge of Post-Modernism', *Architectural Design*, vol. 47, no. 4, 1977, pp. 275, 286

Stirling, J.: *James Stirling, Buildings and Projects*, ed. P. Arnell and T. Bickford, Architectural Press, London, 1984

——, *Writings on Architecture*, ed. R. Maxwell, Skira, Milan, 1998

Streiter, R., 'Das deutsche Kunstgewerbe und die english-amkerikanische Bewegung' (1896), quoted in Mallgrave, 1993, p. 294

——, 'Aus München' (1896b), quoted in Anderson, 1993, p. 339

Sullivan, L. H., 'Kindergarten Chats' (1901; 1918), in *Kindergarten Chats and Other Writings*, Wittenborn Art Books, New York, 1976

——, 'Inspiration' (1886) and 'What is Architecture?' (1906), in Louis Sullivan, *The Public Papers*, ed. R. Twombly, University of Chicago Press, 1977, pp. 174–196

—— (1924a) *The Autobiography of an Idea* (1924), Dover Publications, New York, 1956

—— (1924b) *A System of Architectural Ornament according with a Philosophy of Man's Powers*, New York, 1924

Summers, D., 'Form and Gender', in N. Bryson, M.-A. Holly and K. Moxey (eds), *Visual Culture. Images and Interpretations*, Hanover, New Hampshire, 1994

Summerson, J., *The Classical Language of Architecture* (1963), Thames and Hudson, London, 1980

Swain, H., 'Building for People', *Journal of the Royal Institute of British Architects*, vol. 68, Nov. 1961, pp. 508–10

Swenarton, M., *Artisans and Architects, The Ruskinian Tradition in Architectural Thought*, Macmillan, Basingstoke, 1989

Swift, J., *Gulliver's Travels* (1726), Clarendon Press, Oxford, 1928

Switzer, S., *Ichnographia Rustica*, 3 vols., 1718 and 1742; excerpts in Hunt and Willis, *The Genius of the Place*, 1988, pp. 152–63

Szambien, W., *Symétrie Goût Caractère: Théorie et Terminologie de l'Architecture à l'Age Classique*, Picard, Paris, 1986

Tafuri, M., *Theories and History of Architecture* (1968; 1976), trans. G. Verrecchia, Granada Publishing, London, 1980

——, *History of Italian Architecture, 1944–1985*, trans. J. Levine, MIT Press, Cambridge MA and London, 1989

——, and Dal Co, F., *Modern Architecture* (1976),

trans. R. E. Wolf, Harry N. Abrams, New York, 1979

Taut, B., *Die neue Baukunst in Europa und Amerika*, Stuttgart, 1929. (trans. as *Modern Architecture*, The Studio, London, 1929)

Teige, K., 'Mundaneum' (1929), trans. L. and E. Holovsky, *Oppositions*, no. 4, 1975, pp. 83–91

Teut, A., 'Editorial', *Daidalos*, no.1, 1981, pp. 13–14

Thomson, D., *Renaissance Architecture. Critics, Patrons, Luxury*, Manchester University Press, 1993

Thompson, D'Arcy W., *On Growth and Form* (1917), abridged edn, ed. J. T. Bonner, Cambridge University Press, Cambridge, 1961

Tönnies, F., *Community and Association* (1887), trans. C. P. Loomis (1940), Routledge and Kegan Paul, London, 1955

Trésor de la Langue Française, Paris, Éditions du Centre National de la Recherche Scientifique, 1977

Tschumi, B., *Architecture and Disjunction*, MIT Press, Cambridge, MA, and London, 1996.

——, 'The Architectural Paradox' (1975), in *Architecture and Disjunction*, pp. 27–51

——, 'Architecture and Transgression' (1976), in *Architecture and Disjunction*, pp. 65–78

——, 'The Pleasure of Architecture' (1977), in *Architecture and Disjunction*, pp. 81–96

——, 'Architecture and Limits' (1980–81), in *Architecture and Disjunction*, pp. 101–18

——, *Manhattan Transcripts*, Academy editions, London, 1981

——, 'Illustrated Index. Themes from the Manhattan Manuscripts', *AA Files*, no. 4, 1983, pp. 65–74

——, 'La Case Vide', *AA Files*, no. 12, 1986, p. 66

——, 'Disjunctions' (1987), in *Architecture and Disjunction*, pp. 207–13

——, 'Six Concepts' (1991), in *Architecture and Disjunction*, pp. 226–59

——, *Architecture in/of Motion*, NAI, Rotterdam, 1997

Ungers, O. M., *Architecture as Theme*, Electa, Milan, 1982

Unwin, R., *Town Planning in Practice*, Fisher Unwin, London, 1909

Ure, A., *The Philosophy of Manufactures*, Charles Knight, London, 1835

van Brunt, H., *Architecture and Society, Selected Essays of Henry van Brunt*, ed. W. A. Coles, Belknap Press of Harvard University Press, Cambridge, MA, 1960

van de Ven, C., *Space in Architecture* (1977), Van Gorcum, Assen/Maastricht, 3rd edition, 1987

van Eyck, A., 'The Medicine of Reciprocity Tentatively Illustrated', *Forum*, vol. 15, 1961, nos 6–7, pp. 237–38

——, 'A Step towards a Configurative Discipline', *Forum*, vol. 16, 1962, no. 2, pp. 81–89

Vasari, G., *Le vite de piu eccelenti pittori, scultori ed architetti* (1550; 1568), ed. G. Milanesi, 9 vols, Florence, 1878

——, *The Lives of the Artists*, a selection, trans. G. Bull, Penguin Books, Harmondsworth, 1965

Venturi, R., *Complexity and Contradiction in Architecture* (1966), Architectural Press, London, 1977

——, Scott Brown, D., and Izenour, S., *Learning from Las Vegas* (1972; 1977), MIT Press, Cambridge, MA, and London, 1982

Vesely, D., 'Architecture and the Conflict of

Representation', *AA Files*, no. 8, 1985, pp. 21–38

——, 'Architecture and the Poetics of Representation', *Daidalos*, no. 25, Sept. 1987, pp. 25–36

Vidler, A., 'The Third Typology', *Oppositions*, no. 7, 1977, pp. 1–4

——, 'The Idea of Type: the Transformation of the Academic Ideal 1750–1830', *Oppositions*, no. 8, 1977, pp. 95–115

——, *Claude-Nicolas Ledoux*, MIT Press, Cambridge, MA, and London, 1990

——, *The Architectural Uncanny. Essays in the Modern Unhomely*, MIT Press, Cambridge, MA, and London, 1992

Viel, C.F., *Principes de l'ordonnance et de composition des bâtiments*, Paris, 1797

Viollet-le-Duc, E.-E., *Dictionnaire raisonné de l'architecture française* (10 vols, 1854–1868); selected entries in *The Foundations of Architecture*, trans. K.D. Whitehead, George Braziller, New York, 1990

——, *Lectures on Architecture*, 2 vols (1863 and 1872), trans. B. Bucknall (1877 and 1881), Dover Publications, New York, 1987

Vischer, R., 'On the Optical Sense of Form: a Contribution to Aesthetics' (1873), in Mallgrave and Ikonomou, *Empathy, Form and Space*, pp. 89–123

Vitruvius, *De Architectura*, trans. F. Granger, Loeb Classical Library, Harvard University Press, Cambridge, MA, and William Heinemann, London, 1970

Wagner, O., *Sketches, Projects and Executed Buildings* (1890), ed. P. Haiko, London, 1987

——, *Modern Architecture* (1896; 1902), trans. H. F. Mallgrave, Getty Center, Santa Monica, CA, 1988

Walpole, H., *The History of the Modern Taste in Gardening*, 1771

Watkin, D., *Morality in Architecture*, Clarendon Press, Oxford, 1977

——, *Sir John Soane, Enlightenment Thought and the Royal Academy Lectures*, Cambridge University Press, Cambridge, 1996

Weeks, J., 'Indeterminate Architecture', *Transactions of the Bartlett Society*, vol. 2, 1963–4, pp. 85–106

Whately, T., *Observations on Modern Gardening*, Dublin, 1770; excerpts in Hunt and Willis, *The Genius of the Place*, pp. 37–38, 301–7

White, H., *Metahistory, The Historical Imagination in Nineteenth Century Europe* (1973), Johns Hopkins University Press, Baltimore and London, 1975

Willett, J., *The New Sobriety, Art and Politics in the Weimar Period, 1917–1933*, Thames and Hudson, London, 1978

Williams, R., *Keywords A Vocabulary of Culture and Society* (1976), revised edition, Fontana Press, London, 1989

Willis, R., *Remarks on the Architecture of the Middle Ages, especially of Italy*, Cambridge, 1835

——, 'On the Construction of Vaults in the Middle Ages', *Transactions of the Institute of British Architects*, vol. 2, 1842, pp. 1–69

Winckelmann, J. J., *On the Imitation of the Painting and Sculpture of the Greeks* (1755), trans. H. Fuseli, in G. Schiff (ed.), *German Essays on Art History*, Continuum, New York, 1988, pp. 1–17

——, *The History of Ancient Art* (1764; 1776), trans. G. H. Lodge, London, 1850

Wölfflin, H., 'Prolegomena to the Psychology of Architecture' (1886), in Mallgrave and Ikonomou, *Empathy, Form and Space*, pp. 149–90

——, *Renaissance and Baroque* (1888), trans. K. Simon, Collins, London, 1984

——, *Principles of Art History* (1915; 1929), trans. M. D. Hottinger, Dover Publications, New York, 1950.

Woods, L., 'Neil Denari's Philosophical Machines', *A+U*, March 1991, pp. 43–44

Worringer, W., *Abstraction and Empathy* (1908), trans. M. Bullock, International Universities Press, New York, 1953

Wotton, Sir H., *The Elements of Architecture*, London, 1624

Wurman, R. S., *What Will Be Has Always Been: The Words of Louis I. Kahn*, Access Press and Rizzoli, New York, 1986

Wright, Frank Lloyd, *Collected Writings*, 4 vols., ed. B. B. Pfeiffer, Rizzoli, New York, 1992–94

Yates, F., *The Art of Memory*, Routledge, London, 1966

Zhdanov, A., 'Speech to the Congress of Soviet Writers' (1934), in C. Harrison and P. Wood, *Art in Theory*, pp. 409–12

Index

Numbers in *italic* refer to illustrations.
Words in **bold** type refer to terms that
are discussed specifically in the text.